Computational Econometrics

GAUSS Programming
for Econometricians and Financial Analysts

To: Ayse ;

Kuan-Pin Lin

ETEXT

Los Angeles

www.etext.net

COMPUTATIONAL ECONOMETRICS GAUSS Programming for Econometricians and Financial Analysts

Copyright © 2001 by K. –P. Lin

ISBN 0-9705314-3-5

Published by ETEXT Textbook Publisher, www.etext.net.

All rights reserved. No part of this book and the accompanying software may be reproduced, stored in a retrieval system, translated or transcribed, in any form or by any means—electronic, mechanical, photocopying, recording, or otherwise—without the prior written permission of the copyright owner.

For permission requests or further information, see www.etext.net or email etext@etext.net.

Printed in the United States of America.

Limit of Liability and Disclaimer of Warranty

Although every precaution has been taken in the preparation this book and the accompanying software, the publisher and author make no representation or warranties with respect to the accuracy or completeness of the contents, and specifically disclaim any implied warranties of merchantability or fitness for any particular purpose, and shall in no event be liable for any loss of profit or any damages arising out of the use of this book and the accompanying software.

Trademarks

GAUSS is a trademark of Aptech Systems, Inc. GPE2 is a product name of Applied Data Associates. All other brand names and product names used in this book are trademarks, registered trademarks, or trade names of their respective holders.

Preface

Computational Econometrics is an emerging field of applied economics which focuses on the computational aspects of econometric methodology. To explore an effective and efficient approach for econometric computation, *GAUSS Programming for Econometricians and Financial Analysts* (GPE) was originally developed as the outcome of a faculty-student joint project. The author developed the econometric program and used it in the classroom. The students learned the subject materials and wrote about their experiences in using the program and GAUSS.

We know that one of the obstacles in learning econometrics is the need to do computer programming. Who really wants to learn a new programming language while at the same time struggling with new econometric concepts? This is probably the reason that "easy-to-use" packages such as RATS, SHAZAM, EVIEWS, and TSP are often used in teaching and research. However, these canned packages are inflexible and do not allow the user sufficient freedom in advanced modeling. GPE is an econometrics package running in the GAUSS programming environment. You write simple codes in GAUSS to interact with GPE econometric procedures. In the process of learning GPE and econometrics, you learn GAUSS programming at your own pace and for your future development.

Still, it takes some time to become familiar with GPE, not to mention the GAUSS language. The purpose of this GPE project is to provide hands-on lessons with illustrations on using the package and GAUSS. GPE was first developed in 1991 and has since undergone several updates and revisions. The first version of the project, code-named LSQ, started in the summer of 1995 with limited functions of least squares estimation and prediction. This book and CDROM represent a major revision of this work in progress, including linear and nonlinear regression models, simultaneous linear equation systems, and time series analysis.

Here, in your hands, is the product of GPE. The best way to learn GPE is to read the book, type in and run each lesson, and explore the sample programs and output. For your convenience, all the lessons and data files are available on the distribution disk.

During several years of teaching econometrics using the GPE package, many students contributed to the ideas and codes in GPE. Valuable feedback and suggestions were incorporated into developing this book. In particular, the first LSQ version was a joint project with Lani Pennington, who gave this project its shape. Special thanks are due to Geri Manzano, Jennifer Showcross, Diane Malowney, Trish Atkinson, and Seth Blumsack for their efforts in editing and proofreading many draft versions of the manuscript and program lessons. As always, I am grateful to my family for their continuing support and understanding.

Table of Contents

I

Introduction

GAUSS Programming for Econometricians and Financial Analysts (GPE) is a package of econometric procedures written in GAUSS, and this book is about GAUSS programming for econometric analysis and applications using GPE. To explore the computational aspects of applied econometrics, we adopt the programming environment of GAUSS and GPE.

As you probably know, GAUSS is a programming language designed for matrix-based operations and manipulations, suitable for high level statistical and econometric computation. Many universities and research institutions have used GAUSS in their econometrics curricula. Unfortunately, GAUSS is not an easy language to learn and master, particularly for those without computer programming experience. GPE is designed to provide access to the full power of GAUSS without the intimidation of learning a new programming language. By using GPE, getting acquainted with techniques for econometric analysis as well as the GAUSS programming environment is fast and easy. This book was written so that you could easily use GAUSS as a tool for econometric applications.

You cannot learn econometrics by *just* reading your textbook or by *just* writing GAUSS code or programs. You must interact with the computer and textbook by working through the examples. That is what this book is all about—learning by doing.

Why GAUSS?

GAUSS is a programming language similar to C or Pascal. GAUSS code works on matrices as the basis of a complete programming environment. It is flexible and easily applies itself to any kind of matrix-based computation.

GAUSS comes with about 400 intrinsic commands ranging from file input/output (I/O) and graphics to high-level matrix operations. There are many GAUSS libraries and application packages, which take advantage of these built-in commands and procedures for implementing accurate and efficient computations.

The use of libraries and packages hides complex programming details and simplifies the interface with a set of extended procedures and control variables. For instance, GAUSS supports publication quality graphics by use of a library which extends the main system with a set of control variables manipulated on the defined graphic procedures.

What is GPE?

GPE is a GAUSS package for linear and nonlinear regression useful for econometric analysis and applications. GPE contains many econometric procedures controllable by a few groups of global variables. It covers most basic econometric computations including single linear equation estimation and prediction, systems of simultaneous linear equations, nonlinear models, and time series analysis.

However, beyond econometric computation, GPE does not provide a user interface for data input and output nor are there any procedures for data transformation. Both of these operations and other related topics, which build the interaction between GPE and the GAUSS programming environment, will be discussed in the next chapter on GAUSS Basics. Using the GPE package in a GAUSS environment is first introduced in Chapter III on linear least squares estimation and is the foundation of the rest of the book.

Using GPE

This book and CDROM were developed based on the latest version of GAUSS for Windows (version 3.5). Before using the GPE package, it must be properly installed with your GAUSS program. Install GPE according to the instructions given with the distribution CD. Make sure that the version number of GPE matches with that of your GAUSS program.[1]

Following the completion of GPE installation, the compiled GPE program named **GPE2.GCG** should reside in the GAUSS directory. **GPE2.GCG** is a compiled GAUSS program. It is an encoded binary file, which requires the correct version of GAUSS. In addition, a GPE subdirectory is created and stores all the lesson programs and data files. GPE is the working directory for all the empirical lessons. By going through this book lesson by lesson, program files may be overwritten and additional output files are generated. If you want a fresh start, just reinstall the GPE package.

All the GPE lesson programs are written with direct reference to the GPE subdirectory created during installation. Using the default GPE subdirectory is convenient because all the lesson programs and data files are already there for you to explore. Alternately, you may want to use a working diskette for the practice of creating each lesson. If you don't mind typing, using a working diskette is not only portable but also a true hands-on experience. You need only to change the references of the GPE subdirectory in each lesson program to the floppy drive your working diskette resides on (**a:** is assumed). That is, in the beginning of each lesson program, replace **gpe** with **a:**. You may also need to copy the required data files to the working diskette. A working diskette is recommended especially if you are using GAUSS in a laboratory environment.

It is important to recognize that this book is not a GAUSS how-to manual or program documentation, for which you are advised to consult *GAUSS for Windows User Guide* and *GAUSS Language References* supplied from Aptech Systems. Also, this is not a book on econometrics, although many fundamental formulas for econometric computation are introduced in order to use the implemented algorithms and routines. There are many textbooks on econometrics that describe the technical details. Rather, this is a book on computational aspects of implementing econometric methods. We provide step by step instruction using GPE and GAUSS, complete with explanations and sample program codes. GAUSS program codes are given in small chunks in a piece-meal construction. Each chunk, or lesson, offers hands-on practice for

---

[1] GPE is also available for earlier versions of GAUSS.

economic data analysis and econometric applications. Most examples can be used on different computer platforms without modification.

Conventions Used in this Book

To distinguish our explanations from your typing, as seen on your video display, all program code and output are in the monospace font Courier. For reference purposes, each line of program code is numbered. Menu items in the Windows interface, directory paths, file names, and key-stroke combinations are in **bold**. In addition, the following icons are used to designate special information:

 Extra notes and additional information are given here.

 This warns of common mistakes causing programming errors.

 Hints or remarks specific to GAUSS and GPE.[2]

A number of abbreviations for statistical and econometric terms are used in this text. Although all are defined upon their first appearance, we provide a list of these abbreviations below for reference purposes:

2SLS	*two*-*s*tage *l*east *s*quares
3SLS	*three*-stage *l*east *s*quares
ACF	*a*utocorrelation *f*unction
ADF	*a*ugmented *D*ickey-*F*uller test
AIC	*A*kaike *I*nformation *C*riterion
AOV	*A*nalysis *o*f *V*ariance
ARCH	*a*uto*r*egressive *c*onditional *h*eteroscedasticity
ARDL	*a*uto*r*egressive *d*istributed *l*ag
ARMA	*a*uto*r*egressive *m*oving *a*verage
BFGS	*B*royden-*F*letcher-*G*oldfarb-*S*hanno quasi-Newton optimization method
BHHH	*B*erndt-*H*all-*H*all-*H*ausman maximum likelihood estimation method
BIC	Schwartz *B*aysian *I*nformation *C*riterion
DF	*D*ickey-*F*uller test
DGP	*d*ata *g*enerating *p*rocess
FIML	*f*ull *i*nformation *m*aximum *l*ikelihood
GARCH	*g*eneralized *a*uto*r*egressive *c*onditional *h*eteroscedasticity
GMM	*g*eneralized *m*ethod of *m*oments
IV	*i*nstrumental *v*ariable estimation
LIML	*l*imited *i*nformation *m*aximum *l*ikelihood
LM	*L*agrangian *m*ultiplier
LR	*L*ikelihood *R*atio
ML	*m*aximum *l*ikelihood
OLS	*o*rdinary *l*east *s*quares
PACF	*p*artial *a*utocorrelation *f*unction

---

[2] We thank Aptech Systems for permission to use their GAUSS 3.2 "hammer on numbers" icon.

QHC	*q*uadratic *h*ill-*c*limbing optimization method
RSS	*r*esidual *s*um-of-*s*quares
SUR	*s*eemingly *u*nrelated *r*egressions
VAR	*v*ector *auto*regression
VIF	*V*ariance *I*nflation *F*actors

II
GAUSS Basics

GAUSS is a high-level computer language suitable for mathematical and matrix-oriented problem solving. It can be used to solve any kind of mathematical, statistical, or econometric model. Since GAUSS is a computer language, it is flexible. But it is also more difficult to learn than most *canned* (prewritten) econometric programs such as EVIEWS, SHAZAM, and TSP.

In this chapter we begin with the basics of starting GAUSS for Windows. After learning how to get in and out of GAUSS, we discuss much of the GAUSS language. At the end of the chapter, we introduce the GPE (GAUSS Programming for Econometricians and Financial Analysts) package and briefly describe its capacity for econometric analysis and applications.

Getting Started

Start GAUSS for Windows in one of the following ways:

- Click the short-cut (an icon with GAUSS logo) on the desktop.
- From Start button at the lower left corner, select and run GAUSS.
- Use Windows Explorer or File Manager to locate the GAUSS directory[3] and execute the file **GAUSS.EXE**

To quit and exit GAUSS for Windows, do either one of the following:

- Click and select **File/Exit** from the menu bar.
- Click on the "close" button (the box with the "X") in the upper right-hand corner of the GAUSS main window.

Windows Interface

If you are new to the GAUSS programming environment, you need to spend some time to familiarize yourself with the GAUSS Windows interface. From the menu bar, go to **Help/Contents** to learn about the interface. Understanding the working function of each button on the menu bar, toolbar (below the menu bar), and status bar (bottom bar of the main window) is the crucial beginning of GAUSS programming. A good reference is *GAUSS for Windows User Guide*.

Briefly, GAUSS for Windows runs in two modes: Command and Edit. Each mode has its own window. The Command window (or Command mode) is for running

---

[3] GAUSS directory refers to the directory in which you have successfully installed the GAUSS program in your computer. Assuming **C:** is your boot drive, by default installation, the GAUSS directory may be **C:\GAUSS** (for Version 3.2), **C:\GAUSS35** (for Version 3.5), **C:\GAUSSL** (for Light Version 3.2), or **C:\GAUSSLT** (for Light Version 3.5). In the following, we refer to **C:\GAUSS** as the GAUSS directory.

single-line commands or program files. It is more commonly referred as the *interactive* mode. The Edit window (or Edit mode) is for modifying or editing program and data files. A file is created from the menu bar **File/New**. An existing file can be open and edited from the menu bar **File/Open**. There is only one Command window, but you can open as many as Edit windows as needed for the program, data, output, etc. The title of each Edit window consists of the directory path and file name to indicate where the contents came from. From the **Action** button on the menu bar, a program file is executed. Your program output can be displayed either in the Command window (if Output mode is set to **Cmnd I/O**) or in a separate Output window (if Output mode is set to **Split I/O**). The ability to work simultaneously with multiple program and data files in GAUSS allows straightforward monitoring of project development. Screen displays of GAUSS Command and Edit Windows look like the following (your screen may be slightly different because of differences in the configuration setup of the Windows environment you use):

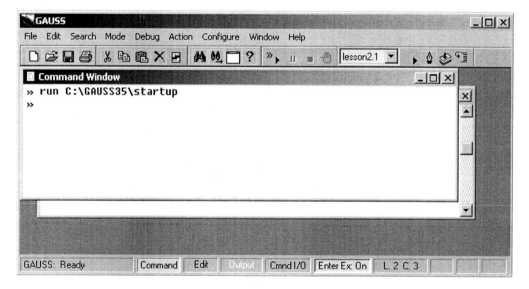

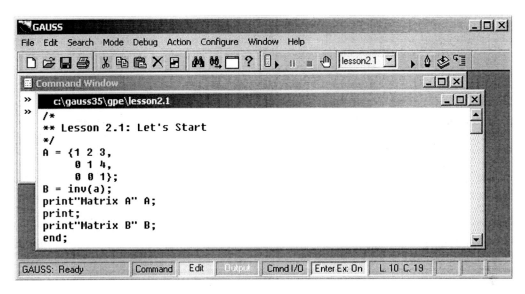

You may want to configure the programming environment to fit your taste as desired. This is done from the menu bar buttons **Mode** and **Configure**. In the GAUSS programming environment, you can also trace and debug a program file in the Debug window. This is more suited for a programmer in developing a large program, which we will not cover in this book.

An Introduction to GAUSS Language[4]

The rest of this chapter covers the basics of GAUSS language. It is written for anyone who has no prior or only limited computer programming knowledge. Only the basics of GAUSS programming are introduced, followed by discussions of more advanced topics useful for econometric analysis. We aspire to promote a reasonable proficiency in reading and understanding procedures that we will write in the GAUSS language. If you are in a hurry to use the econometric package GPE for the project at hand, you can skip the rest of this chapter and go directly to the next chapter on linear regression models and least squares estimation. However, we recommend that later, at your leisure, you come back for a thorough overview of the GAUSS language.

We have seen that GAUSS commands are either written in the Command or Edit mode. Command mode executes each line of code as it is written. Simple GAUSS commands can be typed and executed (by pressing the carriage return or **Enter** key) line by line at the ">>" prompt in the Command window.[5] In the beginning, to

---

[4] This session is written based on introductory materials for MathWorks' MATLAB prepared by William F. Sharpe for his finance course at Stanford (http://www.stanford.edu/~wfsharpe/ mia/mat/mia_mat3.htm). We thank Professor Sharpe for his helpful comments and suggestions. Both GAUSS and MATLAB are matrix programming languages, and they are syntactically similar. Translation programs between GAUSS and MATLAB are available. For example, see http://www.goodnet.com/~dh74673/gtoml/maingtm.htm.

[5] The carriage return or Enter key in the Command window is configurable within GAUSS. The default setting is "Enter always execute." See the GAUSS user guide or online help for more information.

introduce the basic commands and statements of GAUSS, we shall stay in the Command window and use the Command or interactive mode.

Matrices as Fundamental Objects

GAUSS is one of a few languages in which each variable is a matrix (broadly constructed), and the language knows what the contents are and how big it is. Moreover, the fundamental operators (e.g. addition, multiplication) are programmed to deal with matrices when required. The GAUSS environment handles much of the bothersome housekeeping that makes all this possible. Since so many of the procedures required for economic and econometric computing involve matrices, GAUSS proves to be an extremely efficient language for implementation and computation.

First of all, each line of GAUSS code must end with a semi-colon (;).

Consider the following GAUSS expression:

```
C = A + B;
```

If both A and B are scalars (1 by 1 matrices), C will be a scalar equal to their sum. If A and B are row vectors of identical length, C will be a row vector of the same length. Each element of C will be equal to the sum of the corresponding elements of A and B. Finally, if A and B are, say, 3×4 matrices, C will also be a 3×4 matrix, with each element equal to the sum of the corresponding elements of A and B.

In short the symbol "+" means "perform a matrix addition." But what if A and B are of incompatible sizes? Not surprisingly, GAUSS will complain with a statement such as:

```
(0) : error G0036 : matrices are not conformable
```

So the symbol "+" means "perform a matrix addition if you can and let me know if you can't." Similar rules and interpretation apply to matrix operations such as "−" (subtraction) and "*" (multiplication).

Assignment Statements

GAUSS uses a pattern common in many programming languages for assigning the value of an expression to a variable. The variable name is placed on the left of an equal sign and the expression on the right. The expression is evaluated and the result assigned to the variable. In GAUSS, there is no need to declare a variable before assigning a value to it. If a variable has previously been assigned a value, a number, or a string, the new value overrides the predecessor. Thus if A and B are of size 20×30, the statement:

```
C = A + B;
```

creates a variable named C that is also 20×30 and fills it with the appropriate values obtained by adding the corresponding elements in A and B. If C already existed and was, say, 20×15 it would be replaced with the new 20×30 matrix. Therefore, matrix variables in GAUSS are not fixed in size. In GAUSS, unlike some languages, there is no need to *pre-dimension* or *re-dimension* variables. It all happens without any explicit action on the part of the user.

Variable Names

The GAUSS environment is case insensitive. Typing variable names in uppercase, lowercase, or a combination of both does not matter. That is, GAUSS does not distinguish between uppercase and lowercase except inside double quotes. A variable name can have up to 32 characters, including letters, numbers and underscores. The first character must be alphabetic or an underscore. Therefore the variable `PersonalDisposableIncome` is the same as `personaldisposableincome`. While it is tempting to use long names for easy reading, small typing errors can mess up your programs. If you do mistype a variable name, you may get lucky (e.g. the system will complain that you have asked for the value of an undefined variable) or you may not (e.g. you will assign the new value to a newly created variable instead of the old one desired). In programming languages there are always tradeoffs. You don't have to declare variables in advance in GAUSS. This avoids a great deal of effort, but it allows for the possibility that nasty and difficult-to-detect errors may creep into your programs.

Showing Values

If at any time you wish to see the contents of a variable, just type its name. GAUSS will do its best, although the result may extend beyond the Command or Output window if the variable is a large matrix (remember that you can always resize the window). If the variable, say x, is not defined or has not previously been given a value, a message such as:

```
Undefined symbols:
      x                            (0)
```

---

will appear.

GAUSS will not show you the result of an assignment statement unless you specifically request for it. Thus if you type:

```
C = A + B;
```

No values will be shown although C is now assigned with values of the sum of A and B. But, if you type:

```
C;
```

or, equivalently (though verbosely):

```
print C;
```

GAUSS will show you the value of C. It may be a bit daunting if C is, say, a 20 by 30 matrix. If the variable C is not of interest, and what you want to see is the result of A plus B, simply type:

```
A + B;
```

That is, if an expression has no assignment operator (=), it will be assumed to be an implicit print statement. Note that the value shown will be represented in accordance with the format specified. If there is no explicit format used, by default GAUSS will show the numeric value in 16 fields with 8 digits of precision.

Initializing Matrices

If a matrix is small enough, one can provide initial values by simply typing them in the Command window. For example:

```
a = 3;
b = {1 2 3};
c = {4, 5, 6};
d = {1 2 3, 4 5 6};
```

Here, a is a scalar, b is a 1×3 row vector, c a 3×1 column vector, and d is a 2×3 matrix. Thus, typing

```
d;
```

produces:

1.0000000	2.0000000	3.0000000
4.0000000	5.0000000	6.0000000

The system for indicating matrix contents is very simple. Values separated by spaces belong on the same row; those separated by commas are on separate rows. All values are enclosed in brace brackets.

The alternative to creating a matrix using constants is to use the GAUSS built-in command let. If dimensions are given, a matrix of that size is created. The following statement creates a 2×3 matrix:

```
let d[2,3] = 1 2 3 4 5 6;
```

Note that dimensions of d are enclosed in square brackets, not curly brace brackets. If dimensions are not given, a column vector is created:

```
let d = 1 2 3 4 5 6;
```

If curly braces are used, the let is optional. That is, the following two expressions will create the same matrix d:

```
let d = {1 2 3, 4 5 6};
d = {1 2 3, 4 5 6};
```

Making Matrices from Matrices

The general scheme for initializing matrices can be extended to combine or concatenate matrices. For example,

```
a = {1 2};
b = {3 4};
c = a~b;
print c;
```

gives a row vector:

| 1.0000000 | 2.0000000 | 3.0000000 | 4.0000000 |

While

```
a = {1 2 3};
b = {4 5 6};
d = a|b;
print d;
```

gives a 2×3 matrix:

| 1.0000000 | 2.0000000 | 3.0000000 |
| 4.0000000 | 5.0000000 | 6.0000000 |

Matrices can easily be *pasted* together in this manner, a process that is both simple and easily understood by anyone reading a procedure. Of course, the sizes of the matrices must be compatible. If they are not, GAUSS will tell you.

Note that by putting variables in brace brackets such as:

```
c = {a b};
```

or

```
d = {a,b};
```

will not work. It produces a syntax error message.

Using Portions of Matrices

Frequently one wishes to reference only a portion of a matrix. GAUSS provides simple and powerful ways to do so. To reference a part of a matrix, give the matrix name followed by square brackets with expressions indicating the portion desired. The simplest case arises when only one element is wanted. For example, using matrix d in the previous section,

```
d[1,2];
```

equals:

| 2.0000000 |

While

```
d[2,1];
```

equals:

| 4.0000000 |

In every case the first bracketed expression indicates the desired row (or rows), while the second expression indicates the desired column (or columns). If a matrix is a vector, a single expression may be given to indicate the desired element, but it is often wise to give both row and column information explicitly.

The real power of GAUSS comes into play when more than a single element of a matrix is wanted. To indicate "all the rows" use a dot for the first expression. To indicate "all the columns," use a dot for the second expression. Thus,

```
d[1,.];
```

equals:

1.0000000	2.0000000	3.0000000

That is, d[1, .] yields a matrix containing the entire first row of d. While,

```
d[.,2];
```

equals:

2.0000000
5.0000000

That is, d[. , 2] yields a matrix containing the entire second column of d. In fact, you may use any expression in this manner as long as it includes a valid row or column numbers. For example,

```
d[2,2:3];
```

equals:

5.0000000	6.0000000

And

```
d[2,3:2];
```

equals:

6.0000000	5.0000000

Variables may also be used as *subscripts*. Thus,

```
z = {2,3};
d[2,z];
```

equals:

5.0000000	6.0000000

Another useful example is

```
d[1:2, 2:3];
```

which equals:

```
2.0000000        3.0000000
5.0000000        6.0000000
```

This is the same as

```
d[.,2:3];
```

Try the following:

```
d[.,1 3];
```

Recall that "." is a wildcard symbol and may be used when indexing a matrix, rows, or columns, to mean "any and all."

Text Strings

GAUSS is wonderful with numbers. It deals with text too, but one can tell that its heart isn't in it.

A variable in GAUSS is one of two types: numeric or string. A string is like any other variable, except the elements in it are interpreted as ASCII numbers. Thus the number 32 represents a space, and the number 65 a capital A, etc. To create a string variable, enclose a string of characters in double quotation marks. Thus:

```
stg = "This is a string";
```

The variable named `stg` is assigned a string of characters: "This is a string." Since a string variable is in fact a row vector of numbers, it is possible to create a list of strings by creating a matrix in which each row or column is a separate string. As with all standard matrices, each element of a string matrix can only have up to 8 characters long, which is exactly the 32-bit size number can hold. To print a string matrix, the variable must be prefixed with a dollar sign ($). Thus the statement

```
x = {"ab", "cd"};
print $x;
```

produces:

```
ab
cd
```

While

```
x = {"ab" "cd"};
print $x;
```

produces:

```
ab              cd
```

as always.

To see the importance of including the dollar sign in front of a variable, type:

```
print x;
```

and see what GAUSS gives you.

Matrix and Array Operations

The term "matrix operation" is used to refer to standard procedures such as matrix multiplication, while the term "array operation" is reserved for element-by-element computations.

Matrix Operations

Matrix transposition is as easy as adding a prime (apostrophe) to the name of the matrix. Thus

```
x = {1 2 3};
print x';
```

produces:

```
1.0000000
2.0000000
3.0000000
```

To add two matrices of the same size, use the plus (+) sign. To subtract one matrix from another of the same size, use a minus (–) sign. If a matrix needs to be "turned around" to conform, use its transpose. Thus, if A is 3×4 and B is 4×3, the statement

```
C = A + B;
```

results in the message:

```
(0) : error G0036 : matrices are not conformable
```

While

```
C = A + B';
```

will get you a new 3×4 matrix C.

In GAUSS, there are some cases in which addition or subtraction works when the matrices are of different sizes. If one is a scalar, it is added to or subtracted from all the elements in the other. If one is a row vector and its size matches with the number of columns in the other matrix, this row vector is swept *down* to add or subtract the corresponding row elements of the matrix. Similarly, if one is a column vector and its size matches with the number of rows in the other matrix, this column vector is swept *across* to add or subtract the corresponding column elements of the matrix. For instance,

```
x = {1 2 3};
y = {1 2 3, 4 5 6, 7 8 9};
x + y;
```

produces

2.0000000	4.0000000	6.0000000
5.0000000	7.0000000	9.0000000
8.0000000	10.000000	12.000000

While,

```
x' + y;
```

produces

2.0000000	3.0000000	4.0000000
6.0000000	7.0000000	8.0000000
10.000000	11.000000	12.000000

These situations are what we call "array operation" or *element-by-element compatibility* to be discussed below. GAUSS does not make syntactical distinction between matrix addition (subtraction) and array addition (subtraction).

Matrix multiplication is indicated by an asterisk (*), commonly regarded in programming languages as a "times sign." The usual rules of matrix multiplication from linear algebra apply: the inner dimensions of the two matrices being multiplied must be the same. If they are not, you will be told so. The one allowed exception is the case in which one of the matrices is a scalar and one is not. In this instance, every element of the non-scalar matrix is multiplied by the scalar, resulting in a new matrix of the same size as the non-scalar matrix.

GAUSS provides two notations for matrix division which provide rapid solutions to simultaneous equation or linear regression problems. They are better discussed in the context of such problems later.

Array Operations

To indicate an array (element-by-element) multiplication, precede a standard operator with a period (dot). Thus,

```
x = {1 2 3};
y = {4 5 6};
x.*y;
```

produces:

4.0000000	10.000000	18.000000

which is the "dot product" of two row vectors x and y.

You may divide all the elements in one matrix by the corresponding elements in another, producing a matrix of the same size, as in:

```
C = A ./ B;
```

In each case, one of the operands may be a scalar or the matrices must be *element-by-element compatible*. This proves handy when you wish to raise all the elements in a matrix to a power. For example:

```
x = {1 2 3};
x.^2;
```

produces

1.0000000   4.0000000   9.0000000

GAUSS array operations include multiplication (.*), division (./) and exponentiation (.^). Since the operation of exponentiation is obviously element-by-element, the notation ".^" is the same as "^". Array addition and subtraction are discussed earlier using the same matrix operators "+" and "−".

Logical and Relational Operations on Matrices

GAUSS offers six relational operators:

- LT or <   Less than
- LE or <=   Less than or equal to
- GT or >   Greater than
- GE or >=   Greater than or equal to
- EQ or ==   Equal
- NE or /=   Not equal

Note carefully the difference between the double equality and the single equality. Thus A==B should be read "A is equal to B," while A=B should be read "A is assigned the value of B." The former is a logical relation, the latter an assignment statement. For comparisons between character data and comparisons between strings, these operators should be preceded by a dollar sign ($).

Whenever GAUSS encounters a relational operator, it produces a one (1) if the expression is true and a zero (0) if the expression is false. Thus the statement,

```
x = 1 < 3;
print x;
```

produces:

1.0000000

While

```
x = 1 > 3;
print x;
```

produces:

0.0000000

Relational operators can be used on element-by-element compatible matrices. For element-by-element comparisons of two matrices, the relational operator is preceded by a dot (.). If the relational operator is not preceded by a dot (.), then the result is always a scalar 1 (*true*) or 0 (*false*), based upon a comparison of *all* elements in the two matrices. If the relational operator is preceded by a dot (.), then the operation is performed element-by-element, resulting a matrix with ones in positions for which the relation is true and zeros in positions for which the relation is false. Thus, for example:

```
A = {1 2, 3 4};
A > 2;
```

produces:

0.0000000

This is because there is at least one element of A that is not greater than 2. While

```
A .> 2;
```

produces:

0.0000000   0.0000000
1.0000000   1.0000000

Similarly,

```
A = {1 2, 3 4};
B = {3 1, 2 2};
A > B;
```

produces:

0.0000000

While

```
A .> B;
```

produces:

0.0000000   1.0000000
1.0000000   1.0000000

You may also use logical operators of which we will only mention the frequently used ones in passing:

- not
- and

- or

If the logical operator is preceded by a dot (.), the result will be a matrix of 1's and 0's based on an element-by-element logical comparison of two matrices. Each operator works with matrices on an element-by-element basis and conforms to the ordinary rules of logic, treating any non-zero element as true and a zero element as false.

Relational and logical operators are used frequently with if statements (described below) and scalar variables, as in more mundane programming languages. But the ability to use them with matrices offers major advantages in statistical and econometric applications.

Creating and Editing a GAUSS Program

So far, we have seen the working of GAUSS in the Command mode. That is, at the ">>" prompt in the Command window, you enter a statement and press the carriage return (the **Enter** key) and the statement is immediately executed. GAUSS remembers all the variable names and their assigned values. Upon the execution of a statement, the available result is displayed in the Command window or in the Output window depending on the Output mode you use. Given the power that can be packed into one GAUSS statement, this is no small accomplishment. However, for many purposes it is desirable to store a set of GAUSS statements for use when needed. The simplest form of this approach is the creation and modification of a program file: a set of commands in a file. You need to get to the Edit mode to create and edit the file. Once such a file exists in the current directory, you can simply load and run the program file. The statements stored in the file will then be executed, with the results displayed.

GAUSS for Windows provides a consistent and convenient window interface for program development. From the menu bar **File/New** (or by clicking on the blank page icon from the toolbar), you can open a blank Edit window to create a file from scratch. If the file exists, from the menu bar **File/Open** (or by clicking on the open folder icon from the toolbar), then select the name of the file to load its contents into the Edit window. You can also open a file in the Edit window by typing the file name in the Command window, including the directory in which the file is stored. This Edit window will then "pop up" and layer over the Command window. Note that the title of the Edit window is the name of the file you open for editing. After editing, clicking **Run Current File** from the **Action** menu button saves and runs the program file, with outputs shown in the Command or Output window. If you are not running the program file after editing, do not forget to save it.

A group of program and data files may be involved in a project. They can be created, loaded, and edited each in their separate Edit windows. GAUSS keeps track of two types of files: an *active file* and a *main file*. The *active file* is the file that is currently displayed (in the front highlighted Edit windows). The *main file* is the file that is executed to run the current job or project. An active program file can be executed, and put in the main file list (that is, in the pull-down menu on the toolbar). The *main file list* contains the program files you have been running (the results of which appear in the Command window or in the Output window). Any files on the main file list can be selected, edited, and executed repeatedly. The list of main files may be retained or cleared anytime as you wish.

Many Edit/Run cycles are involved in the writing and testing of a GAUSS program. The convention adopted in this book is that all example lessons (with only a few exceptions such as the first one below) will be set up to have two files. The first (program) file contains the GAUSS code, and the second (output) file will contain all output from running the program in the first file. You will see not only the results in the Command or Output window, but also the output is stored in a file you specified. The benefit of using Edit mode is the ability to have a record of each line of code. This is especially helpful when troubleshooting a long or complicated program.

Lesson 2.1 Let's Begin

To get into the Edit mode, from the menu bar, select **File/Open**. Find and select the file named **lesson2.1** in the GPE subdirectory.

 Alternatively, a file can be opened from the Command window by typing the file name at the ">>" prompt:

```
edit gpe\lesson2.1;
```

Press **Enter** key to load **gpe\lesson2.1** into the Edit window.

You are now ready for program editing. The full path of file name **c:\gauss\gpe\lesson2.1** (or something like that depending on your GAUSS installation) shows up as the title of the Edit window. **lesson2.1** is just the name of the program file for the following exercise. GAUSS will create a file named **lesson2.1** in the **c:\gauss\gpe** directory if it does not already exist. If a file named **lesson2.1** does exist, GAUSS will simply bring the file to the Edit window. When working on your own project, you should use the name of your file.

The purpose of this lesson is to demonstrate some basic matrix and array operations in the GAUSS language we have learned so far and to familiarize you with the Edit/Run dual mode operation of GAUSS. If you are typing the following lesson for practice, *do not type the line number* in front of each line of code. The numbering system is for reference and discussion only.

```
      /*
      ** Lesson 2.1: Let's Begin
      */
 1    A = {1 2 3,
           0 1 4,
           0 0 1};
 2    C = {2,7,1};
 3    print"Matrix A" A;
 4    print;
 5    print "Matrix C" c;
 6    print "A*C" a*c;
 7    print "A.*C" a.*c;
 8    print "A.*C'" a.*c';
 9    end;
```

From the menu bar, click on the **Action** button and select **Run Current File**. This will save and run the program. The name of the program file **lesson2.1** appears in the main file list located on the toolbar as a pull-down menu item. As of now, **lesson2.1** is the active file. You can run, edit, compile, and debug the main file all by clicking on the four buttons next to the main file list.

Each line of code *must* end with a semi-colon (;). In line 1, we have typed in the numbers in matrix form to be easier to read. Spaces separate columns while commas separate rows. Carriage return is *not* seen by GAUSS. That is,

```
A = {1 2 3, 0 1 4, 0 0 1};
```

is read by GAUSS in the same way as

```
A = {1 2 3,
     0 1 4,
     0 0 1};
```

The GAUSS command, print, is used to print output to the screen. You may have wondered about the extra print statement in line 4. This creates an empty line between matrix A and matrix C, making the output easier to read. The rest of **lesson2.1** demonstrates the difference between matrix multiplication (*) and element-by-element array multiplication (. *) with matrices. In addition, the use of matrix transpose notation (') is demonstrated.

After running **lesson2.1**, the following output should be displayed:

```
Matrix A
1.00000000        2.0000000        3.0000000
0.00000000        1.0000000        4.0000000
0.00000000        0.0000000        1.0000000

Matrix C
          2.0000000
          7.0000000
          1.0000000
A*C
          19.000000
          11.000000
          1.0000000
A.*C
2.0000000         4.0000000        6.0000000
0.00000000        7.0000000        28.000000
0.00000000        0.00000000       1.0000000
A.*C'
2.0000000         14.0000000       3.0000000
0.00000000        7.0000000        4.0000000
0.00000000        0.00000000       1.0000000
```

Notice that matrix multiplication requires that the number of columns in the first matrix equals the number of rows in the second matrix. Element-by-element array multiplication requires that both matrices have the same number of rows or columns. It "sweeps across" each row, multiplying every element of matrix A by the corresponding element in matrix C (line 7). Element-by-element array multiplication is "swept down" each column if C is transposed first (C') into a horizontal row vector as shown in line 8.

Programming Tips

Just a few comments on programming in general. Professional programmers judge their work by two criteria: Does it do what it is supposed to? Is it efficient? We would like to add a third criterion: Will you be able to understand what your program is supposed to be doing six months from now? Adding a blank line between sections in your program will not affect how it runs, but it will make reading your program easier. Describing the function of each section within comment symbols will benefit you not only in troubleshooting now, but also in understanding your program in the future. To do so in GAUSS, put the comment statement between a pair of "at" (@) signs or in between "/*" and "*/" symbols. Notice that the "*" is always adjacent to the comment text. Everything between the sets of "@" signs or between "/*" and "*/" symbols will be ignored by GAUSS. Comments can extend more than one line as desired. The difference between these two kinds of comments is shown in the following:

```
/* This kind of
      /* comment */
          can be nested */
@ This kind of comment cannot be nested @
```

Another important programming style observed throughout this book is that we will keep each program small. Break down your problem into smaller tasks, and write sub-programs for each task in separate blocks of a larger program or in separate programs. Avoid long lines of coding. Write clear and readable code. Use indention where applicable. Remember that programming is very fluid, and there are always multiple routes to achieve any desired task.

File I/O and Data Transformation

File input and output operations (I/O) and data transformation in a GAUSS programming environment are important prerequisites for econometric modeling and statistical analysis. The file I/O chapter of *GAUSS for Windows User Guide* describes various types of file formats available in the GAUSS programming environment.

Most useful programs need to communicate and interact with peripheral devices such as a file storage device, console display, printer, etc. A typical GAUSS program will read input data from the keyboard or a file, perform the computation, show results on the screen, and send outputs to a printer or store in a file.

GAUSS can handle at least three kinds of data formats: GAUSS data sets, GAUSS matrix files, and text (or ASCII) files. The first two data file formats are unique and efficient in GAUSS. For file transfer (import and export) between GAUSS and other application software or across platforms, the text file format is preferred. Although we do not limit the use of any particular file format, we focus here on text-formatted file input and output. For the use of data set and matrix files, see *GAUSS Language References* or on-line help for more information.

Data Input

The most straightforward way to get information into GAUSS is to type it in the Command window as we have been doing in the first part of this chapter. This approach is useful for a small amount of data input. For example:

```
prices = {12.50  37.875  12.25};
assets = {"cash", "bonds", "stocks"};
holdings = {100 200,
            300 400,
            500 600};
```

21

For long series of data, it is recommended that your create a text file for the data series using the GAUSS editor. That is, create the file and type the data in the Edit window. Such a file should have numeric ASCII text characters, with each element in a row separated from its neighbor with a space and each row on a separate line.

Now, we will introduce a text data file named **longley.txt** which comes with the GPE package. If you installed GAUSS and GPE correctly, this data file should be located in the GPE subdirectory of the GAUSS directory. The easiest way to bring it into the Edit window is to click on the menu bar button **File/Open** and select the file name **longley.txt** located in the GPE directory.

 The alternative is typing the following in the Command window at the ">>" prompt:

```
edit gpe\longley.txt;
```

and pressing**Enter** key.

The data matrix is arranged in seventeen rows and seven columns, and there are no missing values. The first row contains only variable names, so it must not be included in statistical operations. Each variable name is short, no longer than four characters in this case. All values, except the first two columns (YEAR and PGNP), are too large to handle easily. Scaling these variables may make interpreting the resulting data easier. The bottom of the file contains the data source and description for reference purposes. Of course, the descriptive information should not be included for statistical analysis.

To load the data into GAUSS, the following statement:

```
load data[17,7] = gpe\longley.txt;
```

will create a matrix named `data` containing the data matrix.

 Alternatively, it can be re-coded as the following two lines using GAUSS command `reshape` to form the desired 17×7 matrix:

```
load data[]=gpe\longley.txt;
data=reshape(data,17,7);
```

 Notice that the size of a matrix created with `load` must be equal to the size of the file being loaded (not counting optional reference information at the bottom of the file). If the matrix is larger than the actual file size, bogus data will be read. If it is smaller, part of the data series will be discarded. In either case, computations will be inaccurate.

Data Output

A simple way to output data is to display a matrix. This can be accomplished by either giving its name in interactive mode or using the print function as we have shown so far.

```
print data;
```

You can use the `format` statement to control the formats of matrices and numbers printed out. For prettier output, the GAUSS function `printfm` can print a matrix using different format for each column of the matrix.

If you want to save essentially everything that appears on your screen (i.e. the output from your GAUSS program), issue the following command:

```
output file = [filename] [option];
```

where `[filename]` represents the name of a new file that will receive the subsequent output. When using the command `output file` you must designate one of three options in `[option]`: `Reset`, `On`, or `Off`. The option `Reset` clears all the file contents so that each run of the program stores fresh output; `On` is cumulative, each output is appended to the previous one; `Off` creates an output file, but no data are directed to it. An output file is not created if none of these three options is used. When you are through directing output, don't forget to issue the command:

```
output off;
```

You may want to examine the output files. To create a text file containing the data from a matrix use `output` and `print` statements in combination. For example:

```
output file = gpe\output2.1 reset;
print data;
output off;
```

will save the matrix named `data` in the file named `output2.1` in the directory GPE.

Sending output to a printer is as easy as sending output to a file:

```
output file = lpt1 reset;
```

If you are in the Edit mode to write a program file, it is a good habit to end your program with the statement:

```
end;
```

This will automatically perform `output off` and graciously close all the files still open.

Lesson 2.2: File I/O

In Lesson 2.2, we will demonstrate how to direct program output to a file and how to input data from a text file. In addition we will slice a matrix into column vectors, which can be useful for working on individual variables. Columns (or rows) can be joined as well. This is achieved through horizontal (or vertical) concatenation of matrices or vectors.

Click on the menu bar button **File/Open** and select the file name **lesson2.2** located in the GPE directory.

Alternatively, at the ">>" prompt in the Command window, type:

```
edit gpe\lesson2.2;
```

and press **Enter**.

Make sure that the highlighted Edit window, with the title **c:\gauss\gpe\lesson2.2**, is layered over the Command window and stays in the front. To run it, click on menu bar button **Action/Run Current File**.

```
     /*
     ** Lesson 2.2: File I/O
     */
1    output file = gpe\output2.2 reset;
2    load data[17,7] = gpe\longley.txt;
3    data = data[2:17,.];

4    PGNP = data[.,2];
5    GNP = data[.,3]/1000;
6    POPU = data[.,6]/1000;
7    EM = data[.,7]/1000;

8    X = PGNP~GNP~POPU~EM;
9    print X;
10   end;
```

 For those of you who are using a working diskette (**a:** is assumed) and want to type in the program, type these lines exactly as written. Misspellings, missing semicolons, or improper spaces will all result in error messages. Be warned that each type of bracket, { }, [ ], or ( ), is interpreted differently. Errors commonly result from using the wrong bracket.

The first line of the program code tells GAUSS to direct the output of this program to a file named `output2.2` located in the GPE subdirectory. If you want a printed copy of your work, just change it to:

```
output file = lpt1 reset;
```

Let's examine the code for data loading. In line 2, a matrix named `data`, containing 17 rows and 7 columns, is created using the GAUSS command `load`. A text file located in the GPE subdirectory named **longley.txt** is then loaded into the variable `data`.

Remember that the first row of `data` contains variable names. Chopping off the first row, or indexing the matrix, is one way to remove these names from statistical analysis. In line 3, the new `data` takes from the old `data` the second row through the seventeenth row. After line 3, the matrix named `data` contains 16 rows and 7 columns. Now try to make some sense about what line 4 is doing. It assigns PGNP to the second column of the modified `data` matrix. Notice that when a matrix is being created, the brackets are to the left of the equal sign. When a matrix is indexed, the brackets are to the right of the equal sign. In general, information is taken from the right side of an equal sign and assigned to either a matrix or variable on the left side of the equal sign.

The next few lines, 4 through 7, create new variables by picking the corresponding columns of `data`. For easier handling of large numbers, quantity variables are scaled down by 1000-fold: GNP is now in billions of 1954 dollars; POPU and EM are in millions of persons. PGNP is kept as given. Note that only the variables needed for study are named and identified.

We now have four variables (vectors) that have been scaled down to a workable size. Statistical operations can be done on each variable separately, or they can be joined together and then operated on with one command. Line 8 concatenates all of the four variables horizontally with a "~" symbol, forming a new data matrix named X.

Line 9 prints the matrix X as follows:

83.000000	234.28900	107.60800	60.323000
88.500000	259.42600	108.63200	61.122000
88.200000	258.05400	109.77300	60.171000
89.500000	284.59900	110.92900	61.187000
96.200000	328.97500	112.07500	63.221000
98.100000	346.99900	113.27000	63.639000
99.000000	365.38500	115.09400	64.989000
100.00000	363.11200	116.21900	63.761000
101.20000	397.46900	117.38800	66.019000
104.60000	419.18000	118.73400	67.857000
108.40000	442.76900	120.44500	68.169000
110.80000	444.54600	121.95000	66.513000
112.60000	482.70400	123.36600	68.655000
114.20000	502.60100	125.36800	69.564000
115.70000	518.17300	127.85200	69.331000
116.90000	554.89400	130.08100	70.551000

If your output extends beyond your screen (in the Command or Output window), you can resize the window for a better view. You can also try another font such as New Courier, size 10, from the **Configure/Preferences** button on the menu bar.

Lesson 2.3: Data Transformation

In Lesson 2.2 above, we have seen the utility of scaling data series to a more manageable unit of measurement for analysis. For econometric applications, some variables may be transformed for considerations of theoretical and empirical interpretation. Exponential, logarithmic, and reciprocal transformations are frequently used functional forms in econometrics. The data transformation chapter of *GAUSS for Windows User Guide* emphasizes the use of GAUSS internal data sets. Interested readers should refer to this chapter for more details.

Lesson 2.3 below demonstrates the use of logarithmic functional transformation as a way to scale the size of each data series.

For those of you who are using a working diskette (**a:** is assumed), the first two blocks of code in **lesson2.2** can be used again. Duplicating and renaming **lesson2.2** to **lesson2.3** and then editing it will save typing and time. To do that, just start with **lesson2.2** in the Edit window and click on **File/Save As**. Since your working diskette is in **a:**, make sure that in the "Select File to Save…" dialog window the "Save In:" line shows: "3 ½ Floppy (A):". Type **a:\lesson2.3** in the "File Name" line and click on "Save."

Here is the program **lesson2.3**:

```
/*
** Lesson 2.3: Data Transformation
*/
1   output file = gpe\output2.3 reset;
2   load data[17,7] = gpe\longley.txt;
```

```
 3 | data = data[2:17,.];

 4 | PGNP = ln(data[.,2]);
 5 | GNP = ln(data[.,3]/1000);
 6 | POPU = ln(data[.,6]/1000);
 7 | EM = ln(data[.,7]/1000);

 8 | X = PGNP~GNP~POPU~EM;
 9 | print X;
10 | end;
```

Running **lesson2.3**, the printout of matrix X looks like this:

4.4188406	5.4565554	4.6784950	4.0997135
4.4830026	5.5584715	4.6879660	4.1128719
4.4796070	5.5531689	4.6984146	4.0971905
4.4942386	5.6510812	4.7088904	4.1139347
4.5664294	5.7959818	4.7191683	4.1466365
4.5859874	5.8493219	4.7297743	4.1532265
4.5951199	5.9009516	4.7457492	4.1742180
4.6051702	5.8947113	4.7554763	4.1551417
4.6170988	5.9851169	4.7654847	4.1899426
4.6501436	6.0383004	4.7768857	4.2174025
4.6858281	6.0930482	4.7911932	4.2219899
4.7077268	6.0970535	4.8036111	4.1973974
4.7238417	6.1794036	4.8151555	4.2290940
4.7379513	6.2197966	4.8312534	4.2422472
4.7510006	6.2503092	4.8508733	4.2388921
4.7613189	6.3187771	4.8681573	4.2563359

Lines 4 through 7 introduce the logarithmic transformation of each variable in addition to simple scaling. Line 8 concatenates all these variables into a matrix named X. This is simply the logarithmic transformation of the data matrix presented in the previous Lesson 2.2. In GAUSS, ln computes a natural log transformation of a data matrix while log is a base 10 log transformation. We suggest the use of natural log transformation for data scaling if needed.

GAUSS Built-In Functions

GAUSS has a large number of built-in functions or procedures—many of which are very powerful. Without knowing it, you have been using some of them such as let, print, load, and output. Most functions take some input arguments and return some outputs. Before the outputs of a function are used, they must be retrieved. To get all the outputs from a function, use a multiple assignment statement in which the variables that are to receive the outputs are listed to the left of the equal sign, separated by commas, and enclosed in brace brackets. The name of the function is on the right of the equal sign, which takes input arguments separated by commas and enclosed in round brackets. Typically, a function is *called* (initiated) in one of the following two ways:

```
output1=functionName(input1);
{output1,output2,...}=functionName(input1,input2,...);
```

In case the function outputs are not of interest, the command call is used to call the requested function or procedure without using any returned values. The syntax is,

```
call functionName(input1,input2,...);
```

Data Generating Functions

The following functions are particularly useful for creating a new matrix. Their usage is explained by example:

- **ones**   Creates a ones matrix, here a 2x4 matrix:
  ```
  ones(2,4);
  ```

- **zeros**   Creates a zeros matrix, here a 4x4 matrix:
  ```
  zeros(4,4);
  ```

- **eye**   Creates an identity matrix, here a 3x3 matrix:
  ```
  eye(3);
  ```

- **rndu**   Creates a matrix of uniform random numbers, here a 6x3 matrix:
  ```
  rndu(6,3);
  ```

- **rndn**   Creates a matrix of normal random numbers, here a 6x3 matrix:
  ```
  rndn(6,3);
  ```

- **seqa**   Creates a vector of additive sequence of numbers starting at a given value and increasing with a given increment. For instance,
  ```
  seqa(0,0.1,10);
  ```
  creates a 10x1 vector beginning at 0 and increasing with a 0.1 increment (i.e. 0, 0.1, ... , 0.9).

- **seqm**   Creates a vector of multiplicative sequence of numbers starting at a given value and increasing by a given multiplier. For instance,
  ```
  seqm(2,2,10);
  ```
  creates a 10x1 vector beginning at 2 and increasing with a multiplier of 2 (i.e. 2, 4, ... , 1032 or 2^{10}).

To convert or reshape an existing matrix to a new matrix of different size, use the reshape function as in the following example: ...

```
x=seqa(1,1,5);
print x;
y=reshape(x,5,5);
print y;
```

Creation of a sub-matrix based on some selection or deletion criteria is accomplished by selif and delif functions, respectively. For example:

```
x=rndn(100,4);
y=selif(x, x[.,1] .> 0.5);
print y;
```

Equivalently,

```
y=delif(x, x[.,1] .<= 0.5);
print y;
```

There are other useful functions for vector or matrix conversion:

- **vec**   Stacks columns of a matrix into a column vector.

- **vech**   Stacks only the lower triangular portion of matrix into a column vector.

- **xpnd**   Expands a column vector into a symmetric matrix.

- **submat**   Extracts a sub-matrix from a matrix.

- **diag**   Retrieves the diagonal elements of a matrix.

- **diagrv**   Replaces diagonal elements of a matrix.

Matrix Description Functions

To describe a matrix, such as a matrix x defined as

```
x=rndu(10,4);
```

the following functions can be used:

- **rows**   Returns the number of rows of a matrix:
  ```
  rows(x);
  ```

- **cols**   Returns the number of columns of a matrix:
  ```
  cols(x);
  ```

- **maxc**   Returns the maximum elements of each column of a matrix:
  ```
  maxc(x);
  ```

- **minc**   Returns the minimum elements of each column of a matrix:
  ```
  minc(x);
  ```

To find the maximum and minimum of a matrix, try these:

```
maxc(maxc(x));
minc(minc(x));
```

There are many other GAUSS functions like maxc and minc which work on the columns of a matrix. For example:

```
x = {1, 2, 3};
y = sumc(x) + 10;
print y;
```

Since sumc computes the sum of each column of a matrix, this will produce:

```
16.000000
```

If a matrix is given as an argument to sumc function, the summation is applied separately to each column, and a column vector of results is returned. Thus, typing

```
x = {1 2 3, 4 5 6};
sumc(x);
```

will result in:

```
5.0000000
7.0000000
9.0000000
```

To compute the cumulative sum of elements in each column of a matrix, use the function cumsumc as follows:

```
cumsumc(x);
```

Similar to sumc and cumsumc, there are:

- prodc   Computes the product of all elements in each column of a matrix.

- cumprodc   Computes the cumulative product of elements in each column of a matrix.

We further list a few descriptive statistics functions which are applied to each column of a matrix:

- meanc   Computes the mean for each column of a matrix.

- median   Computes the median for each column of a matrix.

- stdc   Computes the standard error for each column of a matrix.

Matrix Sorting Functions

To sort a matrix in ascending order, use one of the following sort functions:

- sortc   Sorts a matrix using quick sort algorithm.

- sorthc   Sorts a matrix using heap sort algorithm.

These functions will sort the rows of a matrix with respect to a specified column. That is, they will sort the elements of a column and will arrange all rows of the matrix in the same order as the sorted column. The sort is in ascending order.

Another useful sort function, sortind, returns the sorted index of a column vector. This can be used to sort several matrices in the same way that some other reference matrix is sorted. For example,

```
x = {5, 2, 8};
idx = sortind(x);
y = x[idx];
print idx~y;
```

produces two columns containing the ordering index of the original x and the sorted x:

```
2.0000000       2.0000000
1.0000000       5.0000000
3.0000000       8.0000000
```

Basic Matrix Computation

The following functions are related to several basic matrix computations:

- `det`   Computes the determinant of a square matrix.

- `inv`   Computes the inverse of a general square matrix.

- `invpd`   Computes the inverse of a symmetric, positive definite square matrix.

- `corrx`   Computes a correlation matrix.

- `vcx`   Computes a variance-covariance matrix.

- `cond`   Computes the condition number of a matrix.

- `rank`   Computes the rank of a matrix.

Solving Systems of Linear Equations

The problem is to find x from A*x = b, where A is a nxn matrix, b is a nx1 (or nxm in general) matrix, and x has the same size as b. If A is a non-singular matrix, then x = A^{-1}b. Consider the following example:

```
a = { 6 8,
     -2 4};
b = {2, 1};
x = inv(a)*b;
print x;
```

If the matrix A is symmetric positive definite, use the GAUSS function solpd to solve for x. Note that the solpd function takes two arguments. The first is the matrix on the right-hand side of the matrix equation, while the second is the matrix being inverted. For example:

```
a = {40 40,
     40 72};   @ a is symmetric positive definite @
b = {2, 1};
x = solpd(b,a);
print x;
```

Therefore, if the matrix A is nxk and n is equal or greater than k, solving x from A*x = b is equivalent to solving x from (A'A)*x = (A'*b). In other words, x = invpd(A'A)*(A'b). Using the solpd function:

```
a = { 6 8,
     -2 4};
b = {2, 1};
x = solpd(a'b,a'a);
print x;
```

This is exactly the GAUSS division (/) operator for finding the *least squares* (LS) solution of A*x = b:

```
x = b/a;
```

```
print x;
```

Another useful application of the `solpd` function is to find the inverse of a symmetric positive definite matrix, which is equivalent to the `invpd` command:

```
x = solpd(eye(2),a'a); @ equivalent to invpd(a'a) @
print x;
```

Characteristic Roots and Vectors

Given a square matrix A, finding x from the characteristic equation $(A-\lambda I)x = 0$ is a two-step procedure: First, solve $|A-\lambda I| = 0$ for λ (characteristic roots or eigenvalues). Then, for each λ, solve $(A-\lambda I)x = 0$ for x (characteristic vectors or eigenvectors). Since we are interested in the case of real eigenvalues and eigenvectors, A is assumed to be a real symmetric matrix only. Two GAUSS functions are used for the computation of eigenvalues and eigenvectors of a real symmetric matrix:

- eigrs   Computes the eigenvalues of a real symmetric matrix.

- eigrs2   Computes the eigenvalues and eigenvectors of a real symmetric matrix.

Consider the following example:

```
a = {41 -23,
     -23  13};  @ a is real and symmetric @
r = eigrs(a);
{r,v} = eigrs2(a);
print r~v;
```

We note that the function `eigrs2` returns two values: the first is a vector of eigenvalues, while the second is a matrix of the corresponding eigenvectors. The returned results are listed to the left of the equal sign, enclosed in brace brackets. Running the above block of codes, we have:

0.074175964	-0.48992502	-0.87176457
53.925824	-0.87176457	0.48992502

The first column of the matrix is the vector of two eigenvalues. The last two columns of eigenvectors correspond to each of the two eigenvalues, respectively.

A useful application of eigenvalues is to compute the condition number of a data matrix—an indicator of multicollinearity for a least squares regression model. Let X be the data matrix of regressors. The condition number of X is computed as follows:

```
xx = x'x;
r = eigrs(xx);
cn = sqrt(maxc(r)./minc(r));
print cn;
```

The condition number, cn, is defined as the square root of the ratio of the largest eigenvalue to the smallest. Compared with the GAUSS built-in function cond, the identical result is:

```
print cond(x);
```

31

Not listed, but of great use, are the many functions that provide data plotting in two or three dimensions, as well as a number of more specialized functions. To whet the econometrician's appetite, let's name a few more in the following:

- pdfn   Computes the standard normal *probability density function* (pdf).

- cdfn   Computes the complement of *cumulative distribution function* (cdf) of standard normal distribution (i.e., the integral of normal distribution in the lower tail).

- cdftc   Computes the complement of cdf of t-distribution.

- cdffc   Computes the complement of cdf of F-distribution.

- cdfchic   Computes the complement of cdf of Chi-square distribution.

- gradp   Computes the first derivative or *gradient* of a function.

- hessp   Computes the second derivative or *hessian* of a function.

- intsimp   Computes the integration of a function by Simpson's method.

- dstat   Computes descriptive statistics of a data matrix.

- ols   Computes a typical least squares regression.

- eqsolve   Solves a system of nonlinear equations.

- sqpsolve   Solves the nonlinear programming problem using the sequential quadratic programming method.

The full list of functions and information on each one can be obtained via GAUSS's on line help system.

Lesson 2.4: Data Analysis

In Lesson 2.4 we write a GAUSS program to review what we have learned so far. First we load the data matrix from the file **longley.txt.** Recall that the first row of this data matrix consists of variable names, therefore it will not be used in statistical calculations. We define y as the last (7th) column of the data matrix. In addition, we select all values of the first 6 variables and add a column of ones (constant vector) to form the matrix x.

First, we call the built-in function dstat to report the descriptive statistics of all data series including y and x. Then the ordinary least squares (OLS) estimator of y on x is computed. Finally, the data matrix x is checked for its condition number. Here is the program:

```
/*
** Lesson 2.4: Data Analysis
*/
```

```
 1 | output file = gpe\output2.4 reset;
 2 | load x[17,7]=gpe\longley.txt;
 3 | y=x[2:17,7];
 4 | x=x[2:17,1:6]~ones(16,1);
 5 | call dstat(0,y~x);
   |
 6 | b=y/x;  @ b=invpd(x'x)*x'y=solvpd(x'x,x'y) @
 7 | print b;
   |
 8 | xx=x'*x;
 9 | r=eigrs(xx);
10 | cn=sqrt(maxc(r)./minc(r));
11 | print cn cond(x);
12 | end;
```

Note that in line 5, dstat is a GAUSS built-in procedure which when called prints descriptive statistics of a data matrix into a table. The output is arranged row-wise for each variable. In dstat, the first input argument 0 means that the data to be used involve a matrix defined earlier in the program. In this case, it is the matrix y~x defined in line 3 for y and line 4 for x.

Line 6 demonstrates a simple way to obtain the least squares estimator: b = y/x. To compute the condition number of x, we first get the eigenvalues of x'x (line 9) and then take the square root of the ratio of maximum and minimum eigenvalues (line 10). The result of the formal calculation of the condition number should be the same as that from calling the GAUSS built-in function cond. We leave the rest of running the program and interpreting the results to you as an exercise.

Controlling Execution Flow

It is possible to do a great deal in GAUSS by simply executing statements involving matrix expressions, one after the other. However, there are cases in which one simply must substitute some non-sequential order. To facilitate this, GAUSS provides several standard methods for controlling program flow. These are For Loops, Do Loops, and If statements.

For Loops

The For Loop is easy to use. The most common use of a For Loop arises when a set of statements is to be repeated a fixed number of times, as in:

```
for i (0, 9, 1);

    . . . . . . .

endfor;
```

where i is the counter integer followed by a pair of parentheses which enclose three arguments. The first argument is the initial value of the counter, the second is its final value, and the last is the increment value. The statements within the loop will be executed 10 times starting from the counter i at value 0 through 9, each time with increment of 1. Note that a For Loop ends with endfor statement.

There are fancier ways to use For Loops, but for our purposes, the standard one suffices.

Do Loops

There are two kinds of Do Loops: `do while` and `do until`. The difference between a `do while` loop and a `do until` loop is that the former will continue the loop execution when the condition is true, while the latter will execute the loop when the condition is false (or until the condition becomes true). A Do Loop always ends with `endo` statement.

A `do while` loop contains statements to be executed as long as a stated condition remains true, as in:

```
do while x <= 0.5;

    . . . . . . .

endo;
```

Similarly, a `do until` loop contains statements to be executed as long as a stated condition remains false, as in:

```
do until x > 0.5;

    . . . . . . .

endo;
```

The statements `break` and `continue` are used within Do Loops to control execution flow. When `break` is encountered, the execution will jump to the statement following the `endo`. This terminates the loop. When `continue` is encountered, the execution will jump to the top of the loop and reevaluate the `do while` or `do until` expression. It reiterates the loop without executing any more of the statements inside the loop. For the For Loops, both `break` and `continue` statements work the same way as described for the Do Loops.

In contrast to the For Loop, there is no counter variable that is automatically incremented in a Do Loop. If one is used, it must be set to its initial value before the loop is entered and explicitly incremented or decremented inside the loop.

 It is, of course, crucial that at some point a statement will be executed that will cause the condition in the `do while` (or `do until`) statement to be false (true). If this is not the case, you have created an infinite loop—one that will go merrily on until you pull the plug.

For readability, it is sometimes useful to create variables for *true* and *false*, then use them in a `do while` or `do until` loop. For example:

```
true = 1==1;
false = 1==0;
. . . . .
done = false;
do while not done;

    . . . . . . . .

endo;
```

Of course, somewhere in the loop there should be a statement that will at some point setdone equal to `true`.

If Statements

An `If` statement provides a method for executing certain statements if a condition is true and other statements (or none) if the condition is false. A complicated `if` section can come with `elseif` and `else` statements, but it always ends with an `endif` statement. For example:

```
if x > 0.5;

      . . . . . . .

elseif x > 0;

      . . . . . . .

else;

      . . . . . . .

endif;
```

In this case, if x is greater than 0.5 the first set of statements will be executed; if not, x is checked again for a positive value. If x is greater than 0, the second set of statements will be executed. Otherwise, the last set of statements will be executed.

A simpler version omits the `elseif` section, as in:

```
if x > 0.5;

      . . . . . . .

else;

      . . . . . . .

endif;
```

In this case, if x is greater than 0.5 the first set of statements will be executed; if not, the second set will be executed. An even simpler version omits the `else` section, as in:

```
If x > 0.5;

      . . . . . . .

endif;
```

Here, the statements will be executed if (and only if) x exceeds 0.5.

Nesting

All of these flow control structures allow nesting, in which one type of structure lies within another. For example:

```
j = 1;
do until j > n;
    for k (1,n,1);
```

```
        if x[j,k] > 0.5;
            x[j,k] = 1.5;
        endif;
    endfor;
    j=j+1;
endo;
```

The indentation is for the reader's benefit, but is highly recommended in this and other situations for purposes of clarity. It is wise to pair up `endo` (`endfor`, `endif`) statements with preceding `do` (`for`, `if`) statements in a last-come-first-served manner. It is up to the programmer to ensure that this will give the desired results. Indenting can help, but hardly guarantees success on every occasion.

While it is tempting for those with experience in traditional programming languages to take the easy way out, using Do Loops for mathematical operations, this temptation should be strenuously resisted in GAUSS. For example, instead of

```
value = 0;
j = 1;
do while j <= n;
    value = value + price[j] * quantity[j];
    j=j+1;
endo;
```

write:

```
value = price'*quantity;
```

The latter is more succinct, far clearer, and will run much, much faster. GAUSS performs matrix operations at blinding speed, but is downright glacial at times when loops are to be executed a great many times, since it must do a certain amount of translation of each statement every time it is encountered.

A Practical Example

Do you know the accuracy of your computer's numerical calculation? The following example addresses this important problem. Suppose e is a known small positive number, and the 5×4 matrix X is defined as follows:

```
1   1   1   1
e   0   0   0
0   e   0   0
0   0   e   0
0   0   0   e
```

Verify that the eigenvalues of $X'X$ are $4+e^2$, e^2, e^2, and e^2. How small a value of e can your computer use and still successfully invert $X'X$? Try to make some sense out of the following segment of code:

```
one=ones(1,4);
e=1.0;
do until e<1.0e-16;
    x=one|(e.*eye(4));
    print "e = " e;
    print invpd(x'x);
    e=e./10;
endo;
end;
```

Writing Your Own Functions

The power of GAUSS really comes into play when you add your own functions or procedures to enhance the language. There are two kinds of user-defined functions in GAUSS. Single-line functions that return one item can be defined with the `fn` statement. A multi-line procedure is a group of GAUSS statements put together to perform a given task. It is better to create a program file to hold the procedures for future use. Procedures are declared with the `proc` statement. A single-line function returns only one argument, while a multi-line procedure can return one or more arguments. Once a function or procedure is written, debugged, and placed in the library, it is for all practical purposes part of your version of GAUSS.

Single-Line Functions

A single-line function starts with a `fn` statement declaring the function, followed by the name of the function with its arguments enclosed in parentheses. The "guts" of the function are defined on the right-hand side of the equal sign, all in one line. It is called the same way as GAUSS built-in functions. However, it returns only one argument. For example:

```
fn value(p,q) = p'*q;
```

This `value` function takes two arguments, p and q, to produce the inner product of them. The result may be a scalar, a vector, or a matrix. Of course, this will only work if p and q vectors or matrices are compatible for matrix multiplication. A more complex multi-line version (or procedure) could examine the sizes of these two matrices p and q, then use transpositions, etc., as required.

It is important to note that the argument and output names used in a function are strictly local variables that exist only within the function itself. Thus, in a program one could write the following statement to use the `value` function defined above:

```
cost = value(price,quantity);
```

In this calling statement, the function `value` takes two arguments, `price` and `quantity`, which become assigned to matrices p and q of the function, respectively. This function returns an output, called `cost`, which is assigned to the output argument (`value`). There is no need for the names to be the same in any respect. Moreover, the function cannot change the original arguments in any way. It can only return information via its output.

A powerful example of a single-line function for time series conversion is the following:

```
fn qtoal(x) = meanc(reshape(x,rows(x)/4,4)');
```

This function converts a quarterly time series into an annual series by taking the average of every four data points. Of course, this function will work only if the input data series starts from the first quarter, and it is designed to handle one series at a time. That is, the input argument x is a column vector of quarterly series, and the function returns a column vector of annual series. Note that if the last year does not have a complete quarterly series of four data points for conversion, it is ignored.

As another example of defining and using a single-line function statement, consider the following scalar-valued function of one variable:

$$f(x) = ln(x) - x^2$$

The maximal of f(x) is found at $x = \sqrt{\frac{1}{2}}$ or 0.707. This can be checked by evaluating its first and second derivatives, respectively:

$$f'(x) = 1/x - 2x$$
$$f''(x) = -1/x^2 - 2$$

Let's write these three single-line functions in GAUSS:

```
fn f(x) = ln(x) - x^2;
fn f1(x) = 1/x -2*x;
fn f2(x) = -1/(x^2) -2;
```

Now we check the maximum $x = \sqrt{\frac{1}{2}}$ for which f1(x) = 0 and f2(x) < 0:

```
xmax = sqrt(0.5);
f(xmax);
f1(xmax);
f2(xmax);
```

Remember the built-in procedures gradp and hessp serve the same purpose of finding the first and second derivatives, the gradient vector, and hessian matrix of a user defined function without writing their analytical forms f1 and f2 as above. Try this:

```
gradp(&f,xmax);
hessp(&f,xmax);
```

The use of gradp and hessp procedures to numerically evaluate the first and second derivatives of a function is particularly useful when the analytical forms of derivatives are difficult to write. Consider the following function of two variables:

$$g(x) = (x_1^2 + x_2 - 11)^2 + (x_1 + x_2^2 - 7)^2$$

With the 2×1 parameter vector x, the function is easily defined in GAUSS:

```
fn g(x) = (x[1]^2 + x[2] - 11)^2 + (x[1] + x[2]^2 -7)^2;
```

Writing out the analytical formulas of the first and second derivatives using single-line functions may be difficult. For this function, there are four minima: (3, 2), (3.5844, -1.8481), (-3.7793, -3.2832), and (-2.8051, 3.1313). Using gradp and hessp to check them is easy.

At this point you may be tempted to try using a graph to find the minima of the above function. GAUSS is not good at graphics. Nevertheless, there are functions available to do pblication quality graphics in GAUSS. See *GAUSS for Windows User Guide* or the on-line help menu for more details.

Procedures

A procedure in GAUSS is basically a user-defined function which can be more than one line and as complicated as necessary to perform a given task. Any GAUSS built-in command or function may be used in a procedure, as well as any user-defined function or other procedure. Procedures can refer to any global variable and declare local variables within. The basic structure of a GAUSS procedure consists of the following components:

1. `proc` statement   Procedure declaration

2. `local` statement   Local variable declaration

3. Body of procedure   ...

4. `retp` statement   Return from procedure

5. `endp` statement   End of procedure definition

There is always one `proc` statement and one `endp` statement in a procedure definition. Anything that comes between these two statements is part of the procedure. `local` and `retp` statements are optional, and may occur more than once in a procedure. GAUSS does not allow nested procedure definitions. That is, a procedure cannot be defined within another procedure.

Variables other than input and output arguments may be included in procedures as needed. There are global and local variables. A global variable is already declared and used outside the procedure. A local variable is only *visible* to the procedure and has no existence outside the procedure. Indeed, a local variable in one procedure may have the same name as a different local variable in another function or procedure; the two will coexist with neither bothering the other.

A procedure can return multiple arguments of output through `retp` statements and by specifying the number of returned items in the beginning of the `proc` statement. As an example, the procedure version of the `value` function takes inputs of p and q and returns the total (called s) and average (called m) values as follows:

```
proc (2) = value(p,q);
    local s, m;
    s = p'*q;
    m = s./sumc(q);
    retp(s,m);
endp;
```

 In the `proc` statement, the syntax of an equal sign preceded with the number of returned arguments enclosed in parentheses (that is, " (2) = " in the above example) is not needed for a procedure with single output argument (the default case).

To use the multiple output arguments of a procedure call, simply assign them names in the declaration line, as in:

```
{sum,mean} = value(price,quantity);
```

Here, variables `price` and `quantity` are assigned to the input arguments p and q, respectively. Similarly, `sum` and `mean` are assigned to the output arguments s and m. All the input and output arguments are local variables.

Note that as with inputs, the correspondence between outputs in the calling statement and the procedure itself is strictly by order. When the procedure has finished its work, its output values are assigned to the variables in the calling statement.

If a procedure does not return any items or you want to discard the returned items, just `call` it as we have demonstrated in the above example lessons. For example:

```
call value(price,quantity);
```

Now let's extend the earlier single-line version of time series conversion function `qtoal` to a multi-line procedure so that it can handle the conversion of a more general data matrix. The working method of the following procedure `qtoa` is to take a data matrix x which consists of quarterly data series in columns and convert it into a matrix of the yearly averages. The procedure takes advantage of the previously defined single-line function `qtoal` to compute the annual average series from each column of the quarterly data matrix, all in a Do Loop. Here is the procedure:

```
proc qtoa(x);
    local r,c,y,i;
    r = rows(x);
    c = cols(x);
    y = qtoal(x[.,1]);
    i = 2;
    do until i > c;
        y = y~qtoal(x[.,i]);
        i = i+1;
    endo;
    retp(y);
endp;
```

Of course, the above time series conversion function and procedure are limited to a quarterly data series. We can make them more flexible by specifying the number of periods of each seasonal cycle as an input argument in addition to the data matrix.

The following function `tss1` and procedure `tss` are essentially the same as `qtoal` and `qtoa`, respectively. The difference is that now the number of periods n for time series conversion is specified as one of the input arguments. Depending on the seasonal cycle of the data series, you can use the same procedure for either quarterly or monthly conversion.

```
fn tss1(x,n) = meanc(reshape(x,rows(x)/n,n)');

proc tss(x,n);
    local r,c,y,i;
    r = rows(x);
    c = cols(x);
    y = tss1(x[.,1],n);
    i = 2;
    do until i > c;
        y = y~tss1(x[.,i],n);
        i = i+1;
    endo;
    retp(y);
endp;
```

As an exercise, write the procedures to compute the analytical first and second derivatives of this scalar-valued function of two variables:

$$g(x) = (x_1^2 + x_2 - 11)^2 + (x_1 + x_2^2 - 7)^2$$

User Library

The purpose of writing functions and procedures is to keep tasks organized and self-contained. Each function or procedure will perform a few given tasks and nothing else. To make programmers' work easier, procedures allow programmers to build on their previous work and on the work of others rather than starting over again and again to perform related tasks. One way to organize the work is to collect a group of functions and procedures into a program file and register the file and its contents with the GAUSS library system. Note that you must have your own copy of GAUSS installed on your own computer in order to access and modify the GAUSS library facility. We will assume that your GAUSS comes with the User Library, to which you can add your creative functions and procedures.

First, let's put the function `tss1` and procedure `tss` together in a file named **TSS.SRC** (SRC is the default file extension name for GAUSS source codes, although you can use any other name you want). Put the program file **TSS.SRC** in the **SRC** subdirectory of GAUSS path. Next, we will add the following lines to the library file **USER.LCG** located in the **LIB** directory of the GAUSS path:

```
TSS.SRC
    tss1  :  fn
    tss   :  proc
```

Similar to the idea of using a dictionary, the function `tss1` and procedure `tss` defined in the program file **TSS.SRC** are now part of GAUSS library system, which will be searched for name recognition every time GAUSS executes a program. You can also add variable names as matrices or strings in the library. Refer to *GAUSS Language References* or the on-line help system for more details on using and maintaining the library system.

From now on, both `tss1` and `tss` functions are an integral part of your version of GAUSS. You have just extended the environment for GAUSS programming!

GPE Package

The other way of extending GAUSS is to use a package, which is a set of compiled GAUSS libraries for special purposes. *GAUSS Programming for Econometricians and Financial Analysts* (GPE) is a GAUSS package of econometric procedures. The GAUSS command `use` is used to load a package at the beginning of your program. For example,

```
use gpe2;
```

will load the GPE package (version 2) for econometric analysis and applications. Note that `use` can only appear *once* and must occur at the *top* of a program.

GPE consists of three main procedures (`estimate`, `forecast`, and `reset`) along with global control variables that modify the econometric routines. The procedure `estimate` computes linear and nonlinear regressions, while `forecast` performs least squares prediction. `reset` initializes global control variables to their default values. Global control variables are of two types: input and output. Global input variables control the execution behavior of the called procedure. For example, they can modify `estimate` and `forecast` to use linear restrictions, weighted variables, instrumental variables, lagged dependent and independent variables, etc.

Output global variables are the results of calling `estimate` and `forecast`. They can be assigned to new variables for further analysis. Depending on the input global variables used which control the econometric routines, not all the output global variables will be available. The name of an input control variable starts with a single underscore (for example, _b), while an output control variable starts with a double underscore (for example, __b). Refer to Appendix A for a complete list of GPE global control variables and their default or predefined values.

A template for a typical program using GPE is given below:

```
/*
** Comments on program title, purposes,
** and the usage of the program
*/

use gpe2;  @ using GPE package (version 2) @
@ this must be the first executable statement @

/*
** Writing output to file or sending it to printer:
** specify file name for output
*/

/*
** Loading data:
** read data series from data files.
*/

/*
** Generating or transforming data series:
** create and generate variables with
** data scaling or transformation
** (e.g. y and x are generated here and will be used below)
*/

call reset;  @ initialize global variables @

/*
** Set input control variables for model estimation
** (e.g. _names for variable names, see Appendix A)
*/

call estimate(y,x); @ do model estimation @
@ variables y, x are generated earlier @

/*
** Retrieve output control variables for
** model evaluation and analysis
*/

/*
** Set more input control variables if needed,
** for model prediction
** (e.g. _b for estimated parameters)
*/
```

```
call forecast(y,x); @ do model prediction @

end; @ important: don't forget this @
```

Using the GPE package in a GAUSS environment is the main focus of the rest of this book, which begins in the next chapter on linear regression models. If you are already familiar with linear least squares estimation, you can jump to the nonlinear models discussion which begins in Chapter VI. The topic of simultaneous equation systems is covered in Chapter XIII. In addition to many classical econometric methods, modern approaches such as generalized method of moments (Chapter XII), autoregressive conditional heteroscedasticity (Chapter XV), and panel data analysis (Chapter XVI), are programmed and solved with GPE (version 2) for GAUSS.

Don't forget that we are learning GAUSS as a tool to do econometrics. The package GPE written in GAUSS acts as a bridge between the domain knowledge (econometrics) and the programming environment (GAUSS). With this approach, only a limited knowledge of computer programming is required in the beginning. After gaining experience with GPE and GAUSS in general, you should be ready for your own programming adventure in advanced econometrics, by either extending GPE or writing new programs.

III
Linear Regression Models

GPE (*GAUSS Programming for Econometricians and Financial Analysts*) is a GAUSS package for linear and nonlinear regressions useful for econometric analysis and applications. The purpose of this chapter is to show you how to use GPE for basic linear least squares estimation.

Least Squares Estimation

A linear regression model can be written either in a matrix form:

$$Y = X\beta + \epsilon$$

or, in a vector form:

$$Y = X_1\beta_1 + X_2\beta_2 + \ldots + X_K\beta_K + \epsilon$$

where Y is the dependent variable, X_k is the k-th independent (explanatory) variable, and β_k is the corresponding parameter (coefficient), k = 1, 2, ... , K. Given a sample of N data observations, both X_k's and Y are N-vectors of sample data. Denote X = $[X_1 X_2 \ldots X_K]$. Typically, we assume the last column of data matrix X, that is X_K, is a constant one-vector. For parameter estimation of a linear regression model, the random error term ϵ is assumed to be identically independently distributed (iid). For statistical inference, an assumption of probability density will be necessary. For example, ϵ is normally identically independently distributed (nid) with zero mean and constant variance σ^2.

The ordinary least squares regression amounts to the following estimation results:

$b = (X'X)^{-1}X'Y$	Estimator of β.
$\text{Var}(b) = s^2(X'X)^{-1}$	Estimated variance-covariance matrix of β.
$e = Y - Xb$	Estimated errors ϵ or residuals.
$s^2 = e'e/N-K$	Estimated regression variance σ^2. N is the number of sample data; K the is the number of parameters.

Consider the simple case of regressing the dependent variable Y against one independent variable X in addition to a constant:

$$Y = \alpha + \beta X + \epsilon$$

where ϵ is the difference between known Y and estimated Y, or the *residual*. The parameter α is the *intercept* and β is the *slope* of the linear regression equation.

Continuing with the text data file **longley.txt** we used in Chapter II, Lesson 3.1 introduces the use of GPE to estimate a simple regression equation. Lesson 3.2

examines a set of regression statistics obtained from the simple regression. Lesson 3.3 is a multiple regression model.

Lesson 3.1: Simple Regression

This lesson estimates a simple regression relationship between employment EM in millions of persons and RGNP or real GNP expressed in billions of 1954 dollars. Note that the 1954 observation of PGNP is 100, which is the base year of the deflator. All data series are read from the text data file **longley.txt**.

```
    /*
    ** Lesson 3.1: Simple Regression
    */
 1  use gpe2;        @ using GPE package (version 2) @
 2  output file = gpe\output3.1 reset;
 3  load data[17,7] = gpe\longley.txt;
 4  data = data[2:17,.];

 5  PGNP = data[.,2];
 6  GNP = data[.,3]/1000;
 7  EM = data[.,7]/1000;
 8  RGNP = 100*GNP./PGNP;

 9  call reset;
10  _names = {"EM","RGNP"};
11  call estimate(EM,RGNP);
12  end;
```

In order to use GPE package for econometric analysis and applications, the first executable statement in your GAUSS program must be:

```
use gpe2;
```

This tells GAUSS where to look when GPE commands are used. However, remarks enclosed in comment symbols are permitted before the first line of program code.

A linear regression model is estimated using the GPE econometric procedure, estimate. Before calling estimate, it is recommended to initialize all the global control variables first by calling the procedure reset. Between the two procedures, reset and estimate, the required GPE input control variables for model estimation are set.

In Lesson 3.1, line 9 initializes all the GPE global control variables by calling reset procedure. Then, in line 10, the input control variable _names is defined to be a list of character names for variables used in the regression (dependent variable first, followed by independent variables in the order of appearance in the equation). In this example, EM is the dependent variable, RGNP the independent variable, and _names is a character vector of variable names as:

```
_names = {"EM", "RGNP"};
```

Not starting GPE input control variables such as _names with an underline (_) is a common mistake. GAUSS ignores them without warning or an error message. Your program using GPE just will not work like it should. See Appendix A for more information about the usage of _names and other input control variables.

If _names is not specified, then the *default* variable names are used for the procedure estimate. That is, Y for the name of the dependent variable and X# for the names of the independent variables (# indicates the number in sequence, i.e., 1, 2, …).

The GPE econometric procedure estimate is called in line 11. It takes the dependent variable as the first argument, and the list of independent variables as the second. A constant vector for the estimated intercept term is automatically added to the model estimation.

Now, let's look at the output from running this program:

```
Least Squares Estimation
------------------------
Dependent Variable = EM
Estimation Range =   1          16
Number of Observations = 16
Mean of Dependent Variable = 65.317
Standard Error of Dependent Variable = 3.5120

R-Square = 0.97320      R-Square Adjusted = 0.97129
Standard Error of the Estimate = 0.59511
Log-Likelihood = -13.331
Log Ammemiya Prediction Criterion (APC) =   -0.92023
Log Akaike Information Criterion (AIC) =   -0.92154
Log Schwarz Bayesian Information Criterion (BIC) =   -0.82497
```

Sum of Squares	SS	DF	MSS	F	Prob>F
Explained	180.05	1	180.05	508.39	2.1048E-012
Residual	4.9582	14	0.35416		
Total	185.01	15	12.334		

Variable Name	Estimated Coefficient	Standard Error	t-Ratio 14 DF	Prob >|t|	Partial Regression
RGNP	0.058726	0.0026045	22.547	2.1048E-012	0.97320
CONSTANT	43.264	0.98931	43.732	2.2494E-016	0.99273

The basic output of estimate is presented in four blocks. The first block gives general information about the regression. Goodness of fit of the estimated regression and several model selection criteria are given in block two. Block three is the standard Analysis of Variance (AOV) . The following discussion focuses on the last block of output information. Values of the estimated coefficient, standard error, and t-ratio for each variable are given row-wise. Reading the output for each variable gives the estimated model as:

EM	=	43.264 +	0.059 RGNP
s.e.		(0.989)	(0.0026)
t-ratio		43.7	22.5

Interpreting this output tells us that, on average for each one billion dollar increase of RGNP (measured in 1954 value), there will be an increase of about 59 thousand in people employed (EM).

Since the expected value of the residuals is zero, it is not in the estimated regression equation. However, a list of error values for each observation is available for further analysis to be discussed in later lessons.

Testing of the simple hypothesis that a given coefficient is equal to zero takes the estimated coefficient's t-ratio and compares it with the critical value from the Student's t distribution listed for the given degrees of freedom (DF). Prob > |t| is the corresponding P-value, or the probability of a type II error (that is, the probability of not rejecting the null (false) hypothesis that the corresponding coefficient equals zero). We know that RGNP's coefficient is statistically significant from its t-ratio of 22.5 and our chance of being wrong is 2×10^{-12}, or very close to zero.

The partial regression coefficient measures the marginal contribution of the variable when the effects of other variables have already been taken into account. For a linear regression including only one independent variable, this is just the R-square (0.9732 in this case) of the regression.

The GPE estimate routine is the foundation of most models that you will use to estimate a regression equation. Global control variables are then added in different combinations to check, test, and hopefully correct the fitted regression. In the next several lessons, further analysis of the regression is achieved through the use of input control variables for the estimate procedure. Again, refer to Appendix A for a more detailed description of GPE input control variables.

Lesson 3.2: Residual Analysis

How good are the results of the simple regression from Lesson 3.1? Of course, the measurement of R-square is a popular yardstick to judge the goodness of fit. One more tool for evaluating just how good an estimated regression fits a set of observations is to analyze residuals, the difference between the actual and estimated dependent variable. GPE provides several options in conjunction with the estimate procedure to analyze and evaluate residuals. This lesson explores three ways to perform residual analysis.

```
   /*
   ** Lesson 3.2: Residual Analysis
   */
1  use gpe2; @ using GPE package (version 2) @
2  output file = gpe\output3.2 reset;
3  load data[17,7] = gpe\longley.txt;
4  data = data[2:17,.];

5  PGNP = data[.,2];
6  GNP = data[.,3]/1000;
7  EM = data[.,7]/1000;
8  RGNP = 100*GNP./PGNP;

9  call reset;      @ initialize control variables @
10 _rstat = 1;      @ report residual statistics @
11 _rlist = 1;      @ list residuals @
12 _rplot = 1;      @ plot residuals @
13 _names = {"EM","RGNP"};
14 call estimate(EM,RGNP);
15 end;
```

Before using global control variables, as we have mentioned earlier, you need to call the reset procedure once to initialize them. Calling reset returns all GPE global control variables to their default setting.

The reset option used with an output file has nothing to do with a called reset in GPE. The latter is a GPE procedure, while the former is an option associated with the GAUSS command output. They are simply two different concepts.

_rstat is the residual analysis tool most frequently used in conjunction with GPE's estimate. Setting the GPE input control variable to a non-zero value (the convention is 1, meaning *true* or *ye*) provides a set o f simple residual statistics. These statistics are: squared correlation of the observed (actual) and predicted (fitted) values of the dependent variable, sum-of-squared residuals, sum of absolute residuals, sum of residuals, and the serial correlation coefficient, first-order Rho. The well-known Durbin-Watson test statistic is useful for testing the presence of first-order serial correlation. The output of residual statistics is:

```
Squared Correlation of Observed and Predicted = 0.97320
Sum of Squared Residuals = 4.9582
Sum of Absolute Residuals = 7.6446
Sum of Residuals = 5.32197E-012
First-Order Rho = 0.23785
Durbin-Watson Test Statistic = 1.4408
```

The option _rlist = 1 lists the observed (actual) and predicted (fitted) values of the dependent variable. The residual is computed as the difference between the actual and fitted values. Each observation of residual and its standard error is listed as well.

```
List of Observed, Predicted and Residuals
     Obs      Observed    Predicted    Residual    Std Error
      1        60.323       59.841      0.48195      0.52253
      2        61.122       60.479      0.64314      0.53477
      3        60.171       60.446     -0.27506      0.53419
      4        61.187       61.938     -0.75124      0.55639
      5        63.221       63.347     -0.12561      0.56955
      6        63.639       64.037     -0.39762      0.57341
      7        64.989       64.938      0.050585     0.57597
      8        63.761       64.588     -0.82719      0.57531
      9        66.019       66.329     -0.31005      0.57446
     10        67.857       66.798      1.0588       0.57246
     11        68.169       67.251      0.91781      0.56979
     12        66.513       66.826     -0.31280      0.57232
     13        68.655       68.439      0.21576      0.55933
     14        69.564       69.110      0.45430      0.55112
     15        69.331       69.565     -0.23401      0.54454
     16        70.551       71.140     -0.58873      0.51511
```

Plotting is a quick way to evaluate the result of model estimation. Setting _rplot = 1 will return a plot of estimated residuals, while setting _rplot = 2 produces both the residual graph and fitted-vs.-actual dependent variable series. The graph is shown in a separate window when running the program. By viewing the plot of residuals, the correlation patterns in residuals may indicate a need to re-specify the model.

Plot of Residuals

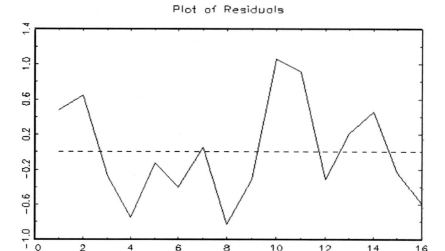

Lesson 3.3: Multiple Regression

Evaluating output from Lesson 3.2 shows it was in general a good model, but could adding more explanatory variables make it better? Let's see what happens when an additional variable, POPU (that is, population in millions of persons), is included in the regression.

In the following, we add a few new twists to both the programs of Lesson 3.1 and 3.2. In addition to _rstat, _rplot, _rlist, this lesson introduces the use of another input control variable, _vcov. By setting it to a non-zero value (i.e., 1), the regression output will include a variance-covariance matrix as well as a correlation matrix of the estimated coefficients. It is often useful to examine the relationship among estimated coefficients in a multiple regression.

```
     /*
     ** Lesson 3.3: Multiple Regression
     */
1    use gpe2; @ using GPE package (version 2) @
2    output file = gpe\output3.3 reset;
3    load data[17,7] = gpe\longley.txt;
4    data = data[2:17,.];

5    PGNP = data[.,2];
6    GNP = data[.,3]/1000;
7    POPU = data[.,6]/1000;
8    EM = data[.,7]/1000;
9    RGNP = 100*GNP./PGNP;

10   call reset; @ initialize control variables @
11   _vcov = 1;      @ print var-covar matrix @
12   _rstat = 1;     @ report residual statistics @
13   _rlist = 1;     @ list residuals @
14   _rplot = 2;     @ plot data and residuals @
15   _names = {"EM","RGNP","POPU"};
16   call estimate(EM,RGNP~POPU);
17   end;
```

Remember how to use "~" to horizontally concatenate vectors or matrices? RGNP~POPU is the data matrix of independent variables for this multiple regression. Line 16 indicates that the dependent variable EM is the first argument of the estimate procedure, followed by the data matrix of independent variables RGNP~POPU as the second argument. The list of respective variable names used in the regression is defined by _names, an input control variable, in line 15. Note that a constant vector for the estimated intercept is automatically added to the model estimation.

Including POPU has changed our estimated regression, but is it better? Analyzing the following result will tell the story.

```
Least Squares Estimation
------------------------
Dependent Variable = EM
Estimation Range =  1          16
Number of Observations = 16
Mean of Dependent Variable = 65.317
Standard Error of Dependent Variable = 3.5120

R-Square = 0.97434      R-Square Adjusted = 0.97039
Standard Error of the Estimate = 0.60430
Log-Likelihood = -12.983
Log Ammemiya Prediction Criterion (APC) =  -0.83552
Log Akaike Information Criterion (AIC) =  -0.84001
Log Schwarz Bayesian Information Criterion (BIC) =  -0.69515
```

Sum of Squares	SS	DF	MSS	F	Prob>F
Explained	180.26	2	90.131	246.81	4.5725E-011
Residual	4.7473	13	0.36518		
Total	185.01	15	12.334		

Variable Name	Estimated Coefficient	Standard Error	t-Ratio 13 DF	Prob >|t|	Partial Regression
RGNP	0.068698	0.013386	5.1322	0.00019257	0.66954
POPU	-0.086282	0.11353	-0.76001	0.46081	0.042542
CONSTANT	49.651	8.4631	5.8667	5.5306E-005	0.72585

```
Variance-Covariance Matrix of Coefficients
RGNP          0.00017918
POPU         -0.0014897    0.012888
CONSTANT      0.10764     -0.95400      71.624
                 RGNP        POPU      CONSTANT

Correlation Matrix of Coefficients
RGNP          1.0000
POPU         -0.98029      1.0000
CONSTANT      0.95017     -0.99293      1.0000
                 RGNP        POPU      CONSTANT

Squared Correlation of Observed and Predicted = 0.97434
Sum of Squared Residuals = 4.7473
Sum of Absolute Residuals = 7.4704
Sum of Residuals = -5.47779E-010
First-Order Rho = 0.32776
Durbin-Watson Test Statistic = 1.2602
```

List of Observed, Predicted and Residuals				
Obs	Observed	Predicted	Residual	Std Error
1	60.323	59.758	0.56493	0.51924
2	61.122	60.416	0.70616	0.53666
3	60.171	60.279	-0.10802	0.49591

4	61.187	61.925	-0.73787	0.56470
5	63.221	63.474	-0.25252	0.55371
6	63.639	64.178	-0.53860	0.55192
7	64.989	65.075	-0.086161	0.55650
8	63.761	64.568	-0.80739	0.58361
9	66.019	66.504	-0.48502	0.53598
10	67.857	66.937	0.92024	0.55198
11	68.169	67.319	0.85001	0.57167
12	66.513	66.692	-0.17851	0.55364
13	68.655	68.457	0.19823	0.56749
14	69.564	69.068	0.49565	0.55697
15	69.331	69.387	-0.055654	0.50068
16	70.551	71.036	-0.48547	0.50510

Our estimated multiple regression equation is

EM	=	49.65	+ 0.069 RGNP	-	0.086 POPU
s.e.		(8.46)	(0.013)		(0.114)
t-ratio		5.87	5.13	-	0.76

RGNP still has about the same influence on EM, as reported in the previous lesson. Based on residual statistics, the model has a similar performance to the simple regression without the POPU variable.

Pay special attention to the "Partial Regression Coefficient," which gauges the marginal contribution of each variable when the effects of other variables have already been taken into account. In terms of model interpretation, the negative slope coefficient of POPU is not what we would expect. POPU has an extremely low partial regression coefficient and it is not statistically significant as seen by its near zero t-ratio. Looking at the outputs of the variance-covariance matrix and the correlation matrix of coefficients, the estimated coefficient of POPU has a relatively large variance and it is strongly correlated with that of RGNP. Therefore, our regression is better without POPU.

Estimating Production Function

So far this handbook has given cut and dried examples of what each GAUSS or GPE command does. Now we will attempt to show the flexibility that GPE has to offer. In the following sections, we will estimate the famous Cobb-Douglas production function with time series of U.S. real output and inputs. To do so, a new data set named **cjx.txt** is introduced; it also comes with the GPE package and is installed in the GPE subdirectory. **cjx.txt** contains six annual data series from 1929 to 1967. Let's look at the contents of **cjx.txt**. The data matrix has 40 rows and 6 columns, with no missing values. The first row contains variable names and should not be included for analysis. The bottom of the file contains descriptive information and also should not be used. Why is looking at each data file so important? Troubleshooting problems caused by imperfect data files is very difficult. Error messages caused by loading imperfect data are not always obvious and can show up anywhere in your program.

Out of the **cjx.txt** data series we will use only the following selected variables:

GNP in constant dollars (X);
Number of persons, adjusted for hours of work and educational level (L1);

Capital stock, adjusted for rate utilization (K1).

To make our following presentation easier, L1 has been renamed L and K1 has been renamed K. With the introduced notations, a simple two-input Cobb-Douglas production function is written as

$$X = \alpha\, L^{\beta 1}\, K^{\beta 2}\, exp(\varepsilon)$$

To transform the model into a more useful form, natural logarithms are taken on both sides of the equation:

$$ln(X) = \beta_0 + \beta_1\, ln(L) + \beta_2\, ln(K) + \varepsilon$$

where $\beta_0 = ln(\alpha)$ is the intercept of the log model, and the slopes β_1 and β_2 are interpreted as input *elasticities*. Econometric estimation of this Cobb-Douglas production function is the focus of the following few lessons.

Lesson 3.4: Cobb-Douglas Production Function

We will first estimate the unrestricted influences of labor input L and capital input K on real output X. Then, the economic theory of constant returns to scale (CRS) is formulated and tested with the use of linear restrictions. Testing CRS is done by restricting the summation of the two slope coefficients to 1 in the log specification of the model. That is, $\beta_1 + \beta_2 = 1$. To test the hypothesis of CRS, we need to check how residuals from both the first unrestricted and second restricted regressions compare.

```
   /*
   ** Lesson 3.4: Cobb-Douglas Production Function
   */
1  use gpe2;
2  output file = gpe\output3.4 reset;
3  load data[40,6] = gpe\cjx.txt;

4  year = data[2:40,1];
5  X = ln(data[2:40,2]);
6  L = ln(data[2:40,3]);
7  K = ln(data[2:40,5]);

8  call reset;
9  _names = {"X","L","K"};
10 call estimate(X,L~K);
11 _restr = {1 1 1};
12 call estimate(X,L~K);
13 end;
```

 Optional residual analysis: _rstat=1, _rplot=2, _rlist=1, _vcov=1 may be added to the program.

Before examining the output, let's look at the programming style. This program is efficient, that is, many actions are combined in few lines of code. Line 4 removes the first row (variable names) of the data file and indexes the matrix data into a vector, all in one step. Lines 5, 6, and 7 go one step further. In addition to indexing the matrix, they take the natural logarithm of each variable.

Line 10 estimates the basic, unrestricted, least squares regression output:

```
Least Squares Estimation
------------------------
Dependent Variable = X
Estimation Range =  1          39
Number of Observations = 39
Mean of Dependent Variable = 5.6874
Standard Error of Dependent Variable = 0.46096

R-Square = 0.99463      R-Square Adjusted = 0.99433
Standard Error of the Estimate = 0.034714
Log-Likelihood = 77.286
Log Ammemiya Prediction Criterion (APC) =   -6.6471
Log Akaike Information Criterion (AIC) =   -6.6474
Log Schwarz Bayesian Information Criterion (BIC) =   -6.5195
```

Sum of Squares	SS	DF	MSS	F	Prob>F
Explained	8.0310	2	4.0155	3332.2	1.3921E-041
Residual	0.043382	36	0.0012051		
Total	8.0744	38	0.21248		

Variable Name	Estimated Coefficient	Standard Error	t-Ratio 36 DF	Prob >|t|	Partial Regression
L	1.4508	0.083228	17.431	3.9260E-019	0.89407
K	0.38381	0.048018	7.9930	1.7130E-009	0.63960
CONSTANT	-3.9377	0.23700	-16.615	1.8332E-018	0.88464

The estimated model is:

$ln(X)$	=	- 3.94	+	1.45 $ln(L)$	+	0.38 $ln(K)$
s.e.		(0.24)		(0.083)		(0.048)
t-ratio		- 16.62		17.43		7.99

Interpreting the estimation result of the log model takes into account that estimated slope coefficients translate directly into elasticities. In other words, the influence of labor L and capital K on output GNP (X) is expressed in terms of "percentage change." For every one percent increase in labor input L, GNP increases by 1.45 percent. When capital input K is increased by one percent, GNP increases 0.38 percent.

An adjusted R^2 of .994 reveals a very good fit of the regression equation. Large t-ratios and small P-values for all variables show that the chance of the elasticity coefficients being zero is also small. Moreover, partial regression coefficients are strong enough for both $ln(L)$ and $ln(K)$. The resulting model is the basis for many lessons to come.

Now, let's consider the theory of constant returns to scale often assumed in many classical productivity studies. Restricted least squares is the technique used to estimate models with linear restrictions. GPE's estimate procedure can be modified to perform restricted least squares with the use of the input control variable _restr (see Appendix A for details).

The last part of the program (lines 11 and 12) demonstrates a simple example of restricting $\beta_1 + \beta_2 = 1$, in order to test for CRS. To understand what line 11 is doing, we need to describe a little matrix algebra. Linear restrictions on least squares coefficients can be expressed by the equation

$$R\beta = q$$

where R is the restriction matrix specifying a set of linear relationships among estimated coefficients. It tells which coefficients are to be restricted. β is the column vector of estimated coefficients, and q is the column vector of values that the linear combination of β's are restricted to. In most cases, restrictions are imposed on slope coefficients. Separating the intercept term from the slope coefficients, the matrix representation of linear restrictions is rewritten as:

$$[\, R_s \; R_0 \,] \begin{bmatrix} \beta_s \\ \beta_0 \end{bmatrix} = q$$

where β_s is the vector of slope coefficients and R_s is the restriction matrix corresponding to β_s. Similarly, β_0 is the intercept coefficient and R_0 corresponds to β_0. The input control variable _restr in GPE is implemented according to the restrictions on slope coefficients defined below:

$$\_restr = [\, R_s \; q \,]$$

Linear restrictions involving the intercept term will necessitate the explicit inclusion of a constant column as part of the data matrix of independent variables and will estimate the model without an intercept. This is done by setting the input control variable _const = 0 before calling the estimate procedure.

Back to our CRS example, line 11:

```
_restr = {1 1 1};
```

Now let's look at the matrix to the right of the equal sign, {1 1 1}. Each row of _restr specifies a single restriction. Therefore, only one restriction is called out (i.e. $\beta_1 + \beta_2 = 1$) in this example. The number of columns of _restr comes from the number of slope coefficients β_s plus the one column of the restricted value q. The first two columns of 1's in _restr (β_s) select β_1 and β_2. When multiplied with corresponding slope coefficients, it is the sum of β_1 and β_2. The last column of 1's in _restr (q) specifies that the resulting sum of β_1 and β_2 equals 1. In other words, the _restr matrix calculates:

$$[\, 1 \; 1 \,] \begin{bmatrix} \beta_1 \\ \beta_2 \end{bmatrix} = 1*\beta_1 + 1*\beta_2 = 1.$$

Restricting $\beta_1 = \beta_2$ is the same as $\beta_1 - \beta_2 = 0$. Using the information from the program **lesson3.4**, the GPE command for the restriction $\beta_1 - \beta_2 = 0$ is:

```
_restr = {1 -1 0};
```

That is, $[\, 1 \; -1 \,] \begin{bmatrix} \beta_1 \\ \beta_2 \end{bmatrix} = 1*\beta_1 - 1*\beta_2 = 0.$

More complicated cases may have several restrictions. To demonstrate such a situation, assume a model with four slope coefficients $\beta_1, \beta_2, \beta_3, \beta_4$. Imposing the restrictions $\beta_2 = 0$ and $\beta_3 + \beta_4 = 1$ would use:

```
_restr ={0 1 0 0 0,
         0 0 1 1 1};
```

That is, $\begin{bmatrix} 0 & 1 & 0 & 0 \\ 0 & 0 & 1 & 1 \end{bmatrix} \begin{bmatrix} \beta_1 \\ \beta_2 \\ \beta_3 \\ \beta_4 \end{bmatrix} = \begin{bmatrix} 0*\beta_1 + 1*\beta_2 + 0*\beta_3 + 0*\beta_4 \\ 0*\beta_1 + 0*\beta_2 + 1*\beta_3 + 1*\beta_4 \end{bmatrix} = \begin{bmatrix} 0 \\ 1 \end{bmatrix}$

Look at the output produced by restricted least squares estimation (line 12):

```
Least Squares Estimation
------------------------
Dependent Variable = X
Estimation Range =  1          39
Number of Observations = 39
Mean of Dependent Variable = 5.6874
Standard Error of Dependent Variable = 0.46096

WARNING: Linear Restrictions Imposed.
R-Square, AOV, SE, and t may not be reliable!
Wald F-Test for Linear Restrictions
F(   1,  36)      Prob>F
     427.66  1.4430E-021

R-Square = 0.93080      R-Square Adjusted = 0.92893
Standard Error of the Estimate = 0.12289
Log-Likelihood = 27.451
Log Ammemiya Prediction Criterion (APC) =   -4.1189
Log Akaike Information Criterion (AIC) =   -4.0918
Log Schwarz Bayesian Information Criterion (BIC) =   -3.9638
```

Sum of Squares	SS	DF	MSS	F	Prob>F
Explained	6.2806	1	6.2806	415.91	1.0185E-021
Residual	0.55874	37	0.015101		
Total	8.0744	38	0.21248		

Variable	Estimated	Standard	t-Ratio	Prob	Partial
Name	Coefficient	Error	37 DF	>|t|	Regression
L	-0.15051	0.10802	-1.3933	0.17183	0.049854
K	1.1505	0.10802	10.651	8.0037E-013	0.75405
CONSTANT	0.95015	0.061657	15.410	1.1067E-017	0.86520

Before testing for CRS, let's look at the format of the output. Notice the warning near the top. Due to the imposed restrictions, standard statistics based on residuals are reliable only when the restrictions are correct. The Wald test statistic of linear restrictions is given along with its P-value, directly under the warning near the top of the output. The Wald test statistic uses residual sum-of-squares (RSS) from both unrestricted and restricted models to check if the stated restrictions yield a model that is statistically different from the model without the restrictions.

The Wald test statistic is:

$$\frac{\frac{RSS^* - RSS}{J}}{\frac{RSS}{N\text{-}K}} \sim F(J, N\text{-}K)$$

where RSS* is the restricted residual sum-of-squares with $\beta_1 + \beta_2 = 1$; RSS is the unrestricted residual sum-of-squares; J is the number of restrictions; K is the number of variables, including the constant (do not confuse K with the variable name for capital input in this program); and N is the number of total observations. That is,

$$\frac{\frac{0.55874 - 0.04338}{1}}{\frac{0.04338}{39\text{-}3}} = 427.66 \sim F(1, 39\text{-}3)$$

At a 5% level of significance, the F critical value of 4.17 places our computed value, 427.66, in the right-tail rejection region of the F distribution. Together with a near zero P-value for the Wald statistic, this result leads us to reject the linear restriction $\beta_1 + \beta_2 = 1$.

Based on this simple two-input Cobb-Douglas specification of the production technology, the data series from **cjx.txt** does not support the theory of constant returns to scale. As a matter of fact, the U.S. production technology exhibited the pattern of increasing returns to scale (i.e., $\beta_1 + \beta_2 > 1$) at least from 1929 to 1967.

Having thrown away the hypothesis of constant returns to scale, the next interesting issue about the production function is presented. Is there any difference in factor productivity between pre-war and post-war periods?

Lesson 3.5: Testing for Structural Change

The goal of this lesson is to determine if real output, measured by GNP from **cjx.txt**, underwent structural change over the time period between 1929 to 1967, starting in 1948. That is, is there a difference between the estimated coefficients when one regression spans the entire time period versus when two separate regressions are estimated? One way to determine if there is a difference is to use the Chow test. The Chow test compares the results of the regression of the entire time period (1929-1967) against the regression data from 1929-1948 and then 1949-1967. If a statistically significant difference is found, we can assume that there was a structural change in productivity after 1948.

```
    /*
    ** Lesson 3.5: Testing for Structural Change
    */
1   use gpe2;
2   output file = gpe\output3.5 reset;
3   load data[40,6] = gpe\cjx.txt;

4   year = data[2:40,1];
5   X = ln(data[2:40,2]);
6   L = ln(data[2:40,3]);
7   K = ln(data[2:40,5]);
8   call reset;
9   _names = {"X", "L", "K"};
10  call estimate(X,L~K);        @ whole sample @
```

```
11 | _begin = 1;      @ sub-sample: 1929-1948 @
12 | _end = 20;
13 | call estimate(X,L~K);

14 | _begin = 21;     @ sub-sample: 1949-1967 @
15 | _end = 39;
16 | call estimate(X,L~K);
17 | end;
```

Run the above program to analyze the output. It calls estimate three times. The first time it estimates the entire sample (the default case):

```
Least Squares Estimation
------------------------
Dependent Variable = X
Estimation Range =  1          39
Number of Observations = 39
Mean of Dependent Variable = 5.6874
Standard Error of Dependent Variable = 0.46096


R-Square = 0.99463      R-Square Adjusted = 0.99433
Standard Error of the Estimate = 0.034714
Log-Likelihood = 77.286
Log Ammemiya Prediction Criterion (APC) =  -6.6471
Log Akaike Information Criterion (AIC) =  -6.6474
Log Schwarz Bayesian Information Criterion (BIC) =  -6.5195
```

Sum of Squares	SS	DF	MSS	F	Prob>F
Explained	8.0310	2	4.0155	3332.2	1.3921E-041
Residual	0.043382	36	0.0012051		
Total	8.0744	38	0.21248		

Variable Name	Estimated Coefficient	Standard Error	t-Ratio 36 DF	Prob >|t|	Partial Regression
L	1.4508	0.083228	17.431	3.9260E-019	0.89407
K	0.38381	0.048018	7.9930	1.7130E-009	0.63960
CONSTANT	-3.9377	0.23700	-16.615	1.8332E-018	0.88464

The first regression is named the restricted model because it restricts the entire time period to having the same structure. The estimated restricted model is:

$ln(X)$	=	- 3.94	+	1.45 $ln(L)$	+	0.38 $ln(K)$
s.e.		(0.24)		(0.083)		(0.048)
t-ratio		- 16.62		17.43		7.99

Sub-samples for the second and for the third regression estimations are controlled by _begin and _end, set to the desired observation numbers, respectively. _begin and _end allow regressions of varying sizes to be estimated from a single data series. Since the default value of _begin is 1, it really is not necessary in line 11. The next line _end = 20 tells GPE to use up to, and including, the 20th row of data for estimate. Here is the output of the second regression equation:

```
Least Squares Estimation
------------------------
Dependent Variable = X
Estimation Range =  1          20
Number of Observations = 20
Mean of Dependent Variable = 5.3115
Standard Error of Dependent Variable = 0.27867
```

```
R-Square = 0.97590        R-Square Adjusted = 0.97307
Standard Error of the Estimate = 0.045732
Log-Likelihood = 34.945
Log Ammemiya Prediction Criterion (APC) =  -6.0301
Log Akaike Information Criterion (AIC) =  -6.0324
Log Schwarz Bayesian Information Criterion (BIC) =  -5.8831
```

Sum of Squares	SS	DF	MSS	F	Prob>F
Explained	1.4399	2	0.71996	344.24	1.7649E-014
Residual	0.035555	17	0.0020915		
Total	1.4755	19	0.077656		

Variable Name	Estimated Coefficient	Standard Error	t-Ratio 17 DF	Prob >|t|	Partial Regression
L	1.6167	0.20897	7.7367	5.7391E-007	0.77881
K	0.21967	0.22995	0.95530	0.35281	0.050947
CONSTANT	-4.0576	0.35722	-11.359	2.3202E-009	0.88358

Notice that the estimation range is from 1 to 20, using 20 observations. Running the regression using only the time period from 1929 to 1948 returns the following model:

$$ln(X) \quad = \quad -4.06 \quad + \quad 1.62\ ln(L) \quad + \quad 0.22\ ln(K)$$

s.e.	(0.36)	(0.21)	(0.23)
t-ratio	-11.36	7.74	0.96

The third regression with _begin = 21 (line 14) and _end = 39 (line 15) tells GPE to estimate the model from the 21st row of the data series up to, and including, the last or the 39th row. Let's look at the regression result:

```
Least Squares Estimation
------------------------
Dependent Variable = X
Estimation Range =  21          39
Number of Observations = 19
Mean of Dependent Variable = 6.0832
Standard Error of Dependent Variable = 0.21025

R-Square = 0.99578        R-Square Adjusted = 0.99525
Standard Error of the Estimate = 0.014484
Log-Likelihood = 55.132
Log Ammemiya Prediction Criterion (APC) =  -8.3228
Log Akaike Information Criterion (AIC) =  -8.3255
Log Schwarz Bayesian Information Criterion (BIC) =  -8.1763
```

Sum of Squares	SS	DF	MSS	F	Prob>F
Explained	0.79237	2	0.39618	1888.5	1.0026E-019
Residual	0.0033566	16	0.00020979		
Total	0.79572	18	0.044207		

Variable Name	Estimated Coefficient	Standard Error	t-Ratio 16 DF	Prob >|t|	Partial Regression
L	1.0090	0.14403	7.0054	2.9675E-006	0.75413
K	0.57909	0.055248	10.482	1.4222E-008	0.87288
CONSTANT	-2.4981	0.53122	-4.7025	0.00023960	0.58021

Now, notice that the estimation range is from 21 to 39, using 19 observations. Regressing only the time period from 1949 to 1967 returns the following model:

$$ln(X) \quad = \quad -2.50 \quad + \quad 1.01 \; ln(\text{L}) \quad + \quad 0.58 \; ln(\text{K})$$

s.e.	(0.53)	(0.14)	(0.055)
t-ratio	-4.70	7.01	10.48

Back to the question at hand, was there a structural change in productivity between the years of 1929 and 1967? We have processed our raw data using 1948 as the break point, and only need to apply the formal Chow test on the results. Computing the Chow test statistic as follows:

$$\frac{\dfrac{RSS^* - (RSS1 + RSS2)}{J}}{\dfrac{RSS1 + RSS2}{N - 2K}} \quad \sim \quad F(K, \; N\text{-}2K)$$

where RSS* is the restricted residual sum-of-squares for the whole sample (1929-1967); RSS1 is the residual sum-of-squares for the first sub-sample (1929-1948); RSS2 is the residual sum-of-squares for the second sub-sample (1949-1967); K is the number of variables, including constant, in each regression (again, do not confuse K with the variable name for capital input in this program); and N is the number of observations for the whole sample.

Plugging in the numbers yields:

$$\frac{\dfrac{0.04338 - (0.03555 + 0.00336)}{3}}{\dfrac{0.03555 + 0.00336}{39 - 6}} \quad = \quad 1.27 \sim F(3, \; 39\text{-}6)$$

At a 5% level of significance, comparing the Chow test statistic (1.27) against the F critical value of 2.92 leads us to conclude that, based on the Cobb-Douglas specification, there was no structural change in productivity between 1929 and 1967.

Lesson 3.6: Residual Diagnostics

From the previous two lessons on the study of the Cobb-Douglas production function using U.S. input and output data series from **cjx.txt**, we concluded that production technology did not exhibit constant returns to scale. As a matter of fact, from 1929 to 1967, there was a pattern of increasing returns to scale (see Lesson 3.4). By dividing the sample into pre-war (1929-1948) and post-war (1949-1967) periods, we did not find any structural differences in these two periods (see Lesson 3.5). It is better to estimate the production function using the whole sample.

This returns us to our original least squares estimation of the model:

$$ln(X) \quad = \quad -3.94 \quad + \quad 1.45 \; ln(\text{L}) \quad + \quad 0.38 \; ln(\text{K})$$

or in exponential form:

$$X = 0.02 \; L^{1.45} \; K^{0.38}$$

For the purpose of statistical inference, the log-model is assumed to be normally distributed. In other words, X is log-normally distributed. Do the estimated errors, or residuals, in fact follow a normal distribution? Are there any *dominant* observations of residuals that distort the distribution of the remaining residuals? The former is a question about the underlying normality assumption of the model, while the latter relates to issues of influential observations and outliers.

Besides examining standard residual statistics and plotting residual series, GPE offers a set of diagnostic information to check the characteristics of residuals in depth.

The first half of the program below is the same as that of **lesson3.4**. After removing _rplot and setting _rstat to typical values, we add the following two lines:

```
_bjtest = 1;
_rlist = 2;
```

Setting _bjtest = 1 (meaning yes or true) will carry out the Bera-Jarque normality test on the residuals.

We have seen the use of _rlist = 1 which lists each observation of the residuals and their standard errors, in addition to observed (actual) and predicted (fitted) data series. With _rlist = 2, in addition to residuals and their standard errors, useful information on influential observations and outliers is available.

```
      /*
      ** Lesson 3.6: Residual Diagnostics
      */
1     use gpe2;
2     output file = gpe\output3.6;
3     load data[40,6] = gpe\cjx.txt;

4     year = data[2:40,1];
5     X = ln(data[2:40,2]);
6     L = ln(data[2:40,3]);
7     K = ln(data[2:40,5]);
8     names = {"X", "L", "K"};

9     call reset;
10    _rstat = 1;
11    _rlist = 2;      @ check influential obs. @
12    _bjtest = 1;     @ normality test @

13    call estimate(X,L~K);
14    end;
```

Running the above program, the output file output3.6 is generated. For model evaluation, we now refer to output3.6. After reporting basic residual statistics, the Bera-Jarque Wald test for normality computes the statistic based on the measurements of *skewness* and *kurtosis* for the residuals as follows:

```
Bera-Jarque Wald Test for Normality
Asymptotic Standard Error of Residuals = 0.033352
Skewness of Residuals = 0.84226
Kurtosis of Residuals = 4.7072
Chi-Sq(   2)   Prob>Chi-Sq
0.0093379
```

The resulting test statistic follows the Chi-squared probability distribution with 2 degrees of freedom. The computed value of 9.35 for the Bera-Jarque test statistic is far greater than the critical value for either a 5 or 10 percent level of significance (or, less than 1% in its P-value). The null hypothesis of residual normality is rejected! For a perfect normal distribution, residual skewness should be 0 and residual kurtosis should be 3. The rejection of normality is not a surprise. However, non normal residuals render potential problems for statistical inference.

The last part of the output reports the regression diagnostics for influential observations and outliers:

Residual Diagnostics for Influential Observations and Outliers
(Valid for Checking Ordinary Least Squares Residuals Only)

Obs	Leverage	Standardized Residual	Studentized Residual	DFFITS
1	0.048570	-0.37556	-0.37103	-0.083832
2	0.069668	-1.2819	-1.2938	-0.35406
3	0.092468	-1.2069	-1.2149	-0.38779
4	0.20093	-0.41784	-0.41300	-0.20710
5	0.18527	-0.97098	-0.97019	-0.46265
6	0.12035	-0.61196	-0.60656	-0.22435
7	0.088917	-0.23985	-0.23669	-0.073941
8	0.063757	0.30955	0.30563	0.079757
9	0.064645	-0.076541	-0.075477	-0.019842
10	0.067310	1.3562	1.3727	0.36876
11	0.057612	1.4644	1.4889	0.36815
12	0.048564	1.2914	1.3039	0.29458
13	0.045681	0.54239	0.53701	0.11749
14	0.049876	-0.51380	-0.50848	-0.11650
15	0.044225	0.036933	0.036417	0.0078335
16	0.048269	1.9447	2.0269	0.45646
17	0.049727	3.2828	3.8671	0.88462
18	0.14309	0.41797	0.41313	0.16882
19	0.13632	-2.0428	-2.1422	-0.85110
20	0.11090	-1.8036	-1.8646	-0.65853
21	0.064225	-0.61213	-0.60673	-0.15895
22	0.055357	0.035430	0.034935	0.0084570
23	0.056146	-0.79457	-0.79042	-0.19278
24	0.050215	-0.95665	-0.95549	-0.21970
25	0.043698	-0.69982	-0.69478	-0.14852
26	0.032275	0.32336	0.31930	0.058311
27	0.037287	0.43459	0.42964	0.084554
28	0.042054	-0.44591	-0.44089	-0.092378
29	0.046087	-0.29348	-0.28972	-0.063681
30	0.056159	0.42446	0.41957	0.10235
31	0.058795	0.010363	0.010218	0.0025538
32	0.064299	-0.41384	-0.40902	-0.10722
33	0.078586	0.11346	0.11190	0.032679
34	0.084366	0.36577	0.36132	0.10968
35	0.083668	0.75412	0.74951	0.22648
36	0.094336	0.69948	0.69443	0.22412
37	0.097121	0.56208	0.55667	0.18257
38	0.10356	0.017775	0.017526	0.0059569
39	0.11562	-0.91018	-0.90796	-0.32830
Mean	0.076923	-0.0072089	0.0067883	-0.024796

To check for influential observations and outliers, we first take a look at the column "Leverage," which measures the influence of each observation on the regressors. We check for leverage which is greater than $2\times(K/N)$ where K is the number of estimated coefficients and N is the number of observations. In this case, $2\times(K/N) = 2\times(3/39) = 0.154$. Observations 4 and 5 (leverage 0.201 and 0.185, respectively) are quite influential.

Standardized (or normalized) residuals should follow a standardized normal distribution, provided that the Bera-Jarque test statistic confirms the distribution assumption. Unfortunately, this is not the case as shown by the test results above. Observations 17 and 19 (3.283 and –2.043, respectively) are greater than 2 standard errors from the mean.

A more robust measure of outliers uses the studentized residuals (or standardized predicted residuals) which follows the Student's t distribution with N-K-1 degrees of freedom. Given the critical value of 1.69 at a 5% level of significance, observations 16, 17, 19, and 20 are candidates for outliers.

The last column, "DFFITS," measures the contribution of each observation to the prediction of the model. The cutoff value $2 \times (K/N)^{0.5}$ is suggested (that is, 0.555 in the case of this Cobb-Douglas production model). The contribution of observations 17, 19, and 20 are rather large.

Materials of this lesson on influential observations and outliers can be found in Judge et al. (1988) and Maddala (1988). In summary, for our study of the Cobb-Douglas production function, the model is sensitive to the use of data near the end of World War II (i.e., observations 17, 19, and 20). The model may be better explained without them.

IV
Dummy Variables

Dummy variables are widely used in econometrics to isolate sub-group effects in a given sample. These sub-groups may be geographical regions, yearly quarters, gender, or periods in time. How dummy variables are used in regression estimation determines in which way the sub-groups differ. The so-called dummy variables themselves remain vectors of ones and zeros. A one indicates the presence of a given characteristic, while a zero indicates its absence. In most cases, one less dummy variable is used than there are sub-groups. Estimated regressions from these sub-groups may have an additive difference, a multiplicative difference, or a combined additive and multiplicative difference. An additive difference refers to a parallel shift in the level of an estimated regression. This shift is reflected in a change of the intercept term, while the other coefficients remain unchanged. The slope coefficients will vary with their associated multiplicative dummy variables. The estimated changes in slope coefficients among sub-groups are measured by the coefficients of multiplicative dummy variables. A combined additive and multiplicative difference in sub-groups is achieved by a change in all coefficients, both intercept and slope terms.

Since entire chapters on dummy variables are written in excellent academic references detailing the interpretation of the results from using dummy variables, we will only give brief interpretations of our results. Instead, we explore in detail the generation of dummy variables using GAUSS.

Seasonality

Determining seasonal patterns in time series data is one application of dummy variables. A new text data file named **almon.txt** will be used to study quarterly seasonality. It has three variables. The first column is the date, in years and quarters (YEARQT). The second column is capital expenditures in millions of dollars (CEXP). The last column holds capital appropriations in millions of dollars (CAPP). The basic Almon model describes the simple relationship between capital expenditures and appropriations as follows:

$$CEXP = \beta_0 + \beta_1 \, CAPP + \varepsilon$$

There are 60 observations in total, although Almon's original study used the first 36 observations from 1953 to 1961. Lesson 4.1 is devoted to the study of seasonal differences with Almon's quarterly time series on capital appropriations and expenditures.

Does the use of dummy variables matter? Lesson 4.1 continues the hypothesis testing procedure for significant differences in quarterly seasonality. It is achieved by comparing regression results from restricted (without seasonal dummy variables) and unrestricted (with seasonal dummy variables) least squares.

In Lesson 4.2, the notorious problem of the "dummy variable trap" is discussed with an alternative use and interpretation of dummy variables in conjunction with the regression without intercept.

Lesson 4.1: Seasonal Dummy Variables

In this lesson, we introduce the use of additive dummy variables to remove seasonality in Almon's quarterly time series data.

First of all, seasonality implies that the best-fitting regression for each season (quarter) may be different. In other words, the intercept and slope terms that provide the best fit for one quarter may not provide the best fit for different quarters. Before generating the seasonal dummy variable matrix, you need to have some idea of what it should look like. It has a repeating set pattern of four columns, one for each quarter. Consider all 60 observations of time series data in **almon.txt**; a pattern of 0's and 1's is created to represent one cycle of seasonality (that is, one year). The pattern is reshaped into a 4-column matrix with the desired 60 rows:

```
pattern = {1 0 0 0,
           0 1 0 0,
           0 0 1 0,
           0 0 0 1};
D = reshape(pattern,60,4);
q1 = D[.,1];
q2 = D[.,2];
q3 = D[.,3];
```

To avoid perfect collinearity with the constant column associated with the intercept, only three columns of the dummy variable matrix D will be used. That is, four quarters are indicated with only three dummies: q1, q2, and q3. Lesson 4.2 on the dummy variable trap explains why we must do this.

Now the model with three quarterly dummy variables is:

$$CEXP = \beta_0 + \beta_1 CAPP + \delta_1 Q1 + \delta_2 Q2 + \delta_3 Q3 + \varepsilon$$

Or, in four equations (one for each quarter) as follows:

Quarter 1: $CEXP = (\beta_0 + \delta_1) + \beta_1 CAPP + \varepsilon$
Quarter 2: $CEXP = (\beta_0 + \delta_2) + \beta_1 CAPP + \varepsilon$
Quarter 3: $CEXP = (\beta_0 + \delta_3) + \beta_1 CAPP + \varepsilon$
Quarter 4: $CEXP = \beta_0 + \beta_1 CAPP + \varepsilon$

We also will address the significance of seasonal differences in the model by testing when the three coefficients δ_1, δ_2, and δ_3 are jointly equal to zero. This is a test procedure for the presence of seasonality in the model we will examine later.

```
/*
** Lesson 4.1: Seasonal Dummy Variables
*/
1  use gpe2;
2  output file = gpe\output4.1 reset;
3  load almon[61,3] = gpe\almon.txt;

4  cexp = almon[2:61,2];
5  capp = almon[2:61,3];
```

```
 6 │ qt = almon[2:61,1];

 7 │ pattern = {1 0 0 0,
 8 │            0 1 0 0,
 9 │            0 0 1 0,
10 │            0 0 0 1};
11 │ D = reshape(pattern,60,4);
12 │ q1 = D[.,1];    @ quarterly seasonal dummies @
13 │ q2 = D[.,2];
14 │ q3 = D[.,3];

15 │ call reset;
16 │ _names = {"cexp", "capp", "q1", "q2", "q3"};
17 │ call estimate(cexp,capp~q1~q2~q3);
18 │ _restr = {0 1 0 0 0,
19 │            0 0 1 0 0,
20 │            0 0 0 1 0};
21 │ call estimate(cexp,capp~q1~q2~q3);
22 │ end;
```

The estimation is carried out with three quarter dummy variables named q1, q2, and q3. The fourth quarter is the base case, and the coefficients of three dummy variables identify the additive differences from that of the fourth quarter, or the intercept term.

There are many ways to generate the dummy variables other than the suggested use of the `reshape` command. A simple alternative is to rely on the quarter indicator qt, appearing in the first column of the data file **almon.txt**. Lines 7 through 14 of the above program can be replaced by the following three lines:

```
q1 = (qt%10) .== 1;
q2 = (qt%10) .== 2;
q3 = (qt%10) .== 3;
```

The modulo division "`%`" returns the remainder of the integer division, and the notation "`.==`" in GAUSS performs element-by-element equality comparison. In other words, each line compares the last digit of qt to a given quarter, placing a one in the dummy variable if the comparison turns out to be true.

GAUSS has its own commands for creating dummy variables: `dummy`, `dummybr`, `dummydn`. The command `dummy` creates a matrix of dummy variables by breaking a vector of data into multiple groups. To make sense of this example, lines 7 through 11 of the above program may be replaced by the following:

```
seasons = {1,2,3,4};
D = dummy(qt%10, seasons);
```

where the column vector `seasons` containing four quarter indicators is used to compare with the last digit of the variable qt. The GAUSS command `dummy` creates a matrix of four columns of dummy variables, D. It compares each data observation of qt%10 to the breakpoints designated in the vector `seasons`. If the data are in the range designated, a one is placed in the corresponding element of matrixD, if not, a zero is placed.

Running the program **lesson4.1** will produce two sets of regression results in the output file `output4.1`. The first estimated model looks like this:

CEXP = 670.93 + 0.737 CAPP - 13.69 Q1 - 50.60 Q2 - 31.53 Q3

s.e.	(230.9)	(0.053)	(204.5)	(204.3)	(204.2)
t-ratio	2.91	13.95	- 0.067	- 0.248	- 0.154

We can also write the estimated model as four separate equations, one for each quarter:

Quarter 1:	CEXP = (670.93 - 13.69) + 0.737 CAPP
Quarter 2:	CEXP = (670.93 - 50.60) + 0.737 CAPP
Quarter 3:	CEXP = (670.93 - 31.53) + 0.737 CAPP
Quarter 4:	CEXP = 670.93 + 0.737 CAPP

We have estimated the linear relationship between capital expenditures (CEXP) and appropriations (CAPP) with varying intercept terms to represent the seasonal differences in the model. Is there a real or significant difference among the four estimated regression equations? Analyzing both the t-ratios and the P-values reveals that the coefficients of dummy variables are not statistically significantly different from zero. Furthermore, the partial regression values are very small for the dummy variables. A more formal procedure is to test the hypothesis that all of the coefficients of dummy variables are jointly equal to zero. The hypothesis is that $\delta_1 = 0$, $\delta_2 = 0$, and $\delta_3 = 0$ hold simultaneously. The GPE input control variable _restr (lines 18,19, and 20) defines Almon's equation with the three quarterly dummy variables jointly equaling zero.

```
_restr = {0 1 0 0 0,
          0 0 1 0 0,
          0 0 0 1 0};
```

Then, restricted least squares estimation is carried out in line 21. Here is the second set of estimation results in which the coefficients of three quarterly dummy variables are restricted to zero:

```
Least Squares Estimation
------------------------
Dependent Variable = CEXP
Estimation Range =  1          60
Number of Observations = 60
Mean of Dependent Variable = 3092.4
Standard Error of Dependent Variable = 1151.9

WARNING: Linear Restrictions Imposed.
R-Square, AOV, SE, and t may not be reliable!
Wald F-Test for Linear Restrictions
F(   3,   55)       Prob>F
   0.023130       0.99518

R-Square = 0.78006      R-Square Adjusted = 0.77626
Standard Error of the Estimate = 544.88
Log-Likelihood = -462.15
Log Ammemiya Prediction Criterion (APC) =  12.681
Log Akaike Information Criterion (AIC) =  12.734
Log Schwarz Bayesian Information Criterion (BIC) =  12.908
```

Sum of Squares	SS	DF	MSS	F	Prob>F
Explained	6.1072E+007	1	6.1072E+007	205.70	9.9398E-021
Residual	1.7220E+007	58	2.9689E+005		
Total	7.8291E+007	59	1.3270E+006		

Variable Name	Estimated Coefficient	Standard Error	t-Ratio 58 DF	Prob >|t|	Partial Regression

CAPP	0.73684	0.051375	14.342	9.9398E-021	0.78006
Q1	-6.1284E-014	0.00000	0.00000	0.00000	0.00000
Q2	2.6290E-013	0.00000	0.00000	0.00000	0.00000
Q3	-1.2079E-013	0.00000	0.00000	0.00000	0.00000
CONSTANT	646.48	184.48	3.5044	0.00088917	0.17474

By comparing regression results from restricted (without seasonal dummy variables) and unrestricted (with seasonal dummy variables) least squares, the computed Wald test statistic for the above three linear restrictions is a negligible 0.02, implying insignificant seasonal variation in the model. It is further confirmed with an extremely large P-value 0.99 of the test statistic. We can conclude safely that there is no difference in the estimated Almon equations for the different quarters.

Lesson 4.2: Dummy Variable Trap

Here comes a technical question. When we estimated Almon's model in Lesson 4.1, we only explicitly included three quarterly dummy variables in the regression equation. Why would we drop the fourth dummy variable? If you keep the constant term and use a dummy variable for each group, your program will generate an error message similar to the following:

```
C:\GAUSS\SRC\GPE2.SRC(1250) : error G0121 : Matrix not positive definite
Currently active call: _lsqest [1250]
```

This condition is called the "dummy variable trap." The dummy variable trap gets just about everyone at some time. Understanding how the dummy variable trap happens will make avoiding it easier. Remember that a typical regression equation contains a constant vector of ones associated with the intercept coefficient. Now, if there is a dummy variable for each group, summing all the dummy variables together equals one. The problem of perfect collinearity exists! Dropping one dummy variable is not the only solution to stay out of the "trap." The alternative is to include all dummy variables but to estimate the regression without the intercept term. In GPE, regression estimation without intercept is carried out by setting the input control variable:

```
_const = 0;
```

The following program is a slightly modified version of the previous program. It includes all four quarterly dummy variables, but the model is estimated without the intercept term.

```
/*
** Lesson 4.2: Dummy Variable Trap
*/
1  use gpe2;
2  output file = gpe\output4.2 reset;
3  load almon[61,3] = gpe\almon.txt;

4  cexp = almon[2:61,2];
5  capp = almon[2:61,3];
6  qt = almon[2:61,1];

7  pattern = {1 0 0 0,
8             0 1 0 0,
9             0 0 1 0,
10            0 0 0 1};
11 D = reshape(pattern,60,4);
```

69

```
12   call reset;
13   _const = 0;      @ regression without intercept @
14   _names = {"cexp","capp","q1","q2","q3","q4"};
15   call estimate(cexp,capp~D);
16   end;
```

Run this program, and refer to the output file output4.2 for details. The important catch is the statement of line 13:

```
_const = 0;
```

Without it, you will fall into the "dummy variable trap"! The estimated model can be summarized as follows:

CEXP = 0.737 CAPP + 657.23 Q1 + 620.32 Q2 + 639.40 Q3 + 670.93 Q4
s.e.   (0.053)   (222.4)   (222.7)   (222.4)   (230.9)
t-ratio 13.95   2.95   2.74   2.80   2.91

The interpretation of the coefficients associated with four quarter dummy variables is directly reflected as the intercept values of each equation:

Quarter 1:   CEXP = 657.23 + 0.737 CAPP
Quarter 2:   CEXP = 620.32 + 0.737 CAPP
Quarter 3:   CEXP = 639.40 + 0.737 CAPP
Quarter 4:   CEXP = 670.93 + 0.737 CAPP

A careful eye will see that these results are the same as those of the first regression equation in Lesson 4.1 using three dummies and a constant term.

Structural Change

In the next lesson, we will use a dummy variable approach to estimate and test for structural change previously studied in the production function of Lesson 3.5. Recall that a simple Cobb-Douglas production functionwas estimated using time series of U.S. real output (X), labor (L) and capital (K) inputs obtained from the data file **cjx.txt**. The question was, is there a change in both intercept and slope terms during post-war expansion after 1948? In Lesson 3.5, a Chow test was formulated and performed with two separate samples: 1929-1948 and 1949-1967. The alternative approach is to use a dummy variable for sample separation, and check for the difference in intercept and slope terms of the regression for each sub-sample. To check for the intercept difference, the use of an additive dummy variable would suffice. To check for the slope difference, a multiplicative dummy variable associated with each explanatory variable should be used.

Lesson 4.3: Testing for Structural Change: Dummy Variable Approach

When breaking the time series data in **cjx.txt** into two sub-groups, only one dummy variable named D is created (one less than the number of sub-groups). D is a vector whose entries are equal to zero for all observations in the first time period (1929-1948), and one for all observations in the second period (1949-1967). One way to create D is to compare a given vector available in the original time series to a set value. In this lesson we create a dummy variable D by comparing each observation in the vector YEAR to the value 1948. For every observation greater than 1948, D is set to one, otherwise D is set to zero. Notice that the dot (.) before the ">" means element-by-element greater-than comparison:

```
D = year.>1948;
```

 If the number of continuing observations designed for the base and alternative situations are known, concatenating a vector of zeros vertically to a vector of ones is a simple method of creating the dummy variable D. In this case,

```
D = zeros(20,1)|ones(19,1);
```

```
      /*
      **   Lesson 4.3: Testing for Structural Change
      **   Dummy Variable Approach
      */
 1    use gpe2;
 2    output file = gpe\output4.3 reset;
 3    load data[40,6] = gpe\cjx.txt;

 4    year = data[2:40,1];
 5    X = ln(data[2:40,2]);
 6    L = ln(data[2:40,3]);
 7    K = ln(data[2:40,5]);

 8    D = year.>1948;
 9    DL = D.*L;
10    DK = D.*K;

11    call reset;
12    _names = {"X","L","K","DL","DK","D"};
13    call estimate(X,L~K~DL~DK~D);
14    _restr = {0 0 1 0 0 0,
15              0 0 0 1 0 0,
16              0 0 0 0 1 0};
17    call estimate(X,L~K~DL~DK~D);
18    end;
```

Line 8 creates the additive dummy variable named D. Lines 9 and 10 use D to set up multiplicative dummy variables in association with the other two explanatory variables L and K, respectively. Thus, for entries of D equal to one, the corresponding entry in DL equals L and the corresponding entry in DK equals K. Otherwise, the entries of DL and DK are zeros. The three dummy variables, one additive and two multiplicative, are added to estimate in line 13. In this example, our model can be written in two ways. It may be written with two separate regressions, one for years before 1948, and one for the years after. This example demonstrates how to construct both situations into one combined regression as follows:

$$X = \beta_0 + \beta_1 L + \beta_2 K + \delta_0 D + \delta_1 DL + \delta_2 DK + \varepsilon$$

When D equals zero (that is, for the period 1929-1948), we have what is called the base case. When D equals one (that is, 1949-1967), the estimated coefficients of the dummy variables are added to the estimated coefficients of the independent variables including the constant vector. In other words,

For 1929-1948, $X = \beta_0 + \beta_1 L + \beta_2 K + \varepsilon$;
For 1949-1967, $X = (\beta_0 + \delta_0) + (\beta_1 + \delta_1) L + (\beta_2 + \delta_2)K + \varepsilon$

Run the program so that we can check out the first estimated regression from the output:

```
Least Squares Estimation
------------------------
Dependent Variable = X
Estimation Range =  1          39
Number of Observations = 39
Mean of Dependent Variable = 5.6874
Standard Error of Dependent Variable = 0.46096

R-Square = 0.99518      R-Square Adjusted = 0.99445
Standard Error of the Estimate = 0.034338
Log-Likelihood = 79.407
Log Ammemiya Prediction Criterion (APC) =  -6.5999
Log Akaike Information Criterion (AIC) -  -6.6023
Log Schwarz Bayesian Information Criterion (BIC) =  -6.3464

Sum of Squares       SS          DF         MSS          F        Prob>F
Explained        8.0355          5      1.6071     1362.9   3.2814E-037
Residual         0.038911       33   0.0011791
Total            8.0744         38     0.21248

Variable      Estimated    Standard     t-Ratio         Prob       Partial
Name        Coefficient       Error       33 DF         >|t|     Regression
L                1.6167     0.15690      10.304   7.6101E-012      0.76288
K                0.21967    0.17266       1.2723     0.21217       0.046758
DL              -0.60772    0.37578      -1.6172     0.11535       0.073433
DK               0.35942    0.21672       1.6584     0.10670       0.076935
D                1.5595     1.2876        1.2111     0.23444       0.042559
CONSTANT        -4.0576     0.26822     -15.128   2.1113E-016      0.87397
```

Interpreting the output gives us the estimated model;

X = - 4.06 + 1.62 L + 0.22 K - 0.61 DL + 0.36 DK + 1.56 D
s.e.   (0.27) (0.16) (0.17)   (0.38)   (0.22)   (1.29)
t-ratio - 15.1   10.3   1.27   - 1.62   1.66   1.21

In terms of two separate samples:

For 1929 - 1948, X = -4.06 + 1.62 L + 0.22 K (base case)
For 1949 - 1967, X = (-4.06 + 1.56) + (1.62 -0.61) L + (0.22 + 0.36) K
        or, X = -2.50 + 1.01 L + 0.58 K

One look at t-ratios and P-values tells us that the dummy variables are not statistically significant. To test for the structural change, we need to verify that the coefficients of both additive and multiplicative dummy variables are all zero. In other words, we must show that $\delta_0 = 0$, $\delta_1 = 0$, and $\delta_2 = 0$ jointly. The GPE input control variable _restr, defines these three dummy variables in a 3 by 6 matrix as shown in lines 14 through 16:

```
_restr = {0 0 1 0 0 0,
          0 0 0 1 0 0,
          0 0 0 0 1 0};
```

Line 17 estimates the restricted model (restricting all coefficients associated with dummy variables to zeros) in which no structural change is assumed. Here is the result of the restricted least squares estimation:

```
Least Squares Estimation
------------------------
Dependent Variable = X
Estimation Range =  1          39
Number of Observations = 39
Mean of Dependent Variable = 5.6874
Standard Error of Dependent Variable = 0.46096

WARNING: Linear Restrictions Imposed.
R-Square, AOV, SE, and t may not be reliable!
Wald F-Test for Linear Restrictions
F(    3,   33)        Prob>F
       1.2639        0.30275

R-Square = 0.99463      R-Square Adjusted = 0.99433
Standard Error of the Estimate = 0.034714
Log-Likelihood = 77.286
Log Ammemiya Prediction Criterion (APC) =  -6.5781
Log Akaike Information Criterion (AIC) =  -6.4936
Log Schwarz Bayesian Information Criterion (BIC) =  -6.2376
```

Sum of Squares	SS	DF	MSS	F	Prob>F
Explained	8.0310	2	4.0155	3332.2	1.3921E-041
Residual	0.043382	36	0.0012051		
Total	8.0744	38	0.21248		

Variable Name	Estimated Coefficient	Standard Error	t-Ratio 36 DF	Prob >|t|	Partial Regression
L	1.4508	0.083228	17.431	3.9260E-019	0.89407
K	0.38381	0.048018	7.9930	1.7130E-009	0.63960
DL	-5.1890E-012	0.00000	0.00000	0.00000	0.00000
DK	2.3426E-012	0.00000	0.00000	0.00000	0.00000
D	1.6888E-011	1.7378E-007	9.7182E-005	0.99992	2.6234E-010
CONSTANT	-3.9377	0.23700	-16.615	1.8332E-018	0.88464

Comparing the result of Chow test presented in Lesson 3.5 to the above output shows an identical computed Wald F-test statistic of 1.27 for three linear restrictions on dummy variables. In other words, based on the Cobb-Douglas log specification of the production function, there is no reason to believe that there was a structural change in output productivity between the years of 1929 and 1967. Both Lesson 3.5 (sample separation approach) and Lesson 4.3 (dummy variable approach) reach the same conclusion. However, to a careful eye, there are subtle differences in the estimated standard errors and t-ratios for the regression coefficients obtained from these two approaches. Why?

V
Multicollinearity

Multicollinearity is a data problem due to a group of highly correlated explanatory variables used in the regression equation. The consequence of multicollinearity is large standard errors of the coefficient estimates. The size of these errors suggest that there are too many explanatory variables and some of them may not be needed. Then the question is how to identify and treat the irrelevant explanatory variables in the regression.

The famous Longley data are known for the problem of multicollinearity. Instead of constructing a meaningful model, we will demonstrate a hypothetical relationship with the dependent variable (EM), regressed against a set of four other variables (YEAR, PGNP, GNP, and AF).

Detecting Multicollinearity

Given the regression equation:

$$EM = \beta_0 + \beta_1 \, YEAR + \beta_2 \, PGNP + \beta_3 \, GNP + \beta_4 \, AF + \varepsilon$$

the focus of this chapter is to examine how closely the four explanatory variables (YEAR, PGNP, GNP, and AF) are related. Lessons 5.1, 5.2, and 5.3 address the techniques of detecting multicollinearity. These include: condition number and correlation matrix (Lesson 5.1), Theil's measure of multicollinearity (Lesson 5.2), and Variance Inflation Factors (Lesson 5.3).

Lesson 5.1: Condition Number and Correlation Matrix

We have seen the regression outputs from previous lessons, which include a column of partial correlation coefficients. Technically, it is computed using the formula:

$$\frac{t^2}{t^2 + DF}$$

where t is the vector of t-ratios of coefficient estimates, and DF is the degrees of freedom of the estimated regression. The partial correlation coefficient, as its name suggests, measures the marginal or partial contribution of the designated variable when the influence of other variables is already considered. The smaller the partial correlation coefficient, the less important the variable would be in the regression equation. It is a useful approach to identify the irrelevant variable as a candidate for deletion.

Another useful tool to check for the problem of multicollinearity is the data correlation matrix, which describes the simple pair-wise correlation among all the variables used in the regression. The built-in GAUSS command `corrx` can do exactly that, but the GPE package offers the convenience of a data correlation matrix by setting the following input control variable:

```
_corr = 1;
```

The condition number of a normalized data matrix of explanatory variables is computed as well. The normalization is necessary so that the condition number is independent of the unit of measurement for each variable. A large condition number indicates multicollinearity. Large values of pair-wise correlation coefficients may hint at the source of the problem.

Using the Longley data, the following program estimates the model with the dependent variable (EM) regressed against a set of four other variables (YEAR, PGNP, GNP, and AF). The problem of multicollinearity is detected by examining the partial regression coefficients, as well as the condition number and correlation matrix of the explanatory variables.

```
   /*
   ** Lesson 5.1: Condition Number and Correlation Matrix
   */
1  use gpe2;
2  output file = gpe\output5.1 reset;
3  load data[17,7] = gpe\longley.txt;
4  data = data[2:17,.];

5  year = data[.,1];
6  pgnp = data[.,2];
7  gnp = data[.,3];
8  af = data[.,5];
9  em = data[.,7];

10 call reset;
11 _corr = 1;   @ cond# and correlation matrix @
12 _names = {"em","year","pgnp","gnp","af"};
13 call estimate(em,year~pgnp~gnp~at);
14 end;
```

Running the above program returns the following output:

```
Least Squares Estimation
------------------------
Dependent Variable = EM
Estimation Range =  1          16
Number of Observations = 16
Mean of Dependent Variable = 65317.
Standard Error of Dependent Variable = 3512.0

R-Square = 0.97352      R-Square Adjusted = 0.96389
Standard Error of the Estimate = 667.34
Log-Likelihood = -123.76
Log Ammemiya Prediction Criterion (APC) =   13.279
Log Akaike Information Criterion (AIC) =   13.257
Log Schwarz Bayesian Information Criterion (BIC) =   13.498
```

Sum of Squares	SS	DF	MSS	F	Prob>F
Explained	1.8011E+008	4	4.5028E+007	101.11	1.3458E-008
Residual	4.8987E+006	11	4.4534E+005		
Total	1.8501E+008	15	1.2334E+007		

Variable Name	Estimated Coefficient	Standard Error	t-Ratio 11 DF	Prob >|t|	Partial Regression
YEAR	-576.46	433.49	-1.3298	0.21049	0.13850

PGNP	-19.768	138.89	-0.14233	0.88940	0.0018381
GNP	0.064394	0.019952	3.2275	0.0080515	0.48638
AF	-0.010145	0.30857	-0.032878	0.97436	9.8262E-005
CONSTANT	1.1691E+006	8.3590E+005	1.3986	0.18949	0.15098

```
Condition Number of Explanatory Variables = 15824.
Correlation Matrix of Dependent and Explanatory Variables
EM            1.0000
YEAR          0.97133     1.0000
PGNP          0.97090     0.99115     1.0000
GNP           0.98355     0.99527     0.99159     1.0000
AF            0.45731     0.41725     0.46474     0.44644     1.0000
                 EM         YEAR        PGNP         GNP          AF
```

With the exception of the variable GNP, small partial regression coefficients are strong indications of irrelevant explanatory variables. The added information from the use of the input control variable _corr = 1 (line 11) includes the condition number and correlation matrix of the explanatory variables. The correlation coefficients between the dependent variable and each independent variable are given in the first column of the correlation matrix. These measure the individual effect of each independent variable on the dependent variable. With the exception of the variable AF, the explanatory variables have a rather high correlation with the dependent variable. However, these variables are also highly correlated among themselves, as seen from the rest of the correlation matrix. In addition, the condition number of explanatory variables is extremely large, suggesting severe multicollinearity for this set of variables.

Lesson 5.2: Theil's Measure of Multicollinearity

Similar to the concept of partial regression coefficients, Theil's measure of multicollinearity uses the R-square from multiple partial regressions to determine if multicollinearity is present in a regression equation.

Theil's measure of multicollinearity is a formula derived from

$$R^2 - \sum_{j=2,\ldots,K} (R^2 - R_{\cdot j}^2)$$

where R^2 is the R-square (that is, coefficient of determination) of the full model, including all explanatory variables. $R_{\cdot j}^2$ is the R-square of the same regression model excluding the j-th explanatory variable. Therefore, the difference $R^2 - R_{\cdot j}^2$ measures the net contribution of the j-th explanatory variable in terms of R-square. K is the number of explanatory variables of the full regression, in which the first one is the constant term. Notice that the index j for summation does not count the constant term. In the ideal case of no multicollinearity, Theil's measure equals or is close to zero.

The first regression in the following program (lines 10-13) estimates the full model with dependent variable (EM) on a set of four independent variables (YEAR, PGNP, GNP, and AF). The rest of the program (lines 14-33) estimates four regression equations; each corresponds to the partial model with one of the independent variables removed. The R-squares from the full model and from the four partial models are then used to compute the Theil's measure of multicollinearity.

Instead of showing the lengthy results of each regression estimation, we explain the use of output control variables in GPE for keeping track of the information from each of the regression runs. The use of an output control variable is first introduced in line 13. In GPE, output control variables take on new values each time estimate or forecast is called. An output control variable is identified with a name beginning with a double underscore (__). For example, __r2 is the value of R-square computed in the previous estimation. Therefore, in line 13, assigning __r2 to a variable named r2 allows us to use that value later in the program. See Appendix A for a complete list of output control variables available in GPE.

```
     /*
     ** Lesson 5.2: Theil's Measure of Multicollinearity
     */
1    use gpe2;
2    output file = gpe\output5.2 reset;
3    load data[17,7] = gpe\longley.txt;
4    data = data[2:17,.];
5    year = data[.,1];
6    pgnp = data[.,2];
7    gnp = data[.,3];
8    af = data[.,5];
9    em = data[.,7];
10   call reset;
11   _names = {"em","year","pgnp","gnp","af"};
12   call estimate(em,year~pgnp~gnp~af);
13   r2 =__r2;
14   call reset;
15   print"Partial Regression 1: EM = PGNP GNP AF";
16   _names = {"em","pgnp","gnp","af"};
17   call estimate(em,pgnp~gnp~af);
18   r2x1 = __r2;
19   print"Partial Regression 2: EM = YEAR GNP AF";
20   _names = {"em","year","gnp","af"};
21   call estimate(em,year~gnp~af);
22   r2x2 = __r2;
23   print"Partial Regression 3: EM = YEAR PGNP AF";
24   _names = {"em","year","pgnp","af"};
25   call estimate(em,year~pgnp~af);
26   r2x3 = __r2;
27   print"Partial Regression 4: EM = YEAR GNP PGNP";
28   _names = {"em","year","gnp","pgnp"};
29   call estimate(em,year~gnp~pgnp);
30   r2x4 = __r2;
31   print "Theil's Measure of Multicollinearity =";;
32   print r2-sumc(r2-(r2x1|r2x2|r2x3|r2x4));
33   end;
```

From four partial regressions, we repeat the use of output variable __r2, to keep track of the R-square of each regression. By renaming each __r2 and subtracting it from the R-square of the full model, these net differences are concatenated and then summed using a GAUSS command sumc (see line 32). Running the program, the output displays the results of all the regressions before the line:

```
Theil's Measure of Multicollinearity =      0.94414
```

In summary, the near unity of the Theil's measure confirms the problem of multicollinearity.

Lesson 5.3: Variance Inflation Factors (VIF)

Relating to the correlation matrix of explanatory variables, Variance Inflation Factors (VIF) indicate the ratio of a variable's actual variance to the perfect variance of zero collinearity. VIF is defined as:

$$\frac{1}{1 - R_j^2}$$

It can be used to detect multicollinearity, where R_j^2 is the R-square from regressing the j-th explanatory variable on all the other explanatory variables. A near unity R_j^2 and hence a high value of VIF indicates a potential problem of multicollinearity with the j-th variable.

The following program computes VIF for each explanatory variable through a set of four auxiliary regressions similar to the procedure used in computing Theil's measure of multicollinearity.

```
     /*
     ** Lesson 5.3: Variance Inflation Factors (VIF)
     */
 1   use gpe2;
 2   output file = gpe\output5.3 reset;
 3   load data[17,7] = gpe\longley.txt;
 4   data = data[2:17,.];
 5   year = data[.,1];
 6   pgnp = data[.,2];
 7   gnp = data[.,3];
 8   af = data[.,5];
 9   em = data[.,7];
10   call reset;
11   print "Aux Regression 1: YEAR = PGNP GNP AF";
12   y = year;
13   x = pgnp~gnp~af;
14   _names = {"year","pgnp","gnp","af"};
15   call estimate(y,x);
16   r2x1 = __r2;
17   print "Aux Regression 2: PGNP = YEAR GNP AF";
18   y = pgnp;
19   x = year~gnp~af;
20   _names = {"pgnp","year","gnp","af"};
21   call estimate(y,x);
22   r2x2 = __r2;
23   print "Aux Regression 3: GNP = YEAR PGNP AF";
24   y = gnp;
25   x = year~pgnp~af;
26   _names = {"gnp","year","pgnp","af"};
27   call estimate(y,x);
28   r2x3 = __r2;
29   print "Aux Regression 4: AF = YEAR GNP PGNP";
30   y = af;
31   x = year~gnp~pgnp;
32   _names = {"af","year","gnp","pgnp"};
33   call estimate(y,x);
34   r2x4 = __r2;
35   r2=r2x1|r2x2|r2x3|r2x4;
36   print "Variance Inflation Factors:";
37   print "        Model      R-Square             VIF";;
38   print seqa(1,1,4)~r2~(1/(1-r2));
39   end;
```

The first part of the program performs four auxiliary regression estimations. Each corresponds to the regression of one selected explanatory variable against the rest of the others. Only the R-squares from the four estimated regressions are of interest in computing the VIF. First, these values are retained using the output variable __r2, then they are concatenated into a vector (line 35) for calculating the VIF of each variable (line 38). Based on the R-square measure of each auxiliary regression, VIF for each explanatory variable is reported as follows:

Variance Inflation Factors:		
Model	R-Square	VIF
1.0000	0.99303	143.46
2.0000	0.98678	75.671
3.0000	0.99245	132.46
4.0000	0.35616	1.5532

Again, all explanatory variables except variable AF (Model 4) have higher than normal values of VIF, indicating a severe problem of multicollinearity.

Correction for Multicollinearity

What to do with the problem of multicollinearity? Besides tweaking the appropriate explanatory variables and data transformation, techniques such as ridge regression and principal components are suggested in the literature. The ridge regression approach seeks to find a set of "stable" coefficient estimates with a "shrinkage parameter," while the principal components approach is to extract a smaller number of independent variables (principal components) that explain most of the variation of regressors. The resulting coefficient estimates from these methods are biased and difficult to interpret, even though they may be more precise (efficient) than their ordinary least squares counterparts. Since multicollinearity is a data problem, data adjustment and variable transformation should be considered in favor of mechanical correction methods for estimation. Nevertheless, the following lesson illustrates the correction mechanics of ridge regression and principal components.

Lesson 5.4: Ridge Regression and Principal Components

GPE's estimate procedure does not offer either ridge regression or principal components. Given the estimates obtained from ordinary least squares, however, it is rather straightforward to implement the computation of ridge regression and principal components. Many standard econometrics textbooks outline the formula. For examples, see Judge, et al. (1988, Chap. 21) and Greene (1999, Chap. 6).

Given a shrinkage parameter of $r>0$, the coefficient estimates b_r of ridge regression are related to the ordinary least squares estimate b of β in the regression equation $Y = X\beta + \varepsilon$ as follows:

$$b_r = (I + r(X'X)^{-1})^{-1}b$$

Therefore, the corresponding estimated variance-covariance matrix $Var(b_r)$ is:

$$Var(b_r) = (I + r(X'X)^{-1})^{-1}Var(b)\,(I + r(X'X)^{-1})^{-1}$$
$$= s^2(I + r(X'X)^{-1})^{-1}X'X\,(I + r(X'X)^{-1})^{-1}$$

Where Var(b)is the estimated variance-covariance matrix and s^2 is the regression variance of the ordinary least squares estimates. By varying the shrinkage parameter r, we can find the most "stable" coefficient estimates.

The method of principal components is to extract sufficient variation of independent variables to explain the dependent variable of a regression equation. Let X be the data matrix of the explanatory variables, including the constant term. Principal components of X are derived from linear combinations of characteristic vectors of X'X. We will use only the principal components which satisfy a minimum size requirement of the characteristic roots of X'X. Let V be the matrix of such characteristic vectors. Then, the coefficient estimates of principal components b_{pc} are related to the least squares estimates b as follows

$$b_{pc} = VV'b$$

and the corresponding estimated variance-covariance matrix Var(b_{pc}) is:

$$Var(b_{pc}) = (VV')Var(b)(VV')$$

lesson5.4 is a GAUSS program which implements the ridge regression and principal components based on the hypothetical regression equation with the Longley data as described in the previous lessons 5.1 to 5.3. After obtaining the ordinary least squares result, we introduce several GAUSS commands to perform ridge regression and principal components estimation. For detailed explanations of the GAUSS commands used therein, refer to the GAUSS Command References or consult the on line help menu.

```
     /*
     ** Lesson 5.4: Ridge Regression and Principal Components
     */
1    use gpe2;
2    output file = gpe\output5.4 reset;
3    load data[17,7] = gpe\longley.txt;
4    data = data[2:17,.];
5    year = data[.,1];
6    pgnp = data[.,2];
7    gnp = data[.,3];
8    af = data[.,5];
9    em = data[.,7];
10   call reset;
11   _names = {"em","year","pgnp","gnp","af"};
12   call estimate(em,year~pgnp~gnp~af);

     /* explanatory variables including constant */
13   x = year~pgnp~gnp~af~ones(rows(year),1);
     /* ridge regression */
14   r=0.3;
15   a = invpd(eye(cols(x))+r*invpd(x'x));
16   br = a*__b;
17   vbr = a*__vb*a';
18   print "Ridge Regression Model:";
19   print " Coefficient    Std Error";;
20   print br~sqrt(diag(vbr));

     /* Principal Components */
     @ compute char. roots and vectors of X'X @
21   {r,v}=eigrs2(x'x);
22   v = selif(v',r.>0.1)';
23   bpc = v*v'__b;
24   vbpc = v*v'__vb*v*v';
```

```
25 | print;
26 | print "Principal Components Model:";
27 | print " Coefficient    Std Error";;
28 | print bpc~sqrt(diag(vbpc));
29 | end;
```

First we estimate the equation using ordinary least squares (lines 10-12), then from line 13 on we focus on the data matrix of explanatory variables including the constant term, to perform ridge regression and principal components. Ridge regression is obtained for a shrinkage parameter of 0.3 (lines 14-20). We could try several small positive values for a shrinkage parameter to find the most "stable" coefficient estimates. The following output is the result of ridge regression:

```
Ridge Regression Model:
 Coefficient    Std Error
     29.750       3.8485
    -99.844       124.85
    0.043571     0.013233
     0.16452      0.28191
      2.5061       1.7759
```

We continue on to perform the principal components method (lines 21-28). To compute the principal components of the data matrix X of regressors, we pick only the characteristic vectors which correspond to the characteristic roots of X'X with values greater than 0.1 (line 22). We notice that the computation of characteristic roots and vectors and therefore the result of principal components are sensitive to the scale of measurement used in the data matrix.

The resulting estimates of principal components are:

```
Principal Components Model:
 Coefficient    Std Error
     29.784       3.8893
    -100.92       126.19
    0.043684     0.013372
     0.16499      0.28202
    0.022451     0.010768
```

As we can see from the above example, the computation of ridge regression and principal components is easy, but the interpretation of the resulting coefficient estimates will be difficult.

VI
Nonlinear Optimization

To find an optimal (maximal or minimal) solution of a scalar-valued function is at the core of econometric methodology. The technique of least squares estimation is an example of solving the nonlinear "sum-of-squares" objective function. For a linear regression model, the exact solution is derived using the analytical formula of matrix algebra. However, the problem may be more complicated if the regression equation is nonlinear in the parameters. In this case, approximation or iterative methods of nonlinear optimization will be necessary. We will consider only the case of unconstrained optimization. In most cases, simple equality constraints can be substituted into the objective function so that the problem is essentially the unconstrained one. Nonlinear optimization with inequality constraints is difficult, though not impossible.

From elementary differential calculus, an optimal solution can be found by setting the first derivatives (gradient) of the objective function with respect to the function's variables equal to zero and solving for the variables. Then to verify a minimum (maximum), the second derivative's matrix (hessian) must be positive (negative) definite. When the functional form is simple, the analytical approach of working out the derivatives is useful. The techniques of numerical approximation and iteration are more practical for solving large and complex optimization problems. GPE offers practical techniques for finding numeric solutions of a general nonlinear objective function.

Although the nonlinear optimization of GPE is designed with statistical or econometric problems in mind, it can be used for solving mathematical functions as well. The first step is to define the objective function as mathematical or statistical. The next step is to solve the function through numerical optimization by calling the procedure `estimate`.

Solving Mathematical Functions

Without going into the details of optimization theory, we first describe how to define and write an objective function suitable for solving its optimum (or optima). Recall that a simple function can be defined with a single-line `fn` statement in GAUSS (see Chapter II). Since GPE is designed for econometric or statistical problem-solving, an objective function is defined with a set of sample data and a vector of unknown parameters. Typically a one line `fn` or multi-line `proc` statement is declared as:

```
fn FunctionName(Data,Parameters) = ...;
```

or

```
proc FunctionName(Data,Parameters);
...
endp;
```

where `FunctionName` is the name of the function, `Data` are the sample observations of data series, and `Parameters` are the parameters or coefficients of the function. For a statistical model, both `Data` and `Parameters` are used to define the function `FunctionName`. For a mathematical function, only the `Parameters` matter, therefore `Data` can be set to 0 (or a dummy value) in this case.

The actual computation of solving the function `FunctionName` is carried out by calling the procedure `estimate`, as follows:

```
call estimate(&FunctionName,Data);
```

Here, `&FunctionName` denotes the code *address* (holding place) of the function `FunctionName` we declared earlier, which itself is defined with `Data` (a set of sample data) and `Parameters` (a vector of initial values of parameters).

Using GPE for nonlinear functional optimization (or estimation), the following input control variables are required:

- `_nlopt`
- `_b`
- `_iter`

The GPE input control variable `_nlopt` defines the type of optimization problem involved. `_nlopt=0` indicates a minimization problem, while `_nlopt=1` indicates a maximization problem. Since numerical iteration is used for solving a nonlinear model, the solution found can be at best a *local* one. The input variable `_b` provides the initial guess of parameters as the starting point of iterations. Different starting values of `_b` may lead to different (local) solutions. In an effort to find a global solution for the function, several different values of `_b` should be tried. The variable `_iter` sets the maximal number of iterations allowed for a particular problem. Usually we keep `_iter` low for testing the function. When the function is debugged and ready for solving, `_iter` should be set large enough to ensure the convergence of an iterative solution.

Calling the procedure `estimate` for nonlinear model estimation (or optimization) is similar to the case of the linear regression model. The differences are that under nonlinear estimation or optimization, the first argument of `estimate` is now an address for the objective function and the second argument (for the data matrix) is more forgiving in its structure. Remember that the objective function must be defined with both data and parameters before calling the `estimate` procedure.

Lesson 6.1: One-Variable Scalar-Valued Function

Consider a scalar-valued function of one variable,

$$f(x) = ln(x) - x^2$$

The single maximum of f(x) is found at $x = \sqrt{1/2}$. First we translate the mathematical function f(x) into a GAUSS `fn` statement as in line 3 of the following program:

```
     /*
     ** Lesson 6.1: One-Variable Scalar-Valued Function
     ** f(x) = ln(x) - x^2
     */
1    use gpe2;
2    output file=output6.1 reset;

3    fn f(data,x)=ln(x)-x^2;

4    call reset;
5    _nlopt=1;
6    _iter=100;
7    _b=0.5;

8    call estimate(&f,0);
9    end;
```

Line 5 indicates the maximization problem involved, and line 6 sets the iteration limit for finding the solution. The estimation (maximization, in particular) of function f starts with the initial value of x at 0.5 as shown in line 7. The GPE input variable _b controls the starting value of iteration. Notice that here we do not use sample data or parameter names in defining the function and its maximization. Running the above lesson program, we obtain the following result:

```
Non-Linear Optimization: Maximization Problem
---------------------------------------------
Number of Parameters = 1

Maximum Number of Iterations = 100
Step Size Search Method = 0
Convergence Criterion = 0
Tolerance = 0.001

Initial Result:
Function Value =      -0.94315
Parameters =       0.50000

Using Steepest-Ascent Algorithm
Iteration =  1   Step Size =  0.2500  Value =      -0.85018
Parameters =       0.75000
Iteration =  2   Step Size =  0.5000  Value =      -0.84991
Parameters =       0.66667
Iteration =  3   Step Size =  0.2500  Value =      -0.84658
Parameters =       0.70833
Iteration =  4   Step Size =  0.5000  Value =      -0.84658
Parameters =       0.70588
Iteration =  5   Step Size =  0.2500  Value =      -0.84657
Parameters =       0.70711
Iteration =  6   Step Size =  0.2500  Value =      -0.84657
Parameters =       0.70711

Final Result:
Iterations = 6              Evaluations = 38
Function Value =      -0.84657
Parameters =       0.70711
Gradient Vector = -4.2549e-006
Hessian Matrix =      -4.0000
```

Starting at $x = 0.5$ with function value -0.94315, it takes six iterations to reach the convergence of a solution. The solution 0.70711 is indeed a maximum with function value -0.84657, where the gradient is almost zero at $-4.2549e{-}06$ and the hessian is negative at -4.0.

You may want to define the function's analytical derivatives and use them for solving the function. For this example, they are:

```
fn f1(data,x) = 1/x - 2*x;
fn f2(data,x) = -1/(x^2) - 2;
```

The functions f1 and f2 are the first and second derivatives of f, respectively. It may be necessary to write a multi-line procedure for the derivatives of a more complicated function. To solve the function with analytical derivatives, just horizontally concatenate the function and derivatives together as a row vector and put them in the first argument of the procedure estimate as below:

```
call estimate(&f~&f1~&f2,0);
```

There is no need to use both first and second derivatives. Using only the first derivative will work. The use of analytical derivatives will speed up the computation and increase the numerical precision of the solution. However, for a complicated function, it is often a difficult task to write and code the analytical formulas of derivatives.

The bare-bones program of Lesson 6.1 does not take advantage of the many options available in GPE to fine tune the optimization process. For a simple problem, as the one shown above, the default settings of the optimization method (i.e., steepest-ascent method) and convergence criteria (i.e., convergence in function value and solution relative to the tolerance level of 0.001) may be acceptable.

We now explain some of the GPE input control variables, which provide the option to select one of many optimization methods and control its behavior in order to find the optimal solution for a more complicated and difficult function. These control variables are:

- _method
- _step
- _conv
- _tol
- _restart

By default, _method is set to 0 if we do not specify any method of optimization in the program. For a mathematical problem, the default method is the steepest descent or ascent method. For a statistical model, it is the Gauss-Newton method for nonlinear least squares, or the steepest descent method for maximum likelihood (ML) estimation. The following lists the more sophisticated optimization methods available :

_method=1	Broyden-Fletcher Goldfarb-Shanno (BFGS) quasi-Newton method.
_method=2	Davidon-Fletcher Powell (DFP) quasi-Newton method.
_method=3	Greenstadt method.
_method=4	Newton-Raphson method.
_method=5	Quadratic hill-climbing (QHC) method.
_method=6	Modified quadratic hill-climbing method.

All the optimization or estimation methods should be combined with a line search to determine the step size of optimization for each iteration. The default line search method is a simple cutback method (_step=0). Setting _step=1 causes the quadratic step size to be used in the search. Readers interested in a more detailed discussion and comparison of different optimization methods should check the references (e.g., Quandt, 1983; Judge, et al., 1985, Appendix B; Greene, 1999, Chapter 5) for details.

The other optional input variables control the accuracy and convergence of the solution. The variable _tol sets the tolerance level of convergence. Typically _tol is a small number (default value 0.001). The variable _conv checks for two consecutive iterations to reach convergence, relative to the tolerance level. When _conv=0 (default), only the function values and solutions are checked for convergence with _tol; when _conv=1, the convergence of function values, solutions, and zero gradients are checked with _tol. Finally, the variable _restart sets the number of times to restart the computation when the function value fails to improve. A maximum of 10 restarts is allowed, with no restart as the default (_restart=0).

As will be demonstrated in many example lessons below, we use all sorts of different optimization methods or algorithms for different types of problems. It is not unusual that a different (local) solution may be found due to the particular algorithm in use. Although there is no clear indication which method should be used for what type of problem, we recommend a mixed bag of optimization methods in conjunction with a variety of options controlling the numerical optimization. It is a matter of experimentation to find the best suite of solution tools for a particular problem.

Lesson 6.2: Two-Variable Scalar-Valued Function

This example demonstrates the use of GPE input control variables. We now consider a two-variable scalar-valued function:

$$g(x) = g(x_1,x_2) = (x_1^2 + x_2 - 11)^2 + (x_1 + x_2^2 - 7)^2.$$

There are four minima, (3,2), (3.5844, -1.8481), (-3.7793, -3.2832), and (-2.8051, 3.1313) with the same function value 0, although we can only find one minimum at a time. With various initial starting values of the variables, we are able to find all of the four solutions. Also, the maximal function value 181.62 is found at the solution (-0.27084, -0.92304). Be warned that sometimes the solutions are difficult to find because there are several saddle points, (0.08668, 2.88430), (3.38520, 0.07358), and (-3.07300, -0.08135), in the way. Here is the program:

```
      /*
      ** Lesson 6.2: Two-Variable Scalar-Valued Function
      ** g(x) = (x[1]^2+x[2]-11)^2 + (x[1]+x[2]^2-7)^2
      */
1     use gpe2;
2     output file=output6.2 reset;

3     fn g(data,x)=(x[1]^2+x[2]-11)^2+(x[1]+x[2]^2-7)^2;

4     call reset;
5     _nlopt=0;
6     _method=1;
7     _iter=100;
```

```
 8 │ _step=1;
 9 │ _conv=1;
10 │ _b={3,-2};

11 │ call estimate(&g,0);
12 │ end;
```

Line 3 defines the one-line objective function g. Again, data is not used for defining such a function, in which only the vector of parameters x matters. In this example, a version of the quasi-Newton method (BFGS, i.e., _method=1) is used (line 6) for optimization. It takes seven iterations to find one of the four minima (3.58, -1.85) from the initial starting point _b=(3, -2) given in line 10. Run this program, and refer to the output file output6.2 for more details.

For pedagogical purposes, we write out the procedures for analytical first and second derivatives g1 and g2, although we do not use them in the optimization. We note that g1 is a row-vector gradient and g2 is a hessian matrix:

```
proc g1(data,x); @ 1st derivative of g(x) @
    local f1,f2;
    f1=4*x[1]*(x[1]^2+x[2]-11)+2*(x[1]+x[2]^2-7);
    f2=2*(x[1]^2+x[2]-11)+4*x[2]*(x[1]+x[2]^2-7);
    retp(f1~f2);
endp;

proc g2(data,x); @ 2nd derivative of g(x) @
    local f11,f22,f12;
    f11=12*x[1]^2+4*x[2]-42;
    f22=4*x[1]+12*x[2]^2-26;
    f12=4*(x[1]+x[2]);
    retp((f11~f12)|(f12~f22));
endp;
```

By changing the initial values of the parameters in line 10 of **lesson6.2**, all solutions may be found. We suggest the following values and the corresponding minima to which they converge. Try them out:

Initial Value (Line 10)	Minimum	Function Value
(3, -2)	(3.58, -1.85)	0
(-3, 2)	(-2.81, 3.13)	0
(-3, -2)	(-3.78, -3.28)	0
(2, 2)	(3, 2)	0

Unfortunately, without knowing the solution ahead of time, the search is rather a blind process. The general rule of thumb is to try as many different initial values as possible. As an exercise, modify the program of Lesson 6.2 to find the maximum (-0.27, -0.92) with function value 181.62. Hint: Try _nlopt=1 (line 5) and _b={0,0} (line 10).

Estimating Probability Distributions

The main use of nonlinear optimization in GPE is statistical model estimation, in which the underlying probability distribution of the random variables is estimated. The characteristics of a random variable (e.g., mean and variance, etc.) may be evaluated through the joint probability density of a finite sample. This joint density function, or the *likelihood function*, is defined as the product of N independent density functions $f(X_i, \theta)$ of sample observations X_i (i=1,2,...,N) and an unknown parameter vector θ. That is, $\prod_{i=1,2,...,N} f(X_i, \theta)$, or equivalently in log form:

$ll(\theta) = \sum_{i=1,2,...,N} ln\ f(X_i, \theta)$

The problem is to maximize the log-likelihood function $ll(\theta)$ so that the solution θ characterizes the probability distribution of the random variable X under consideration. To find the θ that maximizes $ll(\theta)$ is the essence of maximum likelihood estimation. The corresponding variance-covariance matrix of θ is derived from the information matrix (negatives of the expected values of the second derivatives) of the log-likelihood function as follows:

$$Var(\theta) = [-E\left(\frac{\partial^2 ll}{\partial\theta\partial\theta'}\right)]^{-1}$$

The familiar example is the likelihood function derived from a normal probability distribution:

$$f(X, \theta) = \frac{1}{\sqrt{2\pi\sigma^2}} exp\left[\frac{(X-\mu)^2}{2\sigma^2}\right]$$

where $\theta = (\mu, \sigma^2)$ represents the distribution parameters. It is straightforward to show that the maximum likelihood solution is $\mu = E(X) = \frac{1}{N}\sum_{i=1,...,N} X_i$ (the sample mean), and $\sigma^2 = Var(X) = \frac{1}{N}\sum_{i=1,...,N} (X_i - \mu)^2$ (the sample variance).

Another example is based the log-normal distribution of X (or equivalently, normal distribution of $ln(X)$) defined as:

$$f(X, \theta) = \frac{1}{\sqrt{2\pi\sigma^2}} \frac{1}{X} exp\left[\frac{(ln(X)-\mu)^2}{2\sigma^2}\right]$$

with the solution $\mu = \frac{1}{N}\sum_{i=1,...,N} ln(X_i)$ and $\sigma^2 = \frac{1}{N}\sum_{i=1,...,N} (ln(X_i)- \mu)^2$, the corresponding mean and variance of X are $E(X) = exp(\mu+\sigma^2/2)$ and $Var(X) = exp(2\mu+\sigma^2) [exp(\sigma^2)-1]$, respectively. Many economic variables are described with a log-normal instead of a normal probability distribution. If μ is re-parameterized in terms of a set of non-random variables Z and additional parameters β, $\mu = Z\beta$ for example, we get the statistical regression model, to be discussed in the next section.

Of course, maximum likelihood estimation is not limited to models with normal or log-normal probability distribution. In many situations, the probability distribution of a random variable may be non-normal. For example, to estimate the gamma distribution of a nonnegative random variable $X \geq 0$, the distribution function is

$$f(X, \theta) = \frac{\lambda^\rho}{\Gamma(\rho)} exp^{-\lambda X} X^{\rho-1}$$

where $\theta = (\lambda, \rho)$ is the parameter vector with $\lambda > 0$ and $\rho > 0$. The mean of X is ρ/λ, and the variance is ρ/λ^2. Many familiar distributions, such as the exponential and Chi-square distributions, are special cases of the gamma distribution.

As with the normal distribution, the technique of maximum likelihood can be used to estimate the parameters of the gamma distribution. Sampling from N independent observations from the gamma distribution, the log-likelihood function is:

$$ll(\theta) = N [\rho \, ln(\lambda) - ln\Gamma(\rho)] - \lambda \, \Sigma_{i=1,2,...,N} \, X_i + (\rho-1) \, \Sigma_{i=1,2,...,N} \, ln(X_i)$$

With the normal, log-normal, and gamma probability distributions, the characteristics of the random variable X may be described in terms of the estimated mean and variance for each probability distribution as follows:

	Normal Distribution	Log-Normal Distribution	Gamma Distribution
Mean E(X)	μ	$exp(\mu+\sigma^2/2)$	ρ/λ
Variance Var(X)	σ^2	$exp(2\mu+\sigma^2)[exp(\sigma^2)-1]$	ρ/λ^2
Where:	$\mu = \frac{1}{N} \Sigma_{i=1,...,N} \, X_i$	$\mu = \frac{1}{N} \Sigma_{i=1,...,N} \, ln(X_i)$	
	$\sigma^2 = \frac{1}{N} \Sigma_{i=1,...,N} (X_i - \mu)^2$	$\sigma^2 = \frac{1}{N} \Sigma_{i=1,...,N} (ln(X_i) - \mu)^2$	

Lesson 6.3: Estimating Probability Distributions

In the following we use the hypothetical income data series of Greene (1999, Chapter 4, Table 4.1), and estimate its mean and variance under the assumption of three probability distributions. The data are replicated in the text file **yed20.txt**. In **lesson6.3** below, these 20 observations of two variables INCOME and EDUCATION are loaded first. Only the variable INCOME scaled by a factor 10 (here it is called x) will be analyzed. Data scaling is useful for nonlinear model estimation. We estimate the parameters of three probability distributions (normal, log-normal, and gamma) by maximizing the corresponding log-likelihood function.

```
    /*
    ** Lesson 6.3: Estimating Probability Distributions
    ** See Greene (1999), Chapter 4
    */
1   use gpe2;
2   output file=output6.3 reset;
3   load data[21,2]=gpe\yed20.txt;
4   x=data[2:21,1]/10; @ income data: scaling may be helpful @

    /* normal probability distribution: b[1]=mu, b[2]=sigma */
5   fn llfn(x,b)=sumc(ln(pdfn((x-b[1])/b[2])./b[2]));
6   fn llfln(x,b)=sumc(ln(pdfn((ln(x)-b[1])/b[2])./(b[2].*x)));

    /* gamma probability distribution: b[1]=rho, b[2]=lambda */
7   fn pdfg(x,b)=((b[2]^b[1])./gamma(b[1])).*exp(-b[2]*x).*x^(b[1]-1);
8   fn llfg(x,b)=sumc(ln(pdfg(x,b)));
```

```
 9 | call reset;
10 | _nlopt=1;
11 | _method=4;
12 | _iter=100;
13 | _b={3.0,2.0};
14 | call estimate(&llfn,x);
15 | _b={1.0,0.5};
16 | call estimate(&llfln,x);
17 | _b={2.0,0.5};
18 | call estimate(&llfg,x);
19 | end;
```

By definition, the log-likelihood function is just the summation of the logarithmic probability distribution function over the sample observations. Based on a normal probability distribution, line 5 defines the corresponding log-likelihood function in which the unknown parameters are μ and σ. Similarly, line 6 is the log-likelihood function of the underlying log-normal distribution. We note that the GAUSS built-in normal probability density function, pdfn, is used to compute the log-likelihood functions of normal and log-normal distributions. For the case of the gamma distribution, the definition of probability distribution function is given in line 7, which uses the built-in gamma function of GAUSS.

For all cases of maximum likelihood estimation of probability distributions, we use the Newton-Raphson optimization method (_method=4), for up to 100 iterations (_iter=100) as shown in lines 10 through 12. To estimate the parameters μ and σ of the underlying normal distribution, we maximize the corresponding log-likelihood function as carried out in line 14, with initial values 3.0 and 2.0 for μ and σ (line 13). The estimation result below shows that final solution of (μ, σ) is obtained at (3.1278, 2.1809) with the log-likelihood function value -43.974.

```
Non-Linear Optimization: Maximization Problem
- - - - - - - - - - - - - - - - - - - - - - - - - - - - - - - - - - - - - - - -
Assuming Maximum Likelihood Function
Number of Observations = 20
Number of Parameters = 2

Maximum Number of Iterations = 100
Step Size Search Method = 0
Convergence Criterion = 0
Tolerance = 0.001

Initial Result:
Function Value =        -44.174
Parameters =        3.0000       2.0000

Using Newton-Raphson Algorithm
Iteration =  1   Step Size = 1.2100  Value =        -43.974
Parameters =        3.1323       2.1747
Iteration =  2   Step Size = 1.0000  Value =        -43.974
Parameters =        3.1278       2.1809
Iteration =  3   Step Size = 1.0000  Value =        -43.974
Parameters =        3.1278       2.1809

Final Result:
Iterations = 3              Evaluations = 39
Function Value =        -43.974
Parameters =        3.1278       2.1809
Gradient Vector =  -0.00010836   0.00040791

                    Asymptotic     Asymptotic
```

	Parameter	Std. Error	t-Ratio
X1	3.1278	0.48766	6.4139
X2	2.1809	0.34483	6.3247

For the case of log-normal distribution, starting from the initial values of (μ, σ) at (1.0, 0.5) in line 15, the maximum likelihood solution is found at (0.9188, 0.6735) as shown in line 16. The maximal value of log-likelihood function is –38.849. Here is the output:

```
Non-Linear Optimization: Maximization Problem
---------------------------------------------
Assuming Maximum Likelihood Function
Number of Observations = 20
Number of Parameters = 2

Maximum Number of Iterations = 100
Step Size Search Method = 0
Convergence Criterion = 0
Tolerance = 0.001

Initial Result:
Function Value =      -41.299
Parameters =       1.0000      0.50000

Using Newton-Raphson Algorithm
Iteration =  1   Step Size = 1.9487  Value =      -38.858
Parameters =       0.89823       0.67385
Iteration =  2   Step Size = 1.0000  Value =      -38.849
Parameters =       0.91884       0.67317
Iteration =  3   Step Size = 1.0000  Value =      -38.849
Parameters =       0.91880       0.67349

Final Result:
Iterations = 3            Evaluations = 44
Function Value =      -38.849
Parameters =       0.91880       0.67349
Gradient Vector =   -0.0018227      0.027819
```

		Asymptotic	Asymptotic
	Parameter	Std. Error	t-Ratio
X1	0.91880	0.15053	6.1039
X2	0.67349	0.10637	6.3317

For the gamma distribution, the estimation of parameters λ and ρ is implemented in line 18 starting with the initial values 0.5 and 2.0 for λ and ρ, respectively (line 17). The maximum likelihood estimator of (λ, ρ) is obtained at (0.7707, 2.4106) where the log-likelihood function value is –39.324. The output looks like this:

```
Non-Linear Optimization: Maximization Problem
---------------------------------------------
Assuming Maximum Likelihood Function
Number of Observations = 20
Number of Parameters = 2

Maximum Number of Iterations = 100
Step Size Search Method = 0
Convergence Criterion = 0
Tolerance = 0.001

Initial Result:
Function Value =      -40.628
```

```
Parameters =          2.0000        0.50000

Using Newton-Raphson Algorithm
Iteration =   1    Step Size =  1.4641  Value =        -39.366
Parameters =          2.2115        0.71252
Iteration =   2    Step Size =  1.1000  Value =        -39.324
Parameters =          2.4112        0.77079
Iteration =   3    Step Size =  1.0000  Value =        -39.324
Parameters =          2.4106        0.77070

Final Result:
Iterations = 3              Evaluations = 42
Function Value =        -39.324
Parameters =          2.4106        0.77070
Gradient Vector =    -0.0036550       0.0078771

                              Asymptotic    Asymptotic
                 Parameter    Std. Error     t-Ratio
X1                  2.4106       0.71610       3.3663
X2                  0.77070      0.25442       3.0293
```

To summarize the statistical characteristics of the random variable INCOME (divided by 10) under consideration, we compute the estimated mean and variance of the maximum likelihood estimates of parameters from the normal, log-normal, and gamma probability distributions. We also compare the maximal values of the log-likelihood functions associated with these probability distributions. It is interesting to note that the variable INCOME is more likely drawn from log-normal or gamma distributions, as their log-likelihood function values are greater than that of the normal distribution.

	Normal Distribution	Log-Normal Distribution	Gamma Distribution
Mean	3.1278	3.1443	3.1278
Variance	4.7563	5.6745	4.0584
Log-likelihood	-43.974	-38.849	-39.324

Lesson 6.4: Mixture of Probability Distributions

It is possible that a random variable is drawn from a mixture of probability distributions (two or more, same or different types of distributions). For simple exploration, consider X distributed with a mixture of two normal distributions:

$$f_1(X, \mu_1, \sigma_1) = \frac{1}{\sqrt{2\pi\sigma_1^2}} exp\left[\frac{(X-\mu_1)^2}{2\sigma_1^2}\right],$$

$$f_2(X, \mu_2, \sigma_2) = \frac{1}{\sqrt{2\pi\sigma_2^2}} exp\left[\frac{(X-\mu_2)^2}{2\sigma_2^2}\right].$$

Then the likelihood function is

$$f(X,\theta) = \lambda\, f_1(X,\mu_1,\sigma_1) + (1-\lambda)\, f_2(X,\mu_2,\sigma_2)$$

where λ is the probability that an observation is drawn from the first distribution $f_1(X,\mu_1,\sigma_1)$, and $1-\lambda$ is the probability of that drawn from the second distribution. $\theta = (\mu_1,\mu_2,\sigma_1,\sigma_2,\lambda)$ is the unknown parameter vector that must be estimated.

Continuing from the previous example, suppose each observation of the variable INCOME is drawn from one of two different normal distributions. There are five parameters, the first two are the mean and standard error of the first normal distribution, while the second pair of parameters corresponds to the second distribution. The last parameter is the probability that the data are drawn from the first distribution. Lines 12 to 17 of **lesson6.4** below define the log-likelihood function for the mixture of two normal distributions.

```
   /*
   ** Lesson 6.4: Mixture of Two Normal Distributions
   ** See Greene (1999), Chapter 4
   */
1  use gpe2;
2  output file=output6.4 reset;
3  load data[21,2]=gpe\yed20.txt;
4  x=data[2:21,1]/10; @ income data: scaling may help @

5  call reset;
6  _nlopt=1;
7  _method=5;
8  _iter=100;
9  _b={3,3,2,2,0.5};
10 call estimate(&llf,x);

11 end;
   /*
   mixture of two normal distributions
   mu1=b[1], mu2=b[2]
   se1=b[3], se2=b[4]
   prob.(drawn from the 1st distribution)=b[5]
   */
12 proc llf(x,b);
13     local pdf1,pdf2;
14     pdf1=pdfn((x-b[1])/b[3])/b[3];
15     pdf2=pdfn((x-b[2])/b[4])/b[4];
16     retp(sumc(ln(b[5]*pdf1+(1-b[5])*pdf2)));
17 endp;
```

The problem is to maximize the log-likelihood function (_nlopt=1 in line 6) using the QHC algorithm (_method=5 in line 7) with the initial estimates of the parameters given in line 9. After 11 iterations, we obtain the following result (to save space, we print only the first and last iterations):

```
Non-Linear Optimization: Maximization Problem
---------------------------------------------
Assuming Maximum Likelihood Function
Number of Observations = 20
Number of Parameters = 5

Maximum Number of Iterations = 100
Step Size Search Method = 0
Convergence Criterion = 0
Tolerance = 0.001

Initial Result:
Function Value =      -44.174
Parameters =      3.0000     3.0000     2.0000     2.0000    0.50000
```

```
Using Quadratic Hill-Climbing Algorithm
Iteration =  1   Step Size =  2.3579  Value =      -43.996
Parameters =         3.0542        3.0542    2.1325        2.1325        0.50000
...
Iteration = 11   Step Size =  1.0000  Value =      -38.309
Parameters =         2.0495        5.7942    0.81222       2.2139        0.71204

Final Result:
Iterations = 11              Evaluations = 406
Function Value =       -38.309
Parameters =         2.0495        5.7942    0.81222       2.2139        0.71204
Gradient Vector =    1.1441e-005          0.00000  2.1870e-005  5.1351e-006  -
4.7899e-005
```

	Parameter	Asymptotic Std. Error	Asymptotic t-Ratio
X1	2.0495	0.24421	8.3922
X2	5.7942	1.4988	3.8659
X3	0.81222	0.19424	4.1816
X4	2.2139	0.90617	2.4431
X5	0.71204	0.14456	4.9254

With the maximum log-likelihood function value of –38.309, the variable INCOME when drawn from the mixtures of two different normal probability distributions is as convincing as when that variable is drawn from a single non-normal distribution (log-normal or gamma) as demonstrated in Lesson 6.3.

Statistical Regression Models

Estimating probability distributions of a random variable is interesting, but econometric modeling focuses on statistical causal relationships within a group of variables. The GPE package is designed specifically for statistical model estimation. If the sample data, in addition to the parameters, are used to define the scalar-valued objective function, estimate assumes nonlinear least squares for a minimization problem and maximum likelihood for a maximization problem. In addition to reporting the optimization process and outcome, the estimated results are interpreted according to these two types of statistical regression models. If your problem is neither a least squares nor a maximum likelihood, your own scrutiny into the classical statistical interpretation of the model is necessary.

For a statistical model, the estimated variance-covariance matrix of the parameters may be requested by setting a positive value to the input control variable _vcov. Typically, the estimated variance-covariance matrix is derived from the approximated hessian (_vcov=1). A recalculated exact hessian matrix is used instead if we set _vcov=2. Nevertheless, the estimated variance-covariance matrix may only be meaningful in the contexts of nonlinear least squares and maximum likelihood problems.

As with the linear regression model, values of several output control variables are available after nonlinear least squares or maximum likelihood estimation:

- __b   Estimated parameters or solution

- __vb   Estimated variance of the parameters

- • __e   Estimated regression residuals

- • __rss   Sum-of-squares function value at minimum

- • __ll   Log-likelihood function value at maximum

- • __g   Gradient vector of objective function at optimum

- • __h   Hessian matrix of objective function at optimum

Appendix A, GPE Control Variables, lists and explains the usage of these input and output control variables.

Lesson 6.5: Minimizing Sum-of-Squares Function

The following example is taken from Judge, et al., (1988, Chapter 12, p.512). Consider a CES production function of a single output (Q) using two factors, labor (L) and capital (K), as follows:

$$ln(Q) = \beta_1 + \beta_4\, ln\, (\beta_2 L^{\beta_3} + (1-\beta_2) K^{\beta_3}) + \varepsilon$$

where ε is the error term and β's are the unknown parameters. The data matrix X = (L, K, Q) is available in the text file **judge.txt**. The method of least squares estimation is to find the vector $\beta = (\beta_1, \beta_2, \beta_3, \beta_4)$ so that the sum-of-squared errors $S(\beta) = \varepsilon'\varepsilon$ is minimized.

Here is the program:

```
     /*
     ** Lesson 6.5: Minimizing Sum-of-Squares Function
     ** Estimating a CES Production Function
     ** See Judge, et al. (1988), Chapter 12
     */
 1   use gpe2;
 2   output file=output6.5 reset;
 3   load x[30,3]=gpe\judge.txt;

 4   call reset;
 5   _nlopt=0;
 6   _method=5;
 7   _iter=100;
 8   _tol=1.0e-5;
 9   _vcov=1;
10   _b={1.0,0.5,-1.0,-1.0};
11   call estimate(&cessse,x);

12   end;

     /* Objective Function */
13   proc cessse(data,b);  @ sum-of-squares function @
14       local l,k,q,e;
15       l=data[.,1];
16       k=data[.,2];
17       q=data[.,3];
18       e=ln(q)-b[1]-b[4]*ln(b[2]*l^b[3]+(1-b[2])*k^b[3]);
19       retp(sumc(e^2));
20   endp;
```

The objective function cessse, sum-of-squared errors, is defined as a procedure in lines 13 through 20. It is evident that both data matrix data and parameter vector b are used to specify the functional form. The address of function &cessse is used in calling estimate in line 11, where x is the data matrix (see also line 3). Line 5 indicates that the problem is to minimize the objective function cessse, and line 6 requests the quadratic hill-climbing (QHC, i.e., _method=5) optimization method. In line 8, the convergence of function value and solutions are checked relative to a smaller tolerance level of 0.00001. The vector of initial parameter values _b is given in line 10, which is rather a random guess. Finally, at the end of optimization, the variance-covariance matrix of estimated parameters will be computed because _vcov=1, as shown in line 9.

We keep the definition of objective function cessse outside (beyond the end statement) of the main program. There is no strict rule dictating where to place the functions you define. Putting the function or procedure outside of the main program makes the function accessible to other procedures you write for other purposes.

The final solution is found after 36 iterations. To save space, we report only the final result of the iterations. The output file output6.5 contains the details of all the iterations for reference.

In your program, setting _print=0 will suppress the printing of iteration outputs to the file and the screen.

```
Non-Linear Optimization: Minimization Problem
---------------------------------------------
Assuming Nonlinear Least Squares Function
Number of Observations = 30
Number of Parameters = 4

Maximum Number of Iterations = 100
Step Size Search Method = 0
Convergence Criterion = 0
Tolerance = 1e-005

Initial Result:
Function Value =        37.097
Parameters =        1.0000      0.50000      -1.0000      -1.0000

Using Quadratic Hill-Climbing Algorithm

Final Result:
Iterations = 36              Evaluations = 1012
Function Value =        1.7611
Parameters =        0.12449      0.33668      -3.0109      -0.33631
Gradient Vector =   2.6755e-006  4.6166e-007  2.5664e-006  1.7166e-006
Hessian Matrix =
        60.000       -5.7563        35.531       295.65
        -5.7563       19.377        -3.4569      -23.595
        35.531        -3.4569       35.461       298.10
        295.65        -23.595       298.10       2509.4

                               Asymptotic
                   Parameter   Std. Error      t-Ratio
X1                 0.12449     0.074644        1.6678
X2                 0.33668     0.10809         3.1147
X3                 -3.0109     2.2904          -1.3145
X4                 -0.33631    0.26823         -1.2538
```

```
Asymptotic Variance-Covariance Matrix
X1            0.0055717
X2           -0.0013729      0.011684
X3           -0.065566       0.16893       5.2462
X4            0.0071194     -0.019797     -0.61389      0.071948
                    X1            X2            X3            X4
```

Both the gradient and hessian of the solution confirm that the solution indeed minimizes the sum-of-squares objective function at the value 1.761. The estimated model is presented as follows:

$$ln(Q) \; = \; 0.125 \; - \; 0.336 \; ln \, (0.337 \, L^{-3.01} + 0.663 \, K^{-3.01})$$
$$\text{s.e.} \quad\quad (0.075) \quad\quad (0.268) \;\; (0.108) \; (2.29)$$

Lesson 6.6: Maximizing Log-Likelihood Function

The same problem can be estimated by maximizing the likelihood objective function. Assuming the model error ε follows a normal probability distribution with zero mean and constant variance σ^2, the log output $ln(Q)$ is normally distributed with the following distribution function:

$$\frac{N}{\sqrt{2\pi\sigma^2}} \, exp \left[\frac{\varepsilon(X,\beta)' \, \varepsilon(X,\beta)}{2\sigma^2} \right]$$

where N is the sample size, and $\varepsilon(X, \beta) = ln(Q) - \beta_1 - \beta_4 \, ln \, (\beta_2 L^{\beta_3} + (1-\beta_2)K^{\beta_3})$. The corresponding log-likelihood function of the unknown parameters $\theta = (\beta, \sigma)$ is written as

$$ll(\theta) = -N/2 \, ln(2\pi) - N/2 \, ln(\sigma^2) - 1/2 \left[\frac{\varepsilon(X,\beta)'}{\sigma} \right] \left[\frac{\varepsilon(X,\beta)}{\sigma} \right]$$

The program below follows the same basic structure as in the previous lesson. The relevant modifications of **lesson6.6** include changing the objective function in the call estimate to cesll (line 11) and setting the variable _nlopt=1 (line 5). The objective log-likelihood function cesll is defined from lines 13 to 21. In addition to β, the standard error of the model σ must be estimated simultaneously. Line 10 sets out the initial values of $\theta = (\beta, \sigma)$.

```
       /*
       ** Lesson 6.6: Maximizing Log-Likelihood Function
       ** Estimating a CES Production Function
       ** See Judge, et al. (1988), Chapter 12
       */
  1    use gpe2;
  2    output file=output6.6 reset;
  3    load x[30,3]=gpe\judge.txt;

  4    call reset;
  5    _nlopt=1;
  6    _method=5;
  7    _iter=100;
  8    _tol=1.0e-5;
  9    _vcov=1;
 10    _b={1.0,0.5,-1.0,-1.0,1.0};
```

```
11  call estimate(&cesll,x);

12  end;

    /* Objective Function */
13  proc cesll(data,b); @ log-likelihood function @
14      local l,k,q,e,n;
15      l=data[.,1];
16      k=data[.,2];
17      q=data[.,3];
18      e=ln(q)-b[1]-b[4]*ln(b[2]*l^b[3]+(1-b[2])*k^b[3]);
19      n=rows(e);
20      retp(-0.5*n*(ln(2*pi)+ln(b[5]^2))-0.5*sumc((e./b[5])^2));
21  endp;
```

Solving the maximization problem of a classical log-likelihood function, the standard error parameter σ is shown to be dependent on β. That is, if β is known, σ^2 is solved as:

$$\sigma^2(\beta) = \varepsilon(X,\beta)'\varepsilon(X,\beta)/N$$

Therefore, the same maximum log-likelihood may be expressed with the *concentrated* log-likelihood function instead:

$$ll^*(\beta) = -N/2 \ (1+ ln(2\pi) - ln(N)) -N/2 \ ln(\varepsilon(X,\beta)'\varepsilon(X,\beta))$$

The advantage of using the concentrated log-likelihood function is that there is one less parameter (that is, σ) to estimate directly.

Running the program **lesson6.6**, we obtain the following result (again, the details of interim iterations can be found in the output file output6.6):

```
Non-Linear Optimization: Maximization Problem
---------------------------------------------
Assuming Maximum Likelihood Function
Number of Observations = 30
Number of Parameters = 5

Maximum Number of Iterations = 100
Step Size Search Method = 0
Convergence Criterion = 0
Tolerance = 1e-005

Initial Result:
Function Value =      -46.117
Parameters =     1.0000      0.50000     -1.0000      -1.0000       1.0000

Using Quadratic Hill-Climbing Algorithm
Final Result:
Iterations = 41         Evaluations = 1419
Function Value =    -0.039074
Parameters =      0.12449      0.33667      -3.0109      -0.33630      0.24229
Gradient Vector  =   8.5614e-006   1.0552e-006  -8.2596e-007   7.3948e-006  -
3.6658e-006
Hessian Matrix =
      -511.05        49.030     -302.63      -2518.3      0.063432
       49.030       -165.04      29.444       200.98      0.020503
      -302.63        29.444     -302.02      -2539.1     -0.037482
      -2518.3        200.98     -2539.1      -21375.      -2.6556
```

	0.063432	0.020503	-0.037482	-2.6556	-1021.5

	Parameter	Asymptotic Std. Error	t-Ratio
X1	0.12449	0.074646	1.6677
X2	0.33667	0.10811	3.1142
X3	-3.0109	2.2911	-1.3142
X4	-0.33630	0.26830	-1.2535
X5	0.24229	0.031295	7.7421

Asymptotic Variance-Covariance Matrix

X1	0.0055721				
X2	-0.0013740	0.011687			
X3	-0.065602	0.16904	5.2493		
X4	0.0071233	-0.019807	-0.61423	0.071984	
X5	-1.5793E-005	4.5442E-005	0.0014036	-0.00016456	0.00097936
	X1	X2	X3	X4	X5

It is no surprise that the solution is identical to the one obtained from minimizing the sum-of-squares function in Lesson 6.5. In addition, the estimated standard error of the normal distribution is found to be 0.2423, or $\sigma^2 = 0.0587$. This also confirms the minimal sum-of-squares $S(\beta) = N\sigma^2 = 1.761$.

Minimizing sum-of-squares and maximizing log-likelihood are popular techniques for econometric model estimation. In the next chapter on nonlinear regression models, for the convenience of classical econometric analysis, it is only the functional form of model error $\varepsilon(X,\beta)$ that we will need to specify. The objective of either minimizing a sum-of-squares or maximizing a log-likelihood is readily available once the specific error structure is given. Nevertheless, as we have learned from this chapter, being able to work on the scalar-valued objective function directly is useful when dealing with difficult optimization problems.

VII
Nonlinear Regression Models

Many economic and econometric problems can be formulated as optimization (minimization or maximization) problems. In econometrics, sum-of-squares minimization and log-likelihood maximization are standard in empirical model estimation. In the previous chapter, we defined a scalar-valued objective function to minimize (maximize) and interpreted the parameter estimates in accordance with the classical least squares (maximum likelihood) model. This approach is flexible enough to encompass many different econometric models. In many situations, however, it becomes troublesome to write out the objective function in detail. It is more desirable to present only the functional form which defines the model directly, such as

$$F(Z,\beta) = \varepsilon$$

where Z is the data matrix, β is the parameter vector, and ε is the error term. Both Z and β are used to define the functional form of the model (that is, the error structure). The data matrix Z can be further decomposed as $Z = [Y, X]$ where Y consists of endogenous (dependent) variables and X is a list of predetermined (independent) variables. For a classical single regression equation, $Y = f(X,\beta) + \varepsilon$ or $\varepsilon = Y - f(X,\beta)$. The special case of linear model is simply $\varepsilon = Y - X\beta$.

Nonlinear Least Squares

The functional form $F(Z,\beta) = \varepsilon$ is of interest in econometric modeling. Consider the sum-of-squares objective function:

$$S(\beta) = \varepsilon'\varepsilon$$

A nonlinear least squares estimator b of β is computed from the first-order condition for minimization (or the zero gradient condition) as follows:

$$\partial S(b)/\partial\beta = 2\varepsilon'(\partial\varepsilon/\partial\beta) = 0$$

In addition, the hessian matrix of second derivatives evaluated at b,

$$\frac{\partial^2 S(b)}{\partial\beta\partial\beta'} = 2\left[(\partial\varepsilon/\partial\beta)'(\partial\varepsilon/\partial\beta) + \sum_{i=1,2,...,N}\varepsilon_i\left(\frac{\partial^2\varepsilon_i}{\partial\beta\partial\beta'}\right)\right]$$

must be positive definite to guarantee the minimum solution. The estimated variance-covariance matrix of the parameters is derived from the expected values of the hessian:

$$Var(b) = S^2\left[1/2\,E\left(\frac{\partial^2 S(b)}{\partial\beta\partial\beta'}\right)\right]^{-1} = S^2\left[(\partial\varepsilon/\partial\beta)'(\partial\varepsilon/\partial\beta)\right]^{-1}$$

where $s^2 = e'e/N$ is the estimated regression variance σ^2, $e = F(Z,b)$ is the estimated error, and N is the sample size used for estimation. It becomes clear that only the information concerning the functional form $F(Z,\beta)$ and its first and second derivatives is needed to carry out the nonlinear least squares estimation of b, e, s^2, and Var(b).

It is straightforward to generalize the technique of nonlinear least squares to consider weighted model errors. Denote the weighting scheme $w = w(Z,\beta)$. The variable w is a scalar or a vector, which in turn may depend on part or all of the data and parameters. Define the weighted error terms as $\varepsilon^* = w\ \varepsilon$. Then the model is estimated by minimizing the sum-of-squared weighted errors: $S^*(\beta) = \varepsilon^{*'}\varepsilon^*$.

Lesson 7.1: CES Production Function

Let's return to the example of Lesson 6.5 estimating a nonlinear CES production function. Instead of defining and minimizing the sum-of-squares objective function, this example demonstrates the use of the error or residual function for model estimation. A residual function is usually more intuitive and easier to write than a sum-of-squares function. Since the computation of least squares relies on the residuals and their derivatives, the advantage of increased numerical precision is another reason of working with the residuals directly.

The setup of input control variables is the same as in Lesson 6.5. The difference is the use of the residual function (instead of the sum-of-squares objective function) in calling the `estimate` procedure (line 12). The residual function `ces` is defined in the block from line 14 to line 20.

```
/*
** Lesson 7.1: CES Production Function Revisited
** Judge, et al. (1988), Chapter 12
*/
1   use gpe2;
2   output file=gpe\output7.1 reset;
3   load x[30,3]=gpe\judge.txt;

4   call reset;

5   _nlopt=0;      @ NLSQ: SSE minimization @
6   _method=5;     @ optimization method @
7   _iter=100;
8   _tol=1.0e-5;
9   _conv=1;
10  _vcov=1;

11  _b={1.0,0.5,-1.0,-1.0};

12  call estimate(&ces,x);

13  end;

14  proc ces(data,b); @ residual function @
15      local l,k,q;
16      l=data[.,1];
17      k=data[.,2];
18      q=data[.,3];
19      retp(ln(q)-b[1]-b[4]*ln(b[2]*l^b[3]+(1-b[2])*k^b[3]));
20  endp;
```

The regression output duplicates that of Lesson 6.5, and it is available in the output file output7.1.

Maximum Likelihood Estimation

To explore the idea of maximum likelihood estimation in the econometric context, we assume a classical normal probability distribution for the independent model error $\varepsilon = F(Z,\beta)$. That is, ε is normally independently distributed with zero mean and constant variance σ^2. Then the probability density function of Y (recall that Z = [Y, X]) is written as:

$$\frac{1}{\sqrt{2\pi\sigma^2}} exp\left[\frac{F(Z,\beta)^2}{2\sigma^2}\right] | J(Z,\beta)|$$

where $J(Z,\beta) = \partial\varepsilon/\partial Y$ is the Jacobian of the transformation from ε to Y. Sampling over N independent observations, the log-likelihood function of the unknown parameter vector $\theta = (\beta,\sigma)$ is:

$$ll(\theta) = -N/2\, ln(2\pi) - N/2\, ln(\sigma^2) - 1/2\left[\frac{F(Z,\beta)}{\sigma}\right]'\left[\frac{F(Z,\beta)}{\sigma}\right] + \sum_{i=1,2,...,N} ln\,|J(Z_i,\beta)|$$

The technique of maximum likelihood estimation is to find the θ that maximizes the log-likelihood function $ll(\theta)$. Usually the computation is performed by substituting out the variance estimate $\sigma^2 = \varepsilon'\varepsilon/N = F(Z,\beta)'F(Z,\beta)/N$. Then the following *concentrated* log-likelihood function is maximized with respect to the parameter vector β:

$$ll*(\beta) = -N/2[1 + ln(2\pi) - ln(N)] - N/2\, ln\left[F(Z,\beta)'F(Z,\beta)\right] + \sum_{i=1,2,...,N} ln\,|J(Z_i,\beta)|$$

Define $\varepsilon^* = \varepsilon/[(\prod_{i=1,2,...,N}|J_i|)^{1/N}]$ or equivalently $F^*(Z,\beta) = F(Z,\beta)/[(\prod_{i=1,2,...,N}|J_i|)^{1/N}]$, where $J_i = J(Z_i,\beta)$. Then the last two terms of the above concentrated log-likelihood function can be combined and the function is rewritten as:

$$ll*(\beta) = -N/2[1 + ln(2\pi) - ln(N)] - N/2\, ln\left[F*(Z,\beta)'F*(Z,\beta)\right]$$

where $F^*(Z,\beta) = \varepsilon^*$ is the weighted error, with the weight being the inverse of the geometric mean of Jacobians (that is, $1/[(\prod_{i=1,2,...,N}|J_i|)^{1/N}]$). Therefore, maximizing the concentrated log-likelihood function $ll^*(\beta)$ is equivalent to minimizing the corresponding sum-of-squared weighted errors $S^*(\beta) = \varepsilon^*'\varepsilon^*$.

The maximum likelihood estimator b of β is obtained from solving from the first-order condition (recall that $S^* = \varepsilon^*'\varepsilon^*$ and $\varepsilon^* = F^*(Z,\beta)$):

$$\partial ll*(b)/\partial\beta = -1/2(N/S*)(\partial S*/\partial\beta) = -(N/S*)[\varepsilon*'(\partial\varepsilon*/\partial\beta)] = 0$$

We must also check that the hessian matrix is negative definite (the second-order condition for maximization) at b:

$$\frac{\partial^2 ll*(b)}{\partial\beta\partial\beta'} = -1/2\,(N/S*)\left[(1/S*)(\partial S*/\partial\beta)'(\partial S*/\partial\beta) - \frac{\partial^2 S*}{\partial\beta\partial\beta'}\right]$$

Since $\partial S*/\partial\beta = 0$, at the maximum the corresponding negative definite hessian matrix is simply:

$$\frac{\partial^2 ll*(b)}{\partial\beta\partial\beta'} = -(N/S*)\left[1/2\left(\frac{\partial^2 S*}{\partial\beta\partial\beta'}\right)\right]$$

$$= -(N/S*)\left[(\partial\varepsilon*/\partial\beta)'(\partial\varepsilon*/\partial\beta) + \sum_{i=1,2,\ldots,N}\varepsilon_i*\left(\frac{\partial^2\varepsilon_i*}{\partial\beta\partial\beta'}\right)\right]$$

Thus the estimated variance-covariance matrix of maximum likelihood estimator b, defined as the inverse of negative expected hessian, is:

$$\mathrm{Var}(b) = \left[-\mathrm{E}\left(\frac{\partial^2 ll*(b)}{\partial\beta\partial\beta'}\right)\right]^{-1} = S^2*\left[(\partial\varepsilon*/\partial\beta)'(\partial\varepsilon*/\partial\beta)\right]^{-1}$$

where $s^2* = e*'e*/N$ and $e* = F*(Z,b) = F(Z,b)/[(\prod_{i=1,2,\ldots,N}|J_i|)^{1/N}]$. Therefore, if the objective is to maximize the log-likelihood function under the assumption of normally independently distributed model error, then we need only to be concerned with the residual function $\varepsilon = F(Z,\beta)$ and its associated Jacobian transformations $J(Z,\beta)$.

We now introduce the GPE input variable _jacob, we have not yet introduced, which controls the use of Jacobians in deriving the objective function (log-likelihood or sum-of-squares) from the residuals. Notice that a Jacobian transformation is nothing but a function of data and parameters. If you define a Jacobian function of your own, then _jacob should be set to the location (address) of the function. An example of a Jacobian function is given later in Lesson 7.2 on Box-Cox variable transformation. If you do not wish to write out the Jacobian analytically, you may set

```
_jacob = 1;
```

Then the numerical Jacobian is computed for each sample observation, which is usually a time consuming process. In case of requesting numerical Jacobians, the first column of the data matrix used to define the residuals must be the dependent variable Y (recall that $J(Z,\beta) = \partial\varepsilon/\partial Y$ and $Z = [Y,X]$).

Here, based on Lesson 7.1 above, we insert the following statement before calling the estimate procedure in line 12:

```
_jacob = 0;
```

Although it is not necessary (_jacob=0 by default), _jacob=0 is used here to make sure that you understand the implication of Jacobian terms in the log-likelihood function. As a matter of fact, for the classical model of the CES production function, there is no need to consider the *vanishing* Jacobian terms in the log-likelihood function.

Lesson7.1 may be modified to carry out maximum likelihood estimation instead. Change the type of problem from minimization to maximization in line 5:

```
_nlopt = 1;
```

It is no surprise that the empirical results are identical for both techniques of nonlinear least squares and maximum likelihood.

 If you ask for the numerical Jacobians to be computed in this example:

```
_jacob = 1;
```

You must be sure that the first column of the data matrix data used to define the residual function ces(data,b) corresponds to the dependent variable of the model, *ln*(Q) in this case. As it was presented in Lesson 7.1, this rule is not followed. You may want to correct the data matrix and rewrite the procedure ces(data,b) so that you can use the numerical Jacobians which are all ones. The estimation result should not be affected.

Box-Cox Variable Transformation

A nonlinear regression equation may involve nonlinearity in both parameters and variables. The Box-Cox variable transformation is a classic example of a nonlinear model in econometrics. The so-called Box-Cox transformation of a data variable X is defined by

$$X^{(\lambda)} = (X^{\lambda}\text{-}1)/\lambda$$

Although the range of λ can cover the whole set of real numbers, $-2 \leq \lambda \leq 2$ is the area of interest in many econometric applications. $\lambda = 2$ corresponds to a quadratic transformation, while $\lambda = \frac{1}{2}$ is a square-root transformation. A linear model corresponds to $\lambda =1$, and the logarithmic transformation is the limiting case where λ approaches 0 (by L'Hôspital's rule, $\lim_{\lambda \to 0} (X^{\lambda}\text{-}1)/\lambda = ln(X)$).

The value of the power transformation parameter λ may not have to be the same for each variable in the model. In particular, the dependent variable and independent variables as a group may need different Box-Cox transformations. Let $\beta = (\alpha,\lambda,\theta)$ be the vector of unknown parameters for a regression model:

$$\varepsilon = F(Z,\beta) = F(Y,X,\beta) = Y^{(\theta)} - X^{(\lambda)}\alpha$$

or, equivalently,

$$Y^{(\theta)} = X^{(\lambda)}\alpha + \varepsilon$$

To estimate the parameters, we assume the error ε is normally independently distributed with zero mean and constant variance σ^2. The log-likelihood function of the random variable Y is

$$ll(\beta) = -N/2\left[ln(2\pi) + ln(\sigma^2)\right] - 1/2\, F(Z,\beta)'\, F(Z,\beta)/\sigma^2 + (\theta - 1)\sum_{i=1,2,...,N} ln(|\,Y_i\,|)$$

$Z = [Y,X]$, $\beta = (\alpha,\lambda,\theta)$, and for each data observation i, the Jacobian term of the function is derived as $J(Y_i,\theta) = \partial\varepsilon_i/\partial Y_i = Y_i^{(\theta-1)}$. By substituting out the variance $\sigma^2 = \varepsilon'\varepsilon/N$, the concentrated log-likelihood function is

$$ll*(\beta) = -N/2[1 + ln(2\pi) - ln(N)] - N/2\,ln\left(F(Z,\beta)' F(Z,\beta)\right) + (\theta-1)\sum_{i=1,2,...,N} ln(|Y_i|)$$

$$= -N/2[1 + ln(2\pi) - ln(N)] - N/2\,ln\left(F*(Z,\beta)' F*(Z,\beta)\right)$$

where $F*(Z,\beta) = \varepsilon* = \varepsilon/[(\prod_{i=1,2,...,N} |Y_i|)^{(\theta-1)/N}]$. Given the values of Box-Cox transformation parameters θ and λ, a wide range of model specifications are possible. Of course, θ and λ must be estimated jointly with α. An efficient estimator of the parameter vector $\beta = (\alpha,\lambda,\theta)$ is obtained by maximizing the above concentrated log-likelihood function. It is equivalent to minimizing the sum-of-squared weighted errors $S(\beta) = \varepsilon*'\varepsilon*$, where $\varepsilon* = w\,\varepsilon$ and $w = w(Y,\theta) = 1/[(\prod_{i=1,2,...,N} |Y_i|)^{(\theta-1)/N}]$.

Lesson 7.2: Box-Cox Variable Transformation

The following example of U.S. money demand equation is taken from Greene (1999, Chapter 10):

$$M^{(\theta)} = \alpha_0 + \alpha_1 R^{(\lambda)} + \alpha_2 Y^{(\lambda)} + \varepsilon$$

As described in Greene's Example 10.9, M is the real money stock M2, R is the discount interest rate, and Y is real GNP. **money.txt** is the data text file consisting of these variables. Several variations of the Box-Cox transformation may be estimated and tested for selecting the most appropriate functional form of the money demand equation:

1. $\theta \to 0$ $ln(M) = \alpha_0 + \alpha_1 R^{(\lambda)} + \alpha_2 Y^{(\lambda)} + \varepsilon$
2. $\theta = 1$ $M = \alpha_0 + \alpha_1 R^{(\lambda)} + \alpha_2 Y^{(\lambda)} + \varepsilon$
3. $\lambda \to 0$ $M^{(\theta)} = \alpha_0 + \alpha_1 ln(R) + \alpha_2 ln(Y) + \varepsilon$
4. $\lambda = 1$ $M^{(\theta)} = \alpha_0 + \alpha_1 R + \alpha_2 Y + \varepsilon$
5. $\theta = \lambda$ $M^{(\lambda)} = \alpha_0 + \alpha_1 R^{(\lambda)} + \alpha_2 Y^{(\lambda)} + \varepsilon$
6. $\theta, \lambda \to 0$ $ln(M) = \alpha_0 + \alpha_1 ln(R) + \alpha_2 ln(Y) + \varepsilon$
7. $\theta, \lambda = 1$ $M = \alpha_0 + \alpha_1 R + \alpha_2 Y + \varepsilon$

The following program considers a general case of Box-Cox variable transformation. In addition to the regression parameters α, there are two power transformation parameters: θ for the left-hand side variable and λ for the right-hand side. All these parameters (α,λ,θ) are estimated jointly. For model estimation, it is typical to scale the variables so that their power transformations do not under- or over-flow in arithmetic computation. This will make the interpretation of the estimated parameters more difficult. The sensible approach is to convert the estimated values of the parameters to unit-free measurements of elasticity. Therefore, for the general model, the estimated elasticity of the interest rate is

$$\frac{\partial ln(M)}{\partial ln(R)} = \frac{R}{M}\frac{\partial M}{\partial R} = \alpha_1 \frac{R^\lambda}{M^\theta}$$

Similarly, the elasticity of GNP is $\dfrac{\partial ln(M)}{\partial ln(Y)} = \alpha_2 \dfrac{Y^\lambda}{M^\theta}$. The elasticity at the means (of data variables) should be reported for model interpretation.

```
     /*
     ** Lesson 7.2: Box-Cox Transformation
     ** U.S. Money Demand Equation
     ** Greene (1999), Chapter 10
     */
 1   use gpe2;
 2   output file=gpe\output7.2 reset;
 3   load x[21,4]=gpe\money.txt;
     @ scale and re-arrange data: m,r,y @
 4   x=(x[2:21,3]/1000)~(x[2:21,2])~(x[2:21,4]/1000);

 5   call reset;
 6   _method=0;
 7   _iter=200;
 8   _step=1;
 9   _conv=1;
10   _jacob=&jf;

     @ starting linear model @
11   b=x[.,1]/(ones(rows(x),1)~x[.,2:3]);
12   _b=b|1.0|1.0;
     /*
     @ starting log model @
     b=ln(x[.,1])/(ones(rows(x),1)~ln(x[.,2:3]));
     _b=b|-0.01|0.01;
     */
13   _nlopt=1; @ MAXLIK @
14   call estimate(&rf,x);
15   end;

16   proc jf(data,b); @ jacobian @
17       local k;
18       k=rows(b); @ the last parameter @
19       retp(data[.,1]^(b[k]-1));
20   endp;

21   proc rf(data,b); @ residual: general model @
22       local r,m,y,e;
         @ box-cox transformation @
23       m=(data[.,1]^b[5]-1)/b[5];
24       r=(data[.,2]^b[4]-1)/b[4];
25       y=(data[.,3]^b[4]-1)/b[4];
26       e=m-b[1]-b[2]*r-b[3]*y;
27       retp(e);
28   endp;
```

The residual function for the general model rf is defined in lines 21 through 28. Notice that the residual function is written in such a way that the first column of the data matrix is the dependent variable. The procedure jf, given in the block from lines 16 to 20, defines the Jacobian terms for the likelihood function. Recall that the Jacobian term is just $Y^{\theta-1}$ for the Box-Cox model, where Y is the left-hand side dependent variable. As we have mentioned earlier in Lesson 7.1, the GPE input variable _jacob controls the use of Jacobian transformation in defining the log-likelihood and sum-of-squares functions. In the case of Box-Cox variable transformation, the residuals are weighted with the inverse of geometric mean of Jacobians: $1/[(\prod_{i=1,2,\dots,N} |J_i|)^{1/N}]$ and $J_i = Y_i^{\theta-1}$. When _jacob=0, the Jacobians are not used (vanishing log-Jacobians is assumed). When _jacob=1, the numerical

Jacobians are computed from the residual function with the assumption that the first column of the data matrix is the dependent variable under consideration. When _jacob is set to the location (address) of a procedure defining the analytical Jacobians, the result of the procedure called is used. Here, in line 10:

```
_jacob = &jf;
```

the input control variable _jacob is assigned the result of the procedure jf(data,b). Therefore, the analytical Jacobian transformation is used for log-likelihood maximization and sum-of-squares (weighted) minimization. By defining and applying the Jacobian transformation, as we have done here, we guarantee that our parameters will be efficiently estimated.

 Although numerical Jacobians may be requested instead, by setting _jacob=1 in line 10, we recommend against using it. The numerical approximation of Jacobian transformation is typically slower and results in less accurate parameter estimates than explicitly defining the analytical formula. As in the case of defining the residual function, the Jacobian function is problem-dependent and it involves differentiation of the residual function with respect to the dependent variable. For optimization, another round of differentiation of the residual and Jacobian functions is needed. Rounding errors due to excess numerical approximation may be too severe to yield an accurate solution.

Two sets of starting values of the parameters may be tried: one from the linear model estimates and the other from log model. In the program, we start with the linear model estimates (lines 11 and 12). The alternative is to start with the log model estimates as given in the comment block immediately below line 12. Just to make sure that you achieve the same solution starting from several different initial values of the parameters, run program **lesson7.2**, and check the following result:

```
Maximum Likelihood Estimation
------------------------------
Number of Observations = 20
Number of Parameters = 5

Maximum Number of Iterations = 200
Step Size Search Method = 1
Convergence Criterion = 1
Tolerance = 0.001

Initial Result:
Sum of Squares =        7.0963
Log Likelihood =       -18.017
Parameters =       -3.1694    -0.014921       1.5881       1.0000       1.0000

Using Berndt-Hall-Hall-Hausman (BHHH) Algorithm

Final Result:
Iterations = 165         Evaluations = 29500
Sum of Squares =       0.11766
Log Likelihood =        22.978
Gradient  of  Log  Likelihood  =   -8.2374e-005  -3.0382e-005  -2.8533e-005     -
0.00032734 -6.0704e-005

                               Asymptotic
                Parameter    Std. Error      t-Ratio
X1              -14.503       12.127        -1.1959
X2              -14.067       50.134        -0.28058
X3               56.399      106.75          0.52831
```

X4	-2.6723	1.8562	-1.4396
X5	-0.96447	0.54949	-1.7552

Model interpretation of Box-Cox variable transformation is more difficult than that of linear models. However, the elasticity at the mean of each variable is computed and interpreted as below:

$$M^{(-0.96)} = -14.5 - 14.07\, R^{(-2.67)} + 56.4\, Y^{(-2.67)}$$

s.e. (0.55)   (12.13)   (50.13) (1.86)   (106.75) (1.86)

Elasticity   - 0.087   4.252

 The same model may be estimated with the technique of weighted least squares. As long as the Jacobian is used, the sum-of-squares function is derived from the residuals, weighted by the inverse of the geometric mean of the Jacobians. Just replace line 13 with:

```
_nlopt=0;
```

This should produce the same result as that from the maximum likelihood estimation. However, if we attempt to minimize the sum-of-squared unweighted residuals, then the estimation result will not be efficient. It can even be biased. Check it out by deleting line 10 or changing it to:

```
_jacob=0;
```

The program of Lesson 7.2 is readily modifiable to accommodate all of the special cases of Box-Cox transformations. For example, for the case $\theta = \lambda$, let's define the residual function rf1 as follows:

```
proc rf1(data,b);
    local r,m,y,e;
    @ box-cox transformation @
    m=(data[.,1]^b[4]-1)/b[4];
    r=(data[.,2]^b[4]-1)/b[4];
    y=(data[.,3]^b[4]-1)/b[4];
    e=m-b[1]-b[2]*r-b[3]*y;
    retp(e);
endp;
```

To run this special case, modify the starting values for the parameters (note that the number of parameters is changed as well) and call estimate with &rf1. That is, the lines from 12 to 14 should read like this:

```
_b=b|1.0;
_nlopt=1;
call estimate(&rf1,x);
```

Other cases such as linear or log transformation on one side of the equation can be estimated as long as the respective residual function is defined and used correctly. You may have to experiment with different combinations of optimization options and starting values to find all the solutions. Also, the last two cases of linear and log models may be more conveniently estimated with linear least squares. We leave the remainder of these special cases to you as exercises.

From Lesson 7.2, we have estimated the general Box-Cox transformation model, together with many special cases. It is useful to tabulate and compare the estimation results of all these models. Based on the sample data series in **money.txt**, what is the most appropriate functional form for the U.S. money demand equation? To answer this question, some knowledge of statistical inference will be necessary.

Statistical Inference in Nonlinear Models

A fundamental assumption of statistical inference is the normality of the model error: $\varepsilon = F(Z, \beta)$. In particular, ε is assumed to be identically independently normally distributed with zero mean and constant variance σ^2, or $\varepsilon \sim nii(0, \sigma^2)$. Thus the estimated least squares or maximum likelihood parameter b of β is normally distributed with the mean as β and the estimated variance-covariance matrix as:

$$\text{Var}(b) = \left[-\text{E}\left(\partial^2 ll(b) / \partial\beta' \partial\beta\right)\right]^{-1}$$
$$= s^2 \left[1/2 \, \text{E}\left(\partial^2 S(b) / \partial\beta' \partial\beta\right)\right]^{-1}$$

where $s^2 = S(b)/N$ is the estimated asymptotic variance of the model. Note that $S(b) = e'e$ and $e = F(Z, b)$.

In many situations, it is of interest to test the validity of a set of J non-sample restrictions of the parameters, linear or nonlinear (continuous and differentiable), expressed as the following vector-valued equation:

$$c(\beta) = 0$$

If there are J active parameter restrictions, let the restricted parameter estimator and its variance-covariance matrix be b* and Var(b*), respectively. For example, the simplest case of a linear restriction $c(\beta) = \beta - \beta^0$ (possibly a vector) confines the parameter vector β to be near β^0. The following three tests are useful for inference about the model restrictions.

Wald Test

Without estimating the constrained model, the unconstrained parameter estimator b is expected to satisfy the constraint equation closely, if the hypothesis is true. That is, $c(b) = 0$. The Wald test statistic:

$$W = c(b)' \left\{ \text{Var}[c(b)] \right\}^{-1} c(b)$$

has a Chi-square distribution with J degrees of freedom (remember that J is the number of restrictions). With the first-order linear approximation of the constraint function $c(\beta)$ at b,

$$W = c(b)' \left\{ [\partial c(b)/\partial\beta][\text{Var}(b)][\partial c(b)/\partial\beta]' \right\}^{-1} c(b)$$

Note that this test statistic does not require the computation of the constrained parameters.

Lagrangian Multiplier (LM) Test

Given the J-element constraint equation $c(\beta) = 0$, let b^* denote the maximum likelihood estimator of the parameter vector β with the constraint in place. The Lagrangian multiplier test is based on the score vector $\partial ll(b^*)/\partial \beta$ of the original parameterization of the log-likelihood function. If the constraints hold, then $\partial ll(b^*)/\partial \beta$ should be close to $\partial ll(b)/\partial \beta$ for the unconstrained parameter estimator b, which is of course zero. The Lagrangian multiplier test statistic is written as:

$$LM = (\partial ll(b^*)/\partial \beta) \, [Var(b^*)] \, (\partial ll(b^*)/\partial \beta)'$$

The estimated variance-covariance matrix of the constrained estimator b^* is computed as follows:

$$Var(b^*) = H^{-1} \, [I - G'(G \, H^{-1}G')^{-1}H^{-1}]$$

where $H = [-\partial ll(b^*)^2/\partial \beta' \partial \beta]$ and $G = [\partial c(b^*)/\partial \beta]$. In practice, the LM test statistic is easily approximated with the following formula:

$$LM = \left\{ [e^{*\prime}(\partial e^*/\partial \beta)] \Big[(\partial e^*/\partial \beta)'(\partial e^*/\partial \beta) \Big]^{-1} [e^{*\prime}(\partial e^*/\partial \beta)]' \right\} / (e^{*\prime} e^* / N)$$

where $e^* = F(Z,b^*)$ is the vector of residuals evaluated at the constrained maximum likelihood solution, and $\partial e^*/\partial \beta = \partial F(Z,b^*)/\partial \beta$. Note that this test statistic is based on the constrained parameters alone.

Likelihood Ratio (LR) Test

If both the constrained and unconstrained maximum likelihood solutions are available, then the Likelihood Ratio (LR) test statistic defined by

$$LR = -2(ll(b^*)-ll(b))$$

follows a Chi-square distribution with J degrees of freedom, in which there are J constraints in the equation $c\beta$) = 0. In terms of sum-of-squares, it is equivalent to

$$LR = N \, ln(S(b^*)/S(b))$$

Lesson 7.3: Hypothesis Testing for Nonlinear Models

Returning to Lesson 7.1 (see also Lesson 6.5) on CES production function,

$$ln(Q) = \beta_1 + \beta_4 \, ln(\beta_2 L^{\beta 3} + (1-\beta_2)K^{\beta 3}) + \varepsilon$$

let's verify the nonlinear equality constraint: $\beta_4 = 1/\beta_3$. The following program implements the Wald, Lagrangian multiplier, and Likelihood Ratio tests, based on constrained and unconstrained maximum likelihood estimates of the parameters. The unconstrained model is the same as in Lesson 7.1 except that we are working with maximum likelihood estimation (instead of sum-of-squares). The constrained residual function rfc is defined in lines 38 through 45 in which the constraint $\beta_4 = 1/\beta_3$ is substituted into the function, eliminating the parameter β_4. The single constraint, expressed as $\beta_4\beta_3 - 1 = 0$, is given in lines 46 through 48 and is named as

111

the eqc procedure. In line 11 and 12, the constrained model is estimated, and the estimated parameters and log-likelihood function value are saved for later use.

```
/*
** Lesson 7.3: Hypothesis Testing for Nonlinear Models
** CES Production Function: b[4]=1/b[3]
** Judge, et al. (1988), Chapter 12
*/
1   use gpe2;
2   output file=gpe\output7.3 reset;
3   load x[30,3]=gpe\judge.txt;

4   call reset;
5   _nlopt=1;  @ MAXLIK: log-likelihood maximization @
6   _method=5;
7   _iter=100;
8   _tol=1.0e-5;
9   _conv=1;
10  _jacob=0;          @ vanishing log-jacobians @

    /* Lagrangian Multiplier Test */
    @ based on constrained estimation @
11  _b={1.0,0.5,-1.0};
12  call estimate(&rfc,x);
13  b1=__b|(1/__b[3]);  @ original parameterization, b[4]=1/b[3] @
14  lll=__ll;           @ log-likelihood @
15  e=rf(x,b1);         @ estimated errors @
16  s2=meanc(e^2);      @ estimated error variance @
17  g=gradp2(&rf,x,b1); @ gradient of error function @
18  lm=(e'g)*invpd(g'g)*(g'e)/s2;

    /* Wald Test */
    @ based on unconstrained estimation @
19  _b={1.0,0.25,-1.0,-1.0};
20  call estimate(&rf,x);
21  b2=__b;             @ estimated parameters @
22  vb2=__vb;           @ estimated var-cov. of parameters @
23  ll2=__ll;           @ log-likelihood @
24  w=eqc(b2)'*invpd(gradp(&eqc,b2)*vb2*gradp(&eqc,b2)')*eqc(b2);

    /* Likelihood Ratio Test */
25  lr=-2*(lll-ll2);

26  print "Wald Test = " w;
27  print "Lagrangian Multiplier Test = " lm;
28  print "Likelihood Ratio Test = " lr;
29  end;

30  proc rf(data,b); @ unconstrained residual function @
31      local l,k,q,e;
32      l=data[.,1];
33      k=data[.,2];
34      q=data[.,3];
35      e=ln(q)-b[1]-b[4]*ln(b[2]*l^b[3]+(1-b[2])*k^b[3]);
36      retp(e);
37  endp;

38  proc rfc(data,b); @ constrained residual function @
39      local l,k,q,n,e;
40      l=data[.,1];
41      k=data[.,2];
42      q=data[.,3];
43      e=ln(q)-b[1]-(1/b[3])*ln(b[2]*l^b[3]+(1-b[2])*k^b[3]);
44      retp(e);
45  endp;
```

```
46 |  proc eqc(b);   @ constraint function @
47 |      retp(b[3]*b[4]-1);
48 |  endp;
```

Here is the estimation result of the constrained model as of line 12 (see also output7.3 for more details):

```
Maximum Likelihood Estimation
-----------------------------
Number of Observations = 30
Number of Parameters = 3

Maximum Number of Iterations = 100
Step Size Search Method = 0
Convergence Criterion = 1
Tolerance = 1e-005

Initial Result:
Sum of Squares =        37.097
Log Likelihood =       -45.753
Parameters =         1.0000        0.50000       -1.0000

Using Quadratic Hill-Climbing Algorithm

Final Result:
Iterations = 11             Evaluations = 7050
Sum of Squares =         1.7659
Log Likelihood =      -0.080162
Gradient of Log Likelihood = -6.2600e-006  3.4304e-006 -5.5635e-007

                                      Asymptotic
             Parameter    Std. Error      t-Ratio
X1             0.11849      0.070742        1.6749
X2             0.32238       0.10324        3.1225
X3             -3.4403        1.7791       -1.9338
```

We now return to the program of Lesson 7.3. To compute the Lagrangian multiplier test statistic, the estimated errors are recalculated from the residual function rf (line 15). In addition, the variance (line 16) and the derivatives (line 17) of estimated errors are needed for implementing the LM formula in line 18. Note that the gradient computation of line 17 is for a function with two arguments, the data matrix as the first and parameter vector as the second. The procedure gradp2 is built into GPE with the consideration that user-defined functions are constructed from the combination of a data matrix and a parameter vector. It serves the same purpose as the GAUSS built-in procedure gradp to compute the gradient vector of a continuous differentiable function with respect to the parameters. The result of gradp2(&rf,x,b1) of line 17 is a 30 by 4 matrix of derivatives of the residual function rf with respect to 4 parameters of b1 over a sample of 30 observations of x.

The Wald test is based on the unconstrained model. The unrestricted regression model is the same as reported in Lesson 7.1. Based on the maximum likelihood estimation using the unconstrained residual function rf (lines 30-37), the Wald test statistic is computed from the constraint function eqc (and its first derivatives gradp(&eqc,b2)) evaluated at the estimated parameter b2 (lines 19-24). Finally, log-likelihood function values of both constrained and unconstrained estimations are used to compute the Likelihood Ratio test statistic in line 25. The following output summarizes the result:

```
Wald Test =        0.078241
Lagrangian Multiplier Test =       0.092612
Likelihood Ratio Test =     0.082175
```

All three test statistics are small and close to 0. Comparing with the critical value of the Chi-square distribution for 1 degree of freedom, we conclude that the restriction $\beta_4 = 1/\beta_3$ should not be rejected. Therefore the CES production function should be represented as follows:

$$\ln(Q) = 0.12 - 1/3.44 \quad ln\,(0.32\,L^{-3.44} + 0.68\,K^{-3.44})$$
$$\text{s.e.} \quad (0.07) \quad\quad\quad (0.10)\,(1.78)$$

Lesson 7.4: Likelihood Ratio Tests of Money Demand Equation

Now back to the question at the end of Lesson 7.2: what is the most appropriate functional form for the U.S. money demand equation? If we have successfully estimated all the models resulting from Box-Cox variable transformations, it is easy to compute the LR test statistics from each pair of nested models. Note that the log transformation is a limiting case where the power coefficient approaches zero, which is not exactly the same as setting the relevant power coefficient to zero. Nevertheless, LR tests are valid asymptotically. The critical value 3.84 is based on the Chi-square distribution of 1 degree of freedom at the 5% level of significance. By applying the general model to this specific example, we demonstrate the strategy for hypothesis testing:

From the general model $\lambda \neq \theta$,
does $\lambda = 1$? No (LR = 5.92)
does $\lambda \to 0$? Yes (LR = 3.37)
does $\theta = 1$? No (LR = 7.09)
does $\theta \to 0$? Yes (LR = 2.44)
does $\lambda = \theta$? Yes (LR = 2.70)

From the model $\lambda = \theta$,
does $\lambda = \theta = 1$? No
does $\lambda = \theta \to 0$? Yes

The conclusion is obvious that the linear equation of a log model ($\theta, \lambda \to 0$) will be the choice for this set of data. The model is linear in the parameters and can be estimated more accurately using linear least squares. The log model is the limiting case of Box-Cox transformation, and the estimates obtained from linear regression are close to those of nonlinear method. The above calculation is based on the following estimation result, which you should be able to duplicate:

	Money Demand Equation	Log-Likelihood
$\theta \neq \lambda$	$M^{(-0.96)} = -14.5 - 14.07\,R^{(-2.67)} + 56.4\,Y^{(-2.67)}$	22.978
1. $\theta \to 0$	$ln(M) = -2.23 + 0.0005\,R^{(1.04)} + 1.22\,Y^{(1.04)}$	21.760
2. $\theta = 1$	$M = -3.03 + 0.0000007\,R^{(4.91)} + 0.023\,Y^{(4.91)}$	19.433
3. $\lambda \to 0$	$M^{(-0.23)} = -3.62 - 0.022\,ln(R) + 3.58\,ln(Y)$	21.289
4. $\lambda = 1$	$M^{(-0.021)} = -3.54 - 0.0002\,R + 1.27\,Y$	20.019

5.	$\theta = \lambda$	$M^{(-0.35)} = -4.34 - 0.065\ R^{(-0.35)} + 5.17\ Y^{(-0.35)}$	21.648
6.	$\theta, \lambda \to 0$	$ln(M) = -3.64 - 0.03\ ln(R) + 3.66\ ln(Y)$	21.833
7.	$\theta, \lambda = 1$	$M = -3.17 - 0.015\ R + 1.59\ Y$	8.022

VIII
Discrete and Limited Dependent Variables

There are many situations in which the dependent variable of a regression equation is discrete or limited (truncated) rather than continuous. As we have seen in the discussion of dummy variables in Chapter IV, some or all of the explanatory variables in a regression model are qualitative in nature, and therefore only take on a limited number of values. In the case of dummy variables, those values are 0 and 1. In this chapter we will consider only the simplest form of qualitative choice models: binary choice and tobit (censored regression) models. The binary choice (or the "yes or no" decision) will take on one of two discrete values, 1 or 0. The censored regression model allows for the dependent variable to follow a mix of discrete and continuous distributions. Here we learn how to implement and estimate the binary choice and tobit limited dependent variable models as applications of nonlinear regression.

Binary Choice Models

Consider a linear regression model $Y = X\beta + \varepsilon$, where

$Y_i = $ 1 with probability P_i
    0 with probability $1-P_i$

It should be clear that X_i *explains* the probability of Y_i equaling 1 or 0. If we let $P_i = \text{Prob}(Y_i=1|X_i) = F(X_i\beta)$, then $1-P_i = \text{Prob}(Y_i=0|X_i) = 1-F(X_i\beta)$.

Since $E(Y_i|X_i) = (1)F(X_i\beta) + (0)(1-F(X_i\beta)) = F(X_i\beta)$, we may interpret the estimated model using the following *marginal effects*:

$$\frac{\partial E(Y_i|X_i)}{\partial X_i} = \frac{\partial F(X_i\beta)}{\partial(X_i\beta)}\beta = f(X_i\beta)\beta$$

where $f(X_i\beta) = \dfrac{\partial F(X_i\beta)}{\partial(X_i\beta)}$. Given a sample of N independent observations, the likelihood function is

$$L(\beta) = \prod_{i=1,2,...,N} P_i^{Y_i}(1-P_i)^{1-Y_i} = \prod_{i=1,2,...,N} F(X_i\beta)^{Y_i}(1-F(X_i\beta))^{1-Y_i}$$

The log-likelihood function is then:

$$ll(\beta) = ln(L(\beta)) = \sum_{i=1,2,...,N} [Y_i \, lnF(X_i\beta) + (1-Y_i) \, ln(1-F(X_i\beta))]$$

To maximize $ll(\beta)$ with respect to β, we solve from the following first-order condition:

$$\frac{\partial ll\,(\beta)}{\partial \beta} = \sum\nolimits_{i=1,2,\ldots,N} \left[\frac{Y_i}{F_i} - \frac{1-Y_i}{1-F_i} \right] f_i X_i$$

$$= \sum\nolimits_{i=1,2,\ldots,N} \left[\frac{Y_i - F_i}{F_i(1-F_i)} \right] f_i X_i = 0$$

where $F_i = F(X_i\beta)$ and $f_i = f(X_i\beta) = \dfrac{\partial F(X_i\beta)}{\partial(X_i\beta)}$. Note that $f_i X_i = \dfrac{\partial F(X_i\beta)}{\partial \beta}$.

Finally, we need the hessian matrix $\left(\dfrac{\partial ll^2\,(\beta)}{\partial\beta\partial\beta'} \right)$ to be negative definite, allowing us

to write the estimated variance-covariance matrix of β as $Var(\beta) = \left[-E\left(\dfrac{\partial ll^2\,(\beta)}{\partial\beta\partial\beta'} \right) \right]^{-1}$.

Linear Probability Model

Let $P_i = F(X_i\beta) = X_i\beta$. It is immediately clear that $E(Y_i|X_i) = X_i\beta$. In addition, with the linear probability model, we are assured of a heterogeneous error structure:

$$
\begin{aligned}
E(\varepsilon_i) \quad &= (1-X_i\beta)P_i + (-X_i\beta)(1-P_i) = P_i - X_i\beta \\
Var(\varepsilon_i) \quad &= E(\varepsilon_i^2) = P_i(1-X_i\beta)^2 + (1-P_i)(-X_i\beta)^2 \\
&= P_i(1-P_i)^2 + (1-P_i)(-P_i)^2 = (1-P_i)P_i = (1-X_i\beta)(X_i\beta)
\end{aligned}
$$

The range of $Var(\varepsilon_i)$ is between 0 and 0.25. Furthermore, since $E(Y_i|X_i) = F(X_i\beta) = X_i\beta$, a linear function, there is no guarantee that the estimated probability P_i or $1-P_i$ will lie within the unit interval. We can get around the problem of P_i taking values outside the unit interval by considering a specific probability distribution or functional transformation for P_i. A commonly used probability distribution is the normal distribution giving rise to the probit model, while a commonly used functional transformation is the logistic curve function giving rise to the logit model.

Probit Model

Let $P_i = F(X_i\beta) = \int_{-\infty}^{X_i\beta} 1/(2\pi)^{1/2} exp(-z^2/2)\ dz$. Then we call P_i (based on the cumulative normal distribution), the *probit* for the i-th observation. The model $Y_i = F^{-1}(P_i) + \varepsilon_i$ is called the *probit model*, where $F^{-1}(P_i) = X_i\beta$ is the inverse of the cumulative normal distribution $F(X_i\beta)$. For those concerned that we chosen the above specification seemingly out of thin air, the probit model can be derived from a model involving a continuous, unobserved, or *latent*, variable Y_i^* such that $Y_i^* = X_i\beta + \varepsilon_i$, where ε_i follows a standard normal density.[6] Suppose the value of the observed binary variable Y_i depends on the sign of Y_i^* as follows:

$$
Y_i = \begin{array}{l} 1\ if\ Y_i^* > 0 \\ 0\ if\ Y_i^* \leq 0 \end{array}
$$

---

[6] If ε_i is a normal random variable with zero mean and standard error σ, then the probability of $Y_i = 1$ is written as $P_i = F(X_i\beta/\sigma)$. Since β/σ appears in the density function as a ratio, they are not separately identified. Therefore, it is convenient to normalize σ to be one. The standard normal distribution is sometimes referred to as the z-distribution, where the random variable is $z_i = \varepsilon_i/\sigma = \varepsilon_i$, given $\sigma = 1$.

Therefore,

P_i = $Prob(Y_i=1|X_i)$ = $Prob(Y_i^*>0|X_i)$ = $Prob(\varepsilon_i > -X_i\beta)$
= $\int_{-X_i\beta}^{\infty} 1/(2\pi)^{1/2} exp(-z^2/2)\ dz$
= $\int_{-\infty}^{X_i\beta} 1/(2\pi)^{1/2} exp(-z^2/2)\ dz$

For maximum likelihood estimation, we solve the following first-order condition:

$$\sum_{i=1,2,\ldots,N}\left[\frac{Y_i-F_i}{F_i(1-F_i)}\right]f_iX_i = 0$$

where f_i and F_i are, respectively, the probability density and cumulative density functions of a standard normal random variable evaluated at $X_i\beta$. That is,

$$F_i = F(X_i\beta) = \int_{-\infty}^{X_i\beta} 1/(2\pi)^{1/2} exp(-z^2/2)dz$$

and,

$$f_i = \frac{\partial F(X_i\beta)}{\partial(X_i\beta)} = 1/(2\pi)^{1/2} exp\left[-(X_i\beta)^2/2\right]$$

Furthermore, it can be shown that for the maximum likelihood estimates of β the expected value of the (negative definite) hessian is

$$E\left(\frac{\partial ll^2(\beta)}{\partial\beta\partial\beta'}\right) = -\sum_{i=1,2,\ldots,N}\frac{f_i^2X_iX_i'}{F_i(1-F_i)}.$$

The estimated variance-covariance matrix of β is computed as the inverse of negative expected hessian.

In interpreting the model, the probability $E(Y_i|X_i) = F(X_i\beta) = P_i$ will be of interest. The marginal effects of the j-th explanatory variable X_{ij} are written as:

$$\frac{\partial E(Y_i|X_i)}{\partial X_{ij}} = \frac{\partial F(X_i\beta)}{\partial(X_i\beta)}\beta_j = f(X_i\beta)\beta_j = f_i\beta_j$$

Lesson 8.1: Probit Model of Economic Education

This example (see Greene 1999, Example 19.1; Spector and Mazzeo, 1980) examines the effect of a new teaching method (known as PSI) on students' grades. The following variables are used:

GRADE	An indicator of whether the student's grade on an examination improved after exposure to the new teaching method.
PSI	An indicator of whether the student was exposed to the new teaching method.
TUCE	Score of a pretest that indicates entering knowledge of the material

prior to the introduction of PSI.

GPA   Grade point average.

The qualitative model is formulated as follows:

$$\text{GRADE} = \beta_0 + \beta_1 \text{GPA} + \beta_2 \text{TUCE} + \beta_3 \text{PSI} + \varepsilon$$

The data file **grade.txt** is used. The following program estimates the probit model specification of the above equation. The log-likelihood function for each data observation is defined in lines 20 through 26 with the procedure named `probitf`. Since the first derivatives of the log-likelihood function are rather straightforward analytically, we also write the procedure `probitf1` to calculate these derivatives (lines 27 to 34). The analytical first derivatives may be used in optimization to improve the accuracy of the solution (see Chapter VI).

If the residual function is defined and called when estimating a nonlinear regression model, the GPE default objective function is the log-likelihood function for maximization and sum-of-squares for minimization. Whether the problem is maximization or minimization is controlled by the value of the input variable `_nlopt`. Setting `_nlopt=1` specifies a maximization problem. Setting `_nlopt=0` indicates a minimization problem. There are certain cases of maximum likelihood estimation in which the log-likelihood function may be defined instead of the residual function for each sample observation. All the qualitative choice models discussed in this chapter fall in this second category. Setting `_nlopt=2` (see line 11) informs GPE that the maximization is performed on the *sum* of the component (log-likelihood) functions. We could write the *total* log-likelihood function to estimate the model, but there may be a loss of numerical accuracy due to compounding running errors in evaluating the function and its derivatives.

```
     /*
     ** Lesson 8.1: Probit Model of Economic Education
     ** Greene (1999), Example 19.1
     ** See also Spector and Mazzeo (1980)
     */
1    use gpe2;
2    output file=gpe\output8.1 reset;

3    n=33;
4    load data[n,4]=gpe\grade.txt;
5    gpa=data[2:n,1];
6    tuce=data[2:n,2];
7    psi=data[2:n,3];
8    grade=data[2:n,4];
9    z=gpa~tuce~psi~ones(rows(grade),1);

10   call reset;

     @ probit model: estimation @
11   _nlopt=2;   @ using component log-likelihood @
12   _method=4;
13   _iter=50;
14   _b={0.5,0.0,0.5,0};
15   call estimate(&probitf,grade~z);
     /*
     call estimate(&probitf|&probitf1,grade~z);
     */

     @ probit model: interpretation @
16   b=__b;
```

```
17  print " Probability                        Slopes";;
18  print cdfn(z*b)~(pdfn(z*b).*b[1:rows(b)-1]');

19  end;

    /* log-likelihood function of probit model */
20  proc probitf(x,b);
21     local k,z,f;
22     k=rows(b);
23     z=x[.,2:k+1]*b;
24     f=cdfn(z);             @ normal cdf @
25     retp(x[.,1].*ln(f)+(1-x[.,1]).*ln(1-f));
26  endp;

    /* 1st derivatives of log-likelihood function of probit model */
27  proc probitf1(x,b);
28     local z,k,f,g;
29     k=rows(b);
30     z=x[.,2:k+1]*b;
31     f=cdfn(z);             @ normal cdf @
32     g=pdfn(z);             @ normal pdf @
33     retp((x[.,1].*(g./f)-(1-x[.,1]).*(g./(1-f))).*x[.,2:k+1]);
34  endp;
```

Running the program, we obtain the estimated probit model as follows (see also output8.1 for the detailed results of interim iterations):

```
Maximum Likelihood Estimation
-----------------------------
Number of Observations = 32
Number of Parameters = 4

Maximum Number of Iterations = 50
Step Size Search Method = 0
Convergence Criterion = 0
Tolerance = 0.001


Initial Result:
Log Likelihood =       -62.697
Parameters =      0.50000      0.00000      0.50000      0.00000

Using Newton-Raphson Algorithm

Final Result:
Iterations = 5            Evaluations = 3808
Log Likelihood =       -12.819
Parameters =      1.6258       0.051729      1.4263       -7.4523
Gradient Vector = -2.5489e-005  -0.00031045 -3.6749e-006 -5.7386e-006

                           Asymptotic   Asymptotic
                Parameter  Std. Error   t-Ratio
X1                1.6258     0.69373      2.3436
X2               0.051729    0.083925     0.61637
X3                1.4263     0.59520      2.3964
X4               -7.4523     2.5467      -2.9263
```

Recall that, given the estimated parameters, we are mostly concerned with the probability or the conditional expected value $E(Y|X)$. With respect to the three explanatory variables, GPA, TUCE, and PSI, the slopes (or marginal effects) are of interest. Lines 16 through 18 of **lesson8.1** calculate and report the probability and the relevant marginal effects. The next part of the output shows these results for each observation:

Probability		Slopes	
0.018171	0.072553	0.0023084	0.063651
0.053081	0.17584	0.0055949	0.15427
0.18993	0.44108	0.014034	0.38696
0.018571	0.073911	0.0023517	0.064843
0.55457	0.64253	0.020443	0.56369
0.027233	0.10207	0.0032476	0.089546
0.018503	0.073683	0.0023444	0.064642
0.044571	0.15292	0.0048656	0.13416
0.10881	0.30333	0.0096511	0.26611
0.66312	0.59360	0.018887	0.52077
0.016102	0.065434	0.0020819	0.057406
0.19356	0.44623	0.014198	0.39148
0.32333	0.58391	0.018579	0.51227
0.19518	0.44851	0.014270	0.39348
0.35634	0.60608	0.019284	0.53172
0.021965	0.085218	0.0027114	0.074762
0.045694	0.15601	0.0049640	0.13687
0.030851	0.11322	0.0036023	0.099327
0.59340	0.63075	0.020069	0.55336
0.65719	0.59758	0.019013	0.52426
0.061929	0.19852	0.0063164	0.17416
0.90454	0.27577	0.0087744	0.24194
0.27319	0.54072	0.017204	0.47438
0.84745	0.38335	0.012197	0.33631
0.83419	0.40485	0.012881	0.35518
0.48873	0.64834	0.020629	0.56880
0.64241	0.60683	0.019308	0.53237
0.32867	0.58783	0.018703	0.51571
0.84002	0.39555	0.012585	0.34702
0.95224	0.16164	0.0051428	0.14180
0.53996	0.64535	0.020533	0.56617
0.12354	0.33195	0.010562	0.29122

If you do not want to see the long list of E(Y|X) (probability) and ∂E(Y|X)/∂X (marginal effects), they may be computed at the means of the explanatory variables. To see what happens, insert the following statement after line 16:

```
z=meanc(z)';
```

Logit Model

Let $P_i = F(X_i\beta) = \dfrac{1}{1 + exp(-X_i\beta)}$, where P_i as defined is the logistic curve. The model $Y_i = X_i\beta + \varepsilon_i = F^{-1}(P_i) + \varepsilon_i$ is called the *logit model*. We can easily derive the logit model from the *odd ratio* model, in which we assume that the log of the ratio of the probabilities (P_i and $1-P_i$) is equal to $X_i\beta$. Thus we assume $ln\left(\dfrac{P_i}{1-P_i}\right) = X_i\beta$. Solving for P_i yields:

$$P_i = \frac{exp(X_i\beta)}{1 + exp(X_i\beta)} = \frac{1}{1 + exp(-X_i\beta)}$$

For maximum likelihood estimation, we solve the first-order condition:

$$\sum_{i=1,2,\ldots,N}\left[\frac{Y_i - F_i}{F_i(1 - F_i)}\right]f_i X_i = 0$$

Because of the logistic functional form in use,

122

$$F_i = F(X_i\beta) = \frac{1}{1 + exp(-X_i\beta)}$$

and

$$f_i = \frac{\partial F(X_i\beta)}{\partial(X_i\beta)} = \frac{exp(-X_i\beta)}{1 + exp(-X_i\beta)} = F_i(1-F_i),$$

the first-order condition amounts to the following simpler expression:

$$\sum_{i=1,2,\dots,N}(Y_i - F_i)X_i = 0.$$

The variance-covariance matrix of β is estimated with

$$Var(\beta) = \left[-E\left(\frac{\partial ll^2(\beta)}{\partial\beta\partial\beta'}\right)\right]^{-1}$$

where the hessian matrix $\left(\dfrac{\partial ll^2(\beta)}{\partial\beta\partial\beta'}\right) = -\sum_{i=1,2,\dots,N}F_i(1-F_i)X_i'X_i$ is negative definite.

To interpret the model, we define the marginal effect of the j-th explanatory variable X_{ij} as:

$$\frac{\partial E(Y_i \mid X_i)}{\partial X_{ij}} = \frac{\partial F(X_i\beta)}{\partial(X_i\beta)}\beta_j = f(X_i\beta)\beta_j = f_i\beta_j = F_i(1-F_i)\beta_j$$

As you can see, the logit model is similar in construction to the probit model. Only the choice of transformation function is different.

Lesson 8.2: Logit Model of Economic Education

We will now rerun the model of Lesson 8.1, using the logit model instead of the probit model. We will need only to change the transformation function from the cumulative normal probability to the logistic curve. Specifically, lines 20-26 define the component log-likelihood function `logitf` for the logit model, while the corresponding first derivative function `logitf1` is defined in lines 27-34.

```
    /*
    ** Lesson 8.2: Logit Model of Economic Education
    ** Greene (1999), Example 19.1
    ** See also Spector and Mazzeo (1980)
    */
1   use gpe2;
2   output file=gpe\output8.2 reset;

3   n=33;
4   load data[n,4]=gpe\grade.txt;
5   gpa=data[2:n,1];
6   tuce=data[2:n,2];
7   psi=data[2:n,3];
```

```
 8   grade=data[2:n,4];
 9   z=gpa~tuce~psi~ones(rows(grade),1);

10   call reset;

     @ logit model: estimation @
11   _nlopt=2;   @ using component log-likelihood @
12   _method=4;
13   _iter=50;
14   _b={0.5,0.0,0.5,0};

15   call estimate(&logitf,grade~z);
     /*
     call estimate(&logitf|&logitf1,grade~z);
     */

     @ logit model: interpretation @
16   p=1./(1+exp(-z*__b));
17   print " Probability                    Slopes";;
18   print p~(p.*(1-p).*__b[1:rows(__b)-1]');

19   end;

     /* log-likelihood function of logit model */
20   proc logitf(x,b);
21       local k,z,f;
22       k=rows(b);
23       z=x[.,2:k+1]*b;
24       f=1./(1+exp(-z));      @ same as: f=exp(z)./(1+exp(z)); @
                                @ logistic distribution function @
25       retp(x[.,1].*ln(f)+(1-x[.,1]).*ln(1-f));
26   endp;

     /* 1st derivatives of log-likelihood function of logit model */
27   proc logitf1(x,b);
28       local z,k,f;
29       k=rows(b);
30       z=x[.,2:k+1]*b;
31       f=1./(1+exp(-z));      @ same as: f=exp(z)./(1+exp(z)); @
32                              @ logistic distribution function @
33       retp((x[.,1]-f).*x[.,2:k+1]);
34   endp;
```

The estimated results are similar to those of the probit model. Instead of showing the detailed output for comparison, we present the estimated probabilities and marginal effects of the probit and logit models, evaluated at the means of three explanatory variables:

		Probit	Logit
Probability		0.26581	0.25282
Marginal Effects	GPA	0.53335	0.53386
	TUCE	0.01697	0.01798
	PSI	0.04679	0.04493

Extensions of binary choice models to the cases with more than two choices are interesting, though the derivations are tedious. Multiple choice models include unordered (independent or nested) and ordered (with a preference rank) choices. Both the probit and logit model specifications for multiple choice are possible, but they are beyond the scope of the current discussion.

Limited Dependent Variable Models

If the random decision variable follows a mixture of discrete and continuous distributions, we have the limited dependent variable (or censored regression) model. Recall the latent variable interpretation of the probit model,

$$Y_i^* = X_i\beta + \varepsilon_i$$

where ε_i follows a normal probability distribution, and

$$Y_i = \begin{array}{l} 1 \text{ if } Y_i^* > 0 \\ 0 \text{ if } Y_i^* \leq 0 \end{array}$$

Suppose, however, that Y_i is *censored*—that is, we restrict the number (or kinds) of values that Y_i can take. As an example, consider the following:

$$Y_i = \begin{array}{ll} Y_i^* & \text{if } Y_i^* > 0 \\ 0 & \text{if } Y_i^* \leq 0 \end{array}$$

That is,

$$Y_i = \begin{array}{ll} X_i\beta + \varepsilon_i & \text{if } X_i\beta + \varepsilon_i > 0 \\ 0 & \text{otherwise} \end{array}$$

This model is called the *tobit* (or Tobin's probit) model. Define f_i and F_i to be the probability density function and cumulative density function of a standard normal random variable evaluated at $X_i\beta/\sigma$. That is,

$$F_i = F(X_i\beta/\sigma) = \int_{-\infty}^{X_i\beta/\sigma} 1/(2\pi)^{1/2} \exp\left(-z^2/2\right) dz$$
$$f_i = f(X_i\beta/\sigma) = 1/(2\pi)^{1/2} \exp\left[-(X_i\beta/\sigma)^2/2\right]$$

For the observations such that $Y_i = 0$ or $Y_i^* = X_i\beta + \varepsilon_i \leq 0$, the likelihood function is

$$\text{Prob}(Y_i = 0) = \text{Prob}(\varepsilon_i \leq -X_i\beta) = \text{Prob}(\varepsilon_i/\sigma \leq -X_i\beta/\sigma) = 1 - F(X_i\beta/\sigma) = 1\text{-}F_i$$

If $Y_i > 0$, on the other hand, then the likelihood function is simply the normal density function:

$$1/(2\pi\sigma^2)^{1/2} \exp\left[-(Y_i - X_i\beta)^2/(2\sigma^2)\right]$$

Therefore the likelihood function for the tobit model is a mixture of the above discrete and continuous distributions depending on the values taken by the dependent variable (i.e., zero or positive):

$$L = \prod_{\{i \,|Yi = 0\}}(1\text{-}F_i) \prod_{\{i \,|Yi > 0\}} 1/(2\pi\sigma^2)^{1/2} \exp\left[-(Y_i - X_i\beta)^2/(2\sigma^2)\right]$$

The corresponding log-likelihood function is

$$ll = \sum_{\{i|Y_i=0\}} ln(1 - F_i) - 1/2 \sum_{\{i|Y_i>0\}} \left[ln(\pi) + ln(\sigma^2) + (Y_i - X_i\beta)^2/\sigma^2\right]$$

Then, for the maximum likelihood estimation, we solve from the following first-order conditions:

$$\partial ll/\partial\beta = -(1/\sigma)\sum_{\{i|Y_i=0\}} f_i X_i/(1-F_i) + (1/\sigma^2)\sum_{\{i|Y_i>0\}} (Y_i - X_i\beta)X_i = 0$$

$$\partial ll/\partial\sigma^2 = 1/2(1/\sigma^3)\sum_{\{i|Y_i=0\}} f_i X_i\beta/(1-F_i) - 1/2(1/\sigma^2)\sum_{\{i|Y_i>0\}} \left[1-(Y_i - X_i\beta)^2/\sigma^2\right] = 0$$

To interpret the estimated coefficients of the model, we may use three conditional expected values:

$E(Y_i^*|X_i)$ $\quad = X_i\beta$

$E(Y_i|X_i,Y_i>0)$ $\quad = X_i\beta + E(\varepsilon_i|Y_i>0)$
$\quad\quad\quad\quad\quad\quad = X_i\beta + E(\varepsilon_i|\varepsilon_i > -X_i\beta)$
$\quad\quad\quad\quad\quad\quad = X_i\beta + \sigma\, f_i/F_i > E(Y_i^*|X_i)$

$E(Y_i|X_i)$ $\quad = F_i\, E(Y_i|X_i,Y_i>0)$
$\quad\quad\quad\quad = F_i\, X_i\beta + \sigma\, f_i$

The first expected value (corresponding to the "uncensored" case) is easy to obtain. The last expected value will be of particular interest if our sample contains many censored observations. Accordingly, for the j-th explanatory variable, the corresponding marginal effects are:

$\partial E(Y_i^*|X_i)/\partial X_{ij}$ $\quad = \beta_j$

$\partial E(Y_i|X_i,Y_i>0)/\partial X_{ij}$ $\quad = \beta_j\,[1- (X_i\beta/\sigma)(f_i/F_i) -(f_i/F_i)^2]$

$\partial E(Y_i|X_i)/\partial X_{ij}$ $\quad = F_i\,\partial E(Y_i|X_i,Y_i>0)/\partial X_{ij} + E(Y_i|X_i,Y_i>0)\,\partial F_i/\partial X_{ij}$
$\quad\quad\quad\quad\quad\quad = F_i\,\beta_j$

We note that the last censored marginal effect differs from the first uncensored one by a scale factor equal to the probability of that observation not being censored. In other words, the scale factor is equal to F_i (recall that F_i is 1-Prob($Y_i = 0$)).

The tobit model is often estimated for comparison with the alternative probit or count model specifications. The model can be easily extended to consider more than one censoring point. For instance, we could censor both tails of the distribution. This is an example of a doubly censored regression.

Lesson 8.3: Tobit Analysis of Extramarital Affairs

This example is taken from Greene (1999, Example 20.12), which is based on Fair (1978). The study examines the qualitative responses to a question about extramarital affairs from a sample of 601 men and women married for the first time. The dependent variable is:

Y   Number of affairs in the past year: 0, 1, 2, 3, 4-10 (coded as 7), 11-365 (coded as 12).

The preponderance of zeros (no affairs) may not render the tobit model to be the best for the study. The complete data set used in the article is available from the text file **fair.txt**, but we present only the restricted model using a subset of five explanatory variables as follows:

Z_2 Age.
Z_3 Number of years married.
Z_5 Degree of religiousness: 1 (anti-religious), ... , 5 (very religious).
Z_7 Hollingshead scale of occupation: 1, ... , 7.
Z_8 Self-rating of marriage satisfaction: 1 (very unhappy), ... , 5 (very happy).

The regression equation is:

$$Y = \beta_0 + \beta_2 Z_2 + \beta_3 Z_3 + \beta_5 Z_5 + \beta_7 Z_7 + \beta_8 Z_8 + \varepsilon$$

The conclusion and interpretation of the estimated model are left to the interested reader. Our emphasis here is the implementation of tobit analysis using GPE and GAUSS. To do so, we need to briefly explain the maximum likelihood estimation procedure. Recall that the likelihood function of the tobit model is a mixture of discrete and continuous normal likelihoods, depending on the censored point (zero) of the dependent variable. Unlike in the probit model, the standard error is an explicit unknown parameter which must be estimated together with the regression parameters. In lines 22 to 28 of the following program, the procedure `tobitf` defines the log-likelihood function for each sample observation. For maximum likelihood estimation, we need to set `_nlopt=2` (line 10), which instructs GPE to maximize the *sum* of the individual log-likelihood functions.[7]

```
     /*
     ** Lesson 8.3: Tobit Analysis of Extramarital Affairs
     ** Greene (1999), Example 20.12
     ** See also R. Fair, JPE, 86, 1978, 45-61
     */
1    use gpe2;
2    output file=gpe\output8.3 reset;
3    n=602;
4    load data[n,15]=gpe\fair.txt;
5    y=data[2:n,13];
6    z=data[2:n,5 6 8 11 12]; @ use z2, z3, z5, z7, z8 @

7    call reset;

     @ Uncensored OLS estimation @
8    call estimate(y,z);

     @ Tobit model estimation @
9    z=z~ones(rows(z),1); @ RHS variables inc. constant @
10   _nlopt=2;    @ using component likelihood function @
11   _method=5;
12   _iter=100;
13   _b=__b|5.0;
14   call estimate(&tobitf,y~z);

     @ Tobit model interpretation based on E(y) @
15   b=__b[1:6];
16   s=__b[7];
17   ey=cdfn(z*b/s).*(z*b)+s.*pdfn(z*b/s);
```

---

[7] Because the size of this nonlinear optimization is beyond the limits of GAUSS Light, the professional version of GAUSS should be used for Lesson 8.3.

```
18   em=cdfn(z*b/s).*b';
19   print "Expected Value                    Marginal Effects";;
20   print ey~em[.,1:5];

21   end;

     /* Log-likelihood function: tobit model */
22   proc tobitf(x,b);
23       local y,z,k;
24       k=rows(b);
25       y=x[.,1];
26       z=(y-x[.,2:k]*b[1:k-1])/b[k];
27       retp((y.==0).*ln(cdfn(z))+(y.>0).*ln(pdfn(z)/b[k]));
28   endp;
```

Remember that tobit is a nonlinear model. First, the uncensored model is estimated by ordinary least squares (line 8). The estimated parameters are then used as the initial values in the tobit model estimation (line 14). Here is the result of the estimated tobit model, which converges after 60 iterations:

```
Maximum Likelihood Estimation
-----------------------------
Number of Observations = 601
Number of Parameters = 7

Maximum Number of Iterations = 100
Step Size Search Method = 0
Convergence Criterion = 0
Tolerance = 0.001

Initial Result:
Log Likelihood =       -886.21
Parameters =      -0.050347       0.16185      -0.47632       0.10601      -0.71224
5.6082        5.0000

Using Quadratic Hill-Climbing Algorithm

Final Result:
Iterations = 60            Evaluations = 1981497
Log Likelihood =       -705.58
Parameters =      -0.17933       0.55414      -1.6862       0.32605      -2.2850
8.1742        8.2471
Gradient   Vector   =    3.0579e-005    3.0303e-006    2.2826e-006    1.4280e-006
2.3271e-006  4.5474e-007 -2.7294e-006
```

	Parameter	Asymptotic Std. Error	Asymptotic t-Ratio
X1	-0.17933	0.079136	-2.2661
X2	0.55414	0.13459	4.1174
X3	-1.6862	0.40378	-4.1761
X4	0.32605	0.25443	1.2815
X5	-2.2850	0.40787	-5.6022
X6	8.1742	2.7419	2.9812
X7	8.2471	0.55363	14.896

For interpretation of the estimated parameters, we compute the expected values of censored observations and the corresponding marginal effects of the explanatory variables (see lines 14-19). The computation is for each sample observation.

To save space we do not list the 601 observations of expected values and marginal effects. One alternative is to calculate the average of the estimated expected values and marginal effects:

```
print meanc(ey~em[.,1:5])';
```

A second alternative is to evaluate the expected values and marginal effects at the means of the explanatory variables by inserting the following statement before line 16:

```
z=meanc(z)';
```

We conclude with an important remark. In Lesson 8.3, the dependent variable is actually more like count data than a continuous variable, for it records the number of occurrences of extramarital affairs within a year. As a matter of fact, this model is well-suited for probit analysis. If we define the dependent variable Y as a binary variable (0 for no affairs and 1 otherwise), then the same data set can be used for either probit or logit analysis. However, the estimated parameters, expected values, and marginal effects of the probit (or logit) model are not directly comparable to those of the tobit model. The dependent variable being "explained" or "predicted" is different under tobit estimation than under probit or logit estimation. With a tobit model, we are predicting the mean number of affairs. With a probit or logit model, we are predicting the probability of an affair occurring within a year. The probit analysis is not concerned with the actual number of affairs. We leave the model comparison to interested readers.

IX
Heteroscedasticity

Heteroscedasticity is a common problem with cross-sectional data, in which unequal model variance is observed. Ordinary least squares estimation with a heterogeneously distributed error structure leads to inefficient estimates of the regression parameters. In order to correct for this inefficiency, the source of heteroscedasticity in relation to one or more variables must be identified.

To illustrate how to test and correct for the problem of heteroscedasticity, the following relationship of public school spending (SPENDING) and income (INCOME) across 50 states in the U.S. is considered:

$$SPENDING = \beta_0 + \beta_1 \, INCOME + \beta_2 \, INCOME^2 + \varepsilon$$

To estimate this equation, which is used for all the lessons in this chapter, a cross-sectional data file **greene.txt** is used.[8] It gives per capita public school expenditure and per capita income by state in 1979. Let's take a look at the data file **greene.txt** we will be dealing with. The data file contains three columns. The first column is the state identifier (STATE), the second column is per capita expenditure on public schools (SPENDING), and the third column is per capita income (INCOME). Viewing **greene.txt** in the Edit window reveals a problem with the data. Notice that WI (Wisconsin) is missing a data observation. The row WI has "NA" for the corresponding value in the SPENDING column. GAUSS sees "NA" as a character string, not suitable for numerical computation. GAUSS has commands that convert character strings, such as "NA," to a symbol that it can interpret as a missing value. The first part of each lesson in this chapter walks you through the process of converting **greene.txt** with its missing values to useable data. Several new GAUSS commands are introduced for this purpose.

Heteroscedasticity-Consistent Covariance Matrix

Assuming heteroscedasticity, the ordinary least squares estimator is unbiased but inefficient. We can keep the unbiased least squares estimator, but correct for inefficiency with an estimated heteroscedasticity-consistent covariance matrix. Lesson 9.1 below demonstrates the use of the input control variable _hacv to correct the covariance matrix.

Lesson 9.1: Heteroscedasticity-Consistent Covariance Matrix

In this lesson, we estimate the regression equation of public school spending (SPENDING) with regressors income (INCOME) and squared income ($INCOME^2$) using the data file**greene.txt** .

---

[8] This example was used in Greene (1997, Chapter 12), but it has been removed from the updated fourth edition (Greene, 1999).

For a heteroscedastic regression model, a consistent estimate of the variance-covariance matrix is obtained by approximating the original heteroscedastic variances with the squares of estimated residuals from ordinary least squares estimation. That is,

$$\text{Var}(\hat{\beta}) = (X'X)^{-1}(X'\hat{\Sigma}X)(X'X)^{-1}$$

where X is the data matrix of regressors, $(\hat{\beta})$ is the ordinary least squares estimator of the parameters vector β, and $\hat{\Sigma}$ is a diagonal variance-covariance matrix (i.e., the estimator of $E(\varepsilon\varepsilon')$ with the elements being the squares of the estimated regression residuals.

From two least squares estimations, one with the ordinary variance-covariance matrix and the other with the heteroscedasticity-consistent covariance matrix, we can directly compare the results of these regressions. In GPE, by setting the input variable _vcov=1 (see line 11 of Lesson 9.1), the details of the variance-covariance matrix are presented. The second regression estimation with the newly introduced input variable _hacv=1 (see line 13 of Lesson 9.1) computes the heteroscedasticity-consistent estimates of the variance-covariance matrix instead of the inefficient one from the ordinary least squares.

```
      /*
      ** Lesson 9.1: Heteroscedasticity-Consistent
      ** Variance-Covariance Matrix
      */
 1    use gpe2;
 2    output file = gpe\output9.1 reset;
 3    load greene[52,3]= gpe\greene.txt;

 4    data = greene[2:52,.];
 5    data = miss(data,"NA"); @ NA to missing value @
 6    data = packr(data); @ deletes row w/miss value@
 7    spending = data[.,2];
 8    income = data[.,3]/10000;

 9    call reset;

      /* Ordinary Least Squares */
10    _names = {"spending","income","income^2"};
11    _vcov = 1;
12    call estimate(spending,income~income^2);

      /* Ordinary Least Squares */
13    _hacv = 1; @ with hetero. consistent var-cov @
14    call estimate(spending,income~income^2);
15    end;
```

Line 5 introduces the miss command of GAUSS. It modifies the matrix data by comparing each element in the matrix data to the character string "NA." If an element in data equals "NA," it is replaced with a dot (.), GAUSS's symbol for a missing value. In the next line, packr(data) deletes any rows that contain any missing values in the matrix data. After data has been packed (line 6), the number of rows in data is reduced to 50. Refer to the GAUSS manual or on-line help to find more information on the commands miss and packr.

Try combining lines 4, 5, and 6 for efficiency:

```
data=packr(miss(greene[2:52,.],"NA"));
```

The result of the first least squares estimation with the option to print out the estimated variance-covariance matrix (lines 10 to 12) is:

```
Least Squares Estimation
------------------------
Dependent Variable = SPENDING
Estimation Range =  1          50
Number of Observations = 50
Mean of Dependent Variable = 373.26
Standard Error of Dependent Variable = 94.553

R-Square = 0.65534     R-Square Adjusted = 0.64068
Standard Error of the Estimate = 56.679
Log-Likelihood Function Value = -271.27
Log Ammemiya Prediction Criterion (APC) =  8.1331
Log Akaike Information Criterion (AIC) =  8.1329
Log Schwarz Bayesian Information Criterion (BIC) =  8.2476
```

Sum of Squares	SS	DF	MSS	F	Prob>F
Explained	2.8709E+005	2	1.4355E+005	44.684	1.3445E-011
Residual	1.5099E+005	47	3212.5		
Total	4.3808E+005	49	8940.3		

Variable Name	Estimated Coefficient	Standard Error	t-Ratio 47 DF	Prob >|t|	Partial Regression
INCOME	-1834.2	828.99	-2.2126	0.031820	0.094335
INCOME^2	1587.0	519.08	3.0574	0.0036770	0.16590
CONSTANT	832.91	327.29	2.5449	0.014275	0.12111

```
Variance-Covariance Matrix of Coefficients
INCOME      6.8722E+005
INCOME^2   -4.2844E+005  2.6944E+005
CONSTANT   -2.7021E+005  1.6709E+005  1.0712E+005
               INCOME      INCOME^2     CONSTANT


Correlation Matrix of Coefficients
INCOME      1.0000
INCOME^2   -0.99567      1.0000
CONSTANT   -0.99591      0.98352      1.0000
               INCOME      INCOME^2     CONSTANT
```

In order to compare the ordinary least squares estimates of standard errors and the variance-covariance matrix with the heteroscedasticity-consistent variance-covariance matrix, we look at a portion of the output from the second regression estimation (lines 13 and 14):

Variable Name	Estimated Coefficient	Standard Error	t-Ratio 47 DF	Prob >|t|	Partial Regression
INCOME	-1834.2	1243.0	-1.4756	0.14673	0.044275
INCOME^2	1587.0	829.99	1.9121	0.061968	0.072177
CONSTANT	832.91	460.89	1.8072	0.077137	0.064972

```
Variance-Covariance Matrix of Coefficients
INCOME      1.5452E+006
INCOME^2   -1.0296E+006  6.8889E+005
CONSTANT   -5.7170E+005  3.7941E+005  2.1242E+005
               INCOME      INCOME^2     CONSTANT
```

```
Correlation Matrix of Coefficients
INCOME           1.0000
INCOME^2        -0.99796      1.0000
CONSTANT        -0.99789      0.99182     1.0000
                 INCOME       INCOME^2    CONSTANT
```

In this example, the estimated heteroscedasticity-consistent standard errors and the variance-covariance matrix of the regression parameters are both larger than their ordinary least squares counterparts. The results indicate that there are smaller t-ratios, leading to the conclusion of statistically insignificant parameter estimates. Such correction to the model is useful when the problem of heteroscedasticity is of unknown form.

Weighted Least Squares

As mentioned earlier, if we can identify one or more of the regressors in the model as the source of heterogeneity in the variances, then a variation of least squares called weighted least squares is recommended. This estimation method adjusts all data series across the regression equation in accordance with the origin of the heteroscedasticity. Lesson 9.2 details the Goldfeld-Quandt approach, while Lesson 9.3 presents more general testing procedures devised by Breusch-Pagan and White.

Lesson 9.2: Goldfeld-Quandt Test and Correction for Heteroscedasticity

Continuing on with the spending-income regression equation of Lesson 9.1, this lesson introduces the Goldfeld-Quandt method to test for heteroscedasticity. It then corrects for this condition by using the method of weighted least squares.

The Goldfeld-Quandt test requires data to be sorted according to the size of the independent variable suspected to be the source of heteroscedasticity. The entire data set is then divided into three parts. The middle group is dropped, and the regression is run using only the groups containing the smallest and largest values. Separate regressions are estimated on each of the groups of smallest and largest values. Residual sum-of-squares (RSS) from both groups are then compared in the Goldfeld-Quandt test statistic.

As in the previous Lesson 9.1, the data are read from **greene.txt** and corrected for missing values. The Goldfeld-Quandt test requires a sorted data series in accordance with the suspected source of heteroscedasticity. Sorting the rows in the matrix, data, by the information in the third column (that is, the variable INCOME) is done in line 7. INCOME is sorted from its smallest value to its largest. The GAUSS Help menu gives greater details about the data sorting commands such as sortc used here.

```
      /*
      ** Lesson 9.2: Goldfeld-Quandt Test and
      ** Correction for Heteroscedasticity
      */
1     use gpe2;
2     output file = gpe\output9.2 reset;
3     load greene[52,3]= gpe\greene.txt;

4     data = greene[2:52,.];
5     data = miss(data,"NA");  @ NA to missing value @
6     data = packr(data);    @ deletes row w/miss value @
```

```
 7 │ data = sortc(data,3); @ sort data (income), in ascending order @
 8 │ spending = data[.,2];
 9 │ income = data[.,3]/10000;

10 │ call reset;

   │ /* Goldfeld-Quandt Test */
11 │ _names = {"spending","income","income^2"};
12 │ _begin = 1;
13 │ _end = 17;
14 │ call estimate(spending,income~income^2);
15 │ mss1 =__rss/14;                @ N-K = 17-3 = 14 @

16 │ _begin = 34;
17 │ _end = 50;
18 │ call estimate(spending,income~income^2);
19 │ mss2 =__rss/14;                @ N-K = 17-3 = 14 @

20 │ print "Goldfeld-Quandt Test Statistic = " mss2/mss1;

   │ /* Weighted Least Squares */
21 │ call reset;
22 │ _weight = 1/income;
23 │ call estimate(spending,income~income^2);
24 │ end;
```

Selecting the first group of the 17 smallest observations to regress for the Goldfeld-Quandt test is done by restricting the data matrix to only include observations from 1 to 17 (lines 12 and 13). The use of the output control variable, __rss, is introduced in line 15. __rss stores the sum-of-squared residuals from the latest regression estimation. Each time when the procedure estimate is called, output control variables are assigned new values. To save the value of __rss/14, the mean sum-of-squares of residuals, for later use in the Goldfeld-Quandt test statistic, it is assigned to variable mss1. Similarly, lines 16, 17, and 18 select the 17 largest observations and run the regression, assigning the resulting __rss/14 to the variable mss2.

Since we are only interested in the RSS from the regressions, the outputs from the first two estimations are not printed here. Instead, the result of Goldfeld-Quandt test statistic from line 20 is given as follows:

```
Goldfeld-Quandt Test Statistic =        1.9444
```

This statistic is computed according to the formula:

$$\frac{\dfrac{RSS_2}{N_2 - K}}{\dfrac{RSS_1}{N_1 - K}}$$

which follows the F-distribution with N_2-K and N_1-K degrees of freedom, where N1 and N2 are the number of observations corresponding to the two separate samples, and K is the number of regressor parameters, including the constant term. Since the Goldfeld-Quandt method requires that the test statistic be greater than 1, the largest RSS (RSS_2) must be in the numerator. The computed value of 1.94 is smaller than the critical value of F(14,14) at a 5% level of significance (that is, 2.40), so we could not reject the hypothesis of homoscedasticity.

Although there seems to be no problem of heteroscedasticity in the spending-income equation based on the Goldfeld-Quandt test, we warn the reader to never totally rely on statistical results from just one single test. We continue on to show you the weighted least squares method for correcting heteroscedasticity.

The problem of heteroscedasticity is corrected using weighted least squares. In line 22, the statement:

```
_weight = 1/income;
```

tells GPE to estimate the model using 1/INCOME as the weight incorporated in the regression estimation called on line 23. All the variables, both dependent and independent, including the constant term, are weighted (or divided by INCOME). The rationale is that the variable INCOME^2 may be used to approximate the heterogeneous variances of the model.

Because input variables _begin and _end had been set to non-default values earlier in the program, calling reset again (line 21) is the simplest way to insure that all control variables are reset to their default values for the new estimation to come.

Delete line 21 or change it to

```
@ call reset; @
```

See what happens. Why?

The regression output corrected for heteroscedasticity is available in the output file output9.2. Compare the earlier ordinary least squares estimation with the heteroscedasticity-consistent covariance matrix from Lesson 9.1,

SPENDING = 832.91 - 1834.2 INCOME + 1587.0 INCOME^2
s.e.   (460.89)   (1243.0)   (829.99)

and with the weighted least squares estimation using 1/INCOME as the weighting variable,

SPENDING = 664.58 - 1399.3 INCOME + 1311.3 INCOME^2
s.e.   (333.61)   (872.07)   (563.71)

Notice that the numbers in parentheses are the estimated standard errors of the coefficients. The results of the two regressions are similar, but in theory, weighted least squares estimation is more efficient.

Lesson 9.3: Breusch-Pagan and White Tests for Heteroscedasticity

In this lesson, we will briefly explain two other methods to test for heteroscedasticity: the Breusch-Pagan and White tests for general heteroscedasticity. Many econometrics references cover the operation of these tests in more detail.

In an auxiliary regression, the Breusch-Pagan test for general heteroscedasticity uses all explanatory variables including the constant term as the regressors to compute the test statistic. The test procedure does not rely on any particular variable or functional form to specify heteroscedasticity. In addition, it does not require the data to be sorted. However, the Breusch-Pagan test does assume residual normality for accurate results. The alternative Koenker-Basset test is more forgiving in regards to the assumption of normality.

The White test is based on the computation of the heteroscedasticity-consistent covariance matrix as described in Lesson 9.1, in which the explanatory variables and their squares and cross products are used to fit the squared residuals in a regression setting. The resulting goodness of fit is the test statistic.

We note that both the Breusch-Pagan and White tests for general heteroscedasticity do not offer information about the source and the form of heteroscedasticity. To correct for this problem, a more specific heteroscedastic structure of the model may be required.

It is quite easy to implement the Breusch-Pagan and White tests for heteroscedasticity in GPE. What you need is to set a positive value to the input control variable _bptest.

```
   /*
   ** Lesson 9.3: Breusch-Pagan and White Tests
   ** for Heteroscedasticity
   */
1  use gpe2;
2  output file = gpe\output9.3 reset;
3  load greene[52,3]= gpe\greene.txt;

4  data = greene[2:52,.];
5  data = miss(data,"NA"); @ NA to missing value @
6  data = packr(data); @ deletes row w/mis value @
7  spending = data[.,2];
8  income = data[.,3]/10000;

9  call reset;

   /* Breusch-Pagan and White Tests */
10 _names = {"spending","income","income^2"};
11 _bjtest = 1;
12 _bptest = 1;
13 call estimate(spending,income~income^2);

14 end;
```

Lines 1 through 10 are similar to **lesson9.1**. Keeping in mind that the working of the Breusch-Pagan test assumes that residuals are normally distributed, so we have included the Bera-Jarque test for residual normality on line 11 (_bjtest=1). Line 12 (_bptest=1) performs the Breusch-Pagan and White tests for general heteroscedasticity.

Let's examine the output now. The regression result from the first estimation (line 13) is the same as the result discussed in the previous Lesson 9.2, with additional pieces of information: the Bera-Jarque test for normality, and the Breusch-Pagan and White tests for heteroscedasticity:

```
Bera-Jarque Wald Test for Normality
Asymptotic Standard Error of Residuals = 54.952
Skewness of Residuals = -0.083322
Kurtosis of Residuals = 3.3877
```

```
Chi-Sq(  2)  Prob>Chi-Sq
    0.37107     0.83066

Breusch-Pagan and White LM Tests for Heteroscedasticity
                        Chi-Sq   DF  Prob>Chi-Sq
Breusch-Pagan Test      18.903    2  7.8553e-005
Koenkar-Basset Test     15.834    2  0.00036454
White Test              21.159    4  0.00029443
```

The result of the Bera-Jarque test reveals normality in the residuals (refer to Lesson 3.6 for details on the Bera-Jarque test for residual normality). The last section of the regression output is what we are interested in: the Breusch-Pagan and White tests for heteroscedasticity. It is set up to test the null hypothesis of homoscedasticity. That is, for the Breusch-Pagan test, if the computed test value is less than the critical value of the Chi-square distribution with two degrees of freedom, we fail to reject the hypothesis that the model error is homogeneously distributed. A similar conclusion is obtained from the White test, which is based on the R^2 statistic of the auxiliary regression with 4 degrees of freedom. Note the low P-values for both the Breusch-Pagan and White test statistics, leading us to reject the hypothesis of homoscedasticity and conclude that heteroscedasticity exits in the model.

 Remember the requirement of residual normality for the Breusch-Pagan test? If the residuals are not normally distributed, we need to use a more general version of the Breusch Pagan test, called the Koenkar-Basset test. The closer to normal the residuals are, the more similar these two test statistics. If absolute normality exists, the computed values of the two tests will be identical. Since the estimated residuals are indeed normally distributed for this example as shown earlier, both tests return rather close values, 18.9 and 15.8, respectively. Our conclusion of heteroscedasticity is the same from both the Breusch-Pagan and Koenkar-Basset test statistics.

Nonlinear Maximum Likelihood Estimation

A more general approach is to consider the regression model, linear or nonlinear, with the heteroscedastic variance-covariance matrix

$$\Sigma = \sigma^2 \Omega$$

where Ω is a positive diagonal matrix representing the proportional variance weight of each data observation. It is impossible to estimate the general matrix Ω. Usually Ω is re-parameterized with a vector α of only a few parameters. By assuming a normal probability distribution for the model's error term, maximum likelihood estimation is implemented to estimate the regression parameters and heteroscedastic variances.

Consider a sample of N data observations $Z = [Y,X]$ in fitting the regression model $F(Z,\beta) = \varepsilon$, where Y is the left-hand side dependent variable, X is the right-hand side independent variable, and β consists of the unknown parameters. For each data observation i, let $\varepsilon_i(\beta) = F(Z_i,\beta)$ and assume $\varepsilon_i(\beta)$ is normally independently distributed with zero mean and positive variance σ_i^2. The log-likelihood function, $ll(\beta,\sigma^2) = ll(\beta,\sigma_1^2,\sigma_2^2,\ldots,\sigma_N^2)$ for brevity, is

$$ll(\beta,\sigma^2) = -N/2\ ln(2\pi) - \tfrac{1}{2} \Sigma_{i=1,2,\ldots,N}\ ln(\sigma_i^2) - \tfrac{1}{2} \Sigma_{i=1,2,\ldots,N} (\varepsilon_i(\beta)^2 / \sigma_i^2)$$

Given the general form of heteroscedasticity, there are too many unknown parameters. For practical purposes, some hypothesis of heteroscedasticity must be assumed:

$$\sigma_i^2 = \sigma^2 \, h(X_i, \alpha)$$

where $\sigma^2 > 0$ and the heteroscedastic function h depends on part or all of the regressors and a vector of parameters α. Given a specific formulation of heteroscedasticity, $h_i(\alpha) = h(X_i, \alpha)$ for brevity, the log-likelihood function is written as:

$$ll(\beta, \alpha, \sigma^2) = \quad -N/2 \, (ln(2\pi) + ln(\sigma^2))$$

$$- \tfrac{1}{2} \Sigma_{i=1,2,\ldots,N} \, ln(h_i(\alpha)) - \frac{1}{2\sigma^2} \Sigma_{i=1,2,\ldots,N} \, (\varepsilon_i(\beta)^2 / h_i(\alpha))$$

Let $\varepsilon_i^*(\beta, \alpha) = \varepsilon_i(\beta) / \sqrt{h_i(\alpha)}$ and substitute out σ^2 with $\varepsilon^*(\beta, \alpha)'\varepsilon^*(\beta, \alpha)/N$, then the concentrated log-likelihood function is

$$ll^*(\beta, \alpha) = -N/2 \, (1 + ln(2\pi) + ln(\varepsilon^*(\beta, \alpha)'\varepsilon^*(\beta, \alpha)/N)) - \tfrac{1}{2} \Sigma_{i=1,2,\ldots,N} \, ln(h_i(\alpha))$$

As the variances must be explicitly estimated, $\sigma_i^2 = \sigma^2 \, h_i(\alpha)$, the objective log-likelihood function is inevitably complicated. To maximize the log-likelihood function, the techniques of nonlinear optimization of Chapter VI are applicable.

Consider the following examples of heteroscedasticity specifications, in which X is assumed to be a single variable for simplicity. The corresponding functional forms of $h(\alpha)$ and ε^* are defined for the concentrated log-likelihood function:

$$ll^*(\beta, \alpha) = -N/2 \, (1 + ln(2\pi) + ln(\varepsilon^{*'}\varepsilon^*/N)) - \tfrac{1}{2} \Sigma_{i=1,2,\ldots,N} \, ln(h_i(\alpha))$$

	σ_i^2	$h_i(\alpha)$	ε_i^*
1.	$\sigma^2(X_i\alpha)$	$X_i\alpha$	$\varepsilon_i / (X_i\alpha)^{\frac{1}{2}}$ (Note: $X_i\alpha > 0$)
2.	$\sigma^2(X_i\alpha)^2$	$(X_i\alpha)^2$	$\varepsilon_i / X_i\alpha$
3.	$\sigma^2 exp(X_i\alpha)$	$exp(X_i\alpha)$	$\varepsilon_i / exp(X_i\alpha)^{\frac{1}{2}}$
4.	$\sigma^2(X_i^{\alpha})$	X_i^{α}	$\varepsilon_i / X_i^{\alpha/2}$

The last two cases may be expressed in log form:

3. $ln(\sigma_i^2) = ln(\sigma^2) + \alpha \, X_i$
4. $ln(\sigma_i^2) = ln(\sigma^2) + \alpha \, ln(X_i)$

Depending on whether the variable X is log-transformed or not, both cases of multiplicative heteroscedasticity are essentially the same. For (3) and (4), if $\alpha = 0$ the model is homoscedastic. If $\alpha = 2$, we have case (2).

Lesson 9.4: Multiplicative Heteroscedasticity

Let's reexamine the heteroscedastic relationship of public school spending (SPENDING) and income (INCOME) of the previous three lessons:

$$SPENDING = \beta_0 + \beta_1 \, INCOME + \beta_2 \, INCOME^2 + \varepsilon$$

The data set is given in **greene.txt**. This time we will find and compare the maximum likelihood estimates based on the following hypothesis of multiplicative heteroscedasticity:

$$\sigma_i^2 = \sigma^2 \; \text{INCOME}_i^{\alpha}$$

Lesson 9.2 has demonstrated the weighted least squares estimation for the case of α = 2. The alternative expression of multiplicative heteroscedasticity is

$$\sigma_i^2 = \sigma^2 \; exp(\alpha \; \text{INCOME}_i)$$

If the variable INCOME is in log form for the alternative expression of heteroscedasticity, the two forms of multiplicative heteroscedasticity are the same.

```
        /*
        ** Lesson 9.4: Multiplicative Heteroscedasticity
        ** Greene (1997), Chap. 12.5
        */
 1   use gpe2;
 2   output file=gpe\output9.4 reset;
 3   load data[52,3]=gpe\greene.txt;
 4   data=data[2:52,2]~(data[2:52,3]/10000); @ scale data @
 5   data=packr(miss(data,"NA")); @ take care of missing obs @
 6   b=data[.,1]/(ones(rows(data),1)~data[.,2]~(data[.,2]^2));

 7   call reset;
 8   _method=4;
 9   _iter=100;
10   _restart=10;
11   _b=b|2.0;
12   _nlopt=1;

13   call estimate(&llf,data);

14   end;

15   proc llf(data,b);
16       local n,y,x,e,h,ll;
17       y=data[.,1]; @ public school spending @
18       x=data[.,2]; @ income @
19       n=rows(y);
20       h=x^b[4];       @ multiplicative hetero @
        /*
           h=exp(b[4]*x);
        */
21       e=(y-b[1]-b[2]*x-b[3]*(x^2))./sqrt(h);
22       ll=-0.5*n*(1+ln(2*pi)+ln(e'e/n))-0.5*sumc(ln(h));
23       retp(ll);
24   endp;
```

The first part of the program loads and scales the data, which are the same as in previous lessons. Line 6 computes the linear model estimates as the starting values of parameters for nonlinear maximum likelihood estimation (see line 11). The objective log-likelihood function `llf` is defined in lines 15 through 23. The specific form of multiplicative heteroscedasticity is given in line 20. Since the estimation has experienced some difficulty in improving the function value in its final iterations, we set `_restart=10` in line 10 to restart the iteration in case of failure. If you have trouble understanding what this program is doing, a review of Chapter VI and the program lessons on nonlinear models there is recommended.

The result of maximum likelihood estimation is given in the following:

```
Non-Linear Optimization: Maximization Problem
---------------------------------------------
Assuming Maximum Likelihood Function
Number of Observations = 50
Number of Parameters = 4

Maximum Number of Iterations = 100
Step Size Search Method = 0
Convergence Criterion = 0
Tolerance = 0.001

Initial Result:
Function Value =       -268.70
Parameters =        832.91      -1834.2       1587.0        2.0000

Using Newton-Raphson Algorithm
Iteration =  1   Step Size = 1.0000  Value =      -268.11
Parameters =         563.08      -1141.3       1150.6        3.2550
Iteration =  2   Step Size = 1.0000  Value =      -268.09
Parameters =         560.95      -1124.8       1132.8        3.2986
Iteration =  3   Step Size = 1.0000  Value =      -268.09
Parameters =         560.69      -1124.1       1132.4        3.2985
Iteration =  4   Step Size = 1.0000  Value =      -268.09
Parameters =         560.69      -1124.1       1132.4        3.2984
Iteration =  5   Step Size = 1.0000  Value =      -268.09
Parameters =         560.69      -1124.1       1132.4        3.2985

Final Result:
Iterations = 5              Evaluations = 126
Function Value =       -268.09
Parameters =         560.69      -1124.1       1132.4        3.2985
Gradient Vector = 2.0276e-008     0.00000      0.00000   1.7233e-006
Hessian Matrix =
   -0.020623    -0.014837    -0.010848   -0.00024046
   -0.014837    -0.010848    -0.0080655   9.0987e-005
   -0.010848    -0.0080655   -0.0061037   -0.00013901
  -0.00024046   9.0987e-005  -0.00013901    -0.58515

                              Asymptotic
            Parameter    Std. Error    t-Ratio
X1            560.69        354.11       1.5834
X2           -1124.1        943.28      -1.1917
X3            1132.4        621.04       1.8233
X4            3.2985        1.3790       2.3920
```

The estimated public school spending-income relationship is summarized as:

SPENDING = 560.69 - 1124.1 INCOME + 1132.4 INCOME^2
s.e.   (354.11)   (943.28)   (621.04)

In addition, the heteroscedastic variance is related to the variable INCOME as follows:

$$\sigma_i^2 = \sigma^2 \, INCOME_i^{3.3}$$

It is easy to modify **lesson9.4** for the alternative (exponential) form of multiplicative heteroscedasticity. Line 20 in the definition of log-likelihood function would be replaced by:

```
h=exp(b[4]*x);
```

which is currently ignored by GAUSS within the comment notations (/* */). Make the change and run the modified program. The resulting regression equation looks like this,

SPENDING = 544.53 − 1076.2 INCOME + 1097.7 INCOME^2
s.e.   (364.97)   (974.17)   (643.10)

and the variance equation is:

$\sigma_i^2 = \sigma^2 \, exp(4.23 \; INCOME_i)$

Refer to the output file generated from the program and verify the above regression results. To summarize the discussion of heteroscedastic regression models, we put together and compare the estimation results of the public school spending-income relationship:

SPENDING = $\beta_0 + \beta_1$ INCOME + β_2 INCOME^2 + ε

	(1) Lesson 9.1	(2) Lesson 9.2	(3) Lesson 9.4	(4) Lesson 9.4
β_1	-1834.2	-1399.3	-1124.1	-1076.2
	(1243.0)	(872.07)	(943.28)	(974.17)
β_2	1587.0	1311.3	1132.4	1097.7
	(829.99)	(563.71)	(621.04)	(643.10)
β_0	832.91	664.58	560.69	544.53
	(460.89)	(333.61)	(354.11)	(364.97)
α	0	2	3.2985	4.2344
			(1.3790)	(1.7364)

The numbers in parentheses are the estimated standard errors of the parameters. To recap the essence of each model: (1) Lesson 9.1 is an ordinary least squares with heteroscedasticity-consistent variance-covariance matrix; (2) Lesson 9.2 is a weighted least squares using 1/INCOME as the weight (i.e., $\sigma_i^2 = \sigma^2$ INCOME$_i^2$); (3) and (4) are the maximum likelihood estimators with multiplicative heteroscedasticity (i.e., $\sigma_i^2 = \sigma^2$ INCOME$_i^\alpha$ and $\sigma_i^2 = \sigma^2 \, exp(\alpha$ INCOME$_i)$, respectively) as presented in Lesson 9.4.

Which one is most accurate? We leave that decision to you.

X

Autocorrelation

Autocorrelation is a problem most likely associated with time series data. It concerns the relationship between previous and current error terms in a regression model. In the simplest case, the serial correlation is of first order where the correlation between current and immediate previous errors is nonzero. A more complicated error structure can include autoregressive (AR) and moving average (MA) terms.

OLS (ordinary least squares) estimation with autocorrelated error structure results in a loss of efficiency. Therefore, statistical inference using t and F test statistics cannot be trusted.

In this chapter, we revisit the multiple regression model of U.S. production function, using the labor (L), capital (K), and output (X) data series of **cjx.txt**:

$$ln(X) = \beta_0 + \beta_1 \, ln(L) + \beta_2 \, ln(K) + \varepsilon$$

Lesson 10.1 below demonstrates the use of the input control variable _hacv to obtain a consistent estimator of the variance-covariance matrix, when ordinary least squares is used. Several tests for the existence of autocorrelation are given in Lesson 10.2. Correction methods for first-order autocorrelation to improve the efficiency of parameter estimates are presented in Lessons 10.3 and 10.4. Since a more complicated structure of autocorrelation may be identified, the estimation of autoregressive and moving average error structures is considered in the last three lessons. Lesson 10.5 is a model with higher-order autocorrelation. The technique of maximum likelihood is introduced in Lesson 10.6, while Lesson 10.7 covers the nonlinear method.

Autocorrelation-Consistent Covariance Matrix

Given the existence of autocorrelation in a regression equation, the ordinary least squares estimator is unbiased but inefficient. Following from the treatment of the heteroscedasticity-consistent covariance matrix introduced in the previous chapter, we can keep the unbiased parameter estimators but correct for the variance-covariance estimator with an autocorrelation-consistent covariance matrix. Combining both problems of heteroscedasticity and autocorrelation, the Newey-West estimator of the heteroscedasticity-autocorrelation-consistent covariance matrix is a simple approach to deal with an unspecified structure of heteroscedasticity and autocorrelation. The drawback is that the order of autocorrelation must be predetermined for the computation of Newey-West estimators.

For a regression model with an unspecified structure of heteroscedasticity and autocorrelation, the consistent estimator of the variance-covariance matrix is

$$Var(\hat{\beta}) = (X'X)^{-1}(X'\hat{\Sigma}X)(X'X)^{-1}$$

where X is the data matrix of regressors, $\hat{\beta}$ is the ordinary least squares estimator of the parameter vector β, and $\hat{\Sigma}$ is the Newey-West covariance estimator for autocorrelated and possibly heterogeneous disturbances. Refer back to Lesson 9.1 for more details on the consistent covariance matrix in the context of heteroscedasticity.

Lesson 10.1: Heteroscedasticity-Autocorrelation-Consistent Covariance Matrix

Based on the Cobb-Douglas production model for U.S. manufacturing introduced in Lesson 3.4, we first repeat the ordinary least squares estimation, printing out the OLS variance-covariance matrix. Then two more least squares estimations are performed, one with an estimated autocorrelation-consistent covariance matrix and the other with a heteroscedasticity-autocorrelation-consistent covariance matrix. Thus, we can directly compare the results of these regression estimations.

Here is the program:

```
       /*
       ** Lesson 10.1: Heteroscedasticity Autocorrelation
       ** Consistent Variance-Covariance Matrix
       */
 1     use gpe2;
 2     output file = gpe\output10.1 reset;
 3     load data[40,6]= gpe\cjx.txt;

 4     year = data[2:40,1];
 5     X = ln(data[2:40,2]);
 6     L = ln(data[2:40,3]);
 7     K = ln(data[2:40,5]);

 8     call reset;

       /* Ordinary Least Squares */
 9     _names = {"X","L","K"};
10     _vcov = 1;
11     call estimate(X,L~K);

       /* Ordinary Least Squares */
12     _hacv = {0,4};@ with auto consistent var-cov @
13     call estimate(X,L~K);

       /* Ordinary Least Squares */
14     _hacv = {1,4};@ w/hetero auto consist var-cov @
15     call estimate(X,L~K);
16     end;
```

Recall that by setting the GPE input variable _vcov = 1 (see line 10), the estimated variance-covariance matrix is presented. Instead of using the inefficient variance-covariance matrix from ordinary least squares, computation of the consistent covariance matrix is controlled by the input variable _hacv. _hacv is either a scalar or a two-element vector. The first element of _hacv is reserved for heteroscedasticity correction as shown earlier in Lesson 9.1, while the second element is the order of autocorrelation to be considered for the estimator of an autocorrelation-consistent variance-covariance matrix. Therefore, line 12 of the program:

```
_hacv = {0,4};
```

will compute the fourth-order autocorrelation-consistent variance-covariance matrix. The mixture of heteroscedasticity and a fourth-order autocorrelation-consistent covariance matrix is obtained by setting line 14 to:

```
_hacv = {1,4};
```

 Why the fourth-order autocorrelation correction? There is no particular reason for this choice. As a matter of fact, we should try different numbers of orders to compute all the consistent covariance matrices, to find the proper order that stabilizes the resulting covariance matrix.

We now analyze the output of three regression estimations. The first least squares estimation with the option to print out the estimated variance-covariance matrix (lines 10 to 11) is as follows:

```
Least Squares Estimation
------------------------
Dependent Variable = X
Estimation Range =   1          39
Number of Observations = 39
Mean of Dependent Variable = 5.6874
Standard Error of Dependent Variable = 0.46096

R-Square = 0.99463      R-Square Adjusted = 0.99433
Standard Error of the Estimate = 0.034714
Log-Likelihood Function Value = 77.286
Log Ammemiya Prediction Criterion (APC) =  -6.6471
Log Akaike Information Criterion (AIC) =  -6.6474
Log Schwarz Bayesian Information Criterion (BIC) =  -6.5195
```

Sum of Squares	SS	DF	MSS	F	Prob>F
Explained	8.0310	2	4.0155	3332.2	1.3921E-041
Residual	0.043382	36	0.0012051		
Total	8.0744	38	0.21248		

Variable Name	Estimated Coefficient	Standard Error	t-Ratio 36 DF	Prob >|t|	Partial Regression
L	1.4508	0.083228	17.431	3.9260E-019	0.89407
K	0.38381	0.048018	7.9930	1.7130E-009	0.63960
CONSTANT	-3.9377	0.23700	-16.615	1.8332E-018	0.88464

```
Variance-Covariance Matrix of Coefficients
L           0.0069270
K          -0.0038020    0.0023057
CONSTANT   -0.018806     0.0092666    0.056169
                L            K          CONSTANT

Correlation Matrix of Coefficients
L           1.0000
K          -0.95134     1.0000
CONSTANT   -0.95338     0.81428     1.0000
                L            K          CONSTANT
```

Since autocorrelation is suspected for most time series data, the second regression estimation (lines 12 and 13) is carried out with the fourth-order autocorrelation-consistent standard errors and the variance-covariance matrix:

Variable Name	Estimated Coefficient	Standard Error	t-Ratio 36 DF	Prob >|t|	Partial Regression

L	1.4508	0.10980	13.213	2.2423E-015	0.82905
K	0.38381	0.058368	6.5756	1.1907E-007	0.54568
CONSTANT	-3.9377	0.33421	-11.782	6.5278E-014	0.79407

Variance-Covariance Matrix of Coefficients

L	0.012055		
K	-0.0060940	0.0034069	
CONSTANT	-0.035362	0.016267	0.11170
	L	K	CONSTANT

Correlation Matrix of Coefficients

L	1.0000		
K	-0.95089	1.0000	
CONSTANT	-0.96366	0.83388	1.0000
	L	K	CONSTANT

Finally, heteroscedasticity and the fourth-order autocorrelation-consistent covariance matrix is the outcome of the last regression estimation (lines 13 and 14):

Variable Name	Estimated Coefficient	Standard Error	t-Ratio 36 DF	Prob >|t|	Partial Regression
L	1.4508	0.11561	12.549	1.0409E-014	0.81392
K	0.38381	0.062253	6.1653	4.1818E-007	0.51358
CONSTANT	-3.9377	0.33788	-11.654	8.9304E-014	0.79048

Variance-Covariance Matrix of Coefficients

L	0.013366		
K	-0.0069673	0.0038755	
CONSTANT	-0.037946	0.018529	0.11416
	L	K	CONSTANT

Correlation Matrix of Coefficients

L	1.0000		
K	-0.96804	1.0000	
CONSTANT	-0.97140	0.88092	1.0000
	L	K	CONSTANT

Putting together the estimated regression equations with the three sets of estimated standard errors, we have

$ln(X)$	= -3.94	+ 1.45 $ln(L)$	+ 0.38 $ln(K)$
s.e. (ols)	(0.24)	(0.08)	(0.05)
s.e. (ac)	(0.33)	(0.11)	(0.06)
s.e. (hac)	(0.34)	(0.12)	(0.06)

In general, the consistent estimators of the covariance matrix are larger than their ordinary least squares counterparts. The consequence is a higher probability of type II error (incorrectly accepting the null hypothesis) for the estimators. In this example, all three estimated variance-covariance matrices of the coefficients are quite similar in spite of the consistency correction for autocorrelation and heteroscedasticity.

Detection of Autocorrelation

Given each observation of a linear regression model

$$Y_i = X_i \beta + \varepsilon_i$$

the linear form of autocorrelated errors is written as:

$$\varepsilon_i = \rho_1\varepsilon_{i-1} + \rho_2\varepsilon_{i-2} + \ldots + \rho_p\varepsilon_{i-p} + \upsilon_i$$

where Y is the dependent variable, X is a vector of explanatory independent variables, and β is the associated parameter vector. The simplest case of autocorrelated error structure is autocorrelation of order 1 (or AR(1)), where p = 1. It is always worthwhile to check for the existence of autocorrelation before considering correcting the problem.

Lesson 10.2: Tests for Autocorrelation

This lesson explores several methods to test for autocorrelation. The most popular test is the Durbin-Watson bounds test, which is designed to check for first-order serial correlation. The convenience of the Durbin-Watson bounds test has its limits: it tests only for first-order autocorrelation and the regression must include a constant term. Additionally, there cannot be lagged dependent variables in the regression equation. The Breusch Godfrey LM test is more forgiving: lagged dependent variables may be included and it can be used to test for higher orders of autocorrelation. Checking the autocorrelation and partial autocorrelation coefficients can reveal a more complicated autoregressive and moving average structure of autocorrelated errors. This is accomplished with the Box-Pierce and Ljung-Box Q test statistics. However, except for the Durbin-Watson bounds test, all tests for autocorrelation need a large sample size to be useful.

The popular Durbin-Watson test statistic is a part of the residual statistics output reported with the regression estimation. That is, it is available with the statement:

```
_rstat = 1;
```

To call the Breusch-Godfrey LM test statistic, we need to specify the order of autocorrelation to be tested. Indeed, this is a cumulative test for no serial correlation up to the order specified. Therefore, we need only to find the autocorrelation at a rather low order to confirm the problem. For example, to test for autocorrelation up to the fourth order, use the statement:

```
_bgtest = 4;
```

Autocorrelation and partial autocorrelation coefficients are typically computed and plotted for a long period of lags. By examining these coefficients and their distribution, a pattern of autoregressive and moving average structures of autocorrelated residuals may be identified. The Chi-square-based Box-Pierce and Ljung-Box Q test statistics work the same way as the Breusch-Godfrey LM test. For example, 12-lag autocorrelation and partial autocorrelation functions are called with the statement:

```
_acf = 12;
```

 The selection of the fourth-order autocorrelation for the Breusch-Godfrey LM test is only a suggestion. What we need is the lowest number of orders to test for autocorrelation. Again, the use of 12 lags for calculating and plotting autocorrelation and partial autocorrelation coefficients is arbitrary. As a rule of thumb, about one quarter of the sample size should offer sufficient information concerning the sample autocorrelation.

Here is the program:

```
      /*
      ** Lesson 10.2: Tests for Autocorrelation
      */
  1   use gpe2;
  2   output file = gpe\output10.2 reset;
  3   load data[40,6]= gpe\cjx.txt;

  4   year = data[2:40,1];
  5   X = ln(data[2:40,2]);
  6   L = ln(data[2:40,3]);
  7   K = ln(data[2:40,5]);
  8   call reset;

  9   _names = {"X","L","K"};
 10   _rstat = 1;
 11   _rplot = 2;
 12   _bgtest = 4;  @ Breusch-Godfrey, 4th order @
 13   _acf = 12;    @ auto & partial auto,12 lags @
 14   call estimate(X,L~K);
 15   end;
```

Looking at the program, the use of input control variables _bgtest (line 12) and _acf (line 13) are new. You may set the value of _bgtest to any order of autocorrelation for the Breusch-Godfrey LM test, in this case up to 4 orders are tested. Similarly, for calculating and plotting autocorrelation and partial autocorrelation functions, the number of lags must be given to the variable _acf. In this example, 12 lags seem sufficient for a data size of about 40 observations.

Let's analyze the first part of the estimation result (which is the same as that of Lesson 10.1), paying attention to the Durbin-Watson test statistic:

```
Squared Correlation of Observed and Predicted = 0.99463
Sum of Squared Residuals = 0.043382
Sum of Absolute Residuals = 0.96779
Sum of Residuals = -9.88614E-011
First-Order Rho = 0.57053
Durbin-Watson Test Statistic = 0.85808
```

The first-order Rho is the estimated first-order serial correlation coefficient (ρ) which ranges from -1 to 1. At a value of 0.57, we can see that autocorrelation is a problem. To test the statistical significance of $\rho = 0$, the Durbin-Watson bounds test is used here. The computed Durbin-Watson statistic of 0.858 lies below the lower bound critical value of 1.382 for a regression using 39 observations and 2 explanatory variables (not including constant term) at a 5% level of significance.

The second part of the result concerns the Breusch-Godfrey LM test of autocorrelation, up to the fourth order:

Breusch-Godfrey LM Test for Autocorrelation

	Chi-Sq	DF	Prob>Chi-Sq
AR(1)	13.205	1	0.00027923
AR(2)	20.331	2	3.8471e-005
AR(3)	22.221	3	5.8666e-005
AR(4)	22.445	4	0.00016339

The Breusch-Godfrey LM test is compared with the critical value of the Chi-square distribution with degrees of freedom equal to the number of orders of autocorrelation. P-values of each order tested are given to simplify the analysis. It becomes clear that autocorrelation exists from the very first order upward. Since the first order exhibits the problem of serial correlation as the Durbin-Watson bounds test suggests, all LM tests for cumulative higher orders will certainly also identify autocorrelation.

The last part of the output lists and displays autocorrelation and partial autocorrelation coefficients for regression residuals up to 12 lags. Standard errors of these coefficients are useful to spot the significance of lags for autoregressive and moving average structures of autocorrelated residuals. In addition, both Box-Pierce and Ljung-Box Q test statistics are computed for each lag. Similar to the Breusch-Godfrey LM test, these accumulative tests follow a Chi-square distribution with degrees of freedom corresponding to each individual number of lags, adjusted for the number of regression coefficients whenever necessary.

```
Autocorrelation and Partial Autocorrelation Functions
ARMA Model Specification
Mean = -2.8701e-012 Standard Error = 0.033788
  Lag       AR    S.E.(AR)        PAR   S.E.(PAR)   Box-Pierce   Ljung-Box
    1    0.55892   0.20411    0.55892     0.16013       12.183      13.145
    2  -0.046422   0.20438   -0.52183     0.16013       12.267      13.238
    3   -0.19341   0.20902    0.27527     0.16013       13.726      14.900
    4   0.054712   0.20939    0.12555     0.16013       13.843      15.037
    5    0.20105   0.21428  -0.093386     0.16013       15.419      16.937
    6   0.047409   0.21455  -0.073459     0.16013       15.507      17.046
    7   -0.20382   0.21946   -0.12344     0.16013       17.127      19.122
    8   -0.32496   0.23147   -0.18444     0.16013       21.246      24.569
    9   -0.20559   0.23610   0.043822     0.16013       22.894      26.822
   10   -0.15817   0.23881   -0.36648     0.16013       23.870      28.202
   11   -0.23694   0.24476  -0.047891     0.16013       26.059      31.407
   12   -0.24987   0.25121   0.010437     0.16013       28.494      35.105
```

Both moving average and autoregressive processes of lower orders are visibly identifiable from the significant values of autocorrelation and partial autocorrelation coefficients, respectively. These include the first lag of autocorrelation as well as the first and second lags of partial autocorrelation coefficients. Moreover, Box-Pierce and Ljung-Box Q test statistics confirm the problem of autocorrelation starting from the first lag.

In summary, all these tests for autocorrelation suggest that our model may need to be re-specified. Moreover, the correct specification may not involve just the simple first-order correction. Nevertheless, the next two lessons will explain the correction mechanisms of autocorrelation for the first-order model. For higher-order autocorrelation and even the mixture of autoregressive and moving average error structure, a proper model specification must first be identified.

Correction for Autocorrelation

The GPE package offers several different methods to correct for autocorrelation. The default is the Prais-Winsten modified Cochrane-Orcutt iterative method, which applies a scaled data transformation $\sqrt{1-\rho^2}$ to the first observation consistent with an AR(1) error structure. Due to the use of this transformation, only the estimation of an AR(1) process is applicable.

In GPE, use the input control variable _ar to specify the order of autocorrelation for estimation. Since the correction mechanism may require several iterations to complete, another control variable _iter must be set to a large enough number to achieve convergence. Therefore the following statements are minimal for estimating a regression model, which corrects for the first-order serial correlation within the limit of 50 iterations:

```
_ar = 1;
_iter = 50;
```

Lesson 10.3 below illustrates the default method of Cochrane-Orcutt iterative estimation of the AR(1) model.

As an alternative to the Prais-Winsten modification, the original Cochrane-Orcutt iterative method does not include the first observation or its transformation. It is simply dropped from the data set used in the regression estimation. Therefore, adding the statement:

```
_drop = 1;
```

will use the traditional Cochrane-Orcutt method to estimate and to correct for an AR(1) error process. As a matter of fact, this method applies to the autocorrelated error structure of both first and higher orders. It just drops more observations in the beginning of the sample, with a cost of inefficiency, partially due to the loss of degrees of freedom. For estimation with higher-order autocorrelation, it is not necessary to specify the variable _drop. For example,

```
_ar = 4;
```

will estimate and correct for the AR(4) process using the traditional Cochrane-Orcutt iterative method in which the initial four observations are dropped automatically.

The Cochrane-Orcutt method only converges to a local solution. In rare cases, there may exist more than one solution for an autocorrelated error structure. The Hildreth-Lu grid search method guarantees that the global solution will be found for an AR(1) model. Similar to the Prais-Winsten modification to the original Cochrane-Orcutt iterative method, the Hildreth-Lu grid search method may include the first observation with proper transformation. Alternatively, dropping the first observation is an option with the cost of a decrease in efficiency. Again, we note that the Hildreth-Lu method applies to an AR(1) model only. The Hildreth-Lu method is activated by letting:

```
_method = 2;
```

Based on the GAUSS program of Lesson 10.3, the Hildreth-Lu grid search method is introduced in Lesson 10.4, in which the global solution for the estimated AR(1) model is ensured.

Both the Cochrane-Orcutt iterative and the Hildreth-Lu grid search methods offer the option of using least squares or maximum likelihood criterion for optimization. They are the same if the first observation is dropped. However, with the transformed first observation included, the use of different optimization criteria may result in finding different solutions, although they are usually close. We have noted the use of the input control variable _method to select different methods of estimation for an

150

autocorrelated error structure. _method can be either a scalar or a 2-element vector. When employing a 2-element vector, the first element of _method selects the estimation method, while the second element selects either least squares or maximum likelihood criterion for optimization. For example,

```
_method = {0,1};
```

calls for the estimation of autocorrelation coefficients using the Cochrane-Orcutt iterative procedure based on maximum likelihood criterion. The default method is the Cochrane-Orcutt iterative method and the default optimization criterion is the least squares. See Appendix A for more information.

There is another method implemented for estimating the first-order autocorrelation, which includes the transformed first observation of data series using maximum likelihood optimization criterion. This method is the Beach-MacKinnon iterative maximum likelihood algorithm, specified by:

```
_method = 1;
```

Lesson 10.3: Cochrane-Orcutt Iterative Procedure

This lesson walks through the Prais-Winsten modified Cochrane-Orcutt iterative procedure based on the least square criterion. Unless otherwise specified, GPE defaults to this method for estimation and correction for a first-order autoregressive error structure. The most basic model is presented here.

```
     /*
     ** Lesson 10.3: Cochrane-Orcutt Iterative Procedure
     */
1    use gpe2;
2    output file = gpe\output10.3 reset;
3    load data[40,6]= gpe\cjx.txt;

4    year = data[2:40,1];
5    X = ln(data[2:40,2]);
6    L = ln(data[2:40,3]);
7    K = ln(data[2:40,5]);
8    call reset;

9    _names = {"X","L","K"};
10   _rstat = 1;
11   _ar = 1;          @ AR(1) error structure @
12   _iter = 50;       @ 50 iter for default C-O @
13   call estimate(X,L~K);
14   end;
```

As shown below, the regression output of this program is more complicated than previous ones without the autocorrelation correction.

```
Least Squares Estimation
------------------------
Dependent Variable = X
Estimation Range =  1         39
Number of Observations = 39
Mean of Dependent Variable = 5.6874
Standard Error of Dependent Variable = 0.46096

Order of Autoregressive Errors = 1
Maximum Number of Iterations = 50
Convergence Tolerance Level = 0.00100
```

```
Using Cochrane-Orcutt Iterative Least Squares Algorithm
Iteration =  0    Sum of Squares =  0.04338    Log Likelihood =  77.28607
       Rho =         0.00000
Iteration =  1    Sum of Squares =  0.02784    Log Likelihood =  85.74134
       Rho =         0.57053
Iteration =  2    Sum of Squares =  0.02702    Log Likelihood =  86.22178
       Rho =         0.66944
Iteration =  3    Sum of Squares =  0.02670    Log Likelihood =  86.37819
       Rho =         0.72411
Iteration =  4    Sum of Squares =  0.02656    Log Likelihood =  86.42820
       Rho =         0.75755
Iteration =  5    Sum of Squares =  0.02649    Log Likelihood =  86.43761
       Rho =         0.77780
Iteration =  6    Sum of Squares =  0.02647    Log Likelihood =  86.43452
       Rho =         0.78976
Iteration =  7    Sum of Squares -  0.02645    Log Likelihood -  86.42949
       Rho =         0.79670
Iteration =  8    Sum of Squares =  0.02645    Log Likelihood =  86.42547
       Rho =         0.80069
Iteration =  9    Sum of Squares =  0.02644    Log Likelihood =  86.42278
       Rho =         0.80297
Iteration = 10    Sum of Squares =  0.02644    Log Likelihood =  86.42112
       Rho =         0.80427
Iteration = 11    Sum of Squares =  0.02644    Log Likelihood =  86.42014
       Rho =         0.80501
```

Rho	Std.Error	t-Ratio
0.80501	0.095517	8.4279

NOTE: R-Square, AOV are computed from original series.

```
R-Square = 0.99673       R-Square Adjusted = 0.99654
Standard Error of the Estimate = 0.027100
Log-Likelihood Function Value = 86.420
Log Ammemiya Prediction Criterion (APC) =  -7.1423
Log Akaike Information Criterion (AIC) =  -7.1426
Log Schwarz Bayesian Information Criterion (BIC) =  -7.0146
```

Sum of Squares	SS	DF	MSS	F	Prob>F
Explained	8.0200	2	4.0100	5460.0	1.9940E-045
Residual	0.026440	36	0.00073443		
Total	8.0744	38	0.21248		

Variable Name	Estimated Coefficient	Standard Error	t-Ratio 36 DF	Prob >|t|	Partial Regression
L	1.0680	0.15125	7.0612	2.7289E-008	0.58072
K	0.55812	0.095595	5.8384	1.1428E-006	0.48635
CONSTANT	-2.7298	0.45549	-5.9931	7.0980E-007	0.49943

```
Squared Correlation of Observed and Predicted = 0.99673
Sum of Squared Residuals = 0.026440
Sum of Absolute Residuals = 0.76731
Sum of Residuals = 3.30995E-002
First-Order Rho = 0.37997
Durbin-Watson Test Statistic = 1.2244
```

Notice that the second block of output reports the Cochrane-Orcutt iterative results set in lines 11, 12, and 13 of the program. Every iteration is listed until convergence is reached. At the end of the iterations, we have the following results: the estimated Rho, standard error, and t-ratio associated with the first-order serial coefficient. In this example, the significant non-zero Rho value of 0.805 is used to correct the least squares regression. In summary,

$$ln(X) = -2.73 + 1.07\,ln(L) + 0.56\,ln(K) + \varepsilon$$
$$\text{s.e.} \quad (0.46) \quad (0.15) \quad (0.10)$$

$$\varepsilon = 0.805\,\varepsilon_{-1}$$
$$\text{s.e.} \quad (0.096)$$

To call for the estimation of autocorrelation coefficients using Cochrane-Orcutt iterative procedure based on the maximum likelihood criterion, add the following line before calling `estimate` in line 13:

```
_method = {0,1};
```

The verbose listing of iterations may be suppressed by setting the control variable `_print=` 0. See Appendix A for details.

If the iterative estimation terminates prematurely due to exceeding the maximum iteration limit, the estimation result may not be reliable. A larger value of `_iter` must be given and the model re-estimated.

There is another optional input control variable `_tol`, which adjusts the convergence tolerance level. Its default value is set to 0.001.

The remaining regression output is familiar, including the Durbin-Watson test statistic computed for the model corrected for an AR(1) error structure. Recall from the test result of Lesson 10.2 that the extent of autocorrelation specification may be more complicated than the estimated AR(1). Indeed, the first-order Rho of 0.38 for the corrected model supports the notion that we may need to specify and correct for higher orders of autocorrelation.

Lesson 10.4: Hildreth-Lu Grid Search Procedure

To be sure that the estimated coefficient of the first-order serial correlation is indeed a global solution, we need only to specify the estimation method in the previous program. Modify the program to call and run the Hildreth-Lu grid search procedure by adding the statement

```
_method = 2;
```

in line 12 as follows:

```
/*
** Lesson 10.4: Hildreth-Lu Grid Search Procedure
*/
1   use gpe2;
2   output file = gpe\output10.4 reset;
3   load data[40,6]= gpe\cjx.txt;

4   year = data[2:40,1];
5   X = ln(data[2:40,2]);
6   L = ln(data[2:40,3]);
7   K = ln(data[2:40,5]);
8   call reset;

9   _names = {"X","L","K"};
10  _rstat = 1;
11  _ar = 1;        @ AR(1) error structure @
```

```
12 | _method = 2;  @ H-L method @
13 | _iter = 50;    @ 50 iterations @
14 | call estimate(X,L~K);
15 | end;
```

To call for the estimation of autocorrelation coefficients using the Hildreth-Lu grid search procedure based on the maximum likelihood criterion, try this in place of line 12:

```
_method = {2,1};
```

Running the above program returns many iterations and lengthy output. Remember that these iterations are controlled by the global variables _iter and _tol. For viewing the estimation result, we refer readers to the output file output10.4.

The estimated model with AR(1) error structure is summarized as follows:

$$ln(X) \;=\; -2.66 \;+\; 1.05\,ln(L) \;+\; 0.56\,ln(K) \;+\; \varepsilon$$
$$\text{s.e.} \qquad (0.47) \qquad (0.15) \qquad\qquad (0.10)$$

$$\varepsilon \;=\; 0.826\,\varepsilon_{-1}$$
$$\text{s.e.} \qquad (0.090)$$

The results are basically the same as those obtained by using the Cochrane-Orcutt method. Although the Hildreth-Lu grid search is costly in terms of computer resources, the global nature of the estimated autocorrelation coefficients is superior to the local solution found with either of the Cochrane-Orcutt methods.

Lesson 10.5: Higher-Order Autocorrelation

As we have seen, many methods and options are available for estimating and correcting an AR(1) model. For higher-order autocorrelation, the traditional Cochrane-Orcutt iterative method is used, with a truncated sample in which initial unusable observations are dropped. Based on the Cochrane-Orcutt method introduced in Lesson 10.3, the first part of this lesson reexamines the estimated AR(1) model and tests for possible higher-order autocorrelation. We recall the use of the Breusch-Godfrey test (_bgtest) and autocorrelation functions (_acf) in addition to the Durbin-Watson bounds test to check for higher-order problems after the AR(1) model is estimated. Higher-order problems are identified and corrected in the second part of this lesson. Further tests for autocorrelation reveal no more information can be extracted from the estimated residuals.

```
   | /*
   | ** Lesson 10.5: Higher-Order Autocorrelation
   | */
 1 | use gpe2;
 2 | output file = gpe\output10.5 reset;
 3 | load data[40,6]= gpe\cjx.txt;

 4 | year = data[2:40,1];
 5 | X = ln(data[2:40,2]);
 6 | L = ln(data[2:40,3]);
 7 | K = ln(data[2:40,5]);

 8 | call reset;

 9 | _names = {"X","L","K"};
```

```
10 │ _rstat = 1;
11 │ _rplot = 2;
12 │ _bgtest = 4;
13 │ _acf = 12;

14 │ _ar = 1;      @ AR(1) error structure @
15 │ _iter = 50;   @ 50 iterations @
16 │ call estimate(X,L~K);

17 │ _ar = 3;      @ AR(3) error structure @
18 │ call estimate(X,L~K);
19 │ end;
```

Lines 12 and 13 add the options to perform tests for higher-order autocorrelation. These include the Breusch-Godfrey LM test up to the fourth order of autocorrelation and a plot of 12-lag autocorrelation functions. The AR(1) model is re-estimated (line 16) with the following test results:

```
Breusch-Godfrey LM Tests for Autocorrelation
                    Chi-Sq     DF    Prob>Chi-Sq
AR(   1)            5.5093     1      0.018916
AR(   2)            14.853     2      0.00059525
AR(   3)            14.883     3      0.0019193
AR(   4)            15.021     4      0.0046572
```

```
Autocorrelation and Partial Autocorrelation Functions
ARMA Model Specification
Mean = 0.00084871   Standard Error = 0.026364
  Lag        AR     S.E.(AR)        PAR    S.E.(PAR)   Box-Pierce   Ljung-Box
   1    0.36888     0.18061     0.36888    0.16013      5.3068       5.7257
   2   -0.29377     0.19247    -0.49754    0.16013      8.6724       9.4552
   3   -0.32527     0.20608    0.031588    0.16013      12.799       14.155
   4   0.058462     0.20651     0.12368    0.16013      12.932       14.311
   5    0.22715     0.21282   -0.015040    0.16013      14.944       16.737
   6   -0.026579    0.21290    -0.15509    0.16013      14.972       16.772
   7   -0.17667     0.21663    0.061130    0.16013      16.189       18.331
   8   -0.15212     0.21935    -0.15998    0.16013      17.092       19.525
   9    0.11512     0.22090     0.19394    0.16013      17.608       20.231
  10    0.10311     0.22213    -0.19689    0.16013      18.023       20.817
  11   -0.14423     0.22451   -0.090591    0.16013      18.834       22.005
  12   -0.21271     0.22962   -0.026934    0.16013      20.599       24.685
```

From the visual display of autocorrelation functions as well as the results of several test statistics (Breusch-Godfrey LM test, Box-Pierce and Ljung-Box Q tests), higher orders of autocorrelation, or a mixture of autocorrelation and moving average processes is suspected. In particular, the coefficients for the first lag of autocorrelation and the first two lags of partial autocorrelation are still statistically significantly different from zero. The second part of Lesson 10.5 goes ahead to estimate the AR(3) model using the traditional Cochrane-Orcutt iterative method. The possibility of a mixed error structure with a moving average process is discussed in the next lesson.

Since the option to test for higher orders of autocorrelation is still included in the program (see lines 12 and 13), the estimated AR(3) model is also tested for problems of autocorrelation. Here are the estimation and test results with the AR(3) error structure:

```
Least Squares Estimation
------------------------
Dependent Variable = X
```

```
Estimation Range =   4          39
Number of Observations = 36
Mean of Dependent Variable = 5.7319
Standard Error of Dependent Variable = 0.45153


NOTE: Estimation Range Has Been Adjusted.

Order of Autoregressive Errors = 3
Maximum Number of Iterations = 50
Convergence Tolerance Level = 0.00100

Using Cochrane-Orcutt Iterative Least Squares Algorithm
Iteration =  0   Sum of Squares =  0.03894    Log Likelihood =  71.84326
       Rho =      0.00000     0.00000    0.00000
Iteration =  1   Sum of Squares =  0.01579    Log Likelihood =  88.09111
       Rho =      1.0537     -0.81992    0.31827
...
Iteration =  12  Sum of Squares =  0.01434    Log Likelihood =  89.82665
       Rho =      1.3540     -0.92057    0.39938

         Rho      Std.Error     t-Ratio
      1.3540      0.14121       9.5891
     -0.92057     0.21656      -4.2508
      0.39938     0.14174       2.8178


NOTE: R-Square, AOV are computed from original series.

R-Square = 0.99799     R-Square Adjusted = 0.99787
Standard Error of the Estimate = 0.020845
Log-Likelihood Function Value = 89.827
Log Ammemiya Prediction Criterion (APC) =  -7.6612
Log Akaike Information Criterion (AIC) =  -7.6616
Log Schwarz Bayesian Information Criterion (BIC) =  -7.5296
```

Sum of Squares	SS	DF	MSS	F	Prob>F
Explained	7.0896	2	3.5448	8157.7	3.4129E-045
Residual	0.014340	33	0.00043453		
Total	7.1357	35	0.20388		

Variable Name	Estimated Coefficient	Standard Error	t-Ratio 33 DF	Prob >|t|	Partial Regression
L	1.0433	0.11306	9.2277	1.1644E-010	0.72070
K	0.54676	0.074920	7.2979	2.2460E-008	0.61743
CONSTANT	-2.5236	0.38943	-6.4802	2.3638E-007	0.55996

```
Squared Correlation of Observed and Predicted = 0.99800
Sum of Squared Residuals = 0.014340
Sum of Absolute Residuals = 0.56667
Sum of Residuals = -1.68421E-012
First-Order Rho = -0.0040825
Durbin-Watson Test Statistic = 1.8661

Breusch-Godfrey LM Tests for Autocorrelation
                     Chi-Sq     DF   Prob>Chi-Sq
AR(   1)             0.41856    1     0.51766
AR(   2)             0.86990    2     0.64730
AR(   3)             3.3268     3     0.34393
AR(   4)             3.4588     4     0.48416

Autocorrelation and Partial Autocorrelation Functions
ARMA Model Specification
Mean = 3.4232e-015  Standard Error = 0.020241
```

Lag	AR	S.E.(AR)	PAR	S.E.(PAR)	Box-Pierce	Ljung-Box
1	-0.0039777	0.16667	-0.0039777	0.16667	0.00056961	0.00061843
2	-0.086337	0.16791	-0.086355	0.16667	0.26892	0.30054
3	-0.20318	0.17460	-0.20543	0.16667	1.7551	2.0119
4	-0.0027129	0.17460	-0.016352	0.16667	1.7554	2.0122

5	0.10710	0.17642	0.074897	0.16667	2.1683	2.5184
6	-0.18193	0.18156	-0.23380	0.16667	3.3599	4.0277
7	0.060756	0.18212	0.073555	0.16667	3.4928	4.2018
8	-0.14740	0.18540	-0.15926	0.16667	4.2749	5.2633
9	0.15411	0.18893	0.092475	0.16667	5.1299	6.4667
10	0.019960	0.18899	0.0049687	0.16667	5.1443	6.4876
11	-0.20234	0.19491	-0.24119	0.16667	6.6182	8.7281
12	-0.24101	0.20302	-0.28134	0.16667	8.7093	12.039

Based on the Breusch-Godfrey LM test up to the fourth order as well as the plot of the 12-lag autocorrelation function and the associated Box-Pierce and Ljung-Box Q test statistics, the estimated model with AR(3) error structure is now free of autocorrelation. The estimated model is superior to that of correcting only for first-order autocorrelation.

In summary,

$$ln(X) = -2.52 + 1.04\, ln(L) + 0.55\, ln(K) + \varepsilon$$
$$\text{s.e.} \quad (0.39) \quad\quad (0.11) \quad\quad\quad (0.08)$$

$$\varepsilon = 1.35\, \varepsilon_{-1} - 0.93\, \varepsilon_{-2} + 0.40\, \varepsilon_{-3}$$
$$\text{s.e.} \quad (0.14) \quad\quad (0.22) \quad\quad (0.14)$$

Autoregressive and Moving Average (ARMA) Models: An Introduction

GPE can handle the estimation of a more complicated regression model involving autoregressive and moving average autocorrelated errors. In addition to the p-th order autoregressive structure AR(p) discussed earlier such as

$$\varepsilon_i = \rho_1 \varepsilon_{i-1} + \rho_2 \varepsilon_{i-2} + \ldots + \rho_p \varepsilon_{i-p} + \upsilon_i$$

the q-th order moving average error structure MA(q) is specified as

$$\varepsilon_i = \upsilon_i - \theta_1 \upsilon_{i-1} - \theta_2 \upsilon_{i-2} - \ldots - \theta_q \upsilon_{i-q}$$

Or in combination with the autoregressive structure, that is ARMA(p,q), we have

$$\varepsilon_i = \rho_1 \varepsilon_{i-1} + \rho_2 \varepsilon_{i-2} + \ldots + \rho_p \varepsilon_{i-p} - \theta_1 \upsilon_{i-1} - \theta_2 \upsilon_{i-2} - \ldots - \theta_q \upsilon_{i-q} + \upsilon_i$$

where the filtered error term υ_i is assumed to be normally independently distributed. Given a mixed error process of AR(p) and MA(q), or ARMA(p,q), the estimation of the p-element AR and q-element MA parameters is typically carried out by a nonlinear optimization algorithm. To be more specific, nonlinear least squares or maximum likelihood is called for in the estimation of an error structure with a moving average component. Without the moving average specification, the estimated autoregressive parameters are computed by the methods described earlier in previous lessons.

With GPE, the following input control variables are relevant to the estimation of an error structure with autoregressive and moving average components:

- _arma   Autoregressive moving average orders
- _nlopt   Nonlinear least squares or maximum likelihood

- • `_method`   Nonlinear optimization method
- • `_iter`   Iteration limit
- • `_conv`   Convergence criteria
- • `_tol`   Convergence tolerance level

Among these control variables, only _arma is new. The other variables are related to nonlinear model estimation discussed in Chapters VI and VII. The variable _arma is used to specify the orders of the autoregressive and moving average components of the error structure. It is a column vector consisting of at least two elements: the first is the order of the autoregressive component, followed by the order of the moving average. For example,

```
_arma = {1,1};
```

specifies an error process of the first-order autoregressive and first-order moving average. A *pure* moving average of q-th order is set by _arma = {0,q}. Obviously, _arma = {p,0} is identical to _ar = p where p is the order number of the autocorrelation. For parameter estimation, providing the initial guess values of autoregressive and moving average parameters will be helpful for the convergence. These values could be appended to the variable _arma, in which the first two elements are always the order of the respective process. We note that the estimated nonlinear ARMA error structure is conditional upon data initialization for the beginning observations necessary to compute the process. For convenience, in GPE, we initialize the data series with the sample mean of model errors.

Lesson 10.6: ARMA(1,1) Error Structure

In normal situations, a higher order of autoregressive structure can be specified with a lower order moving average structure, and vice versa. In order to keep the estimation simple, we recommend the use of a lower order model. Of course, this is a matter of taste and also depends on the theory and computational experience. Earlier lessons on estimating the U.S. production function suggest that the model is better described with an AR(3) error structure (see Lesson 10.5). An alternative would be to estimate the error process using a MA(1) structure or a mixed structure of autoregressive and moving average at a lower order, say, ARMA(1,1). Lesson 10.6 demonstrates the estimation of an ARMA(1,1) model.

```
     /*
     ** Lesson 10.6: ARMA(1,1) Error Structure
     */
1    use gpe2;
2    output file = gpe\output10.6 reset;
3    load data[40,6]= gpe\cjx.txt;

4    year = data[2:40,1];
5    X = ln(data[2:40,2]);
6    L = ln(data[2:40,3]);
7    K = ln(data[2:40,5]);

8    call reset;

9    _names = {"X","L","K"};
10   _rstat = 1;
11   _rplot = 2;
12   _bgtest = 4;
13   _acf = 12;
```

```
14 │ _arma = {1,1};  @ ARMA(1,1) error structure @
15 │ _nlopt = 1;     @ maximum likelihood estimation @
16 │ _method = 5;    @ QHC optimization method @
17 │ _iter = 50;     @ 50 iterations @
18 │ call estimate(X,L~K);
19 │ end;
```

To double check for autocorrelation after the specification of ARMA(1,1) is estimated, we keep _bgtest and _acf (lines 12 and 13) in the program.

The ARMA(1,1) structure is estimated with the nonlinear maximum likelihood method using the quadratic hill-climbing algorithm. It takes 34 iterations to achieve the convergence. Here is the abridged regression output of the estimated Cobb-Douglas production function with an ARMA(1,1) error structure:

```
Least Squares Estimation
------------------------
Dependent Variable = X
Estimation Range =  1          39
Number of Observations = 39
Mean of Dependent Variable = 5.6874
Standard Error of Dependent Variable = 0.46096

Maximum Likelihood Estimation for Nonlinear Error Structure
ARMA(1 ,1 ) Autoregressive Moving Average Process

Maximum Number of Iterations = 50
Step Size Search Method = 0
Convergence Criterion = 0
Tolerance = 0.001

Initial Result:
Sum of Squares =      0.043221
Log Likelihood =        77.359
Parameters =          1.4508      0.38381      -3.9377      0.00000      0.00000

Using Quadratic Hill-Climbing Algorithm
Iteration =  1   Step Size =  2.3579  Log Likelihood =        89.926
Parameters =          1.4410      0.38615      -3.8967      0.45558      -0.46020
Iteration = 34   Step Size =  1.0000  Log Likelihood =        93.016
Parameters =          1.1051      0.54833      -2.8796      0.62424      -0.67141

Final Result:
Iterations = 34          Evaluations = 50154
Sum of Squares =      0.019363
Log Likelihood =        93.016
Parameters =          1.1051      0.54833      -2.8796      0.62424      -0.67141
Gradient of Log Likelihood =       0.022545      0.019469      0.0044089    -
0.00020935   0.00015670


               Parameter   Std.Error    t-Ratio
AR(1 )          0.62424     0.22900      2.7259
MA(1 )         -0.67141     0.17318     -3.8770

NOTE: R-Square, AOV are computed from original series.
R-Square = 0.99760       R-Square Adjusted = 0.99747
Standard Error of the Estimate = 0.022282
Log-Likelihood = 93.016
Log Ammemiya Prediction Criterion (APC) =  -7.4538
Log Akaike Information Criterion (AIC) =  -7.4541
Log Schwarz Bayesian Information Criterion (BIC) =  -7.3261

Sum of Squares        SS         DF         MSS         F         Prob>F
```

Explained	8.0216	2	4.0108	7456.8	7.4158E-048
Residual	0.019363	36	0.00053787		
Total	8.0744	38	0.21248		

Variable Name	Estimated Coefficient	Standard Error	t-Ratio 39 DF	Prob >|t|	Partial Regression
L	1.1051	0.16031	6.8934	3.0026E-008	0.54923
K	0.54833	0.083877	6.5373	9.3096E-008	0.52285
CONSTANT	-2.8796	0.54958	-5.2397	5.8625E-006	0.41314

Squared Correlation of Observed and Predicted = 0.99761
Sum of Squared Residuals = 0.019363
Sum of Absolute Residuals = 0.67628
Sum of Residuals = 1.84261E-002
First-Order Rho = -0.0028812
Durbin-Watson Test Statistic = 1.9895

Breusch-Godfrey LM Tests for Autocorrelation

		Chi-Sq	DF	Prob>Chi-Sq
AR(	1)	0.50222	1	0.47852
AR(	2)	0.86082	2	0.65024
AR(	3)	5.3236	3	0.14958
AR(	4)	5.4880	4	0.24079

Autocorrelation and Partial Autocorrelation Functions
ARMA Model Specification
Mean = 0.00047246   Standard Error = 0.022568

Lag	AR	S.E.(AR)	PAR	S.E.(PAR)	Box-Pierce	Ljung-Box
1	-0.0037201	0.16013	-0.0037201	0.16013	0.00053974	0.00058235
2	-0.049522	0.16052	-0.049537	0.16013	0.096186	0.10657
3	-0.23055	0.16880	-0.23150	0.16013	2.1691	2.4674
4	0.064036	0.16942	0.060518	0.16013	2.3290	2.6547
5	0.24181	0.17805	0.23366	0.16013	4.6095	5.4047
6	-0.13491	0.18065	-0.20050	0.16013	5.3193	6.2865
7	0.032581	0.18080	0.086890	0.16013	5.3607	6.3396
8	-0.26120	0.19023	-0.18931	0.16013	8.0215	9.8587
9	0.18387	0.19474	0.11395	0.16013	9.3400	11.661
10	0.0024843	0.19474	-0.030052	0.16013	9.3403	11.661
11	-0.10407	0.19616	-0.16014	0.16013	9.7627	12.280
12	-0.13637	0.19857	-0.093640	0.16013	10.488	13.381

 If you prefer to use nonlinear least squares instead of maximum likelihood to estimate the ARMA model, just delete line 15 or change it to:

```
_nlopt = 0;
```

The result should be the same. Why?

Summarizing, the estimated model with ARMA(1,1) error structure is:

$$ln(X) = -2.88 + 1.11\,ln(L) + 0.55\,ln(K) + \varepsilon$$
$$\text{s.e.} \quad (0.55) \quad (0.16) \quad (0.08)$$

$$\varepsilon = 0.62\,\varepsilon_{-1} - 0.67\,\upsilon_{-1}$$
$$\text{s.e.} \quad (0.23) \quad (0.17)$$

Both the parameter estimates of AR(1) and MA(1) are statistically significant and useful for correcting autocorrelation. Based on the Breusch-Godfrey LM test up to the fourth order, as well as the 12-lag autocorrelation function plot and the associated Box-Pierce and Ljung-Box Q test statistics, the estimated ARMA(1,1) model is as good as that of the AR(3) specification presented in the Lesson 10.5. Both models are essentially equivalent.

Nonlinear Maximum Likelihood Estimation

It is clear that a regression model with autocorrelation is intrinsically a nonlinear model. Even with the basic linear regression equation, $\varepsilon = Y - X\beta$, the functional form of model error for estimation is nonlinear in the parameters. Consider the AR(1), MA(1), and ARMA(1,1):

	Residual	Residual Function
AR(1)	$\upsilon_i = \varepsilon_i - \rho\,\varepsilon_{i-1}$	$(Y_i - \rho Y_{i-1}) - (X_i - \rho X_{i-1})\beta$
MA(1)	$\upsilon_i = \varepsilon_i + \theta\,\upsilon_{i-1}$	$(Y_i - X_i\beta) + \theta\,\upsilon_{i-1}$
ARMA(1,1)	$\upsilon_i = \varepsilon_i - \rho\,\varepsilon_{i-1} + \theta\,\upsilon_{i-1}$	$(Y_i - \rho Y_{i-1}) - (X_i - \rho X_{i-1})\beta + \theta\,\upsilon_{i-1}$

The nonlinearity of AR(1) is clearly due to the product of parameters β and ρ, while MA(1) is recursively weighted by θ. ARMA(1,1) is a mixed process of AR(1) and MA(1), and therefore contains both of aforementioned nonlinearities. For model estimation, the beginning observation of data series may be lost if not properly initialized. The built-in ARMA estimation of GPE is conditional upon the simple data initialization with the sample mean. We have seen the Prais-Winsten transformation for the first observation of AR(1): $\sqrt{1-\rho^2}\,Y_1$ and $\sqrt{1-\rho^2}\,X_1$. This adds more nonlinear complexity into the model and makes maximum likelihood the preferred method for estimation.

Given N sample data observations of $Z = [Y,X]$, the concentrated log-likelihood function for the AR(1) model is

$$ll^*(\beta,\rho) = -N/2\,(1+2\pi\text{-}ln(N)) - N/2\,ln(\upsilon'\upsilon) + ln(1\text{-}\rho^2)$$

For MA(1), the recursive process starts with the initial residual υ_0 which is typically set to its expected value (i.e., zero) or the sample mean. An alternative is to estimate υ_0 directly. The concentrated log-likelihood function is simpler but conditional to the initialization of υ_0 as follows:

$$ll^*(\beta,\theta,\upsilon_0) = -N/2\,(1+2\pi\text{-}ln(N)) - N/2\,ln(\upsilon'\upsilon)$$

The concentrated log-likelihood function of the mixed process ARMA(1,1) is similar to that of AR(1) in which the residual function depends on both ρ and θ (in addition to β) and is subject to the initialization of υ_0 and transformation for the first data observation.

Lesson 10.7: Nonlinear ARMA Model Estimation

We continue with the previous example of U.S. Cobb-Douglas production function and estimate the three autoregressive error structures: AR(1), MA(1), and ARMA(1,1). Using the method of nonlinear maximum likelihood, the regression parameter β and autoregressive coefficients ρ and/or θ are estimated jointly. For MA(1) and ARMA(1,1), the initialization of residuals with zero expected value is applied. As we have mentioned earlier, the nonlinear method may produce different results compared with the linear iterative approximations as employed in the Cochrane-Orcutt approach (Lesson 10.3) or the GPE built-in method of conditional nonlinear maximum likelihood (Lesson 10.6). However, the results are not drastically different.

This lesson differs from the previous ones in that the program setup is for nonlinear maximum likelihood estimation. Nonlinear maximum likelihood was covered in Chapter VII, and it is helpful to go back for a thorough review of the estimation technique.

For each of three autoregressive models, the residual function must be defined in order to maximize the objective log-likelihood function. The block from line 34 to line 41 defines the residual function for an AR(1) model. The MA(1) specification is given in lines 42 through 48, while the ARMA(1,1) is specified from line 49 to line 57. Notice that AR(1) and ARMA(1,1) require the use of Jacobians in the likelihood function. The Jacobian function is defined in the block from line 29 to line 33.

```
        /*
        ** Lesson 10.7: Maximum Likelihood Estimation
        ** AR(1), MA(1), ARMA(1,1)
        */
1       use gpe2;
2       output file = gpe\output10.7 reset;
3       load data[40,6]= gpe\cjx.txt;

4       year = data[2:40,1];
5       X = ln(data[2:40,2]);
6       L = ln(data[2:40,3]);
7       K = ln(data[2:40,5]);
8       data=X~L~K;

        @ OLS estimates as initial values @
9       b=data[.,1]/(ones(rows(data),1)~data[.,2:3]);

10      call reset;
11      _nlopt=1;
12      _method=0;
13      _iter=100;
14      _conv=1;

15      _b=b|0.5;
16      _jacob=&jcb;
17      _names = {"CONSTANT","LN(L)","LN(K)","AR(1)"};
18      call estimate(&ar,data);

19      _b=b|0;
20      _jacob=0;
21      _names = {"CONSTANT","LN(L)","LN(K)","MA(1)"};
22      call estimate(&ma,data);

23      _b=b|0.5|0;
24      _jacob=&jcb;
25      _names = {"CONSTANT","LN(L)","LN(K)","AR(1)","MA(1)"};
26      call estimate(&arma,data);

27      end;

28      proc jcb(x,b);   @ jacobian for AR(1) and ARMA(1,1) @
29          local j;
30          j=ones(rows(x),1);
31          j[1]=sqrt(1-b[4]^2);
32          retp(j);
33      endp;

34      proc ar(x,b);
```

```
35 |     local n,e,u;
36 |     n=rows(x);
37 |     e=x[.,1]-b[1]-b[2]*x[.,2]-b[3]*x[.,3];
38 |     u=e-b[4]*lagn(e,1);
   |     @ first obs transformation @
39 |     u[1]=sqrt(1-b[4]^2)*e[1];
40 |     retp(u);
41 | endp;

42 | proc ma(x,b);
43 |     local n,e,u;
44 |     n=rows(x);
45 |     e=x[.,1]-b[1]-b[2]*x[.,2]-b[3]*x[.,3];
46 |     u=recserar(e,e[1],b[4]); @ u[1]=e[1] since u[0]=0 @
   | /*
   |     @ recursive computation of errors using @
   |     @ built-in RECSERAR is the same as below: @
   |     u=e;      @ initialize: u[1]=e[1] @
   |     i=2;
   |     do until i>n;
   |         u[i]=e[i]+b[4]*u[i-1];
   |         i=i+1;
   |     endo;
   | */
47 |     retp(u);
48 | endp;

49 | proc arma(x,b);
50 |     local n,e,u,v;
51 |     n=rows(x);
52 |     e-x[.,1]-b[1]-b[2]*x[.,2]-b[3]*x[.,3];
53 |     u=e-b[4]*lagn(e,1);
   |     @ first obs transformation @
54 |     u[1]=sqrt(1-b[4]^2)*e[1];
55 |     v=recserar(u,u[1],b[5]);
56 |     retp(v);
57 | endp;
```

Using the linear least squares estimates as initial values of parameters (line 9), lines 15-18 carry out the estimation for the AR(1) model. Here is the result:

```
Maximum Likelihood Estimation
-----------------------------
Number of Observations = 39
Number of Parameters = 4

Maximum Number of Iterations = 100
Step Size Search Method = 0
Convergence Criterion = 1
Tolerance = 0.001

Initial Result:
Sum of Squares =      0.029940
Log Likelihood =        84.518
Parameters =      -3.9377       1.4508       0.38381       0.50000

Using Berndt-Hall-Hall-Hausman (BHHH) Algorithm

Final Result:
Iterations = 17          Evaluations = 4914
Sum of Squares =      0.027133
Log Likelihood =        86.438
Gradient of Log Likelihood = 4.9312e-005   0.00023054   0.00020964   2.6217e-
005
                              Asymptotic
```

```
                Parameter    Std. Error      t-Ratio
CONSTANT         -2.8220        0.56933       -4.9567
LN(L)             1.0926        0.17753        6.1546
LN(K)             0.54995       0.096866       5.6775
AR(1)             0.77832       0.13059        5.9599
```

The BHHH method is used for log-likelihood function maximization (see line 12), and it converges in 17 iterations. As seen in line 15, the initial value of the AR(1) coefficient is set to 0.5. The solution is close to that of the Cochrane-Orcutt (Lesson 10.3) and Hildreth-Lu (Lesson 10.4) procedures. The crucial point of this model is the use of first observation transformation (line 39) and the resulting Jacobian function must be incorporated for the *exact* maximum likelihood estimation.

Similarly, the MA(1) model is estimated in lines 19-22 with the starting value of the MA(1) coefficient at 0. Here is the estimation result:

```
Maximum Likelihood Estimation
-----------------------------
Number of Observations = 39
Number of Parameters = 4

Maximum Number of Iterations = 100
Step Size Search Method = 0
Convergence Criterion = 1
Tolerance = 0.001

Initial Result:
Sum of Squares =      0.043382
Log Likelihood =        77.286
Parameters =       -3.9377       1.4508      0.38381      0.00000

Using Berndt-Hall-Hall-Hausman (BHHH) Algorithm

Final Result:
Iterations = 29             Evaluations = 8073
Sum of Squares =      0.022342
Log Likelihood =        90.226
Gradient of Log Likelihood =  -0.00016182  -0.00094511  -0.00082061  4.1086e-
005

                          Asymptotic
                Parameter    Std. Error      t-Ratio
CONSTANT         -3.6176        0.27477      -13.166
LN(L)             1.3379        0.094876      14.102
LN(K)             0.44264       0.054316       8.1495
MA(1)            -0.81620       0.095539      -8.5431
```

As the MA(1) model does not use the first-observation transformation of AR(1), the Jacobian function should not be called (see line 20). The residual function is defined with an autoregressive recursive series using the GAUSS built-in function recserar (line 46). The initialization of the recursive series is the expected value of the series, which is zero. Line 46 shows the use of recserar with initialization. Check the GAUSS manual or online help for more information about the procedure recserar. The computation of autoregressive recursive series is also explained in the comment block immediately below line 46.

 Conditional to the initialization of the recursive moving average series

$$\upsilon_i = (Y_i - X_i\beta) + \theta \upsilon_{i-1}$$

we have obtained the maximum likelihood estimates of β and θ as shown above. For $i = 1$, $\upsilon_0 = 0$ is assumed. The alternative is to estimate υ_0 together with β and θ. Simply replace line 46 with the following:

```
u=recserar(e,e[1]+b[5]*b[4],b[4]);
```

where `b[5]` is the unknown υ_0 to be estimated with the rest of the parameters. Starting from the initial guess of (θ, υ_0) at $(0,0)$, in addition to the linear least squares estimator of β, the model is estimated exactly the same way as before except that line 19 should be:

```
_b=b|0|0;
```

How do the estimation results differ from those of Lesson 10.7, which assumed $\upsilon_0 = 0$? We leave this question to you.

For ARMA(1,1), both the first observation transformation of AR(1) and the autoregressive recursive series with initialization of MA(1) are required. The model is estimated in lines 23-26. Here is the estimation result:

```
Maximum Likelihood Estimation
-----------------------------
Number of Observations = 39
Number of Parameters = 5

Maximum Number of Iterations = 100
Step Size Search Method = 0
Convergence Criterion = 1
Tolerance = 0.001

Initial Result:
Sum of Squares =       0.029940
Log Likelihood =         84.518
Parameters =         -3.9377        1.4508        0.38381        0.50000        0.00000

Using Berndt-Hall-Hall-Hausman (BHHH) Algorithm

Final Result:
Iterations = 21            Evaluations = 7059
Sum of Squares =       0.018525
Log Likelihood =         93.879
Gradient  of  Log  Likelihood  =      -0.00012631      -0.00065739      -0.00055447
0.00015394 -1.6021e-006
                                    Asymptotic
                   Parameter    Std. Error      t-Ratio
CONSTANT            -2.6041       0.42941       -6.0644
LN(L)                1.0321       0.12537        8.2320
LN(K)                0.57271      0.071019       8.0641
AR(1)                0.66145      0.14519        4.5559
MA(1)               -0.71077      0.12402       -5.7309
```

Again, for estimating the above ARMA(1,1) model:

$$\upsilon_i = (Y_i - \rho Y_{i-1}) - (X_i - \rho X_{i-1})\beta + \theta \upsilon_{i-1}$$

$\upsilon_0 = 0$ is assumed for $i = 1$. The alternative is to estimate υ_0 together with β, ρ, and θ. Simply replace line 55 with the following:

```
v=recserar(u,u[1]+b[6]*b[5],b[5]);
```

where `b[6]` is the unknown υ_0 to be estimated with the rest of the parameters. Starting from the initial guess of (ρ,θ,υ_0) at $(0.5,0,0)$, in addition to the linear least squares estimator of β, the model is estimated exactly the same way as before except that line 23 should be changed to:

```
_b=b|0.5|0|0;
```

To summarize the discussion of autoregressive regression models, we put together and compare the estimation results of the U.S. Cobb-Douglas production function:

$$ln(X) = \beta_0 + \beta_1\, ln(L) + \beta_2\, ln(K) + \varepsilon$$

where X is output, and the two factor inputs are labor L and capital K. The following table presents the parameter estimates (numbers in parentheses are the estimated standard errors of the parameters) and the corresponding log-likelihood function value *ll* for each model.

	(1) Lesson 10.1	(2) Lesson 10.3	(3) Lesson 10.4	(4) Lesson 10.7	(5) Lesson 10.7	(6) Lesson 10.7	(7) Lesson 10.6
β_1	1.451 (0.083)	1.068 (0.151)	1.050 (0.153)	1.093 (0.178)	1.338 (0.095)	1.032 (0.125)	1.105 (0.160)
β_2	0.384 (0.048)	0.558 (0.096)	0.563 (0.098)	0.550 (0.097)	0.443 (0.054)	0.573 (0.071)	0.548 (0.084)
β_0	-3.94 (0.237)	-2.73 (0.456)	-2.66 (0.465)	-2.82 (0.569)	-3.62 (0.275)	-2.60 (0.429)	-2.88 (0.550)
ρ	0	0.805 (0.096)	0.826 (0.090)	0.778 (0.131)	0	0.661 (0.145)	0.624 (0.229)
θ	0	0	0	0	-0.816 (0.096)	-0.711 (0.124)	-0.671 (0.173)
ll	77.286	86.420	86.379	86.438	90.226	93.879	93.016

The top row of the table identifies the model and its corresponding lesson: (1) Lesson 10.1 is the ordinary least squares estimates without autocorrelation correction; (2) Lesson 10.3 is the AR(1) model using the Cochrane-Orcutt iterative procedure; (3) Lesson 10.4 is the same AR(1) model using Hildreth-Lu grid search method; (4), (5), and (6) are based on Lesson 10.7, using nonlinear maximum likelihood estimation for the model AR(1), MA(1), and ARMA(1,1), respectively. The last column (7) is the ARMA(1,1) model estimated with the GPE built-in conditional maximum likelihood method in Lesson 10.6. All the methods use the entire sample of 39 observations from 1929 to 1967. For model comparison, the statistics of pair-wise Likelihood Ratio will be useful. It is immediately clear that the model must be corrected for autocorrelation. The plain OLS model (1) is rejected based on LR tests with all the other models. Finally, the structure of the autoregressive moving average ARMA(1,1) of both Lessons 10.6 and 10.7 cannot be rejected.

XI
Distributed Lag Models

With the proper use of distributed lags, regression models can be expanded to include dynamic features such as long-run and short-run elasticities and multipliers for analysis. In this chapter we will consider two popular setups of distributed lags: geometric, or Koyck lags, and polynomial, or Almon lags. The former is an infinite distributed lags model with a geometric declining pattern, which in turn can be transformed into a lagged dependent variable model. The latter is a finite distributed lags model with polynomial functional restrictions. The combination of the two is the so-called autoregressive distributed lag (ARDL) model.

Lagged Dependent Variable Models

Applications of lagged dependent variable models include partial adjustment and adaptive expectation estimations. These models relate the long-run and short-run behavior of influential variables. However, regression models with lagged dependent variables may possess some undesirable characteristics. Possible problems include correlated error terms and random regressors. The resulting least squares estimation is biased, inconsistent, and inefficient. The lagged dependent variable model is considered in Lesson 11.1.

For estimating such a model with lagged dependent variables, instrumental variable (IV) estimation is suggested. IV weighs the trade-off between "biasedness" and "inefficiency" and obtains a "consistent" parameter estimator which minimizes the ill effects of using lagged dependent variables. Instrumental variable estimation for a lagged dependent variable model is the focus of Lesson 11.2.

Lesson 11.1: Testing for Autocorrelation with Lagged Dependent Variable

A classical consumption-income relationship based on the Permanent Income Hypothesis is a good example to demonstrate the construction, testing, and estimation of the lagged dependent variable model:

$$C = \beta_0 + \beta_1 Y + \beta_2 C_{-1} + \varepsilon$$

where C is consumption and Y is income. Assuming a simple partial adjustment of short-run consumption towards its long-run equilibrium, the lagged dependent variable C_{-1} is included in the model specification.

To estimate the above consumption-income equation, we introduce a new data file **usyc87.txt**. This data file consists of three variables: YEAR, Y, and C. YEAR is just the time indicator ranging from 1929 to1994. Y is personal disposable income, and C is personal consumption expenditure. Both income and consumption time series are expressed in billions of 1987 dollars. In total there are 66 observations.

In this lesson we will estimate a lagged dependent variable model. The only new input control variable is _dlags, which is used to specify the number of lags desired. For example, by setting _dlags = 1, GPE inserts the first lag of the dependent variable into the regression equation for least squares estimation. The lagged dependent variable is added in front of the other explanatory variables. The Durbin-H test statistic is automatically included in the output of _rstat when _dlags is set to a value greater than zero.

```
/*
** Lesson 11.1: Lagged Dependent Variable Model
** Estimation and Testing for Autocorrelation
*/
1   use gpe2;
2   output file = gpe\output11.1 reset;
3   load z[67,3] = gpe\usyc87.txt;
4   y = z[2:67,2];
5   c = z[2:67,3];

6   call reset;
7   _names = {"c","y"};
8   _rstat = 1;
9   _dlags = 1;
10  call estimate(c,y);

11  _ar = 1;
12  _iter = 50;
13  call estimate(c,y);
14  end;
```

 If more than one lag is needed, just change the value of _dlags to the desired positive number of lags.

To estimate the model is simple, but to evaluate and interpret the effect of a lagged dependent variables is not. Line 9 specifies that the model to be estimated includes the first lag of the dependent variable. The following call to estimate (line 10) proceeds to carry out least squares estimation of the model. Since _rstat is set to 1 in line 8, a summary of residual statistics including the new Durbin-H test statistic is presented.

 Alternatively, you can create the lagged dependent variable and then include it in estimate as an independent variable. In GAUSS, the lagged variable is constructed with the command lag1 or lagn. This method requires the extra step of handling the initial observation lost from lagging the dependent variable explicitly so that the program will run. Setting the GPE control variable _begin to the beginning of the usable sample for estimation may be necessary. In addition, GPE will not treat the variable you created differently from the rest of the explanatory variables. Therefore, the Durbin-H test statistic, unique to the lagged dependent variable model, is not computed. In passing, we note that testing linear restrictions involving lagged dependent variables requires specifying restrictions on those variables explicitly.

The result of the first least squares estimation (line 10) is given below:

Least Squares Estimation

Dependent Variable = C

```
Estimation Range =  2          66
Number of Observations = 65
Mean of Dependent Variable = 1588.2
Standard Error of Dependent Variable = 955.14

NOTE: Estimation Range Has Been Adjusted.
Lagged Dependent Variables Used = 1

R-Square = 0.99927      R-Square Adjusted = 0.99925
Standard Error of the Estimate = 26.154
Log-Likelihood Function Value = -302.86
Log Ammemiya Prediction Criterion (APC) =  6.5731
Log Akaike Information Criterion (AIC) =  6.5731
Log Schwarz Bayesian Information Criterion (BIC) =  6.6734
```

Sum of Squares	SS	DF	MSS	F	Prob>F
Explained	5.8344E+007	2	2.9172E+007	42648.	4.9624E-098
Residual	42410.	62	684.03		
Total	5.8387E+007	64	9.1229E+005		

Variable Name	Estimated Coefficient	Standard Error	t-Ratio 62 DF	Prob >|t|	Partial Regression
C-1	0.69465	0.057390	12.104	5.6098E-018	0.70265
Y	0.29660	0.051205	5.7925	2.4894E-007	0.35114
CONSTANT	-0.56350	6.4092	-0.087920	0.93022	0.00012466

```
Squared Correlation of Observed and Predicted = 0.99927
Sum of Squared Residuals = 42410.
Sum of Absolute Residuals = 1274.2
Sum of Residuals = -1.12485E-008
First-Order Rho = 0.45221
Durbin-Watson Test Statistic = 1.0769
Durbin-H Statistic = 4.1974
```

Notice that the estimation range given in the first block of the output is from 2 to 66, using 65 observations. This is because of the use of the first lag of the dependent variable on the right-hand side of the regression equation. Next is a statement giving the number of lags included in the estimation.

The last line of the first block of output is the Durbin-H statistic. Given the first-order Rho at 0.45 with the Durbin-H test statistic as high as 4.2 (comparing with the critical values of a standardized normal distribution), the problem of autocorrelation is readily apparent. Methods of correction for autocorrelation discussed in the previous chapter should be used to improve the results of the model estimation.

Lines 11 to 13 of the program correct and then re-estimate the model with a first-order autocorrelated error structure. The default Cochrane-Orcutt iterative method is used. We refer the reader to the output file output11.1 for details of the regression results. In summary, here is our estimated lagged dependent variable model with AR(1) error structure:

$$C \quad = \quad -6.284 \quad + \quad 0.487\,Y \quad + \quad 0.484\,C_{-1} \quad + \quad \varepsilon$$
$$\text{s.e.} \qquad (14.61) \qquad\quad (0.065) \qquad\quad (0.073)$$

$$\varepsilon \quad = \quad 0.648\,\varepsilon_{-1}$$
$$\text{s.e.} \qquad (0.098)$$

The correction for first-order autocorrelation is certainly a right step to improve the model. It may not be a bad idea to continue to carry out testing for higher orders of autocorrelation. Remember to use the following statements before the last call of estimate in the above program:

```
_bgtest = 4;
_acf = 12;
```

With the results not shown here, we did not find a significant autocorrelation problem at higher orders.

Lesson 11.2: Instrumental Variable Estimation

The more serious specification problem related to the lagged dependent variable model is random regressors. In Lesson 11.1, although the problem of autocorrelation seems easy to resolve by correcting the first-order serial correlation, the estimated parameters are still biased and inefficient. These problems are due to the ill effects of random regressors that may be involved through the use of lagged dependent variables.

To handle a lagged dependent variable model estimation with instrumental variables, GPE implements an estimation technique which uses the current and lagged explanatory variables as instruments for the lagged dependent variable. If longer lags of the dependent variable are adopted or an autocorrelated error structure is identified, the instrumental variable estimation procedure may need to include more lags of the explanatory variables as well. In the context of a lagged dependent variable model, instrumental variable estimation is activated by setting the following input control variable:

```
_ivar = 1;
```

The alternative is to specify the entire data matrix for the variable _ivar. This is useful for applying instrumental variable estimation in other contexts such as measurement error in the regression model. We note that the matrix specification of _ivar requires that its size (rows and columns) to be at least as large as that of the data matrix of explanatory variables.

We now continue on from the end of Lesson 11.1, adding the option to estimate the model using instrumental variables in the following program:

```
/*
** Lesson 11.2: Lagged Dependent Variable Model
** Instrumental Variable Estimation
*/
1   use gpe2;
2   output file=gpe\output11.2 reset;

3   load z[67,3]=gpe\usyc87.txt;
4   y=z[2:67,2];
5   c=z[2:67,3];

6   call reset;
7   _names={"c","y"};
8   _rstat=1;
9   _dlags=1;
10  _ar=1;
11  _iter=50;
12  call estimate(c,y);
```

```
13 | _ivar=1;
14 | call estimate(c,y);
15 | end;
```

The only new addition to the program is line 13:

```
_ivar = 1;
```

which calls for the use of internal instrumental variables that GPE will construct for the lagged dependent variables. In addition, the autocorrelation correction is requested for the first order (line 10), hence one additional lag of explanatory variables is needed as part of the instrumental variables.

Alternatively, line 13 can be replaced with the explicitly defined instrumental variables as follows:

```
_ivar = y~lagn(y,1)~lagn(y,2)~ones(rows(y),1);
_begin = 3;
```

The advantage is that you have more control over the addition of relevant instrumental variables in order to improve the small-sample properties of the estimator. In contexts other than the lagged dependent variable model, instrumental variable estimation may be requested with the variable _ivar explicitly assigned to a data matrix no smaller than that of explanatory variables.

We note that the scalar definition of _ivar = 1 will only work when specifying a positive number of _dlags. _ivar = 1 without _dlags (or _dlags = 0) will result in a program error.

Looking at the output file output11.2, the results of the first regression in this lesson are the same as the results of the second regression of Lesson 11.1. The second estimation of this lesson performs instrumental variable estimation while at the same time correcting for first-order serial correlation. We will show you only a partial result of the second regression estimation:

```
Least Squares Estimation
------------------------
Dependent Variable = C
Estimation Range =   3        66
Number of Observations = 64
Mean of Dependent Variable = 1604.9
Standard Error of Dependent Variable = 953.09

NOTE: Estimation Range Has Been Adjusted.
NOTE: Lagged Dependent Variables Used = 1
NOTE: Instrumental Variables Used = 4

Order of Autoregressive Errors = 1
Maximum Number of Iterations = 50
Convergence Tolerance Level = 0.00100

Using Cochrane-Orcutt Iterative Least Squares Algorithm
Iteration =  0    Sum of Squares =   50104.92594 Log Likelihood = -304.02779
       Rho =        0.00000
Iteration =  1    Sum of Squares =   31093.47963 Log Likelihood = -289.01518
       Rho =        0.63232
...
Iteration =  8    Sum of Squares =   31055.04449 Log Likelihood = -289.01591
```

```
    Rho =        0.66806

        Rho     Std.Error     t-Ratio
    0.66806     0.097245       6.8699

NOTE: R-Square, AOV are computed from original series.

R-Square = 0.99946      R-Square Adjusted = 0.99944
Standard Error of the Estimate = 22.563
Log-Likelihood = -289.02
Log Ammemiya Prediction Criterion (APC) =  6.2785
Log Akaike Information Criterion (AIC) =  6.2784
Log Schwarz Bayesian Information Criterion (BIC) =  6.3796
```

Sum of Squares	SS	DF	MSS	F	Prob>F
Explained	5.7131E+007	2	2.8566E+007	56110.	2.6192E-100
Residual	31055.	61	509.10		
Total	5.7228E+007	63	9.0838E+005		

Variable Name	Estimated Coefficient	Standard Error	t-Ratio 61 DF	Prob >|t|	Partial Regression
C-1	0.45966	0.094109	4.8843	7.8449E-006	0.28114
Y	0.50728	0.084052	6.0353	1.0194E-007	0.37388
CONSTANT	-3.8035	16.185	-0.23501	0.81499	0.00090457

```
Squared Correlation of Observed and Predicted = 0.99946
Sum of Squared Residuals = 31055.
Sum of Absolute Residuals = 1040.2
Sum of Residuals = -1.67559E+001
First-Order Rho = 0.20383
Durbin-Watson Test Statistic = 1.5864
Durbin-H Statistic = 2.5137
```

 Because instrumental variables are used essentially to replace lagged dependent variables in the model estimation, testing and correction for autocorrelation is now the same as in the classical model. The Durbin-Watson test statistic can be applied as usual.

The model uses four instrumental variables: the original, the first and second lags of the explanatory independent variable Y, and the constant term. The second lag is included due to the first-order serial correlation being specified for model estimation.

Comparing the estimation results obtained when instrumental variables are not used,

$$C = -6.284 + 0.487\,Y + 0.484\,C_{-1} + \varepsilon$$
$$\text{s.e.} \quad (14.61) \quad (0.065) \quad (0.073)$$

$$\varepsilon = 0.648\,\varepsilon_{-1}$$
$$\text{s.e.} \quad (0.098)$$

with our estimated model using instrumental variables,

$$C = -3.804 + 0.507\,Y + 0.460\,C_{-1} + \varepsilon$$
$$\text{s.e.} \quad (16.185) \quad (0.084) \quad (0.094)$$

$$\varepsilon = 0.668\,\varepsilon_{-1}$$
$$\text{s.e.} \quad (0.097)$$

172

we see that their parameter estimates are similar. But the current estimated standard errors of the parameters are slightly larger than the standard errors resulting from not using the instrumental variables. Nevertheless, the conclusions of statistical inferences are not affected in this example.

We will keep the interpretation of the estimated model using instrumental variables brief. First, the short-run marginal propensity to consume is 0.51. With the estimated coefficient 0.46 for the lagged dependent variable, the long-run consumption change is about 0.94 for each dollar increase of income. To realize 50% of the total effect (that is, half of 0.94 or 0.47) will take 0.89 years. This is the concept of median lag frequently used in dynamic analysis. The other measurement is the lag-weighted average or the mean lag, which is computed at about 0.85 years.

 Remember the formula for computing the median lag and mean lag? Let λ be the estimated parameter of the lagged dependent variable. Then the median lag is computed as $\frac{ln(0.5)}{ln(\lambda)}$, and the mean lag is $\frac{\lambda}{1-\lambda}$.

Polynomial Lag Models

By imposing polynomial functional restrictions on the finite distributed lags of some or all explanatory variables, the dynamic model can be estimated with traditional restricted least squares methodology. In this model we specify the polynomial distributed lag structure for each explanatory variable. Given the number of distributed lags q, a polynomial function of order p is used to describe p-1 number of turning points in the lag structure. In addition, we can add end-point restrictions to "tie down" the effects of distributed lags at either or both ends. For a polynomial lag model to be meaningful, p must be greater than 1, and the total number of lags (q) must be greater than the polynomial orders (p). If q equals p, the distributed lag model is without polynomial restrictions.

In GPE, a polynomial lag model is defined with the input control variable _pdl. The variable _pdl is a 3-column matrix with the number of the rows corresponding to the number of explanatory variables. A polynomial lag structure must be defined for each variable (row) in the _pdl matrix. The 3-column entry for each explanatory variable must be separately called out for the lags q, polynomial orders p, and end-point restrictions r in that order. End-point restrictions "tie down" one or both ends of the polynomial's curve, enforcing a theoretical or empirical justification of the lag structure. For variables that do not have the polynomial lag structure, the 3-column entry 0 0 0 should be used. Normally the constant term is not included in the _pdl matrix, unless otherwise specified.

Estimating a model with a polynomial lag structure defined for each explanatory variable is essentially the same as restricted least squares. The number of restrictions is (q-p) polynomial restrictions plus the number of end-point restrictions. Any additional linear restrictions imposed with the variable _restr must take into account the correct structure of right-hand side variables that _pdl may add to the original equation.

Lesson 11.3: Almon Lag Model Revisited

In this lesson, we will revisit the relationship between appropriations (CAPP) and capital expenditure (CEXP) first introduced in Lesson 4.1. The data file **almon.txt** provides quarterly data series containing the values of CEXP and CAPP in the period from 1953 to 1967. In the following, we try to duplicate the original study of S. Almon published in 1965. Almon's regressions were computed using a fourth-order polynomial and lags extending in seven periods. She also included seasonal dummy variables whose four coefficients were constrained to sum to zero. Also, both end-points are restricted on the polynomial lags.

Here is the program:

```
    /*
    ** Lesson 11.3: Polynomial Distributed Lag Model
    ** Almon Lag Model Revisited
    */
1   use gpe2;
2   output file = gpe\output11.3 reset;
3   load almon[61,3] = gpe\almon.txt;

4   cexp = almon[2:61,2];
5   capp = almon[2:61,3];
6   qt = almon[2:61,1];

7   q1=(qt%10).==1;   @ quarterly seasonal dummies @
8   q2=(qt%10).==2;
9   q3=(qt%10).==3;
10  q4=(qt%10).==4;

11  call reset;
12  _rstat = 1;
13  _end = 36;

    /* restrictions on all dummy variables */
14  _const = 0;
15  _restr = {0 0 0 0 0 0 0 0 1 1 1 1 0};
16  _pdl = {7 4 2,
17           0 0 0,
18           0 0 0,
19           0 0 0,
20           0 0 0};
21  _names={"cexp","capp","q1","q2","q3","q4"};
22  call estimate(cexp,capp~q1~q2~q3~q4);
23  end;
```

In her original discussion, Almon used only 36 observations, therefore we end our estimation at 36 (line 13). As you will remember, suppressing the constant term (line 14) is necessary to avoid the dummy variable trap when using all four seasonal dummy variables. The reason for not dropping one dummy variable is so that we can impose a linear restriction, summing the coefficients of these four dummy variables to zero (line 15). Lines 16 through 20 define the polynomial lag structures with _pdl. Each row of _pdl controls a different explanatory variable and rows are separated by commas. Remember that carriage returns are not "seen" by GAUSS. Three columns of _pdl specify the following: q = lags, p = orders, and r = end-point restrictions, respectively. There are four possible settings for end-point restrictions: -1 (beginning), 1 (ending), 2 (both), or 0 (no restriction). The first row of _pdl in line 16 assigns 7 lags, to the fourth order, with both endpoints restricted to the variable CAPP. The four dummy variables are not affected since each entry is set to 0 in lines 17 through 20.

Run the program to see how _pdl works.[9]

```
Least Squares Estimation
------------------------
Dependent Variable = CEXP
Estimation Range =   8          36
Number of Observations = 29
Mean of Dependent Variable = 2568.3
Standard Error of Dependent Variable = 468.69

NOTE: Estimation Range Has Been Adjusted.
Distributed Lags Variables Used = 7

WARNING: Constant Term Suppressed.
R-Square, AOV, SE, and t may not be reliable!

WARNING: Linear Restrictions Imposed.
R-Square, AOV, SE, and t may not be reliable!
Wald F-Test for Linear Restrictions
F(   6,  17)        Prob>F
        1.1338      0.38486

R-Square = 0.91023      R-Square Adjusted = 0.88681
Standard Error of the Estimate = 154.94
Log-Likelihood Function Value = -184.04
Log Ammemiya Prediction Criterion (APC) =   10.432
Log Akaike Information Criterion (AIC) =   10.682
Log Schwarz Bayesian Information Criterion (BIC) =   11.248
```

Sum of Squares	SS	DF	MSS	F	Prob>F
Explained	6.5671E+006	6	1.0945E+006	45.590	1.2384E-011
Residual	5.5218E+005	23	24008.		
Total	6.1508E+006	29	2.1210E+005		

Variable Name	Estimated Coefficient	Standard Error	t-Ratio 23 DF	Prob >|t|	Partial Regression
CAPP	0.086812	0.020858	4.1620	0.00037595	0.42960
CAPP-1	0.12315	0.014384	8.5619	1.3128E-008	0.76118
CAPP-2	0.13424	0.011553	11.620	4.1900E-011	0.85445
CAPP-3	0.13671	0.020442	6.6879	8.0157E-007	0.66041
CAPP-4	0.13859	0.020447	6.7778	6.5118E-007	0.66637
CAPP-5	0.13931	0.011649	11.959	2.3667E-011	0.86146
CAPP-6	0.12972	0.014578	8.8986	6.5882E-009	0.77492
CAPP-7	0.092066	0.020974	4.3894	0.00021327	0.45584
Q1	-13.302	50.453	-0.26365	0.79440	0.0030131
Q2	-7.0170	50.455	-0.13907	0.89060	0.00084023
Q3	-7.6275	50.450	-0.15119	0.88114	0.00099286
Q4	27.946	48.255	0.57915	0.56812	0.014373

```
Squared Correlation of Observed and Predicted = 0.91622
Sum of Squared Residuals = 5.5218E+005
Sum of Absolute Residuals = 3437.7
Sum of Residuals = 1.88769E+002
First-Order Rho = 0.78062
Durbin-Watson Test Statistic = 0.43219
```

In the output, seven lags of CAPP are estimated with the adjusted sample size. Look at the results of hypothesis testing for linear restrictions. Although we have explicitly

---

[9] As pointed out by Greene (1997, Chapter 17), it was not possible to reproduce Almon's original results. Our regression results match with Greene's results.

defined only one restriction to sum all the seasonal effects across four quarters to zero, there are six restrictions. How are the other five restrictions entering the model? Remember the 7 lags and 4 orders of the polynomial lag structure for the variable CAPP? Equivalently, there are 3 restrictions (that is, 7-4). On top of them, there were two end-point restrictions. The computed Wald F-test statistic of 1.13 (with P-value 0.38) suggests these 6 linear restrictions cannot be jointly rejected. We notice the insignificant seasonal effect for all four quarters. The model may be re-estimated without quarterly dummy variables but with a constant.

 Of course, there are problems of model misspecification. As you can see from the Durbin-Watson statistic, autocorrelation is a serious problem that was not addressed in the original Almon study. We leave for an exercise the challenge of refining this model further.

Autoregressive Distributed Lag Models

A polynomial (finite) lag structure may be combined with geometric (infinite) lag to form an ARDL (autoregressive distributed lag) model. The result is a powerful dynamic specification which captures the essences of two types of distributed lag models. The benefit is a better fit of the model with improved (or "whiter") error structure. The cost is the potential problem of random regressors and multicollinearity. Autocorrelation must be evaluated and tested with the presence of lagged dependent variables. By including more lags of the dependent variable, the estimated model is assured of being free of misspecification. Further, the model should be checked for dynamic stability.

To implement an ARDL model using GPE, we need to specify _pdl for the appropriate polynomial lag structure (restricted or unrestricted) of the explanatory variables and _dlags for the number of lags of dependent variable. Additional parameter restrictions may be imposed on these lag variables as well. We have seen the input control variables _pdl and _dlags used separately in previous lessons. For specifying an ARDL model, both _pdl and _dlags are required.

Lesson 11.4: Almon Lag Model Once More

As an example of ARDL model, we will improve upon the Almon Lag Model of Lesson 11.3 by including lags of the dependent variables. First, we need to fix up a few issues from the regression output of Lesson 11.3. The quarterly seasonality is not statistically significant, and the parameter restriction on the seasonal dummy variables is not necessary. We eliminate four quarterly seasonal dummy variables, and in their place insert a constant term (constant is included in the regression by default). In the program **lesson11.4**, line 14, we keep the same polynomial lag structure for the single explanatory variable. That is, we include seven lags with fourth-order polynomials, and with end-point restrictions on both sides. Because quarterly dummy variables are deleted from the model, _pdl consists of only one row (for the explanatory variable). Now we will deal with the autocorrelation problem associated with the polynomial lag model of Lesson 11.3. By adding lags of the dependent variable in the regression equation, serial dependence of the model errors may be reduced. Through trial and error, and testing for no serial correlation, we decide on two augmenting lags of the dependent variable.[10] Line 15 of **lesson11.4** does exactly that.

```
    /*
    ** Lesson 11.4: Autoregressive Distributed Lag Model
    ** Almon Lag Model Once More
    */
 1  use gpe2;
 2  output file = gpe\output11.4 reset;
 3  load almon[61,3] = gpe\almon.txt;

 4  cexp = almon[2:61,2];
 5  capp = almon[2:61,3];
 6  qt = almon[2:61,1];

 7  q1=(qt%10).==1;    @ quarterly seasonal dummies @
 8  q2=(qt%10).==2;
 9  q3=(qt%10).==3;
10  q4=(qt%10).==4;

11  call reset;
12  _rstat = 1;
13  _end = 36;

14  _pdl = {7 4 2};
15  _dlags = 2;

16  _names={"cexp","capp"};
17  call estimate(cexp,capp);
18  end;
```

Running the program, we have the following:

```
Least Squares Estimation
------------------------
Dependent Variable = CEXP
Estimation Range =  8           36
Number of Observations = 29
Mean of Dependent Variable = 2568.3
Standard Error of Dependent Variable = 468.69

NOTE: Estimation Range Has Been Adjusted.
NOTE: Lagged Dependent Variables Used = 2
NOTE: Distributed Lags Variables Used = 7

WARNING: Linear Restrictions Imposed.
R-Square, AOV, SE, and t may not be reliable!
Wald F-Test for Linear Restrictions
F(  5,  18)       Prob>F
    0.77945       0.57735

R-Square = 0.98015      R-Square Adjusted = 0.97584
Standard Error of the Estimate = 72.850
Log-Likelihood = -162.15
Log Ammemiya Prediction Criterion (APC) =  8.8984
```

---

[10] To correct for autocorrelation, we could continue on the model of Lesson 11.3 and assume that the error structure is AR(1) or even higher-order. Such derivation will result in complicated non-linear restrictions involving lagged variables (dependent and independent). We can view it as a restricted version of ARDL model. For example, assuming AR(1) correlation $\varepsilon = \rho\, \varepsilon_{-1} + u$ for the long-run relation $Y = \alpha + \beta X + \varepsilon$ is the same as assuming the

```
Log Akaike Information Criterion (AIC) =  9.1036
Log Schwarz Bayesian Information Criterion (BIC) =  9.6223
```

Sum of Squares	SS	DF	MSS	F	Prob>F
Explained	6.0288E+006	5	1.2058E+006	227.20	8.8193E-019
Residual	1.2206E+005	23	5307.1		
Total	6.1508E+006	28	2.1967E+005		

Variable Name	Estimated Coefficient	Standard Error	t-Ratio 23 DF	Prob >|t|	Partial Regression
CEXP-1	1.2541	0.16540	7.5824	1.0625E-007	0.71426
CEXP-2	-0.62565	0.16853	-3.7124	0.0011458	0.37469
CAPP	0.033586	0.018926	1.7746	0.089205	0.12043
CAPP-1	0.041515	0.016618	2.4982	0.020075	0.21343
CAPP-2	0.038166	0.012788	2.9845	0.0066274	0.27916
CAPP-3	0.033262	0.017913	1.8568	0.076188	0.13036
CAPP-4	0.031873	0.021607	1.4751	0.15373	0.086433
CAPP-5	0.034417	0.021396	1.6086	0.12135	0.10113
CAPP-6	0.036656	0.021233	1.7263	0.097699	0.11471
CAPP-7	0.029698	0.018826	1.5775	0.12833	0.097636
CONSTANT	228.22	160.09	1.4256	0.16742	0.081186

```
Squared Correlation of Observed and Predicted = 0.98015
Sum of Squared Residuals = 1.2206E+005
Sum of Absolute Residuals = 1480.9
Sum of Residuals = -4.66639E-008
First-Order Rho = -0.085940
Durbin-Watson Test Statistic = 2.0420
Durbin-H Statistic = -0.24902
```

The estimated model is a restricted ARDL model. The restrictions come in the form of the fourth-order (of 7 lags) polynomial and end-point restrictions. There are 5 restrictions because of the polynomial lag structure assumed, and these restrictions are statistically significant based on the Wald F-test. The first two lags of the dependent variable, with coefficients 1.25 and –0.63, are statistically significant. The stability of a dynamic equation hinges on the characteristic equation for the autoregressive part of the model. It is easy to show that the model is stable.[11] By augmenting two lags of the dependent variables, the model is free of autocorrelation as required.

---

short run dynamics $Y = a + b X + c X_{-1} + \rho Y_{-1} + u$ with the non-linear restriction $b = -c/\rho$. In other words, given $\varepsilon = \rho \varepsilon_{-1} + u$, we must have $a = \alpha/(1-\rho)$, $b = \beta$, $c = -\beta\rho$.

[11] Solving the characteristic function $1-1.25z + 0.63z^2 = 0$, $z = 0.9921 \pm 0.7766i$. It is obvious that the solutions are greater than 1 in absolute value. Thus two complex solutions of z lie outside of unit circle.

XII
Generalized Method of Moments

Recall from the study of maximum likelihood estimation that assumptions regarding the underlying probability density or likelihood function of a model structure are rather strong, typically including the assumption that the model error is normally distributed. The alternative to the maximum likelihood approach, known as generalized method of moments (GMM), does away with assumptions regarding the probability density or likelihood function. Instead, GMM estimation begins by specifying a set of identities, or moment functions, involving the model variables and parameters, and then finds the set of parameters that best satisfies those identities according to a quadratic criterion function. As a result, the GMM estimator is consistent. For some ideal cases, it can be shown to be as efficient as a maximum likelihood estimator. In addition to the classical least squares and maximum likelihood methods, GMM serves as an alternative for regression parameter estimation. Even for the purpose of estimating the parameters for a probability distribution of a random variable, GMM is a viable alternative to maximum likelihood estimation.

GMM estimation is nonlinear in nature. In the following, we shall revisit the problem of estimating a probability distribution first seen in Lesson 6.3. Instead of using the maximum likelihood method, GMM is introduced to estimate the parameters of a gamma probability distribution. It is generalized to study a nonlinear regression model of rational expectations as done by Hansen and Singleton (1982), where a set of moment equations or orthogonality conditions are estimated. Finally, the special cases of linear regression models are considered. For linear models, GMM is more general than the least squares estimation. It is analogous to an instrumental variable estimator which accounts for heteroscedasticity and autocorrelation. One of the advantages of GMM estimation is that it is less dependent on the underlying probability density or likelihood function. Classical least squares and maximum likelihood estimation methods are special cases of GMM.

GMM Estimation of Probability Distributions

GMM estimation relies on the specification of a set of identities, known as *moment* functions, involving variables and parameters. A moment function is defined as the expectation of some continuous function m of a random variable X with a parameter vector θ:

$$E[m(X,\theta)] = 0$$

Let's consider a simple example. Suppose X is a random variable for which the population mean is defined as $\theta = E(X)$. Then, $E(X) - \theta = E(X - \theta) = 0$. The moment function is $m(X,\theta) = X - \theta = 0$ so that $E[m(X,\theta)] = 0$. In the now familiar maximum likelihood case, $m(X,\theta) = \partial ll(\theta)/\partial\theta$ and $E[\partial ll(\theta)/\partial\theta] = 0$, where $ll(\theta)$ is the log-likelihood function with unknown parameters θ. Moments are used to describe the characteristics of a distribution, and much of the statistical estimation focuses on the problem of moment functions (or in the case above, orthogonality conditions). In addition, a function of moments is also a moment. A more general class of estimators based on moment functions has been shown to exhibit desirable asymptotic (or large-sample) properties. For empirical estimation, GMM estimators are based on the sample moment functions:

$$m(\theta) = 1/N \sum_{i=1,2,...,N} m(X_i,\theta)' = 0$$

where X_i is a sample observation of the random variable and θ is the vector of unknown parameters. If there are K parameters (i.e., $\theta = (\theta_1, \theta_2, ..., \theta_K)'$), we will need at least K moment equations in order to successfully estimate the parameters (i.e., $m(\theta) = (m_1(\theta), m_2(\theta), ..., m_L(\theta))'$, $L \geq K$). In other words, the number of sample moment equations must be at least as large as the number of parameters to be estimated. This is just the classical identification problem. If $L = K$, this model is exactly identified. If $L > K$, the model is over-identified with L-K functional restrictions. The optimization problem is to minimize the quadratic criterion function:

$$Q(\theta) = m(\theta)'W\, m(\theta)$$

where W is a positive definite weighting matrix. Optimally, W is chosen to be the inverse of the estimated consistent covariance matrix of $m(\theta)$. That is, $W = W(\theta) = [Var(m(\theta))]^{-1}$ and $Var(m(\theta)) = 1/N^2 \sum\sum_{i,j=1,2,...,N} m(X_i,\theta)'m(X_j,\theta)$.

To ensure that W is positive definite, we need to say some things about its autocovariance structure. For example,

$$
\begin{aligned}
Var(m(\theta)) = \quad & S_0(\theta) + \sum_{j=1,2,...,p}(1 - j/(p+1))\,(S_j(\theta) + S_j(\theta)') \\
& S_0(\theta) = m(\theta)m(\theta)' = 1/N^2 \sum_{i=1,2,...,N} m(X_i,\theta)'m(X_i,\theta) \\
& S_j = m(\theta)m_{-j}(\theta)' = 1/N^2 \sum_{i=j+1,...,N} m(X_i,0)'m(X_{i-j},0) \\
& j = 1, ..., p < N
\end{aligned}
$$

where p is the degree of autocovariance assumed in the model. This is the White-Newey-West estimator of $Var(m(\theta))$, which guarantees positive definiteness by down-weighting higher-order autocovariances.

For an exactly identified model, the optimal value of Q is zero and therefore the choice of weighting matrix W is irrelevant. For an over-identified case, there are L-K moment restrictions which must be satisfied with a minimal positive value (or *penalty*) of Q. The function of weighting matrix W as constructed is to place the importance of each individual moment function. Typically, the first iteration of GMM estimation starts with the special case of $W = I$ (the identity matrix). In other words, we find the estimator θ^0 of θ that minimizes the quadratic function, $Q(\theta) = m(\theta)'m(\theta)$, with the associated asymptotic covariance matrix:

$$Var(\theta^0) = [G(\theta^0)'G(\theta^0)]^{-1}G(\theta^0)'[Var(m(\theta^0))]\, G(\theta^0)\, [G(\theta^0)'G(\theta^0)]^{-1}$$

where $G(\theta^0) = \partial m(\theta^0)/\partial\theta$ is the L by K matrix of derivatives. With the initial parameter estimates θ^0, let $W = W(\theta^0) = [Var(m(\theta^0))]^{-1}$ and then minimize the quadratic function:

$$Q(\theta) = m(\theta)'W\, m(\theta)$$

The asymptotic covariance matrix for the resulting GMM estimator θ^1 of θ is:

$$\text{Var}(\theta^1) = [G(\theta^1)'W\ G(\theta^1)]^{-1}G(\theta^1)'W\ [\text{Var}(m(\theta^1))]\ WG(\theta^1)\ [G(\theta^1)'W\ G(\theta^1)]^{-1}$$

Updating the weighting matrix $W = W(\theta^1) = [\text{Var}(m(\theta^1))]^{-1}$ and reiterating the optimization process until convergence, the final GMM estimator θ^* of θ is obtained, with the following asymptotic covariance matrix:

$$\text{Var}(\theta^*) = [G(\theta^*)'W(\theta^*)G(\theta^*)]^{-1}$$

We note that convergence is not necessary for a consistent GMM estimator of θ. If our estimate θ^* of θ is to be asymptotically efficient, the optimal weighting matrix $W = W(\theta^*)$ must have been used. In other words, the iterative estimation process must converge on the solution θ^*. With the optimal weighting matrix, θ^* is asymptotically normally distributed with mean θ and covariance $\text{Var}(\theta^*)$. The value of quadratic function Q at the optimal solution θ^* is:

$$Q^* = Q(\theta^*) = m(\theta^*)'W(\theta^*)m(\theta^*)$$

Q^* serves as the basis for hypothesis testing of moment restrictions. If there are L moment equations with K parameters ($L > K$), the Hansen test statistic Q^* follows a Chi-square distribution with L-K degrees of freedom. Justification for including L-K additional moment functions is made based on the value of Q^*.

Lesson 12.1 Gamma Probability Distribution

Recall the classical maximum likelihood method of estimating a probability distribution discussed in Chapter VI. We now return to Lesson 6.3, estimating the two parameters of the gamma distribution of the INCOME variable. Consider four sample moment functions of the gamma probability distribution function with unknown parameters λ and ρ:

$$m_1(\lambda,\rho) = 1/N\ \textstyle\sum_{i=1,2,\ldots,N}\ X_i - \rho/\lambda$$
$$m_2(\lambda,\rho) = 1/N\ \textstyle\sum_{i=1,2,\ldots,N}\ X_i^2 - \rho(\rho+1)/\lambda^2$$
$$m_3(\lambda,\rho) = 1/N\ \textstyle\sum_{i=1,2,\ldots,N}\ ln(X_i) - dln\Gamma(\rho)/d\rho + ln(\lambda)$$
$$m_4(\lambda,\rho) = 1/N\ \textstyle\sum_{i=1,2,\ldots,N}\ 1/X_i - \lambda/(\rho-1)$$

The GMM estimator of $\theta = (\lambda,\rho)$ is obtained from minimizing the weighted sum-of-squares:

$$Q(\theta) = m(\theta)'W\ m(\theta)$$

where $m(\theta) = (m_1(\theta),\ m_2(\theta),\ m_3(\theta),\ m_4(\theta))'$ and W is a positive definite symmetric matrix. Conditional to the weighting scheme W, the variance-covariance matrix of θ is estimated by:

$$\text{Var}(\theta) = [G(\theta)'W\ G(\theta)]^{-1}\ G(\theta)'W\ [\text{Var}(m(\theta))]\ WG(\theta)\ [G(\theta)'W\ G(\theta)]^{-1}$$

If we let W equal the inverse of the covariance matrix of $m(\theta)$, or $[\text{Var}(m(\theta))]^{-1}$, then $\text{Var}(\theta) = [G(\theta)'W\ G(\theta)]^{-1}$.

From here, we can show that the GMM class of estimators includes the maximum likelihood estimator as a special case. Solving from the *score* of the log-likelihood function based on the gamma distribution:

$$\partial ll(X,\theta)/\partial\lambda = N\ (\rho/\lambda) - \Sigma_{i=1,2,...,N}\ X_i = 0$$

$$\partial ll(X,\theta)/\partial\rho = N\ ln(\lambda) - N\ dln\Gamma(\rho)/d\rho + \Sigma_{i=1,2,...,N}\ ln(X_i) = 0$$

where $ll(X,\theta) = N\ [\rho ln(\lambda) - ln\Gamma(\rho)] - \lambda\ \Sigma_{i=1,2,...,N}\ X_i + (\rho-1)\ \Sigma_{i=1,2,...,N}\ ln(X_i)$. Thus, the maximum likelihood estimate of $\theta = (\lambda,\rho)$ is an exactly identified GMM with $m(\theta) = (m_1(\theta), m_3(\theta))$. For this exactly identified case, the weighting matrix W is irrelevant, and the optimal criterion Q is zero.

GMM is a nonlinear estimation method. Nonlinear optimization methods were discussed in Chapter VI. Chapter VII presented the applications of nonlinear least squares and maximum likelihood estimation in econometrics. GMM estimation is a straightforward example of a nonlinear minimization problem. The first part of the program **lesson12.1** sets up a standard nonlinear optimization problem. The data series INCOME is read from the text file **yed20.txt**. As in Lesson 6.3, the INCOME variable is scaled by 10 and renamed x (line 4).[12] The next few lines specify the minimization problem (_nlopt=0 in line 6) to be estimated by the QHC method (_method=5 in line 7) with no more than 100 iterations (_iter=100 in line 8). Line 9 specifies the initial values of the two parameters ρ and λ, respectively.

```
      /*
      ** Lesson 12.1: GMM Estimation of a Gamma Distribution
      ** See Greene (1999), Example 4.26 and Example 11.4
      */
 1    use gpe2;
 2    output file=gpe\output12.1 reset;
 3    load data[21,2]=gpe\yed20.txt;
 4    x=data[2:21,1]/10;        @ income: data scaling may help @

 5    call reset;
 6    _nlopt=0;                 @ it is a minimization problem @
 7    _method=5;
 8    _iter=100;

 9    _b={3,1};                 @ initial values of parameters @
10    _hacv=1;                  @ hetero consistent covariance @
                                @ assuming serially uncorrelated @
11    call estimate(&gmmqw,x);
                                @ using the results of previous estimator @
12    _b=__b;                   @ for initial value of parameters and @
13    gmmw=invpd(gmmv(x,_b));   @ for computing the weight matrix @
14    call estimate(&gmmqw,x);
15    call gmmout(x,__b);       @ print GMM output @
      /*
      _b=__b;
      call estimate(&gmmq,x);
      call gmmout(x,__b);       @ print GMM output @
      */
```

---

[12] Our implementation of this example is slightly different from that of Example 11.4 in Greene (1999). Instead of using the scaled moment equations as Greene did, we scale the data series first and then estimate the original moment equations as described. The numerical results are more stable and easier to evaluate.

```
16  end;

    /*
    User-defined moments equations, must be named mf
    based on gamma distribution: b[1]=rho, b[2]=lambda
    */
17  proc mf(x,b);
18      local n,m;
19      n=rows(x);
20      m=zeros(n,4);
21      m[.,1]=x-b[1]/b[2];
22      m[.,2]=x^2-b[1]*(b[1]+1)/(b[2]^2);
23      m[.,3]=ln(x)-gradp(&lngamma,b[1])+ln(b[2]);
24      m[.,4]=1/x-b[2]/(b[1]-1);
25      retp(m);
26  endp;

    /*
    Log of gamma distribution function
    */
27  fn lngamma(x)=ln(gamma(x));

28  #include gpe\gmm.gpe;
```

Most of the computation details and algorithms of GMM estimation in GAUSS are grouped in a module named **GMM.GPE**. There are many ways to include a module in your program. The simplest is to use the GAUSS compiler directive #include. It will include the specified module during the compilation of your program. We suggest including the module **GMM.GPE** at the end of your program. If you have properly installed the GPE package with your version of GAUSS, **GMM.GPE** is located in the GPE subdirectory. Putting source codes in a separate file hides their implementation "secrets." If you are interested in the programming details, you can examine the program listing of **GMM.GPE** available in Appendix B-1.

The module **GMM.GPE** defines two objective functions, gmmqw and gmmq. The former uses a predefined weighting matrix, while the latter computes the weighting matrix together with the unknown parameters. In addition, the procedure gmmout prints the regression output. Since GMM is a nonlinear optimization method, it requires a user-defined moment function with the name mf which, like the other functions (e.g. residual function for nonlinear least squares or maximum likelihood estimation), depends on a sample data matrix x and a parameter vector b.

Based on the gamma probability distribution, two parameters λ and ρ will be estimated from the four moment functions we defined earlier (see lines 17 through 26 which define the procedure mf(x,b)). One tricky part is computing the derivative of the log of the gamma function for the third moment equation (line 23). The logarithm of the gamma function is defined as a separate one-line function in line 27, so that the GAUSS built-in gradient function gradp is applied in line 23.

One of the key advantages of GMM is that it allows for a flexible specification of covariance structure, including heteroscedasticity and autocorrelation. We have seen the use of the GPE control variable _hacv to compute the heteroscedasticity-autocorrelation-consistent covariance matrix in the context of heteroscedasticity (Chapter IX) and autocorrelation (Chapter X). _hacv is used similarly for nonlinear GMM estimation, except that heteroscedasticity-consistent covariance is the default option here. If we assume first-order autocovariance, then line 10 needs to be modified as follows:

```
_hacv = {1,1};
```

The first element of _havc directs the computation of the heteroscedasticity-consistent covariance matrix, while the second element specifies the order of autocovariance requested. See Appendix A for more information about the global control variable _hacv.

We begin the GMM estimation by minimizing the objective function gmmqw (line 11) with the default weighting matrix I (identity matrix). The estimated parameters are used as starting point for the next iteration. First, we start from the estimated parameters (line 12) and compute the corresponding weighting matrix (line 13). Then the improved consistent parameter estimates are obtained (line 14) and printed (line 15). We could continue on updating the weighting matrix and estimating the parameters until convergence. Equivalently, we could estimate the parameters together with the associated weighting matrix. However, finding a convergent solution is not guaranteed due to a high degree of nonlinearity in the objective function.

Running **lesson12.1**, the first set of GMM estimation results, based on the identity weighting matrix, is as follows:

```
Non-Linear Optimization: Minimization Problem
---------------------------------------------
Assuming Generalized Method of Moments
Number of Observations = 20
Number of Parameters = 2

Maximum Number of Iterations = 100
Step Size Search Method = 0
Convergence Criterion = 0
Tolerance = 0.001

Initial Result:
Function Value =        6.4658
Parameters =        3.0000        1.0000

Using Quadratic Hill-Climbing Algorithm
Iteration =  1   Step Size =  1.0000  Value =        1.9867
Parameters =        3.0010        0.86896
...
Iteration =  8   Step Size =  1.0000  Value =      0.0068077
Parameters =        2.3691        0.74112

Final Result:
Iterations = 8              Evaluations = 123
Function Value =      0.0068077
Parameters =        2.3691        0.74112
Gradient Vector =      -0.21423        0.44266

                              Asymptotic    Asymptotic
                  Parameter    Std. Error     t-Ratio
X1                   2.3691      0.010345      229.02
X2                  0.74112     0.0028050      264.21
```

The second set of GMM estimation results is based on the previous estimates of the parameters and the associated weighting matrix (see lines 12-14 of the program **lesson12.1**). As is standard practice in nonlinear optimization, the estimated standard errors and t-ratios of the parameters are computed from the inverse of the hessian matrix calculated during minimization of the quadratic criterion function. Note that these are not the GMM estimates of the standard errors and t-ratios. The correct estimates of the standard errors and t-statistics of the parameters are computed at the end. In addition, the Hansen test statistic of the moment restrictions is presented. Calling the procedure gmmout (see line 15 of the program **lesson12.1**) gives us the following result:

```
Non-Linear Optimization: Minimization Problem
- - - - - - - - - - - - - - - - - - - - - - - - - - - - - - - - - - - -
Assuming Generalized Method of Moments
Number of Observations = 20
Number of Parameters = 2

Maximum Number of Iterations = 100
Step Size Search Method = 0
Convergence Criterion = 0
Tolerance = 0.001

Initial Result:
Function Value =         13.294
Parameters =        2.3691        0.74112

Using Quadratic Hill-Climbing Algorithm
Iteration =   1   Step Size =  1.0000  Value =         9.3992
Parameters =        3.3687        0.74667
...
Iteration =   5   Step Size =  0.5000  Value =         3.2339
Parameters =        2.8971        0.84839

Final Result:
Iterations = 5            Evaluations = 103
Function Value =         3.2339
Parameters =        2.8971        0.84839
Gradient Vector =      -487.16        -6.2162

                                Asymptotic   Asymptotic
                    Parameter   Std. Error      t-Ratio
X1                     2.8971    0.0079292       365.37
X2                    0.84839    0.062556        13.562

GMM Estimation Result
======================
    Parameter   Std. Error      t-Ratio
    2.8971       0.0044004       658.37
    0.84839      0.11996         7.0721

Hansen Test Statistic of the Moment Restrictions
Chi-Sq(   2) =        4.4604
```

For the two parameters of the gamma distribution, ρ and λ, we now compare their GMM estimators with the maximum likelihood (ML) estimators obtained earlier from Lesson 6.3 in Chapter VI. The standard errors are in parentheses.

	ML	GMM
ρ	2.4106 (0.7161)	2.8971 (0.0044)
λ	0.7707 (0.2544)	0.8484 (0.120)

GMM Estimation of Econometric Models

The GMM estimation of econometric models can be considered as an extension of the IV (instrumental variable) estimation method. IV estimation is widely used for models with random regressors (e.g. lagged dependent variables) which exhibit contemporaneous correlation with the model's errors. The advantage of GMM over IV is that the model need not be homoscedastic and serially independent. The covariance matrix of the averages of sample moments is taken into account for minimizing the GMM criterion function.

For notational convenience, let X be a combined data matrix of endogenous (dependent) and predetermined (independent or explanatory) variables in the model. β is a K-element vector of unknown parameters. Suppose there are L moment equations, $m(X,\beta) = (m_1(X,\beta), ..., m_L(X,\beta))$, where $L \geq K$. The model formulation is not limited to the case of a single equation. Generalization to a system of linear or nonlinear equations is straightforward.

Corresponding to the moment conditions $E(m(X,\beta)) = 0$, we write the sample moment equations as follows:

$$m(\beta) = 1/N \sum_{i=1,2,...,N} m(X_i,\beta)' = 0$$

Recall that the objective function, known as the GMM criterion function, to be minimized is $Q(\beta) = m(\beta)'W\, m(\beta)$. We would optimally choose W to be equal to $[Var(m(\beta))]^{-1}$. To find the β^* which minimizes $Q(\beta)$, we solve the zero-gradient conditions: $\partial Q(\beta^*)/\partial \beta = 0$. Our estimator β^* of β will be asymptotically efficient and normally distributed with mean β and covariance matrix:

$$Var(\beta^*) = \{G(\beta^*)'[Var(m(\beta^*))]^{-1}G(\beta^*)\}^{-1}$$

where $G(\beta^*) = \partial m(\beta^*)/\partial \beta$ and $[Var(m(\beta^*))]$ is the White-Newey-West estimator of the covariance matrix of the sample moments.

Nonlinear IV Estimation

Now we consider the regression model $\varepsilon = \varepsilon(\beta) = F(Y,X,\beta)$ (or Y- $f(X,\beta)$), where Y is the endogenous or dependent variable, and X consists of predetermined (or independent) variables. β is a K-element parameter vector. Let Z be a set of L instrumental variables, for which we assume $L \geq K$. Under the general assumption that $E(\varepsilon) = 0$ and $Var(\varepsilon) = E(\varepsilon\varepsilon') = \Sigma = \sigma^2\Omega$, we can write the model as $E(Z'\varepsilon) = 0$. The sample moment functions are defined by $m(\beta) = 1/N\ Z'\varepsilon(\beta)$ with covariance matrix:

$$Var(m(\beta)) = 1/N^2\ Z'\ E[\varepsilon(\beta)\varepsilon(\beta)']\ Z = 1/N^2\ Z'\Sigma(\beta)Z$$

Therefore, GMM estimation amounts to finding the β^* which minimizes:

$$Q(\beta) = \varepsilon(\beta)'Z\ [Z'\Sigma(\beta)Z]^{-1}Z'\varepsilon(\beta)$$

The resulting GMM estimator β^* is asymptotically normally distributed with mean β and covariance matrix:

$$Var(\beta^*) = \{(\partial\epsilon(\beta^*)/\partial\beta)'Z\ [Z'\Sigma(\beta^*)Z]^{-1}Z'(\partial\epsilon(\beta^*)/\partial\beta)\}^{-1}$$

where $\Sigma(\beta^*)$ is the White-Newey-West estimator of $\Sigma = \sigma^2\Omega$.

Linear IV Estimation

If the model is linear, or $\epsilon = \epsilon(\beta) = Y - X\beta$, then the GMM estimator of β is equivalent to the IV estimator:

$$\beta^* = (X'Z[Z'\Sigma(\beta^*)Z]^{-1}Z'X)^{-1}\ X'Z[Z'\Sigma(\beta^*)Z]^{-1}Z'Y$$
$$Var(\beta^*) = \{X'Z[Z'\Sigma(\beta^*)Z]^{-1}Z'X\}^{-1}$$

If the instrumental variables $Z = X$, then

$$\beta^* = (X'X)^{-1}X'Y$$
$$Var(\beta^*) = (X'X)^{-1}[X'\Sigma(\beta^*)X](X'X)^{-1}$$

Special Cases

If the IV model is homoscedastic and serially uncorrelated, that is $\Sigma = \sigma^2 I$, then

$$\beta^* = (X'Z[Z'Z]^{-1}Z'X)^{-1}X'Z[Z'Z]^{-1}Z'Y$$
$$Var(\beta^*) = \sigma^2(\beta^*)\ \{X'Z[Z'Z]^{-1}Z'X\}^{-1}$$

where $\sigma^2(\beta^*) = 1/N\ \epsilon(\beta^*)'\epsilon(\beta^*)$. If the instrumental variables $Z = X$, this further reduces to the ordinary least squares estimator:

$$\beta^* = (X'X)^{-1}X'Y$$
$$Var(\beta^*) = \sigma^2(\beta^*)\ (X'X)^{-1}$$

Hypothesis Testing

Based on the statistical inference for nonlinear regression models (see Chapter VII, Lesson 7.3 in particular), there are three corresponding test statistics for testing linear or nonlinear restrictions on the GMM estimate of β. Suppose there are J constraint equations written in the form $c(\beta) = 0$. Let β^* be the unconstrained GMM estimator of β, and let b^* be the constrained estimator of β. All the three test statistics discussed below will follow a Chi-square distribution with J degrees of freedom.

Wald Test

The Wald test statistic, based on the unconstrained estimator β^*, is defined as:

$$W = c(\beta^*)'[Var(c(\beta^*))]^{-1}c(\beta^*)$$
$$= c(\beta^*)'\ \{(\partial c(\beta^*)/\partial\beta)\ [Var(\beta^*)]\ (\partial c(\beta^*)/\partial\beta)'\}^{-1}\ c(\beta^*)$$

Lagrangian Multiplier (LM) Test

Let $\alpha = \partial Q(b^*)/\partial\beta = 2\ m(b^*)'W\ G(b^*)$, where $G(b^*) = \partial m(b^*)/\partial\beta$. If the constraints hold, then α approaches to 0. The LM statistic is:

$$\text{LM} = \alpha[\text{Var}(\alpha)]^{-1}\alpha'$$
$$= m(b^*)'W\ G(b^*)[G(b^*)'W\ G(b^*)]^{-1}G(b^*)'W\ m(b^*)$$

Likelihood Ratio (LR) Test

If we estimate both β^* and b^*, the LR test statistic is computed as:

$$\text{LR} = Q(b^*) - Q(\beta^*)$$

We note that both β^* and b^* are computed using the same consistent estimator of the weighting matrix W.

Lesson 12.2 A Nonlinear Rational Expectations Model

An important application of GMM estimation is to estimate the first-order conditions (or Euler equations) of a dynamic optimization problem. As an example, we will use a model common in the finance literature. Suppose a representative stockholder at current time t, who tries to maximize a concave expected utility function of consumption over an indefinite future horizon. This can be modeled as:

$$\sum_{\tau=0,...,\infty} \beta^\tau\, E\{u(C_{t+\tau}) \mid Z_t\}$$

where Z_t is the information available to the consumer at time t and $C_{t+\tau}$ is the consumption τ periods from t. $0 < \beta < 1$ is known as the discount factor of time preference. Given N different stocks, the optimal consumption-investment allocation must satisfy the following condition:

$$u'(C_t) = \beta\, E\{u'(C_{t+1})\ [(P_{i,t+1}+D_{i,t+1})/P_t] \mid Z_t\}$$

for $i = 1,...,N$. $u'(C_t) = \partial u/\partial C_t$ is the marginal utility of consumption at time t. $P_{i,t+1}$ is the price of stock i at time t+1 and $D_{i,t+1}$ is the dividend per share of stock i at t+1. The ratio $(P_{i,t+1}+D_{i,t+1})/P_{i,t}$ represents the returns of investment in stock i between periods t and t+1. In other words, this merely defines the equilibrium condition that the marginal utility of consumption in the current period must equal the expected return next period from investing in stock i. Assume that the utility function exhibits *constant relative risk aversion* as:

$$u(C_t) = C_t^\alpha/\alpha \quad \text{for } \alpha<1$$

where $1-\alpha$ is known as the coefficient of relative risk aversion, and $1-\alpha > 0$. Then, for each $i = 1, ..., N$, the optimal decision-rule is

$$C_t^{\alpha-1} = \beta\, E\{C_{t+1}^{\alpha-1}\ [(P_{i,t+1}+D_{i,t+1})/P_t] \mid Z_t\}$$

Equivalently, for each stock $i = 1, ..., N$, we must have

$$\beta E\{[(C_{t+1}/C_t)^{\alpha-1}]\ [(P_{i,t+1}+D_{i,t+1})/P_t] \mid Z_t\} = 1$$

The hypothesis of rational expectations assumes that the intertemporal decision-making should be independent from the historical information available at the time at which the decision is made. Therefore, the derived orthogonality condition for each stock $i = 1, ..., N$ is:

$$E \left[Z_t \left\{ \beta [(C_{t+1}/C_t)^{\alpha-1}] [(P_{i,t+1}+D_{i,t+1})/P_t] -1 \right\} \right] = 0$$

For more detailed description of the model, see Hansen and Singleton (1982).[13] In terms of our econometric estimation, the model may be expressed with the orthogonality condition: $E[Z \; \varepsilon(X,\theta)] = 0$, where $X = [X_1, X_2, X_3]$, $\theta = (\beta, \alpha)$, and

$$\varepsilon(X, \theta) = [\beta X_1^{\alpha-1} X_2 - 1, \; \beta X_1^{\alpha-1} X_3 - 1]$$

The data file **gmmq.txt** installed in the GPE subdirectory consists of three variables (335 observations from January 1959 to December 1978, though not the original Hansen-Singleton data):

X_1 Ratio of two-period consumption, C_{t+1}/C_t.

X_2 Value-weighted returns of NYSE stock market, $(P_{t+1}+D_{t+1})/P_t$ where P_{t+1} is the price and D_{t+1} is the dividend payoff of stock at $t+1$.

X_3 Risk-free rate of returns (T-Bill rate).

We note that this model consists of a system of two nonlinear equations. The instrumental variables Z consist of one or several lags of X and a constant. The following program **lesson12.2** implements and estimates the Hansen-Singleton rational expectations model. The program structure looks similar to that of Lesson 12.1. The main difference is the model specification described in the block from line 19 to line 27 for the moment function procedure mf(x,b), which reflects exactly the model described above. We use one lag of each of the three variables X_1, X_2, X_3, and a constant as the instrumental variables (see line 22). More lags may be included for the additional instrumental variables. The two orthogonality equations for stock and risk-free returns are concatenated to form the moment functions system (see lines 23 and 24). The rest of the program performs the GMM estimation. First, the initial estimates of (β, α) are obtained by assuming the default identity weighting matrix in the objective function for minimization (line 10). Then, with the resulting covariance matrix of the moment functions, the consistent parameter estimates are calculated (see lines 11-13). An efficient solution is obtained from simultaneously estimating the parameters and the corresponding covariance matrix in the second iteration (see lines 15 and 16).

```
     /*
     ** Lesson 12.2: A Nonlinear Rational Expectation Model
     ** GMM Estimation of Hansen-Singleton Model (Ea, 1982)
     */
1    use gpe2;
2    output file=gpe\output12.2 reset;
3    load x[335,3]=gpe\gmmq.txt;   @ data columns: @
                                   @ (1) c(t+1)/c(t) (2)vwr (3)rfr @
4    call reset;
5    _nlopt=0;
6    _method=5;
7    _tol=1.0e-5;
8    _iter=100;

9    _b={1,0};                     @ GMM estimation with initial @
```

---

[13] For computational implementation of the model and the data file **gmmq.txt** used in this lesson example, see also the Hasen-Heaton-Ogaki GMM package from the American University GAUSS archive at http://www.american.edu/academic.depts/cas/econ/gaussres/GMM/GMM.HTM.

```
10    call estimate(&gmmqw,x);  @ identity weighting matrix @

11    _b=__b;                   @ GMM estimation with external @
12    gmmw=invpd(gmmv(x,__b));   @ covariance weighting matrix @
13    call estimate(&gmmqw,x);

14    call gmmout(x,__b);        @ print GMM output @

15    _b=__b;                    @ there may be a convergent efficient solution
16    @
      call estimate(&gmmq,x);    @ with internal covariance weighting matrix @
17
      call gmmout(x,__b);        @ print GMM output @
18
      end;

      /*
      User-defined moments functions, must be named mf
19    */
20    proc mf(x,b);
21        local z,n,m;
22        n=rows(x);
23        z=ones(n,1)~lagn(x,1);    @ IV @
24        m=z.*(b[1]*(x[.,1]^(b[2]-1)).*x[.,2]-1);
25        m=m~(z.*(b[1]*(x[.,1]^(b[2]-1)).*x[.,3]-1));
26        @ nonlinear multiple equations system @
27        retp(packr(m));
      endp;
28
      #include gpe\gmm.gpe;
```

The first part of the output (the first iteration, using the identity matrix as the weighting matrix) is only preparation for computing the consistent parameter estimates in the second iteration of the GMM estimation. The result of second consistent estimation is shown below:

```
Non-Linear Optimization: Minimization Problem
---------------------------------------------
Assuming Generalized Method of Moments
Number of Observations = 335
Number of Parameters = 2

Maximum Number of Iterations = 100
Step Size Search Method = 0
Convergence Criterion = 0
Tolerance = 1e-005

Initial Result:
Function Value =        55.406
Parameters =       0.99977  -0.00012883

Using Quadratic Hill-Climbing Algorithm
Iteration = 1    Step Size = 1.0000  Value =        19.924
Parameters =        1.0014    0.00045142
...
Iteration = 13   Step Size = 1.4641  Value =         9.4685
Parameters =        0.99919     0.85517

Final Result:
Iterations = 13           Evaluations = 239
Function Value =        9.4685
Parameters =        0.99919     0.85517
Gradient Vector =  -0.00026951    0.00017303
```

```
                             Asymptotic   Asymptotic
                 Parameter   Std. Error    t-Ratio
X1                 0.99919   0.00012573     7946.9
X2                 0.85517    0.044497      19.219


GMM Estimation Result
=====================
  Parameter    Std. Error     t-Ratio
    0.99919    0.00047887      2086.6
    0.85517     0.17853        4.7901

Hansen Test Statistic of the Moment Restrictions
Chi-Sq(  6) =        13.306
```

> The consistent estimates (0.9992, 0.8552) of the two parameters are obtained using 8 instrument variables (4 for each of the two equations). The Hansen test statistic of the extra 6 moment restrictions is barely statistically significant at 5% level (with the critical value 12.59).

```
Non-Linear Optimization: Minimization Problem
---------------------------------------------
Assuming Generalized Method of Moments
Number of Observations = 335
Number of Parameters = 2

Maximum Number of Iterations = 100
Step Size Search Method = 0
Convergence Criterion = 0
Tolerance = 1e-005

Initial Result:
Function Value =       13.306
Parameters =       0.99919       0.85517

Using Quadratic Hill-Climbing Algorithm
Iteration =  1   Step Size =  1.0000  Value =        12.590
Parameters =       0.99934       0.85482
...
Iteration =  7   Step Size =  0.0039  Value =        12.474
Parameters =       0.99950       0.78735

Final Result:
Iterations = 7              Evaluations = 127
Function Value =       12.474
Parameters =       0.99950       0.78735
Gradient Vector =     0.0069545     0.0056644

                             Asymptotic   Asymptotic
                 Parameter   Std. Error    t-Ratio
X1                 0.99950   9.8686e-005    10128.
X2                 0.78735    0.037531      20.979


GMM Estimation Result
=====================
  Parameter    Std. Error     t-Ratio
    0.99950    0.00047957      2084.2
    0.78735     0.17736        4.4393

Hansen Test Statistic of the Moment Restrictions
Chi-Sq(  6) =        12.474
```

The final GMM estimate of (β,α) at $(0.9995, 0.7874)$ is consistent with the result of Hansen and Singleton (1982). Since it is the convergent solution, it is also efficient. However, the 6 moment restrictions are significant only at the 10 percent level.

It may be of interest to perform hypothesis tests on the coefficient of relative risk aversion $1-\alpha$. Two cases that are often of practical interest are α approaching 0 (indicating a logarithmic utility function) and $\alpha = 1$ (indicating a linear utility function), we leave applying hypothesis testing in the GMM framework to interested readers.

Linear GMM

GMM estimation of a linear regression model is essentially the same as IV estimation with a general covariance matrix. In Chapters IX and X, we discussed the computation of White-Newey-West estimates of heteroscedasticity-autocorrelation-consistent covariance by using the GPE control variable _hacv. In the case of the IV approach, Lesson 11.2 introduced the use of another GPE control variable, _ivar, to specify a set of instruments for linear model estimation. _ivar may be internally determined in the case of autocorrelation correction for a lagged dependent variable model. Alternatively, it may be externally specified as a data matrix consisting of a list of instrumental variables. Refer to your econometrics textbook for the requirements and proper use of instrumental variables in a regression model.

In GPE, _ivar may be combined with _hacv to carry out GMM estimation. In addition, as in a nonlinear model estimation, we can set the control variable _iter to allow for iterated computation of the parameter estimates. If the solution converges, it is efficient. Even if it does not converge, the GMM estimator is still consistent.

Lesson 12.3 GMM Estimation of U.S. Consumption Function

In the following, we present a simple example of a consumption function derived from Hall's Life Cycle-Permanent Income Hypothesis (Hall, 1978) with a quadratic utility function. The intertemporal model formulation is similar to that of Lesson 12.2 on the consumption-investment decision-making, with the exception that we consider only the consumption plan with a quadratic utility function. The use of a quadratic functional form leads to a linear consumption function:

$$C_{t+1} = \beta_0 + \beta_1 C_t + \varepsilon_{t+1}$$

C_{t+1} and C_t are expected and current consumption, respectively. Let Z_t be historical information available to the consumer at time t or earlier. Then the orthogonality condition becomes:

$$E(Z_t \varepsilon_{t+1}) = 0$$

From other theories of consumption, the instrumental variables Z may include levels of income Y and consumption C in addition to a constant. That is,

$$Z_t = [\ 1\ C_t\ Y_t]$$

Further lags of C and Y may be added to the model as needed. The consumption-income relationship was studied in Chapter XI with income as the explanatory variable. Based on an Euler equation of a constrained expected utility maximization, in this example, the future consumption is affected indirectly by the current and past income as the instrumental variables. Using the U.S. time series data of **usyc87.txt**, Lesson 12.3 demonstrates GMM estimation of the linear consumption function as follows:

```
   /*
   ** Lesson 12.3: GMM Estimation of U.S. Consumption Function
   ** GMM Estimation of a Linear Regression Model
   */
 1 use gpe2;
 2 output file=gpe\output12.3 reset;

 3 load z[67,3]=gpe\usyc87.txt;
 4 y = z[2:67,2];
 5 c = z[2:67,3];

 6 call reset;
 7 _names={"c","c1"};
 8 _rstat=1;
 9 _rplot=2;
10 _dlags=1;
11 _ivar=ones(rows(y),1)~lagn(c~y,1);
12 _hacv={1,1};
13 _iter=100;

14 call estimate(c,0);

15 end;
```

Two variables, named C and Y, are read from the data file **usyc87.txt**. Line 10, _dlags = 1, specifies the lagged dependent variable model. GMM estimation for the linear autoregressive consumption function is given in line 14, with the instrumental variables _ivar specified in line 11. We use only the first lag of income and consumption variables in addition to a constant as the instruments. The first-order autocovariance structure is specified in line 12, in which the White-Newey-West estimate will be computed. The computation of GMM estimates will be iterated until convergence or until the limit set in line 13, _iter = 100. The empirical results in greater detail can be found in the output file output12.3.

Of course the estimated model is not good enough to be free of misspecification. It serves the purpose for demonstrating GMM estimation of a linear model. To improve the model, either more lags of consumption should be included for a comprehensive autoregressive specification or the model should explicitly correct for serial correlation. We leave the rest of the model improvement task to the interested reader.

XIII

Systems of Simultaneous Equations

GPE can estimate systems of linear and nonlinear equations. For a system of linear equations, you need to define the endogenous and predetermined (including lagged endogenous, current and lagged exogenous) variables. By selecting and identifying the relevant variables for each equation, the procedure `estimate` carries out the system model estimation as in the case of a single equation model. For a system of nonlinear equations, it becomes more involved to define the functional form for the model equations. In this chapter, the classic example of Klein Model I (1950) is used to demonstrate the estimation of a system of linear regression equations. The special case of seemingly unrelated regressions (SUR) is considered with the Berndt-Wood model of energy demand. Finally, re-examining the Klein Model, nonlinear maximum likelihood estimation is shown to be useful for estimating a system of nonlinear equations.

Linear Regression Equations System

We follow the conventional matrix representation of a system of linear equations as:

$$YB + X\Gamma = U$$

Let N be the number of observations, G be the number of endogenous variables (therefore, the number of equations), and K be the number of predetermined variables. Then Y, a N×G matrix, and X, a N×K matrix, are the respective data matrices of endogenous and predetermined variables. The corresponding G×G matrix B associated with the endogenous variable matrix Y, and the G×K matrix Γ associated with predetermined variable matrix X are the sparse parameter matrices in which the unknown nonzero elements need to be estimated. Finally, U is the N×G stochastic error matrix.

Given the data matrices Y and X, the unknown parameters in B and Γ can be estimated using a variety of methods. GPE implements both single equation (limited information) methods and simultaneous equations (full information) methods. Before the parameter estimation, the model of multiple equations must be properly specified to account for the relevant variables and restrictions. In GPE, this is done by specifying the structure of the parameter matrices B and Γ. It uses a couple of specification matrices to define the stochastic equations and fixed identities of the system by representing the parameter matrices of the system as arrays of 1's, 0's, and –1's, signifying the inclusion or exclusion of variables from particular equations. In the following, we discuss the three most important input variables that control the specification and estimation of a simultaneous linear equations model.

- `_eq`
- `_id`
- `_method`

First, the variable _eq specifies the stochastic equation matrix for system model estimation. This is a G_s by $(G+K)$ matrix with elements -1, 0, and 1 arranged in accordance with the order of endogenous variables Y followed by the predetermined variables X. Note that G_s is the number of *stochastic* equations and $G \geq G_s$. For each stochastic equation, there is exactly one row of _eq to define it. In the stochastic equation specification matrix _eq, an element -1 indicates the left-hand side endogenous variable. Only one -1 entry is allowed in each equation. An element 1 indicates the use of an endogenous and/or a predetermined variable on the right-hand side of an equation. The zeros indicate the corresponding unused or excluded variables in the equation. Constant terms are not normally included in the equation specification. If _eq is not specified, or _eq=0 by default, a SUR equations system is assumed. In this case, $G_s = G$, and the _eq matrix consists of a G×G sub-matrix with -1 in the diagonals and zeros elsewhere (endogenous variables portion of _eq), and a G×K sub-matrix consisting entirety of ones (predetermined variables portion of _eq).

The second input variable _id specifies the identity equation specification matrix for a system model. _id is similar in size and setup to _eq, except that its entries can be any value as required by the model. If _id is not specified, or _id=0 by default, there is no identity. To ensure system compatibility, the number of rows in two specification matrices _eq and _id must sum to G, the total number of endogenous variables or equations in the system.

The input variable _method controls the use of the specific method of estimation. In the context of simultaneous linear equations, the available estimation methods are:

_method=0	Ordinary least squares (OLS, the default method)
_method=1	Limited information maximum likelihood (LIML)
_method=2	Two-stage least squares (2SLS)
_method=3	Three-stage least squares (3SLS, may be iterative)
_method=4	Full information maximum likelihood (FIML, may be iterative)

Note that LIML and FIML are not true nonlinear maximum likelihood estimation methods. Instead they are types of instrumental variables estimation. In GPE, three variants of the FIML method are available:

_method={4,0} (or 4)	FIML instrumental variable method (Hausman, 1975)
_method={4,1}	FIML linearized method (Dhrymes, 1970)
_method={4,2}	FIML Newton method

2SLS and 3SLS are flavors of the instrumental variables estimation method, where the instrumental variables used are all the predetermined variables in the system. For estimation of a linear system model, external instrumental variables may be requested and specified in the matrix _ivar. The data matrix _ivar will be combined with all the predetermined variables to form the basis for instrumental variable estimation. A constant term is automatically included in _ivar. For technical details and comparisons of different estimation methods for a linear equations system, refer to your econometrics textbook.

Klein Model I (1950)

The pedagogical example of Klein Model I is typically used to demonstrate the model estimation of a linear regression equations system. It was the first U.S. economy-wide econometric model consisting of three stochastic equations with about 10 variables covering the prewar period from 1920 to 1941. **klein.txt** is a text data file containing these variables which will be used in the Klein Model I. There are several variations of the Klein Model in the literature. For the convenience of illustration, we adopt the following specification of the model:

$$C = \alpha_0 + \alpha_1 P + \alpha_2 P_{-1} + \alpha_3 (W1 + W2) + \varepsilon_1$$
$$I = \beta_0 + \beta_1 P + \beta_2 P_{-1} + \beta_3 K + \varepsilon_2$$
$$W1 = \gamma_0 + \gamma_1 X + \gamma_2 X_{-1} + \gamma_3 A + \varepsilon_3$$
$$X = C + I + G$$
$$P = X - T - W1$$
$$K = K_{-1} + I$$

The variables used are:

C	Consumption in billions of 1934 dollars.
I	Investment.
W1	Private wage bill.
X	Total private income before taxes, or $X = Y + T - W2$ where Y is after-tax income.
P	Private profits.
K	Capital stock in the beginning of year, or capital stock lagged one year.
W2	Government wage bill.
G	Government non-wage spending.
T	Indirect taxes plus net exports.
A	Year – 1931 (a time trend).

The first three equations are stochastic with unknown parameters α's, β's, and γ's, respectively. The remaining three equations are accounting identities. Since the sum of private and public wage bills (W1+W2) appears in the first equation, it is more convenient to introduce one additional endogenous variable W, total wage bill, with the accounting identity:

$$W = W1 + W2$$

The alternative is to impose a linear parameter restriction of identical parameter value for W1 and W2 in the first equation. The resulting model consists of 7 endogenous variables (C, I, W1, X, P, K, W) and 8 predetermined variables (X_{-1}, P_{-1}, K_{-1}, W2, G, T, A, and Constant). Lesson 13.1 below implements the model as described.

Lesson 13.1: Klein Model I

In the program, from line 3 to line 15, the data file **klein.txt** is loaded and each variable used in the model is defined. Data matrix yvar of endogenous variables is defined in line 16. Line 17 defines the data matrix xvar of predetermined variables which includes three lagged endogenous variables and four exogenous variables. By default, a constant term is automatically included in each stochastic equation. Then, in the next two lines, are the two important control variables: _eq and _id. We

197

explain the construction of the first line of these two matrices, and leave you to puzzle out the rest.

First, the _eq matrix (line 21) specifies which variables are to be included in which stochastic equations. Recall the first stochastic equation in the Klein Model I:

$$C = \alpha_0 + \alpha_1 P + \alpha_2 P_{-1} + \alpha_3 (W1 + W2) + \varepsilon_1$$

Then the first line of the _eq matrix is:

```
      @ C   I  W1  X   P  K   W XL PL KL W2  A  G  T  1 @
_eq =  {-1  0   0  0   1  0   1  0  1  0  0  0  0  0  0, ...
```

Note that the column under the variable C contains a −1. This means that C is the left-hand side variable of the first stochastic equation. Since I and W1 are not in the first stochastic equation, we place 0's in their respective columns. Looking again at this equation, we see that the right-hand side variables are: constant, P, P_{-1}, and W (remember that W = W1+ W2). To let GPE know that P, P_{-1}, and W are in the first equation, we place 1's in their respective places in the _eq matrix. This does not mean that their coefficients are restricted to be equal to one, it merely tells GPE to include those particular variables in the equation. GPE includes the constant automatically. All other variables (namely X, K, X_{-1}, K_{-1}, W2, A, G, T) are not in the first equation. Putting 0's in the respective places of these variables in the _eq matrix lets GPE know that it should not include these variables in the first stochastic equation of the system.

```
   /*
   ** Lesson 13.1: Klein's Model I
   ** Simultaneous Equation System of Klein's Model I
   */
1  use gpe2;
2  output file = gpe\output13.1 reset;
3  load data[23,10] = gpe\klein.txt;

4  a=data[2:23,1]-1931;        @ time trend: 1931 = 0 @
5  c=data[2:23,2];             @ consumption @
6  p=data[2:23,3];             @ profit income @
7  w1=data[2:23,4];            @ private wage income @
8  i=data[2:23,5];             @ investment @
9  k1=data[2:23,6];            @ lagged capital stock @
10 x=data[2:23,7];             @ private total income @
11 w2=data[2:23,8];            @ public wage income @
12 g=data[2:23,9];             @ government spending @
13 t=data[2:23,10];            @ tax @

14 k=k1[2:22]|209.4;           @ capital stock @
15 w=w1+w2;                    @ total wage income @

16 yvar=c~i~w1~x~p~k~w;
17 xvar=lag1(x~p~k)~w2~a~g~t;

18 call reset;

19 _names={"c","i","w1","x","p","k","w",
          "x-1","p-1","k-1","w2","a","g","t"};
20 _vcov=1;
      @ C   I  W1  X   P  K   W XL PL KL W2  A  G  T  1 @
21 _eq =  {-1  0   0  0   1  0   1  0  1  0  0  0  0  0  0,
           0  -1  0  0   1  0   0  0  1  1  0  0  0  0  0,
           0   0  -1  1  0  0   0  1  0  0  0  1  0  0};
22 _id =  { 1  1   0  -1  0  0   0  0  0  0  0  0  0  1  0,
```

```
                0   0  -1   1  -1   0   0   0   0   0   0   0   0  -1,
                0   1   0   0   0  -1   0   0   0   1   0   0   0   0,
                0   0   1   0   0   0  -1   0   0   0   1   0   0   0};
```

```
23   _begin=2;

24   _method=0;          @ OLS estimation @
25   call estimate(yvar,xvar);
26   _method=1;          @ LIML estimation @
27   call estimate(yvar,xvar);
28   _method=2;          @ 2SLS estimation @
29   call estimate(yvar,xvar);

30   _iter=100;
31   _method=3;          @ 3SLS estimation (iterative) @
32   call estimate(yvar,xvar);
33   _method=4;          @ FIML estimation @
34   call estimate(yvar,xvar);
35   end;
```

Similarly, line 22 specifies the identity equations of the model. Take the first identity equation as an example:

$$X = C + I + G$$

It involves the variables X, C, I, and G. Therefore, in the first row of the _id matrix, only the relevant columns have non-zero values. Typically these entries are 1 or -1, but they could be any other values as required. Variables not used in the definition of an identity have zeros in the corresponding places of the _id matrix. The first row of the _id matrix looks like this:

```
          @ C   I  W1   X   P   K   W  XL  PL  KL  W2   A   G   T   1 @
   _id =   { 1   1   0  -1   0   0   0   0   0   0   0   0   1   0,  ...
```

The easiest way to understand the construction of the system model described so far is to relate it with the matrix representation:

$$YB + X\Gamma = U$$

where Y corresponds to yvar and X corresponds to xvar in the program. The matrix _eq|_id (vertical concatenation of _eq and _id) is the specification matrix corresponding to the transpose of B|Γ (vertical concatenation of B and Γ).

Because of the use of lag variables, the first observation of the data is lost and estimation must start from the second observation (see line 23). In lines 24 through 34, five estimation methods are carried out. They are OLS, LIML, 2SLS, 3SLS, and FIML. It is of interest to see the covariance matrices of the equations, thus line 20 sets the option _vcov=1 to show the variance-covariance matrix across equations and across parameters as well. Note that 3SLS and FIML are iterative methods, and it is wise to set an iteration limit for the solution to converge. Line 30, _iter=100, does the job.

Running the program of Lesson 13.1 will generate about 20 pages of output. To save space, we will only present the results of 2SLS because of its popularity in the literature. You should run the program in its entirety and check the output file to see the complete results. In a summary table, the parameter estimates of these methods are listed and compared. You need to check your econometrics textbook for the evaluation of the pros and cons of these estimation methods, in particular the differences between limited information and full information estimation methods.

The regression results of a typical linear system model are divided into two parts: the results of the system of equations as a whole, and the results of each separate equation. Here we present only the first part of 2SLS for the estimated parameters, including the variance-covariance matrices across equations. For the rest of regression results by equation, we refer to the output file output13.1.

```
Simultaneous Linear Equations Estimation
-----------------------------------------
Number of Endogenous Variables = 7
Number of Predetermined Variables = 8
Number of Stochastic Equations = 3
Number of Observations = 21
Estimation Range =   2              22

Two Stages Least Squares Estimation

System R-Square = 0.97711
Log-Likelihood = -121.56134
```

Equation Name	Variable Name	Estimated Coefficient	Asymptotic Std Error	t-Ratio
C	P	0.017302	0.11805	0.14657
	W	0.81018	0.040250	20.129
	P-1	0.21623	0.10727	2.0158
	CONSTANT	16.555	1.3208	12.534
I	P	0.15022	0.17323	0.86718
	P-1	0.61594	0.16279	3.7838
	K-1	-0.15779	0.036126	-4.3677
	CONSTANT	20.278	7.5427	2.6885
W1	X	0.43886	0.035632	12.316
	X-1	0.14667	0.038836	3.7767
	A	0.13040	0.029141	4.4746
	CONSTANT	1.5003	1.1478	1.3071

```
Asymptotic Variance-Covariance Matrix of Equations
C            1.0441
I            0.43785        1.3832
W1          -0.38523        0.19261        0.47643
                 C              I              W1
```

```
Asymptotic Variance-Covariance Matrix of Coefficients
P            0.013936
W           -0.0015260      0.0016200
P-1         -0.0095710     -0.00053085      0.011506
CONSTANT    -0.015344      -0.032733       -0.0047520      1.7445
P            0.0040375      0.0012781      -0.0046423     -0.045188      0.030008
P-1         -0.0031110     -0.0011810       0.0051395      0.017372     -0.025772
K-1         -0.00037500     0.00039811     -0.00013045    -0.0080439     0.0041898
CONSTANT     0.057936      -0.082066        0.020400       2.1124       -0.92485
X           -0.0018149      5.1138E-005     0.0011799      0.0092111     0.00059433
X-1          0.0018888     -8.0164E-005    -0.0017884      0.00071044   -0.00058617
A            0.00066034    -0.00052372      0.00047623     0.0027719     0.00047661
CONSTANT    -0.00052229     0.0015772       0.032840      -0.61273      -0.0017044
                 P              W              P-1          CONSTANT          P

P-1          0.026499
K-1         -0.0038717      0.0013051
CONSTANT     0.77760       -0.26903        56.892
X           -0.00033125    -9.0028E-005     0.013436       0.0012696
X-1          0.00061121     9.9812E-005    -0.020120      -0.0011997      0.0015082
```

	P-1	K-1	CONSTANT	X	X-1
A	-0.00066991	0.00017448	-0.032062	-0.00030915	5.1023E-005
CONSTANT	-0.015548	-0.00038089	0.36894	-0.0066842	-0.015405

	A	CONSTANT
A	0.00084920	
CONSTANT	0.015608	1.3174

The system estimation methods such as 3SLS and FIML may be iterated until the convergent solution is found. To control the iteration, as in the case of nonlinear iteration methods, the following input control variables may be applied: _iter, _tol, and _restart. We refer readers to Appendix A for more details of these control variables. For example, the statement _iter=100 of line 30 sets the number of iterations for 3SLS and FIML estimation. This is to ensure the near efficiency (theoretically speaking) of the parameter estimates, if they are found before exhausting the limit of iterations. It will be warned that the results may be unreliable when iterations exceed the limit.

In Lesson 13.1, line 33,

```
_method = 4;
```

indicates that the instrumental variables method of FIML is used for estimation. It is equivalent to state the scalar 4 as a vector {4,0}. The alternatives are either setting _method to {4,1} for a linearized FIML or setting it to {4,2} for the Newton method. It is mind-boggling that, for the same problem, not all the FIML methods will converge to the same solution (provided there is convergence of a solution). It is now common wisdom that different methods may produce different results due to different algorithms in use for nonlinear model estimation.

We now present the summary table of the parameter estimates obtained from five methods we use in estimating the Klein Model I. Numbers in parentheses are asymptotic standard errors.

Eq.	Variable	OLS	LIML	2SLS	3SLS	FIML/IV
C	P	0.19293	-0.22251	0.017302	0.16451	-0.23190
		(0.082065)	(0.20175)	(0.11805)	(0.096198)	(0.23178)
	W	0.79622	0.82256	0.81018	0.76580	0.80182
		(0.035939)	(0.055378)	(0.040250)	(0.034760)	(0.037137)
	P_{-1}	0.089885	0.39603	0.21623	0.17656	0.38545
		(0.081559)	(0.17360)	(0.10727)	(0.090100)	(0.18362)
	Const.	16.237	17.148	16.555	16.559	18.340
		(1.1721)	(1.8403)	(1.3208)	(1.2244)	(1.8637)
I	P	0.47964	0.075185	0.15022	-0.35651	-0.80082
		(0.087377)	(0.20218)	(0.17323)	(0.26015)	(0.35761)
	P_{-1}	0.33304	0.68039	0.61594	1.0113	1.0516
		(0.090747)	(0.18817)	(0.16279)	(0.24876)	(0.30823)
	K_{-1} -	0.11179	-0.16826	-0.15779	-0.26019	-0.14811
		(0.024048)	(0.040798)	(0.036126)	(0.050868)	(0.033826)
	Const.	10.126	22.591	20.278	42.895	27.267
		(4.9175)	(8.5458)	(7.5427)	(10.593)	(7.7850)
W1	X	0.43948	0.43394	0.43886	0.37478	0.23412
		(0.029158)	(0.067937)	(0.035632)	(0.031103)	(0.045546)

X_{-1}	0.14609	0.15132	0.14667	0.19365	0.28464
	(0.033671)	(0.067054)	(0.038836)	(0.032402)	(0.042736)
A	0.13025	0.13159	0.13040	0.16792	0.23487
	(0.028711)	(0.032386)	(0.029141)	(0.028929)	(0.033488)
Const.	1.4970	1.5262	1.5003	2.6247	5.7963
	(1.1427)	(1.1884)	(1.1478)	(1.1956)	(1.7621)
Log-Likelihood	-141.92156	-122.81636	-121.56134	-86.14210	-83.32381

Lesson 13.2: Klein Model I Reformulated

In **lesson13.1**, we saw the use of the input variable _begin (line 23) to control the starting data observation for model estimation, and of _vcov (line 20) to show the estimated variance-covariance matrix of the parameters. There are many other input variables useful for controlling single equation model estimation that are applicable to system model estimation. These include, but are not limited to: _const, _dlags, and _restr. In addition, for presenting the estimation results, control variables such as _rstat and _rplot are useful. For details of using these input control variables, we refer the reader to Appendix A: GPE Control Variables.

lesson13.2 below is a reformulation of Klein Model I. There are no new things added. Instead, it demonstrates the use of a few of the input control variables mentioned above in order to offer an alternative formulation of the model. This may be a more useful representation for the purpose of forecasting and simulation. In the following, we will list the program without running it.

```
     /*
     ** Lesson 13.2: Klein's Model I Reformulated
     ** Using _dlags and _restr
     */
1    use gpe2;
2    output file = gpe\output13.2 reset;
3    load data[23,10] = gpe\klein.txt;

4    a=data[2:23,1]-1931;       @ time trend: 1931 = 0 @
5    c=data[2:23,2];            @ consumption @
6    p=data[2:23,3];            @ profit income @
7    w1=data[2:23,4];           @ private wage income @
8    i=data[2:23,5];            @ investment @
9    k1=data[2:23,6];           @ lagged capital stock @
10   x=data[2:23,7];            @ private total income @
11   w2=data[2:23,8];           @ public wage income @
12   g=data[2:23,9];            @ government spending @
13   t=data[2:23,10];           @ tax @

14   k=k1[2:22]|209.4;          @ capital stock @
15   w=w1+w2;                   @ total wage income @

     @ do not include lagged endog. var. in xvar and _names @
16   yvar=c~i~w1~x~p~k;
17   xvar=w2~a~g~t;

18   call reset;

19   _names={"c","i","w1","x","p","k",
             "w2","a","g","t"};
20   _vcov=1;

     @ do not include lagged endog. var. in _eq and _id @
     @          C  I W1  X  P  K W2  A  G  T  1 @
```

202

```
21   _eq =    {-1  0  1  0  1  0  1  0  0  0,
                0 -1  0  0  1  0  0  0  0  0,
                0  0 -1  1  0  0  0  1  0  0};
22   _id =    { 1  1  0 -1  0  0  0  0  1  0,
                0  0 -1  1 -1  0  0  0  0 -1,
                0  1  0  0  0 -1  0  0  0  0};

     @ using _dlags option to add the specified lagged endog. var. @
     @ after the entire list of endog. var. in _eq and _id @
     @          C  I W1  X  P  K  @
23   _dlags = {0  0  0  0  1  0,
                0  0  0  0  1  1,
                0  0  0  1  0  0,
                0  0  0  0  0  0,
                0  0  0  0  0  0,
                0  0  0  0  0  1};

     @ restriction: W1 and W2 share the same coef. in C eq. @
     @ EQ:              C   |   I   |    W1    @
     @ VAR:     W1 P P1 W2|P P1 K1|X X1  A|q  **incl. lagged endog. @
24   _restr = { 1  0  0 -1  0  0  0 0  0  0 0};

25   _method=2; @ 2SLS estimation @
26   call estimate(yvar,xvar);

27   _iter=100;
28   _method=3; @ 3SLS estimation (iterative) @
29   call estimate(yvar,xvar);

30   _method=4; @ FIML estimation @
31   call estimate(yvar,xvar);
32   end;
```

We notice the use of _dlags in line 23 to specify the lagged endogenous variables in each equation. _dlags is a G×G matrix whose entries indicate the number of lags for each endogenous variable (column) in each equation (row). If there is no lag of a particular endogenous variable in a particular equation, the corresponding entry in _dlags is set to 0. The resulting lag variables are appended to the list of endogenous variables to form the complete system. Instead of hard-coding the relevant lags as in Lesson 13.1, the advantage of using _dlags to specify the model's lag structure is to let GPE control the dynamic specification of the model. This feature will be useful for forecasting and simulation.

Considering linear restrictions of the model's parameters is a cumbersome task in a simultaneous equations system. Whenever possible, it is recommended to substitute out the restrictions (as we did in Lesson 13.1 by defining W = W1+W2). Nevertheless, we recall that linear restrictions are expressed in the form $R\beta=q$, where β is the parameter vector and _restr=[R|q] is the restriction matrix. The number of rows in _restr is the number of restrictions imposed. We first introduced the use of variable _restr in Lesson 3.4, to specify the linear restrictions in a single regression equation. For a system model, in the matrix R, restrictions are stacked horizontally in accordance with the order of equations. q is a column vector of the restricted values. Cross equation restrictions, if any, can be coded accordingly. In general, restrictions on the constant terms are not required. In cases with restrictions involving the constant term, we have to explicitly treat the constant term as one of the exogenous variables. The input control variable _const is used for this purpose. That is, coding the restrictions with the constant term (as one of the exogenous variables) requires setting _const=0 first. Then the restrictions involving the constant term can be specified correctly. Normally, a constant term will be added for each equation, unless otherwise specified. This variable can be a column vector with 0 (no constant) or 1 (with constant) associated with each equation.

Leaving Klein Model I for the moment, let's move on to consider a special class of simultaneous linear regression equations which has broad application. More examples involving the usage of the above mentioned input control variables will follow.

Seemingly Unrelated Regression Equations System (SUR)

Recall the matrix representation of a simultaneous linear equations system: $YB + X\Gamma = U$. Let $B = -I$ (minus identity matrix) and $E = -U$. Then, the resulting system is a seemingly unrelated regression system of equations:

$$Y = X\Gamma + E$$

The system is *seemingly unrelated* because of the correlated error structure of the model due to the embedded parameter restrictions or data constraints. In other words, errors in one equation may be correlated with errors in other equations.

The estimation of a cost-minimizing factor demand system, developed by Berndt and Wood (1975), is an application of seemingly unrelated regression. The system is derived from an indirect translog cost function of four factors: capital (K), labor (L), energy materials (E), and non-energy materials (M). Assuming constant returns to scale and price normalization, the real unit cost function is:

$$ln(c) = \beta_0 + \sum_{i=K,L,E} \beta_i \, ln(p_i) + \tfrac{1}{2} \sum_{i=K,L,E} \sum_{j=K,L,E} \beta_{ij} \, ln(p_i) \, ln(p_j)$$

where $c = (C/P_M)/Q$ is the normalized unit cost (C is total cost and Q is total output), and the normalized factor price is $p_i - P_i/P_M$ for $i = K, L, E$. All the βs are unknown parameters of the cost function. Invoking the Shepard Lemma, we can derive the factor shares as $S_i = P_i X_i/C = \partial ln(c)/\partial ln(p_i)$, where X_i is the quantity demanded of the i-th factor (i = K, L, E). Therefore, adding the error terms, the system of factor demand equations for model estimation is written as:

$$S_i = \beta_i + \sum_{j=K,L,E} \beta_{ij} \, ln(p_j) + \varepsilon_i$$
$$i = K, L, E$$

The symmetry condition, $\beta_{ij} = \beta_{ji}$, must be imposed as parameter restrictions. We note that the factor M is treated as a *numeraire*, and it is clear that $S_M = 1 - \sum_{i=K,L,E} S_i$

Lesson 13.3: Berndt-Wood Model

The price and quantity data of the Berndt-Wood Model come in two files: **bwp.txt** and **bwq.txt**. The time series from 1947 to 1971 covers the period before oil embargo. Quantity series are in billions of dollars, and the price series are the 1947-based indexes.

```
/*
** Lesson 13.3: Berndt-Wood Model
** Seemingly Unrelated Regression Estimation
** Factor Shares System with Symmetry Restrictions
```

```
    */
 1  use gpe2;
 2  output file = gpe\output13.3 reset;

 3  n=26;
 4  load x[n,6] = gpe\bwq.txt;
 5  year=x[2:n,1];
 6  qy=x[2:n,2];
 7  qk=x[2:n,3];
 8  ql=x[2:n,4];
 9  qe=x[2:n,5];
10  qm=x[2:n,6];
11  load x[n,6] = gpe\bwp.txt;
12  py=x[2:n,2];
13  pk=x[2:n,3];
14  pl=x[2:n,4];
15  pe=x[2:n,5];
16  pm=x[2:n,6];

17  tc=pk.*qk + pl.*ql + pe.*qe + pm.*qm;
18  sk=(pk.*qk)./tc;
19  sl=(pl.*ql)./tc;
20  se=(pe.*qe)./tc;
21  sm=(pm.*qm)./tc;
22  pk=ln(pk./pm);
23  pl=ln(pl./pm);
24  pe=ln(pe./pm);

25  yv=sk~sl~se;
26  xv=pk~pl~pe;

27  call reset;

28  _names={"sk","sl","se","pk","pl","pe"};

              @ PK PL PE|PK PL PE|PK PL PE| q @
29  _restr = {  0  1  0 -1  0  0  0  0  0  0,
                0  0  1  0  0  0 -1  0  0  0,
                0  0  0  0  0  1  0 -1  0  0};

30  _method=0;
31  call estimate(yv,xv);
32  _method=1;
33  call estimate(yv,xv);
34  _method=2;
35  call estimate(yv,xv);

36  _iter=50;
37  _method=3;
38  call estimate(yv,xv);
39  _method=4;
40  call estimate(yv,xv);
41  _method={4,1};
42  call estimate(yv,xv);
43  _method={4,2};
44  call estimate(yv,xv);
45  end;
```

The program is rather straightforward. It loads the two data files and calculates the necessary variables such as factor shares and normalized prices needed for model estimation. We do not use either _eq or _id to define the equations system. First, there are no identity equations. All the equations in the model are stochastic. The model is in the form $Y = X\Gamma + E$ where Y corresponds to yv and X corresponds to xv in the program, and all variables in the xv matrix appear in each equation. Recall that this is exactly the default structure of the _eq matrix.

For the Berndt-Wood example of three equations or endogenous variables (factor shares) and three exogenous variable (factor prices), the _eq matrix could be specified as follows:

```
_eq = {-1  0  0  1  1  1,
        0 -1  0  1  1  1,
        0  0 -1  1  1  1};
```

The more challenging task is to specify the symmetry condition for the parameters. As shown in **lesson13.2**, linear restrictions are expressed in $R\beta = q$ and _restr = $[R|q]$. Recall that the number of rows in restr is the number of restrictions imposed. As explained before, the restrictions are stacked horizontally in matrix R, and q is a column vector of the restricted values. There are three symmetry restrictions for the Berndt-Wood Model across three equations: $\beta_{KL} = \beta_{LK}$, $\beta_{KE} = \beta_{EK}$, and $\beta_{LE} = \beta_{EL}$. Line 29 does exactly that by setting the correct entries in the _restr matrix. No restrictions on the constant terms are needed.

The first row of _restr corresponds to the first restriction $\beta_{KL} = \beta_{LK}$. The entry for the variable PL of SK equation is set to 1, while the entry for the variable PK of SL equation is −1. Since there is a zero for the q's column, it amounts to $\beta_{KL} - \beta_{LK} = 0$, or $\beta_{KL} = \beta_{LK}$. By the same token, the other two restrictions, $\beta_{KE} = \beta_{EK}$ and $\beta_{LE} = \beta_{EL}$, are expressed in the second and third rows of _restr, respectively:

```
          @ PK PL PE| PK PL PE| PK PL PE|  q @
_restr = {  0  1  0  -1  0  0   0  0  0   0,
            0  0  1   0  0  0  -1  0  0   0,
            0  0  0   0  0  1   0 -1  0   0};
```

Although we estimate the model with all the available methods, there are only two sets of solutions. One is from the limited information method, and the other from full information. Of course, the single equation method is not appropriate for a seemingly unrelated equations system in which parameter restrictions bind the equations together. Cross equation covariance is of interest in the multiple equations system. Iterative 3SLS and FIML are the methods of choice for this particular class of model. In the literature, the estimated parameters of a production function are rich in terms of elasticity interpretation. Elasticities are simple to compute once the parameters have been estimated according to the formula:

Elasticities of Substitution	Price Elasticities
$\zeta_{ij} = \dfrac{\beta_{ij} + S_i S_j}{S_i S_j}$	$\eta_{ij} = S_j \zeta_{ij}$
$\zeta_{ii} = \dfrac{\beta_{ii} + S_i (S_i - 1)}{S_i^2}$	$i, j = K, L, E, M$

We leave the elasticity interpretation of the production function to the reader. Here is the summary output of 3SLS estimation of the Berndt-Wood Model (see output13.2 for the estimated results by equation):

Simultaneous Linear Equations Estimation

```
Number of Endogenous Variables = 3
Number of Predetermined Variables = 4
Number of Stochastic Equations = 3
Number of Observations = 25
Estimation Range =   1          25

Three Stages Least Squares Estimation
Maximum Number of Iterations = 50
Tolerance = 0.001

Iteration =   1    Log Likelihood =  344.55
Parameters =   0.030634    -0.00035814   -0.0097343    0.057091    -0.00035814
0.075102    -0.0044159     0.25349      -0.0097343    -0.0044159    0.018921
0.044330
Iteration =   2    Log Likelihood =  344.57
Parameters =   0.029791    -0.00038017   -0.010208     0.057029    -0.00038017
0.075403    -0.0044256     0.25340      -0.010208     -0.0044256    0.018761
0.044291


System R-Square = 0.87645
Log-Likelihood = 344.56744
```

Equation Name	Variable Name	Estimated Coefficient	Asymptotic Std Error	t-Ratio
SK	PK	0.029791	0.0059443	5.0117
	PL	-0.00038017	0.0038638	-0.098392
	PE	-0.010208	0.0034011	-3.0014
	CONSTANT	0.057029	0.0013574	42.013
SL	PK	-0.00038017	0.0038638	-0.098392
	PL	0.075403	0.0068108	11.071
	PE	-0.0044256	0.0024401	-1.8137
	CONSTANT	0.25340	0.0021210	119.47
SE	PK	-0.010208	0.0034011	-3.0014
	PL	-0.0044256	0.0024401	-1.8137
	PE	0.018761	0.0053539	3.5042
	CONSTANT	0.044291	0.00088399	50.103

```
Asymptotic Variance-Covariance Matrix of Equations
SK          9.9232E-006
SL          8.0000E-006   2.8720E-005
SE          4.6387E-006   4.7966E-006   3.1884E-006
                 SK            SL            SE
```

Lesson 13.4: Berndt-Wood Model Extended

Extending from the basic system model of factor demand equations, the stochastic unit cost function:

$$ln(c) = \beta_0 + \sum_{i=K,L,E} \beta_i \, ln(p_i) + \tfrac{1}{2} \sum_{i=K,L,E} \sum_{j=K,L,E} \beta_{ij} \, ln(p_i) \, ln(p_j) + \varepsilon_c$$

may be added to the model of Lesson 13.3 to form a four-equation system. The idea is to explicitly estimate the cost function from which the factor share equations are derived. In particular, this model allows us to estimate the scale parameter β_0 of the cost function. In addition, both first-order β_i and second-order β_{ij} parameters are constrained to equal the corresponding parameters of the factor share equations.

The parameter restrictions are certainly more involved in the extended model. Since the restrictions involve constant terms of each equation, we need to address the issue of regression intercept explicitly. In **lesson13.4** below, we first define the constant vector one in line 32, and include it in the list of exogenous variables xv in line 34.

207

The model is then estimated without the constant term or _const=0 (line 38). Line 39 specifies 13 linear restrictions among 23 variables (including constant terms for each equation). Identifying and restricting the parameters of the unit cost function with those of derived factor share equations is accomplished in the first 10 rows of _restr. The last 3 rows are the familiar three symmetry conditions across factor demand equations, as specified in Lesson 13.3.

```
    /*
    ** Lesson 13.4: Berndt-Wood Model Extended
    ** Seemingly Unrelated Regression Estimation
    ** Full System with Restrictions
    */
 1  use gpe2;
 2  output file = gpe\output13.4 reset;
 3  n=26;
 4  load x[n,6] = gpe\bwq.txt;
 5  year=x[2:n,1];
 6  qy=x[2:n,2];
 7  qk=x[2:n,3];
 8  ql=x[2:n,4];
 9  qe=x[2:n,5];
10  qm=x[2:n,6];
11  load x[n,6] = gpe\bwp.txt;
12  py=x[2:n,2];
13  pk=x[2:n,3];
14  pl=x[2:n,4];
15  pe=x[2:n,5];
16  pm=x[2:n,6];

17  tc=pk.*qk + pl.*ql + pe.*qe + pm.*qm;
18  sk=(pk.*qk)./tc;
19  sl=(pl.*ql)./tc;
20  se=(pe.*qe)./tc;
21  sm=(pm.*qm)./tc;
22  c=ln(tc./pm./qy);
23  pk=ln(pk./pm);
24  pl=ln(pl./pm);
25  pe=ln(pe./pm);
26  pkpk=0.5*pk.*pk;
27  pkpl=pk.*pl;
28  pkpe=pk.*pe;
29  plpl=0.5*pl.*pl;
30  plpe=pl.*pe;
31  pepe=0.5*pe.*pe;
32  one=ones(rows(c),1);

33  yv=sk~sl~se~c;
34  xv=pk~pl~pe~pkpk~pkpl~pkpe~plpl~plpe~pepe~one;

35  call reset;
36  _names={"sk","sl","se","c","pk","pl","pe",
            "pkpk","pkpl","pkpe","plpl","plpe","pepe","one"};
37  _iter=50;
38  _const=0;
                    @ |----yv----|-------------xv--------------| @
                    @ SK SL SE  C PK PL PE KK KL KE LL LE EE  1 @
39  _eq[4,14] = {  -1  0  0  0  1  1  1  0  0  0  0  0  0  1,
                    0 -1  0  0  1  1  1  0  0  0  0  0  0  1,
                    0  0 -1  0  1  1  1  0  0  0  0  0  0  1,
                    0  0  0 -1  1  1  1  1  1  1  1  1  1  1};

40  _restr[12,23] =
                                      @ P  P  P  K  K  K  L  L  E @
     @PK PL PE  1|PK PL PE  1|PK PL PE  1|K  L  E  K  L  E  L  E  E  1|q @
      {0  0  0 -1  0  0  0  0  0  0  0  0  1  0  0  0  0  0  0  0  0  0,
```

```
    0   0   0   0   0   0   0  -1   0   0   0   0 0 1 0 0 0 0 0 0 0 0 0,
    0   0   0   0   0   0   0   0   0   0   0  -1 0 0 1 0 0 0 0 0 0 0 0,
   -1   0   0   0   0   0   0   0   0   0   0   0 0 0 0 1 0 0 0 0 0 0 0,
    0   0   0   0   0  -1   0   0   0   0   0   0 0 0 0 0 0 1 0 0 0 0 0,
    0   0   0   0   0   0   0   0   0   0  -1   0 0 0 0 0 0 0 0 1 0 0 0,
    0  -1   0   0   0   0   0   0   0   0   0   0 0 0 0 1 0 0 0 0 0 0 0,
    0   0  -1   0   0   0   0   0   0   0   0   0 0 0 0 0 1 0 0 0 0 0 0,
    0   0   0   0   0   0  -1   0   0   0   0   0 0 0 0 0 0 1 0 0 0 0 0,
    0   1   0   0  -1   0   0   0   0   0   0   0 0 0 0 0 0 0 0 0 0 0 0,
    0   0   1   0   0   0   0   0  -1   0   0   0 0 0 0 0 0 0 0 0 0 0 0,
    0   0   0   0   0   0   1   0   0  -1   0   0 0 0 0 0 0 0 0 0 0 0 0};
```

```
41  _method=3;
42  call estimate(yv,xv);
43  end;
```

The extended Berndt-Wood Model is estimated with 3SLS. To save space, we leave out the lengthy results of the model estimation. You should run the program and check out the results yourself. Instead, we compare the parameter estimates for two versions of the Berndt-Wood Model. We do not expect the parameter estimates to be the same, or close, for the two models, even though the same 3SLS method is used for model estimation. Numbers in the parentheses are standard errors.

Eq.	Variable	Basic Model	Extended Model
S_K	$ln(P_K)$	0.029791 (0.0059443)	0.040482 (0.0048854)
	$ln(P_L)$	-0.00038017 (0.0038638)	0.029914 (0.0031598)
	$ln(P_E)$	-0.010208 (0.0034011)	-0.0043608 (0.0026280)
	Constant	0.057029 (0.0013574)	0.049289 (0.0015800)
S_L	$ln(P_K)$	-0.00038017 (0.0038638)	0.029914 (0.0031598)
	$ln(P_L)$	0.075403 (0.0068108)	0.096927 (0.0065949)
	$ln(P_E)$	-0.0044256 (0.0024401)	0.014914 (0.0019469)
	Constant	0.25340 (0.0021210)	0.24955 (0.0022281)
S_E	$ln(P_K)$	-0.010208 (0.0034011)	-0.0043608 (0.0026280)
	$ln(P_L)$	-0.0044256 (0.0024401)	0.014914 (0.0019469)
	$ln(P_E)$	0.018761 (0.0053539)	0.019229 (0.0047603)
	Constant	0.044291 (0.00088399)	0.039379 (0.0010016)
C	$ln(P_K)$		0.049289 (0.0015800)
	$ln(P_L)$		0.24955 (0.0022281)
	$ln(P_E)$		0.039379 (0.0010016)
	$ln(P_K)ln(P_K)$		0.040482 (0.0048854)
	½ $ln(P_K)ln(P_L)$		0.029914 (0.0031598)
	½ $ln(P_K)ln(P_E)$		-0.0043608 (0.0026280)
	$ln(P_L)ln(P_L)$		0.096927 (0.0065949)
	½ $ln(P_L)ln(P_E)$		0.014914 (0.0019469)
	$ln(P_E)ln(P_E)$		0.019229 (0.0047603)
	Constant		-0.16689 (0.010360)
Log-Likelihood		344.56744	390.87112

Based on the Likelihood Ratio statistic: -2(344.56744-390.87112) = 92.60736, compared with the critical value 18.31 (Chi-square distribution of 10 degrees of freedom at 95% significance level), the gain in efficiency of the parameter estimates using the full system, including the unit cost function and share equations, is obvious.

Nonlinear Maximum Likelihood Estimation

The method of full information maximum likelihood is intrinsically a nonlinear optimization method. We can write a general representation of a system of nonlinear equations as follows:

$$F(Y,X,\beta) = U$$

Assuming N data observations, Y is an N by G data matrix of G endogenous variables, X is an N by K data matrix of K predetermined variables (including exogenous and lagged variables), β is the parameter matrix, and U is an N by G error matrix of G stochastic equations. Let

$$F = [F_1, F_2, ..., F_G]'$$
$$Y = [Y_1, Y_2, ..., Y_G]$$
$$X = [X_1, X_2, ..., X_K]$$
$$U = [U_1, U_2, ..., U_G]'$$
$$\beta = [\beta_1, \beta_2, ..., \beta_G]'$$

Then, the model can be rewritten in G separate stochastic equations as:

$$F_1(Y,X,\beta_1) = U_1$$
$$F_2(Y,X,\beta_2) = U_2$$
$$...$$
$$F_G(Y,X,\beta_G) = U_G$$

Note that identity equations are *substituted out* in order to avoid the complication of using constrained optimization. Also, not all the columns of data matrices Y and X are used in each equation of the system. However, there must be at least one distinct endogenous variable appearing in each equation. The parameter vector β_j effectively selects the variables included in the equation j.

Log-Likelihood Function of Nonlinear Equations System

We now briefly describe the methodology of nonlinear FIML. Chapter VI covered the general framework of nonlinear optimization, and must be reviewed. Many econometrics textbooks and journal articles discuss the implementation in more detail.

Assume U is normally independently distributed with mean 0 (a G-element zero vector) and covariance $\Sigma \otimes I$. That is, $Cov(U_j, U_k) = \sigma_{jk}$, where σ_{jk} is an element of the G by G cross-equation covariance matrix Σ. For each equation j, U_j is zero in mean and it has homogeneous variance σ_{jj} or σ_j^2.

Constructing from the joint normal probability density of U_i and the Jacobian factor $J_i = J_i(\beta) = det(\partial U_i / \partial Y_i)$ for each observation i, the likelihood function is

$$(2\pi)^{-G/2} |det(\Sigma)|^{-1/2} exp(-\tfrac{1}{2}U_i\Sigma^{-1}U_i') |det(J_i)|$$

It follows immediately that the log-likelihood function $ll(\beta,\Sigma|Y,X)$ for a sample of N observations is

$-NG/2\ ln(2\pi)\ -N/2\ ln|det(\Sigma)|\ -\frac{1}{2}\Sigma_{i=1,2,...,N}\ U_i\Sigma^{-1}U_i' + \Sigma_{i=1,2,...,N}\ ln|det(J_i)|$

The concentrated log-likelihood function is obtained by substituting the estimated covariance matrix $\Sigma = U'U/N$ as follows:

$ll^*(\beta|Y,X) = -NG/2\ (1+ln(2\pi))\ -N/2\ ln(det(U'U/N)) + \Sigma_{i=1,2,...,N}\ ln|det(J_i)|$

The FIML estimator of the parameters vector $\beta = [\beta_1, \beta_2, ..., \beta_G]'$ is obtained by maximizing the above concentrated log-likelihood function.

Special Case: Linear Equations System

A linear equations system is typically represented with the matrix form $YB + X\Gamma = U$, where the sparse parameter matrices B and Γ are used to identify the variables included in the respective equations (and the identity restrictions, if any). We adopt the notation β to indicate the combined elements of estimated parameters in B and Γ. To estimate the linear model $YB + X\Gamma = U$, the Jacobian term is the same for each data observation. That is, $J_i = det(\partial U_i/\partial Y_i) = det(B)$ for all $i = 1,2,...,N$. Thus the corresponding concentrated log-likelihood function is

$ll^*(\beta|Y,X) = -NG/2\ (1+ln(2\pi))\ -N/2\ ln(det(U'U/N)) + N\ ln|det(B)|$

Lesson 13.5: Klein Model I Revisited

We are now ready to estimate the Klein Model I using nonlinear FIML. First, we need to eliminate the three identities by substituting them into the stochastic equations so that there are three endogenous variables corresponding to the three stochastic equations in the original presentation of the model. One representation of the model (see Goldfeld and Quandt, 1972, p.34) is

$P = a_0 + a_1\ (W1+W2) + a_2\ (K-K_{-1}+G+W2-T) + a_3\ P_{-1} + u_1$
$W1 = b_0 + b_1\ (P+T) + b_2\ X_{-1} + b_3\ A + u_2$
$K = r_0 + r_1\ P + r_2\ P_{-1} + r_3\ K_{-1} + u_3$

Note that the original Klein model (Klein, 1950) used a variable $G' = G + W2$, and many parameter restrictions have to be built into the system for correct estimation. To represent the model in the form $YB + X\Gamma = U$, we have

$Y = [P\ W1\ K]$

$X = [P_1\ K_1\ X_1\ W2\ (G+W2)\ T\ A\ 1]$

$$B = \begin{bmatrix} -1 & b_1 & r_1 \\ a_1 & -1 & 0 \\ a_1 & 0 & -1 \end{bmatrix} \qquad \Gamma = \begin{bmatrix} a_3 & 0 & r_2 \\ -a_2 & 0 & r_3 \\ 0 & b_2 & 0 \\ a_1 & 0 & 0 \\ a_2 & 0 & 0 \\ -a_2 & b_1 & 0 \\ 0 & b_3 & 0 \\ 1 & 1 & 1 \end{bmatrix}$$

| /*

```
        ** Lesson 13.5: Klein Model I Revisited
        ** Nonlinear FIML Estimation, Goldfeld-Quandt (1972), p.34
        */
 1    use gpe2;
 2    output file=gpe\output13.5 reset;
 3    load data[23,10]=gpe\klein.txt;

 4    a=data[2:23,1]-1931;      @ time trend: 1931 = 0 @
 5    c=data[2:23,2];           @ consumption @
 6    p=data[2:23,3];           @ profit income @
 7    w1=data[2:23,4];          @ private wage income @
 8    i=data[2:23,5];           @ investment @
 9    k1=data[2:23,6];          @ lagged capital stock @
10    x=data[2:23,7];           @ private total income @
11    w2=data[2:23,8];          @ public wage income @
12    g=data[2:23,9];           @ government spending @
13    t=data[2:23,10];          @ tax @

14    k=k1[2:22]|209.4;         @ capital stock @
15    w=w1+w2;                  @ total wage income @

      @ use klein original data @
16    data=packr(p~w1~k~lag1(p~k~x)~w2~(g+w2)~t~a);
17    data=data-meanc(data)'; @ change data format to: @
                              @ deviation-from-mean form @
18    call reset;                      @ reset default control variables @
19    _nlopt=1;
20    _method=6;                       @ modified quadratic hill climbing @
21    _iter=100;                       @ set 50 maximal iterations @
22    _step=1;
23    _tol=1.0e-4;                     @ set tolerance level @
24    _conv=2;                                  @    set    convergence
25    criteria @
26    _vcov=1;
      _b={0.2041,0.1025,0.22967,    @ initial parameter values @
          0.72465,0.23273,0.28341,  @ for nonlinear FIML @
          0.23116,0.541,0.854};
27
28    _names={"a1","a2","a3","b1","b2","b3","r1","r2","r3"};
29    call estimate(&klein,data);
      end;
30
31    proc klein(x,c);                 @ klein model 1 @
32        local n,u,beta,gama,a,b,r,ll;
33        a=c[1 2 3]; b=c[4 5 6]; r=c[7 8 9];
34        n=rows(x);                   @ number of observations @
35        beta=-eye(3);                @ initialize beta @
36        gama=zeros(7,3);     @ initialize gama @
37        beta[2,1]=a[1];      @ assign values to beta and gama @
38        beta[3,1]=a[2];
39        gama[1,1]=a[3];
40        beta[1,2]=b[1];
41        gama[3,2]=b[2];
42        gama[7,2]=b[3];
43        beta[1,3]=r[1];
44        gama[1,3]=r[2];
45        gama[2,3]=r[3];
46        gama[4,1]=a[1];      @ parameter restrictions @
47        gama[5,1]=a[2];
48        gama[6,1]=-a[2];
49        gama[2,1]=-a[2];
50        gama[6,2]=b[1];
          u=x[.,1:3]*beta+x[.,4:10]*gama;  @ stochastic errors @
51        ll=-0.5*n*3*(1+ln(2*pi))+          @ log-likelihood value @
52          -0.5*n*ln(det(u'u/n))+n*ln(abs(det(beta)));
53        retp(ll);
      endp;
```

Gamma is a built-in function in GAUSS to compute the gamma function, therefore we use gama for the variable name in Lesson 13.5 above. It is not a typo.

The first part of the data manipulation is the same as in the linear system of Lesson 13.1. The relevant input variables controlling nonlinear optimization are discussed in chapters VI and VII. The objective log-likelihood function is defined in lines 30 through 53. For nonlinear maximum likelihood estimation, we reduce the size of the problem by using the deviation from the mean of the data series so that the constant terms of each equation are eliminated (see line 17). The following is the result of running **lesson13.5**:

```
Non-Linear Optimization: Maximization Problem
---------------------------------------------
Assuming Maximum Likelihood Function
Number of Observations = 21
Number of Parameters = 9

Maximum Number of Iterations = 100
Step Size Search Method = 1
Convergence Criterion = 0
Tolerance = 0.0001

Initial Result:
Function Value =        -116.37
Parameters =        0.20410       0.10250       0.22967       0.72465       0.23273
0.28341       0.23116       0.54100       0.85400

Using Modified Quadratic Hill-Climbing Algorithm
Iteration =   1    Step Size =  1.0000  Value =        -111.52
Parameters =        0.076508      0.36162       0.45511       0.68255       0.31692
0.22009     0.095885      0.41955       0.96932
...
Iteration =  19   Step Size =  1.0000  Value =        -83.324
Parameters =        -0.16079      0.81143       0.31295       0.30568       0.37170
0.30662    -0.80101       1.0519        0.85190

Final Result:
Iterations = 19              Evaluations = 1369
Function Value =        -83.324
Parameters =        -0.16079      0.81143       0.31295       0.30568       0.37170
0.30662    -0.80101       1.0519        0.85190
```

	Parameter	Asymptotic Std. Error	Asymptotic t-Ratio
A1	-0.16079	0.098663	-1.6297
A2	0.81143	0.38368	2.1149
A3	0.31295	0.11847	2.6417
B1	0.30568	0.16223	1.8843
B2	0.37170	0.049169	7.5596
B3	0.30662	0.047628	6.4378
R1	-0.80101	0.84311	-0.95007
R2	1.0519	0.42533	2.4730
R3	0.85190	0.046840	18.187

Asymptotic Variance-Covariance Matrix

A1	0.0097344				
A2	-0.035851	0.14721			
A3	0.0064035	-0.031598	0.014034		
B1	-0.011472	0.041600	-0.0049678	0.026317	
B2	0.0017000	-0.0066728	0.0015841	-0.0038648	0.0024176
B3	0.00042010	-0.0040841	0.00081371	-0.0036929	-0.00025486
R1	-0.071452	0.30359	-0.066130	0.084909	-0.0091796

R2	0.027921	-0.12886	0.043653	-0.020684	0.0067868
R3	0.0029682	-0.010417	0.0014621	-0.0059803	0.0014133
	A1	A2	A3	B1	B2

B3	0.0022684			
R1	-0.0095885	0.71083		
R2	-0.00072454	-0.30500	0.18091	
R3	0.00081869	-0.015241	0.0034790	0.0021940
	B3	R1	R2	R3

As a mathematical exercise, you may want to verify the relationships of parameters between the two representations of Klein Model I we discussed in Lesson 13.1 and 13.5:

$$a_0 = \alpha_0/(1-\alpha_1) \qquad b_0 = \gamma_0/(1-\gamma_1) \qquad r_0 = \beta_0$$
$$a_1 = (\alpha_2-1)/(1-\alpha_1) \qquad b_1 = \gamma_1/(1-\gamma_1) \qquad r_1 = \beta_1$$
$$a_2 = 1/(1-\alpha_1) \qquad b_2 = \gamma_2/(1-\gamma_1) \qquad r_2 = \beta_2$$
$$a_3 = \alpha_3/(1-\alpha_1) \qquad b_3 = \gamma_3/(1-\gamma_1) \qquad r_3 = \beta_3+1$$

The advantage of nonlinear FIML is to allow for nonlinear equations in a simultaneous system, but the computation becomes more involved in defining the nonlinear function for numerical optimization. Because the Klein Model includes only the linear equations, it is no surprise that the parameter estimates obtained from the nonlinear FIML method and from a variant of linear instrumental variable FIML method (using the option _method=4, as shown in the table at the end of Lesson 13.1) are very close, if not numerically identical.

	Nonlinear FIML	FIML/IV
α_1	-0.2324	-0.23190
α_2	0.80184	0.80182
α_3	0.38568	0.38545
α_0		18.340
β_1	-0.801	-0.80082
β_2	1.0518	1.0516
β_3	-0.1481	-0.14811
β_0		27.267
γ_1	0.23412	0.23412
γ_2	0.28468	0.28464
γ_3	0.23483	0.23487
γ_0		5.7963
Log-Likelihood	-83.324	-83.32381

XIV
Unit Roots and Cointegration

So far the econometric models we have constructed are mostly based on economic theory or empirical evidence. In many situations involving time series data, we will have to rely on information drawn from the data generating process (DGP) . An example of this would be a time series with an autocorrelated error structure.

Considering a time series as a DGP, the data may possess a trend, cycle, or seasonality (or any combination). By removing these deterministic patterns, we would hope that the remaining DGP is stationary. However, most nonstationary data series are stochastic. "Spurious" regressions with a high R-square but a near-two Durbin-Watson statistic, often found in time series literature, are mainly due to the use of stochastic nonstationary data series.

Given a time series DGP, testing for a random walk is a test of stationarity. It is also called a unit roots test. Testing for the problem of unit roots for each time series is more of a process than it is a step. This chapter will chart the procedure to test for unit roots. If a problem is identified, the original data are differenced and tested again. In this way, we are able to identify the order of the integrated process for each data series. Once all data series have completed this process, they are regressed together and tested for a cointegrating relationship.

Since the tests we use, Dickey-Fuller (DF) and augmented Dickey-Fuller (ADF), require the model's error structure to be individually independent and homogeneously distributed, anomalous serial correlation in time series must be treated before these tests can be applied. Therefore, serial correlation is tested and corrected as the pretest step of each unit root test. Instead of directly correcting the error structure through the integration process, we will modify the dynamics of the data generating process with lagged dependent variables.

We follow the "top down" approach to carry out both the DF and ADF tests for unit roots, by testing for the most complicated problems first and then simplifying our model if problems are absent. We will formulate and test a hierarchy of three models. First, we estimate the Random Walk Model with trend and drift, or the Model III, as follows:

$$\Delta X_t = \alpha + \beta\, t + (\rho-1)\, X_{t-1} + \Sigma_{i=1,2,\ldots}\, \rho_i\, \Delta X_{t-i} + \varepsilon_t$$

where the dependent variable $\Delta X_t = X_t - X_{t-1}$ is the first difference of the data series X_t. Using augmented lags of dependent variable $\Sigma_{i=1,2,\ldots}\, \rho_i\, \Delta X_{t-i}$ ensures a white noise ε_t for the unit root test. The optimal lag may be selected based on criteria such as AIC (Akaike Information Criterion) and BIC (Schwartz Baysian Information Criterion). Testing the hypothesis that $\rho = 1$ (so that the coefficient of X_{t-1} is equal to zero) is the focus of the unit root tests.

If the unit root is not found in the Model III, we continue the process by estimating the Random Walk Model with Drift, or the Model II, as follows:

$$\Delta X_t = \alpha + (\rho-1)\, X_{t-1} + \Sigma_{i=1,2,...}\, \rho_i\, \Delta X_{t-i} + \varepsilon_t$$

And finally, if the unit root is not found in the Model II, we estimate the Random Walk Model, or Model I:

$$\Delta X_t = (\rho-1)\, X_{t-1} + \Sigma_{i=1,2,...}\, \rho_i\, \Delta X_{t-i} + \varepsilon_t$$

Testing for unit roots is the first step of time series model building. For a univariate case, several versions of the DF and ADF tests are available. For multivariate time series, after unit root tests for each variable, a cointegration test should be carried out to ensure that the multiple regression model is not spurious. For testing cointegration of a set of variables, the necessary causal relationship among variables may not be available for the single equation ADF-type testing due to Engle and Granger (1987). Johansen's vector autoregression (VAR) representation of the model and the relevant Likelihood Ratio tests are suggested for the multivariate case.

Testing for Unit Roots

The process of the augmented Dickey-Fuller (ADF) test starts from estimating Model III in which autocorrelation has been removed from the data series. The ADF test for unit roots then steps through three models, testing each model's estimated coefficients to see if they are statistically significantly different from zero. Computed t- and F-statistics are compared against critical values from various Dickey-Fuller τ and ϕ distributions. Critical values of ADF τ and ϕ distributions for all three models are given in Appendix C, Statistical Table C-1 and C-2, respectively. We note that unit root tests have low power to reject the null hypothesis. Hence, if the null hypothesis of a unit root is rejected, there is no need to proceed further.

Estimate and Test Model III

$$\Delta X_t = \alpha + \beta\, t + (\rho-1)\, X_{t-1} + \Sigma_{i=1,2,...}\, \rho_i\, \Delta X_{t-i} + \varepsilon_t$$

1. Test $\rho = 1$, using the ADF τ_ρ distribution (t-statistic) for Model III. If the null hypothesis is rejected, we conclude that there are no unit roots in X. Otherwise, continue on to Step 2.

2. Test $\beta = 0$ given $\rho = 1$, using the ADF τ_β distribution (t-statistic) or the ADF ϕ_3 distribution (F-statistic) for Model III. If the null hypothesis is rejected, we need to test $\rho = 1$ again using the normal distribution as follows (see Step 3). Otherwise, go to Estimate and Test Model II.

3. Test $\rho = 1$ using the normal distribution. If the null hypothesis is rejected, we conclude that there are no unit roots. Otherwise, we conclude that the data series is nonstationary, and restart the test process using the differenced data series.

Estimate and Test Model II

$$\Delta X_t = \alpha + (\rho-1)\, X_{t-1} + \Sigma_{i=1,2,...}\, \rho_i\, \Delta X_{t-i} + \varepsilon_t$$

1. Test $\rho = 1$, using the ADF τ_ρ distribution (t-statistic) for Model II. If the null hypothesis is rejected, we conclude that there are no unit roots in X. Otherwise, continue on to Step 2.

2. Test $\alpha = 0$ given $\rho = 1$, using the ADF τ_α distribution (t-statistic) or the ADF ϕ_1 distribution (F-statistic) for Model II. If the null hypothesis is rejected, we need to test $\rho = 1$ again using the normal distribution as follows (see Step 3). Otherwise, go to Estimate and Test Model I.

3. Test $\rho = 1$ using normal distribution. If the null hypothesis is rejected, we conclude that there are no unit roots. Otherwise, we conclude that data series is nonstationary, and restart the test process using the differenced data series.

Estimate and Test Model I

$$\Delta X_t = (\rho - 1) X_{t-1} + \Sigma_{i=1,2,\dots} \rho_i \Delta X_{t-i} + \varepsilon_t$$

Test $\rho = 1$, using the ADF τ_ρ distribution (t-statistic) for Model I. If the null hypothesis is rejected, we conclude that there are no unit roots in X. Otherwise, we conclude that the data series is nonstationary, and restart the test process using the differenced data series.

Many macroeconomic time series have been scrutinized for unit roots and cointegration. In this chapter, two economic time series, Y (real personal disposable income) and C (real personal consumption expenditure), from **usyc87.txt** are used to illustrate the process of ADF tests for unit roots and cointegration. The same data series were used in the example of U.S. income-consumption relationship studied in Chapter XI.

Lesson 14.1: Augmented Dickey-Fuller Test for Unit Roots

Based on time series of personal consumption and personal disposable income from **usyc87.txt**, this lesson performs the ADF unit root test procedure. The program is written to allow straightforward testing of different variables or different transformations of the same variable.

Personal Consumption Expenditure

This program is designed to easily allow the testing of more than one data series. Starting at line 7, the variable X is tested for a unit root. To change data series to be tested, just assign a different data series in line 6 to the variable X. The level (not differenced) series of C, personal consumption, is examined first.

```
   /*
   ** Lesson 14.1: Unit Root Tests
   */
1  use gpe2;
2  output file = gpe\output14.1 reset;
3  load z[67,3] = gpe\usyc87.txt;
4  y = z[2:67,2];
5  c = z[2:67,3];

   /* select one variable to work on */
```

```
 6  x = c;

    /* difference the data if needed */
 7  diff = 0;
 8  j = 1;
 9  do until j > diff;
10                  x = x-lagn(x,1);
11                  j = j+1;
12  endo;

13  x1 = packr(lagn(x,1)); @ sample truncated @
14  dx = packr(x-lagn(x,1));
15  trend = seqa(1,1,rows(dx));

16  call reset;

17  _names={"dx","trend","x1"};
18  _rstat = 1;
19  _dlags = 3; @ augmented terms if needed @

    /* Model III */
20  call estimate(dx,trend~x1);

21  _restr = {0 0 0 1 0 0,
             0 0 0 0 1 0};  @ DF joint test @
22  call estimate(dx,trend~x1);
23  end;
```

Let's walk through the program. Lines 7 through 12 introduce a Do Loop to simplify taking the difference of our data, if needed. Line 7 specifies the number of differences diff on the data series. Then, from line 8 to 12, a Do Loop is used to transform the necessary differences for the data series when the variable diff is greater than 0. In line 7 we begin with the original data series in level:

```
diff = 0;
```

The next two lines (lines 13 and 14) work on the selected variable to compute the lagged and the differenced values necessary for the test specification. A GAUSS command packr is used to eliminate the initial observations of data which are lost due to the lag operation. Next, a trend variable is generated (line 15) and included for the estimation of Model III.

Line 19 is the result of a pretest of the model to ensure a classical or white noise error structure, which is necessary for the ADF test of unit roots. Through a process of trial and error, we found that for the consumption series C, the addition of three lags of the dependent variable to the test equation is enough to remove autocorrelation and maintain the classical assumption for the model error.

Model III is now estimated and tested for unit roots (line 20). Keep in mind that most computed t-statistics will fall in the left tail of the ADF τ distribution and will be negative. The second restricted least squares estimation (lines 21 to 22) is there to carry out the ADF ϕ-test (based on the F-statistic) for the joint hypotheses of unit root and no trend, provided that the first regression equation reveals a unit root. We note that the definition of the restriction matrix of _restr must take into account the three lags of dependent variables included in front of the explanatory independent variables.

The following is the result of the estimated Model III in which three lags of the dependent variable are augmented for analyzing personal consumption.

```
Least Squares Estimation
------------------------
Dependent Variable = DX
Estimation Range =   4          65
Number of Observations = 62
Mean of Dependent Variable = 50.353
Standard Error of Dependent Variable = 37.125

NOTE: Estimation Range Has Been Adjusted.
Lagged Dependent Variables Used = 3

R-Square = 0.51348      R-Square Adjusted = 0.47004
Standard Error of the Estimate = 27.026
Log-Likelihood Function Value = -289.22
Log Ammemiya Prediction Criterion (APC) =   6.6860
Log Akaike Information Criterion (AIC) =   6.6854
Log Schwarz Bayesian Information Criterion (BIC) =   6.8912

Sum of Squares         SS          DF          MSS          F      Prob>F
Explained           43171.          5        8634.1     11.821  7.9646E-008
Residual            40904.         56         730.42
Total               84074.         61        1378.3

Variable        Estimated     Standard     t-Ratio        Prob       Partial
Name            Coefficient     Error        56 DF        >|t|     Regression
DX1              0.32414       0.12529       2.5872     0.012301     0.10676
DX2             -0.16381       0.13150      -1.2457     0.21807      0.026963
DX3             -0.25278       0.12477      -2.0260     0.047541     0.068291
TREND            2.3924        0.98917       2.4186     0.018859     0.094575
X1              -0.020042      0.018215     -1.1003     0.27590      0.021162
CONSTANT         2.7427        7.8871        0.34775    0.72933      0.0021548

Squared Correlation of Observed and Predicted = 0.51348
Sum of Squared Residuals = 40904.
Sum of Absolute Residuals = 1219.9
Sum of Residuals = -6.69331E-012
First-Order Rho = -0.031240
Durbin-Watson Test Statistic = 2.0589
Durbin-H Statistic = -1.4164
```

Because of the use of lagged dependent variables, the sample range is adjusted. As a pretest, we see that the errors for the test model are not autocorrelated, therefore various ADF tests for unit roots are applicable. Starting at Step 1, with the estimated t-statistic of −1.10 for the coefficient of the lagged variable X1 in the test equation (vs. the τ_ρ critical value of −3.5 at 5% level of significance, see Table C-1), the unit root problem is clearly shown. Given the unit root, we continue on to Step 2, testing the zero-value coefficient of the trend variable. Based on the ADF t-statistic for the variable TREND, the hypothesis of no trend is barely rejected at a 10% level of significance. Notice that, from Table C-1, the τ_β critical value is 2.81 and 2.38 at 5% and 10% levels of significance, respectively. However, the joint hypotheses of unit root and no trend may be better served with the ADF ϕ-test based on the F-statistic.

The following F-statistic result is due to the restrictions specified in line 21:

```
WARNING: Linear Restrictions Imposed.
R-Square, AOV, SE, and t may not be reliable!
Wald F-Test for Linear Restrictions
F(  2,  56)       Prob>F
    10.836    0.00010513
```

Compared with the critical value of the ADF ϕ_3 distribution for Model III (6.73 at 5% significance, see Table C-2), the conclusion of unit root and no trend leads to the confirmation of unit root with a traditional normal test. Unit root for the variable C is confirmed, so the level series of C is nonstationary.

Since the level data series is nonstationary, it must be differenced then estimated and tested again for unit roots. Based on the above program, it is easy to make changes to carry out the unit root test for the first differenced consumption series. First, line 7 should read as:

```
diff = 1;
```

The Do Loop of lines 8 through 12 translates the original level series to the first difference series. From this point on, the program will evaluate the data series in the first difference. We also found that there is no need to augment the model with lagged dependent variables, since the model error is already free of correlation. Therefore, line 19 is changed to:

```
_dlags = 0;
```

Model III is estimated and tested for unit roots for the first difference of the consumption series. The ADF test for the joint hypotheses of unit root and no trend in lines 21 to 22 must be modified or deleted. A simple way to remove these lines from being "seen" by GAUSS is to comment them out in between "/*" and "*/". Here is the output of the modified program running the unit root test on the first difference of the consumption series:

```
Least Squares Estimation
------------------------
Dependent Variable = DX
Estimation Range =  1          64
Number of Observations = 64
Mean of Dependent Variable = 2.4109
Standard Error of Dependent Variable = 34.561

R-Square = 0.33553      R-Square Adjusted = 0.31374
Standard Error of the Estimate = 28.630
Log-Likelihood Function Value = -303.96
Log Ammemiya Prediction Criterion (APC) =  6.7547
Log Akaike Information Criterion (AIC) =  6.7547
Log Schwarz Bayesian Information Criterion (BIC) =  6.8559
```

Sum of Squares	SS	DF	MSS	F	Prob>F
Explained	25248.	2	12624.	15.401	3.8510E-006
Residual	50001.	61	819.69		
Total	75250.	63	1194.4		

Variable Name	Estimated Coefficient	Standard Error	t-Ratio 61 DF	Prob >|t|	Partial Regression
TREND	0.91047	0.25521	3.5675	0.00070864	0.17262
X1	-0.66639	0.12008	-5.5496	6.5763E-007	0.33550
CONSTANT	3.0604	7.2425	0.42256	0.67410	0.0029186

```
Squared Correlation of Observed and Predicted = 0.33553
Sum of Squared Residuals = 50001.
Sum of Absolute Residuals = 1373.6
Sum of Residuals = 3.12639E-013
First-Order Rho = 0.069752
Durbin-Watson Test Statistic = 1.8495
```

Based on the ADF t-statistic –5.55 for the lagged variable X1, the conclusion of no unit root in the first difference data is immediate and obvious. Therefore, we conclude that the consumption series is an integrated series of order one. We know this because taking the first difference makes the data stationary.

Personal Disposable Income

We continue on to test the second data series, personal disposable income Y, for unit root. The original program for analyzing consumption level data is used, except the variable of interest now selected in line 6 is Y.

```
x = y;
```

Also, from the pretest for the classical error structure, it appears that augmenting the first lag of the dependent variable is necessary for "whitening" the error term. Therefore, in line 19:

```
_dlags = 1;
```

Accordingly, for computing the F-statistic from the second restricted least squares estimation, we also modify the restriction matrix in line 21:

```
_restr = {0 1 0 0,
          0 0 1 0};
```

Here is the estimation result of Model III for personal income level series:

```
Least Squares Estimation
------------------------
Dependent Variable = DX
Estimation Range =  2          65
Number of Observations = 64
Mean of Dependent Variable = 51.456
Standard Error of Dependent Variable = 46.141

NOTE: Estimation Range Has Been Adjusted.
Lagged Dependent Variables Used = 1

R-Square = 0.33360      R-Square Adjusted = 0.30028
Standard Error of the Estimate = 38.596
Log-Likelihood Function Value = -322.55
Log Ammemiya Prediction Criterion (APC) =  7.3669
Log Akaike Information Criterion (AIC) =  7.3668
Log Schwarz Bayesian Information Criterion (BIC) =  7.5017
```

Sum of Squares	SS	DF	MSS	F	Prob>F
Explained	44744.	3	14915.	10.012	1.9204E-005
Residual	89380.	60	1489.7		
Total	1.3412E+005	63	2128.9		

Variable Name	Estimated Coefficient	Standard Error	t-Ratio 60 DF	Prob >|t|	Partial Regression
DX1	0.13228	0.12474	1.0605	0.29318	0.018399
TREND	3.2200	1.2776	2.5203	0.014404	0.095731
X1	-0.038953	0.022835	-1.7059	0.093203	0.046257
CONSTANT	3.8784	10.136	0.38263	0.70335	0.0024341

```
Squared Correlation of Observed and Predicted = 0.33360
Sum of Squared Residuals = 89380.
Sum of Absolute Residuals = 1827.4
Sum of Residuals = 1.97531E-012
First-Order Rho = -0.010452
```

```
Durbin-Watson Test Statistic = 1.9860
Durbin-H Statistic = 0.86308
```

We see that by comparing the t-statistic of X1 (-1.71) with the corresponding ADF critical values (-3.50 at 5% significance, see Table C-1), there is a unit root. Based on the joint test for unit root and no trend hypotheses, a trend is also presented. This is the purpose of the second regression estimation. The following test result should be checked with the critical values of the ADF ϕ_3 distribution for Model III (6.73 at 5% significance, see Table C-2):

```
WARNING: Linear Restrictions Imposed.
R-Square, AOV, SE, and t may not be reliable!
Wald F-Test for Linear Restrictions
F(   2,  60)        Prob>F
     7.8478    0.00093843
```

The level series of personal disposable income is clearly nonstationary. By modifying the program again in line 7,

```
diff = 1;
```

and deleting the last part of the ADF joint F-test, the first difference of the income series augmented with one lag of dependent variable is reexamined as follows:

```
Least Squares Estimation
------------------------
Dependent Variable = DX
Estimation Range =  2        64
Number of Observations = 63
Mean of Dependent Variable = 2.4413
Standard Error of Dependent Variable = 51.142

NOTE: Estimation Range Has Been Adjusted.
Lagged Dependent Variables Used = 1

R-Square = 0.42924      R-Square Adjusted = 0.40022
Standard Error of the Estimate = 39.608
Log-Likelihood Function Value = -319.11
Log Ammemiya Prediction Criterion (APC) =   7.4196
Log Akaike Information Criterion (AIC) =   7.4194
Log Schwarz Bayesian Information Criterion (BIC) =   7.5555
```

Sum of Squares	SS	DF	MSS	F	Prob>F
Explained	69607.	3	23202.	14.790	2.7151E-007
Residual	92557.	59	1568.8		
Total	1.6216E+005	62	2615.5	Variable	Estimated
Standard	t-Ratio	Prob	Partial		
Name	Coefficient	Error	59 DF	>|t|	Regression
DX1	-0.073578	0.12989	-0.56648	0.57322	0.0054095
TREND	0.99944	0.35282	2.8327	0.0063057	0.11972
X1	-0.79417	0.16721	-4.7496	1.3442E-005	0.27660
CONSTANT	9.4345	10.400	0.90713	0.36803	0.013755

```
Squared Correlation of Observed and Predicted = 0.42924
Sum of Squared Residuals = 92557.
Sum of Absolute Residuals = 1849.6
Sum of Residuals = 4.26326E-014
First-Order Rho = -0.0057744
Durbin-Watson Test Statistic = 1.9309
Durbin-H Statistic = NA
```

Based on the ADF t-test statistic, -4.75, for the lagged variable X1, the first differenced income series is stationary and free of unit roots. As with consumption, personal income is an integrated series of order one.

 The above example of testing for unit roots in the personal consumption and income data series is carried out based on Model III. We did not go down the hierarchy further to test Model II or Model I since most of the test results are clear-cut at the level of Model III. For other macroeconomic time series, you may be required to test Model II or Model I as well.

Below is the summarized result of the unit root tests:

Series	N	Lags	ρ-1 (τ_ρ)	β (τ_β)	ϕ_3
C	62	3	-0.02 (-1.10)	2.39 (2.42)	10.84*
Y	64	1	-0.04 (-1.71)	3.22 (2.52)*	7.85*
ΔC	64	0	-0.67 (-5.55)*		
ΔY	63	1	-0.79 (-4.75)*		

All tests are based on Model III. The following annual data series from 1929 to 1994 are tested (in rows): C = Personal consumption expenditure in billions of 1987 dollars; Y = Personal disposable income in billions of 1987 dollars; ΔC = Annual change in personal consumption expenditure; ΔY = Annual change in personal disposable income. Also the following notations are used (in columns): N = number of observations; Lags = augmented lag terms in the test equation; ρ-1 = estimated coefficient of the lag variable; β = estimated coefficient of the trend variable; τ_ρ = t-statistic hypothesis of unit root; τ_β = t-statistic hypothesis of no trend, given unit root; and ϕ_3 = F-statistic hypotheses of unit root and no trend. The asterisk (*) indicates rejection of the null hypothesis at a 5% statistical significance level based on ADF distributions (see Table C-1 for critical values of t-statistics and Table C-2 for critical values of F-statistics).

As many previous studies have suggested, income and consumption data are nonstationary in level, but their first difference or change series are stationary. In summary, both income and consumption are of the first-order integrated series.

Testing for Cointegrating Regression

The next interesting question is, statistically, can we find a meaningful nonspurious income-consumption relationship as the classical Permanent Income Hypothesis claims? To answer this question, we need to look at the problem in a more general framework of multivariate regression.

Suppose there are M variables, Z_1, ... , Z_M. Let $Y_t = Z_{t1}$ and $X_t = [Z_{t2}, ..., Z_{tM}]$. Consider the following regression equation:

$$Y_t = \alpha + X_t\beta + \varepsilon_t$$

In general, if Y_t, $X_t \sim I(1)$, then $\varepsilon_t \sim I(1)$. But, if ε_t can be shown to be I(0), then the set of variables $[Y_t, X_t]$ is said to be cointegrated, and the vector $[1 -\beta]'$ (or any multiple of it) is called a cointegrating vector. Depending on the number of variables M, there are up to M-1 linearly independent cointegrating vectors. The number of linearly independent cointegrating vectors that exists in $[Y_t, X_t]$ is called the cointegrating rank.

To test for the cointegration of the set of variables $[Y_t, X_t]$, two approaches are used. If the causality of Y on X is clear, then the Engle-Granger or ADF test based on the regression residuals may be applied. The alternative is to work with the VAR system of all variables under consideration. This is the Johansen approach to the cointegration test, to be discussed later.

Cointegration Test: The Engle-Granger Approach

Based on the regression model

$$Y_t = \alpha + X_t\beta + \varepsilon_t$$

the Engle-Granger test for cointegration is to test for unit root for the residuals of the above regression model. That is, based on Model I, the auxiliary test equation is written as:

$$\Delta\varepsilon_t = (\rho-1)\varepsilon_{t-1} + u_t$$

where $\varepsilon_t = Y_t - \alpha - X_t\beta$, and $\Delta\varepsilon_t$ is defined as $\varepsilon_t - \varepsilon_{t-1}$. The rationale is that if the residual ε_t has unit root, regressing Y on X may not completely capture the underlying (nonstationary) trends of all these variables. The estimated model does not reveal the meaningful relationship, although it may fit the data well. This is the crux of the spurious regression problem. However, if a cointegrating vector can be found among the variables that causes the error term ε_t to be stationary or I(0), then we can attach meaning to the estimated regression parameters.

We note that the above unit root test equation on the regression residuals does not have a drift or trend. In order to apply ADF-type testing for a unit root, the model may be augmented with lagged dependent variables as needed:

$$\Delta\varepsilon_t = (\rho-1)\varepsilon_{t-1} + \sum_{j=1,2,...} \rho_{t-j}\Delta\varepsilon_{t-j} + u_t$$

Alternatively, the cointegrating test regression may be expressed as the following *Error Correction Model*:

$$\Delta Y_t = \Delta X_t\beta + (\rho-1)(Y_{t-1} - \alpha - X_{t-1}\beta) + \sum_{j=1,2,...} \rho_{t-j}(\Delta Y_{t-j} - \Delta X_{t-j}\beta) + u_t$$

If we can reject the null hypothesis of unit root on the residuals ε_t, we can say that variables $[Y_t, X_t]$ in the regression equation are cointegrated. The cointegrating regression model may be generalized to include trend as follows:

$$Y_t = \alpha + \gamma t + X_t\beta + \varepsilon_t$$

Notice that the trend in the cointegrating regression equation may be the result of combined drifts in X and/or Y. Critical values of the ADF τ_ρ distribution for spurious cointegrating regression are given in Table C-3 of Appendix C. These values are based on the work of Phillip and Ouliaris (1990), and depend on the number of cointegrating variables and their trending behaviors for large samples.

Furthermore, MacKinnon's table of critical values of cointegration tests for cointegrating regression with and without trend (named Model 2 and Model 3, respectively) is given in Appendix C, Table C-4. It is based on simulation experiments by means of response surface regression in which critical values depend on the type of model, number of variables, and are adjusted for sample size. MacKinnon's table is easier and more flexible to use than that of Phillip and Ouliaris. We note that the univariate case (K=1) of MacKinnon's table (top portion) corresponds to the critical values of ADF distributions (testing unit roots for Models I, II, and III).

Lesson 14.2: Cointegration Test: Engle-Granger Approach

Given that both the income (Y) and consumption (C) series are integrated of order one (that is, I(1)), the long-run relationship:

$$C_t = \beta_0 + \beta_1 Y_t + \varepsilon_t$$

will be meaningful only if the error ε_t is free of unit roots. The test for cointegration between C and Y thus becomes a unit root test on the regression residuals:

$$\Delta\varepsilon_t = (\rho-1)\,\varepsilon_{t-1} + \Sigma_{j=1,2,...}\,\rho_j\,\Delta\varepsilon_{t-j} + u_t$$

```
      /*
      ** Lesson 14.2: Cointegration Test
      ** Engle-Granger Approach
      */
1     use gpe2;
2     output file = gpe\output14.2 reset;

3     load z[67,3] = gpe\usyc87.txt;
4     y = z[2:67,2];
5     c = z[2:67,3];

6     call reset;

7     _names = {"c","y"};
8     call estimate(c,y);

      /* Unit Roots Test on Residuals */
9     x = __e;  @ set x to regression residuals @
10    x1 = packr(lagn(x,1)); @ sample truncated @
11    dx = packr(x-lagn(x,1));
12    _names = {"dx","x1"};

13    _rstat = 1;
14    _dlags = 2; @ augmented terms if needed @
15    _const = 0; @ no intercept term @
16    call estimate(dx,x1);
17    end;
```

The program reads in and uses both income (Y) and consumption (C) data series, and runs a regression of the consumption-income relationship. Here, we are not interested in investigating or refining the error structure of the regression equation (though we must make sure that no autocorrelated structure exists in the error term of the cointegrating regression). Instead, we want to test the residuals for the presence of unit roots. In GPE, residuals are available as the output variable __e immediately after the regression equation is estimated. Line 9 sets the variable X to the vector of residuals:

```
x = __e;
```

and prepares for unit root testing on this variable in the rest of the program. This later portion of codes (lines 10 through 16) is the same as that in **lesson14.1** for testing unit roots of a single variable. Again, line 14 is the result of a pretest to ensure the white noise error structure for unit root test:

```
_dlags = 2;
```

It turns out that we need to have two lags of the dependent variable augmented to the test equation. We recall that both income (Y) and consumption (C) variables include linear trend from our earlier unit roots tests on the respective variable. This fact must be considered when we use the appropriate ADF τ_ρ distribution for cointegration tests (using Model 2a or Model 3 of Table C-3). The alternative is to use MacKinnon's table (Table C-4) for testing the cointegrating regression model. We present only the results relevant to the cointegration test in the following (see the generated output file output14.2 for more details):

```
Least Squares Estimation
------------------------
Dependent Variable = DX
Estimation Range =  3          65
Number of Observations = 63
Mean of Dependent Variable = 0.70448
Standard Error of Dependent Variable = 29.013

NOTE: Estimation Range Has Been Adjusted.
Lagged Dependent Variables Used = 2

WARNING: Constant Term Suppressed.
R-Square, AOV, SE, and t may not be reliable!

R-Square = 0.20697      R-Square Adjusted = 0.16732
Standard Error of the Estimate = 26.264
Log-Likelihood Function Value = -293.75
Log Ammemiya Prediction Criterion (APC) =  6.5829
Log Akaike Information Criterion (AIC) =  6.5828
Log Schwarz Bayesian Information Criterion (BIC) =  6.6849
```

Sum of Squares	SS	DF	MSS	F	Prob>F
Explained	10786.	3	3595.5	5.2123	0.0028932
Residual	41388.	60	689.80		
Total	52190.	63	828.41		

Variable Name	Estimated Coefficient	Standard Error	t-Ratio 60 DF	Prob >|t|	Partial Regression
DX1	0.33306	0.12268	2.7149	0.0086440	0.10941
DX2	0.17315	0.13228	1.3089	0.19555	0.027762
X1	-0.29001	0.082515	-3.5146	0.00084459	0.17073

```
Squared Correlation of Observed and Predicted = 0.20700
Sum of Squared Residuals = 41388.
Sum of Absolute Residuals = 1118.1
Sum of Residuals = -9.96447E+000
First-Order Rho = -0.0042224
Durbin-Watson Test Statistic = 1.9889
Durbin-H Statistic = 0.19258
```

Testing for the cointegration of two variables, C and Y with trend, the computed t-statistic for the lagged variable X1 in the test equation is –3.52, which is right on the borderline of rejecting the null hypothesis of unit root at a 5% level of significance (looking at Table C-3, the critical value of ADF cointegration t-statistic τ_ρ for K=2 at 5% is –3.42 for Model 2a). A similar conclusion is obtained by using the critical values of MacKinnon (Table C-4). Although these results do not give us overwhelming confidence that the long-run income-consumption relationship is legitimate, empirical studies based on the Permanent Income Hypothesis still stand.

Single equation cointegration tests can only be valid when the specific causal relation of the underlying multiple regression is correct. If the causal relationship of C and Y is not as clean-cut as the Permanent Income Hypothesis suggests, we need to run and test the reverse regression equation.

Cointegration Test: The Johansen Approach

The Engle-Granger cointegration test discussed in the previous section is only appropriate when the direction of causality involved in the regression equation is clear. If there are more than two variables involved in a regression model, the direction of causality may not be clear, or one-sided. In this case, we turn to Johansen's multivariate cointegration test.

Given a set of M variables $Z_t=[Z_{t1}, Z_{t2}, ..., Z_{tM}]$, and considering their feedback simultaneity, Johansen's cointegration test based on FIML (full information maximum likelihood) is derived from the following:

- VAR (vector autoregression) System Model Representation
- FIML Estimation of the Linear Equations System
- Canonical Correlations Analysis

Similar to the random walk (unit roots) hypothesis testing for a single variable with augmented lags, we write a VAR(p) linear system for the M variables Z_t:

$$Z_t = Z_{t-1}\Pi_1 + Z_{t-2}\Pi_2 + ... + Z_{t-p}\Pi_p + \Pi_0 + U_t$$

where Π_j, j=1,2,...M, are the MxM parameter matrices, Π_0 is a 1xM vector of deterministic factors (drifts and trends). Moreover, we assume the 1xM error vector U_t is independently normally distributed with a zero mean and a constant covariance matrix $\Sigma = Var(U_t) = E(U_t'U_t)$ across M variables.

The VAR(p) system can be transformed using the difference series of the variables, resembling the error correction model, as follows:

$$\Delta Z_t = \Delta Z_{t-1}\Gamma_1 + \Delta Z_{t-2}\Gamma_2 + ... + \Delta Z_{t-(p-1)}\Gamma_{p-1} + Z_{t-1}\Pi + \Gamma_0 + U_t$$

where I denotes the identity matrix, $\Pi = \sum_{j=1,2,...,p}\Pi_j - I$, $\Gamma_1 = \Pi_1 - \Pi - I$, $\Gamma_2 = \Pi_2 + \Gamma_1$, $\Gamma_3 = \Pi_3 + \Gamma_2$, ... , and $\Gamma_0 = \Pi_0$ for notational convenience. Recall that Γ_0 is a vector of deterministic factors including drifts and trends. If both drift and trend ($\mu_0 + \mu_1 t$) exist in Z_t, then $\Gamma_0 = -\mu_0 \Pi + \mu_1(\Gamma+\Pi) - \mu_1\Pi\, t$ where $\Gamma = I - \sum_{j=1,2,...,p-1}\Gamma_j$.

A few words about the vector Γ_0 (or Π_0) of the deterministic factors. We consider only the case of constant vector Γ_0 that is restricted such that $\mu_1\Pi = 0$ (no trend), then $\Gamma_0 = -\mu_0 \Pi + \mu_1 \Gamma$. It is easy to see that (1) if $\mu_1 = 0$, μ_0 is the only deterministic factor (drift) for Z_t, or $\Gamma_0 = -\mu_0 \Pi$; (2) if $\mu_1 \neq 0$, then the VAR(p) model consists of drift and linear trend components, or $\Gamma_0 = -\mu_0 \Pi + \mu_1 \Gamma$.

If $Z_t \sim I(1)$, then $\Delta Z_t \sim I(0)$. In order for the variables in Z_t to be cointegrated, we must have $U_t \sim I(0)$. That is, we must show the last term in the error correction equation: $Z_{t-1}\Pi \sim I(0)$. By definition of cointegration, the parameter matrix Π must contain r $(0<r<M)$ linearly independent cointegrating vectors such that $Z_t\Pi \sim I(0)$. Therefore, the cointegration test for Z_t amounts to checking the rank of matrix Π, denoted Rank(Π). If Rank(Π) = r > 0, we may impose parameter restrictions $\Pi = -BA'$ where A and B are Mxr matrices. Given the existence of the constant vector Γ_0, there can be up to M-r random walks or drift trends. Such common trends in the variables may be removed in the case of Model II below. We consider the following three models:

- Model I: VAR(p) representation without constant vector, i.e., $\Gamma_0 = 0$.
- Model II: VAR(p) representation with constant vector but the trend removed (drift only, i.e., $\Gamma_0 = -\mu_0\Pi$).
- Model III: VAR(p) representation with constant vector (drift trend, i.e., $\Gamma_0 = -\mu_0\Pi + \mu_1\Gamma$).

For model estimation of the above VAR(p) system, where U_t is independently normally distributed with zero mean and constant covariance matrix Σ, we derive the log-likelihood function for Model III:

$$ll(\Gamma_1,\Gamma_2,..., \Gamma_{p-1},\Gamma_0,\Pi,\Sigma) = -MN/2 \; ln(2\pi) - N/2 \; ln|\det(\Sigma)| - \tfrac{1}{2} \sum_{t=1,2,...,N} U_t\Sigma^{-1}U_t'$$

Since the maximum likelihood estimate of Σ is U'U/N, the concentrated log-likelihood function is written as:

$$ll^*(\Gamma_1,\Gamma_2,..., \Gamma_{p-1},\Gamma_0,\Pi) = -NM/2 \; (1+ln(2\pi)-ln(N)) - N/2 \; ln|\det(U'U)|$$

The actual maximum likelihood estimation can be simplified by considering the following two auxiliary regressions:

1. $\Delta Z_t = \Delta Z_{t-1}\Phi_1 + \Delta Z_{t-2}\Phi_2 + ... + \Delta Z_{t-(p-1)}\Phi_{p-1} + \Phi_0 + W_t$
2. $Z_{t-1} = \Delta Z_{t-1}\Psi_1 + \Delta Z_{t-2}\Psi_2 + ... + \Delta Z_{t-(p-1)}\Psi_{p-1} + \Psi_0 + V_t$

We see that $\Gamma_j = \Phi_j - \Psi_j\Pi$, for j=0,1,2,...,p-1, and $U_t = W_t - V_t\Pi$. If $\Phi_0 = \Psi_0 = 0$, then $\Gamma_0 = 0$, implying no drift in the VAR(p) model. However, $\Gamma_0 = 0$ needs only the restriction that $\Phi_0 = \Psi_0\Pi$.

Plugging in the auxiliary regressions, we can now write the concentrated log-likelihood function as

$$ll^*(W(\Phi_1,\Phi_2,...,\Phi_{p-1},\Phi_0), V(\Psi_1,\Psi_2,...,\Psi_{p-1},\Psi_0),\Pi)$$
$$= -NM/2 \; (1+ln(2\pi)-ln(N)) - N/2 \; ln|\det((W-V\Pi)'(W-V\Pi))|$$

Maximizing the above concentrated log-likelihood function is equivalent to minimizing the sum-of-squares term $\det((W-V\Pi)'(W-V\Pi))$. Conditional on $W(\Phi_1,\Phi_2,...,\Phi_{p-1},\Phi_0)$ and $V(\Psi_1,\Psi_2,...,\Psi_{p-1},\Psi_0)$, the least squares estimate of Π is $(V'V)^{-1}V'W$. Thus,

$$\det((W-V\Pi)'(W-V\Pi)) = \det(W(I-V(V'V)^{-1}V')W')$$
$$= \det((W'W)(I-(W'W)^{-1}(W'V)(V'V)^{-1}(V'W))$$

$$= \quad \det(W'W) \ \det(I-(W'W)^{-1}(W'V)(V'V)^{-1}(V'W))$$
$$= \quad \det(W'W) \ (\prod_{i=1,2,...,M}(1-\lambda_i))$$

where λ_1, λ_2, ..., λ_M are the ascending ordered eigenvalues of the matrix $(W'W)^{-1}(W'V)(V'V)^{-1}(V'W)$. Therefore the resulting double concentrated log-likelihood function (concentrating on both $\Sigma = U'U/N$ and $\Pi = (V'V)^{-1}V'W$) is

$$ll^{**}(W(\Phi_1,\Phi_2,...,\Phi_{p-1},\Phi_0), V(\Psi_1,\Psi_2,...,\Psi_{p-1},\Psi_0))$$
$$= - NM/2 \ (1+ln(2\pi)-ln(N)) - N/2 \ ln|\det(W'W)| - N/2 \ \Sigma_{i=1,2,...,M} \ ln(1-\lambda_i)$$

Given the parameter constraints that there are $0<r<M$ cointegrating vectors, that is $\Pi = -BA'$ where A and B are Mxr matrices, the restricted concentrated log-likelihood function is similarly derived as follows:

$$ll_r^{**}(W(\Phi_1,\Phi_2,...,\Phi_{p-1},\Phi_0), V(\Psi_1,\Psi_2,...,\Psi_{p-1},\Psi_0))$$
$$= - NM/2 \ (1+ln(2\pi)-ln(N)) - N/2 \ ln|\det(W'W)| - N/2 \ \Sigma_{i=1,2,...,r} ln(1-\lambda_i)$$

Therefore, with the degree of freedom M-r, the Likelihood Ratio test statistic for at least r cointegrating vectors is

$$-2(ll_r^{**} - ll^{**}) = -N \ \Sigma_{i=r+1,r+2,...,M} ln(1-\lambda_i)$$

Similarly the Likelihood Ratio test statistic for r cointegrating vectors against r+1 vectors is

$$-2(ll_r^{**} - ll_{r+1}^{**}) = -N \ ln(1-\lambda_{r+1})$$

A more general form of the Likelihood Ratio test statistic for r_1 cointegrating vectors against r_2 vectors $(0 \le r_1 \le r_2 \le M)$ is

$$-2(ll_{r1}^{**} - ll_{r2}^{**}) = -N \ \Sigma_{i=r1+1,r1+2,...,r2} ln(1-\lambda_i)$$

The following table summarizes the two popular cointegration test statistics: the maximal eigenvalue test statistic $\lambda_{max}(r)$ and the trace test statistic $\lambda_{trace}(r)$. By definition, $\lambda_{trace}(r) = \Sigma_{r1=r,r+1,...,M}\lambda_{max}(r_1)$. For the case of $r = 0$, they are the tests for no cointegration. If M=r+1, the two tests are identical.

Cointegrating Rank (r)	H_0: $r_1 = r$ H_1: $r_2 = r+1$	H_0: $r_1 = r$ H_1: $r_2 = M$
0	$-N \ ln(1-\lambda_1)$	$-N \ \Sigma_{i=1,2,...,M} ln(1-\lambda_i)$
1	$-N \ ln(1-\lambda_2)$	$-N \ \Sigma_{i=2,3,...,M} ln(1-\lambda_i)$
...	...	...
M-1	$-N \ ln(1-\lambda_M)$	$-N \ ln(1-\lambda_M)$
Test Statistics	$\lambda_{max}(r)$	$\lambda_{trace}(r)$

The critical values of $\lambda_{max}(r)$ and $\lambda_{trace}(r)$ for testing the specific number of cointegrating vectors or rank r are given in Statistical Table C-5. Three models (no constant, drift only, and trend drift) are presented.

The procedure of Johansen's cointegration Likelihood Ratio tests is implemented as the GPE module program **JOHANSEN.GPE**. The module is located in the GPE subdirectory (see also Appendix B-2). Interested readers can study the details of implementation of the Likelihood Ratio test we outline above. To perform the Johansen's cointegration test, in **lesson14.3**, we include the module at the end of the program (line 17). The test is done by calling the procedure johansen with three input arguments: z = data matrix, p = lags of VAR structure, and c is the model or constant (0=no, 1=drift only, 2=trend drift):

```
call johansen(z,p,c);
```

The lengthy implementation closely follows the theoretical discussion above. We will concentrate on the application of cointegration test statistics, and leave the programming details of the procedure to you.

Lesson 14.3: Cointegration Test: Johansen Approach

Returning to the data series of income (Y) and consumption (C) we have studied so far, the Johansen cointegration test considers a VAR representation of the data matrix, and estimates the model as a simultaneous linear equations system. In **lesson14.3**, line 7 defines the data matrix consisting of two variables: y (income) and c (consumption). A VAR model with 3 lags (i.e., _dlags=3 of line 11) has been shown to best describe the data series under consideration (that is, to "whiten" the residuals). This can be verified by checking the estimation result of the VAR system as specified from line 9 through line 12. Although the estimation is carried out with the system method of 3SLS (line 10), it should be the same as any limited information estimation method (why?).

```
     /*
     ** Lesson 14.3: Cointegration Test
     ** Johansen Approach
     */
1    use gpe2;
2    output file = gpe\output14.3 reset;

3    load z[67,3] = gpe\usyc87.txt;
4    y = z[2:67,2];
5    c = z[2:67,3];
6    ns = {"c","y"};

7    data = y~c;   @ data matrix for cointegration test @

8    call reset;
9    _rstat=1;
10   _method=3;
11   _dlags=3;                @ find the proper order p @
12   call estimate(data,0);   @ for VAR(p) model estimation @

     @ Johansen cointegration test based on VAR(3) model @
13   call johansen(data,3,2); @ model with trend drift @
14   call johansen(data,3,1); @ model with drift only @
15   call johansen(data,3,0); @ model with no drift @
16   end;
17   #include gpe\johansen.gpe;
```

We present only the summary of the estimation results, and leave out the details of each equation. We note that the model estimation is used to determine the lag structure of the VAR system. In this example, VAR(3) has been shown to be the appropriate model.

```
Simultaneous Linear Equations Estimation
----------------------------------------
Number of Endogenous Variables = 2
Number of Predetermined Variables = 7
Number of Stochastic Equations = 2
Number of Observations = 63
Estimation Range =   4          66

NOTE: Estimation Range Has Been Adjusted.
Lagged Endogenous Variables Used = 6

Three Stages Least Squares Estimation

System R-Square = 0.99841
Log-Likelihood = -593.32619
```

Equation Name	Variable Name	Estimated Coefficient	Asymptotic Std Error	t-Ratio
Y1	Y1-1	0.88597	0.16655	5.3196
	Y1-2	0.29313	0.24559	1.1935
	Y1-3	-0.36656	0.18016	-2.0346
	Y2-1	0.59551	0.23153	2.5720
	Y2-2	-0.74215	0.35751	-2.0759
	Y2-3	0.36302	0.23135	1.5691
	CONSTANT	13.691	9.4196	1.4535
Y2	Y1-1	-0.12601	0.12090	-1.0423
	Y1-2	0.36104	0.17828	2.0251
	Y1-3	-0.11330	0.13079	-0.86627
	Y2-1	1.5421	0.16808	9.1748
	Y2-2	-0.93942	0.25952	-3.6198
	Y2-3	0.28254	0.16795	1.6823
	CONSTANT	7.4753	6.8380	1.0932

```
Asymptotic Variance-Covariance Matrix of Equations
Y1           1367.7
Y2           683.05      720.74
             Y1          Y2


Cointegration Test (Model 3):
Cointegrating  Eigv. Test  Trace Test
   Rank   DF   Statistic    Statistic
      0    2     18.958       25.103
      1    1     6.1456       6.1456

Cointegration Test (Model 2):
Cointegrating  Eigv. Test  Trace Test
   Rank   DF   Statistic    Statistic
      0    2     23.890       35.150
      1    1     11.260       11.260

Cointegration Test (Model 1):
Cointegrating  Eigv. Test  Trace Test
   Rank   DF   Statistic    Statistic
      0    2     23.547       33.056
      1    1     9.5092       9.5092
```

Most importantly, cointegration tests based on eigenvalue and trace statistics are given for each of the three models: trend drift (Model 3), drift only (Model 2), and no constant (Model 1), in that order. These computed test statistics are compared with the critical values of Statistical Table C-5 in Appendix C. Consider the case of no cointegration (that is, cointegrating rank equals 0 with 2 degrees of freedom): both $\lambda_{max}(0)$ and $\lambda_{trace}(0)$ statistics are statistically greater than the corresponding critical values at a 5% level significance. We reject the null hypothesis of no cointegration for the data series under consideration. Therefore, the time series income (Y) and consumption (C) are cointegrated, confirming the previous Engle-Granger or ADF test result based on the cointegrating regression residuals.

XV
Time Series Analysis

Continuing from the previous chapter in which we discussed a stationary vs. nonstationary data generating process, in this chapter, we focus on the modeling of stationary time series data. If the data series under consideration is nonstationary, we assume that it is an integrated process and can be made stationary with the proper amount of differencing. A random data generating process which is difference stationary is the subject of modern time series analysis.

Autocorrelation occurs when previous and current observations of a random variable are correlated. Chapter X discussed autocorrelation in detail. Serial correlation in the mean is common in many economic time series, with the simplest case being first-order correlation. More complicated model structures can include autoregressive and moving average terms, known as ARMA processes. However, serial correlation in the mean is not the only problem of autocorrelation in time series. Conditional to the information available, the variance of a data generating process may not be constant for all observations. Nonconstant variance, or heteroscedasticity, was studied in Chapter IX. Even worse is serial correlation in the conditional variance. The phenomenon of conditional variance correlation is often found in high-frequency observations such as those studied in financial economics. Autoregressive conditional heteroscedasticity, or the ARCH process, is another important time series model structure to be studied in this chapter.

Typically, time series analysis is carried out in several steps: model identification, estimation, diagnostic checking, and prediction. In this chapter we emphasize model identification and estimation. Diagnostic checking is the repetition of the identification step on the estimated model. Prediction is taken up later in Chapter XVII. In many circumstances, economic theory offers no *a priori* data generating process for a given variable, so model identification is often a trial and error process. To extract structural information from a random variable, the process of model identification consists of testing and estimation for the mean and variance of the variable under consideration. In Chapter X, we used several procedures to test for autocorrelation in an ARMA model. These tests include the Durbin-Watson bounds test for first-order serial correlation, the Breusch-Godfrey LM test for higher-order autocorrelation, and Box-Pierce and Ljung-Box Q test statistics based on different lags of autocorrelation coefficients. In addition, the autocorrelation function (ACF) and partial autocorrelation function (PACF) gave us useful clues as to the model's structure. Many examples shown in Chapter X demonstrated the use of a combination of the above-mentioned testing procedures and statistics to study the time series.

For ARCH modeling, the idea of variance correlation is new but the mechanics are similar to ARMA analysis. Working on the squares of mean-deviation (or regression) residuals, the corresponding ACF and PACF can assist in detecting the autocorrelation in the variance. The associated Box-Pierce and Ljung-Box statistics are useful to test the potential ARCH process. Analogous to the Breusch-Godfrey

LM test for autocorrelation in the mean, the Engle-Bollerslev LM test statistic is used for testing autocorrelation in the variance.

In the following, we present the basic formulation of ARMA and ARCH models. GPE implementation of model identification and estimation for regression models with ARMA and ARCH effects are illustrated by examples.

Autoregressive and Moving Average Models

Consider a stationary data generating process ARMA(p,q) for a random variable Y:

$$Y_t = \delta + \rho_1 Y_{t-1} + \rho_2 Y_{t-2} + \ldots + \rho_p Y_{t-p} - \theta_1 \varepsilon_{t-1} - \theta_2 \varepsilon_{t-2} - \ldots - \theta_q \varepsilon_{t-q} + \varepsilon_t$$

where ε_t is independently distributed with zero mean and constant variance σ^2, or $\varepsilon_t \sim ii(0,\sigma^2)$, $t = 1,2,\ldots,N$. As described in Chapter X, ARMA(p,q) is a mixed process of AR(p) and MA(q), where p and q represent the highest order of autoregressive and moving average parameters in the model, respectively. The model may also be written as a general linear stochastic process:

$$Y_t = \mu + \varepsilon_t + \psi_1 \varepsilon_{t-1} + \psi_2 \varepsilon_{t-2} + \ldots$$

Recall that stationarity requirements for the process imply that the mean, variance, and autocovariances of the variable must be finite constants:

Mean	$\mu = E(Y_t) < \infty$	
Variance	$\gamma_0 = \sigma^2 \Sigma_{i=0,\ldots,\infty} \psi_i^2 < \infty$	$\psi_0 = 1$
Autocovariance	$\gamma_j = \sigma^2 \Sigma_{i=0,\ldots,\infty} \psi_i \psi_{j+i} < \infty$	

The coefficient of autocorrelation defined by $\phi_j = \gamma_j / \gamma_0$ serves as the foundation for model identification. We have seen examples in chapters X and XI of using autocorrelation and partial autocorrelation coefficients to model the ARMA error structure. In particular, the Box-Pierce and Ljung-Box Q test statistics derived from the autocorrelation coefficients are useful in identifying the autoregressive and moving average time series. For details of model identification, we refer readers to standard econometrics textbooks on time series analysis.

For parameter estimation, the ARMA(p,q) model may be written in the "inverted" form as follows:

$$\rho(B)Y_t = \delta + \theta(B)\varepsilon_t$$

or,

$$\theta(B)^{-1}[-\delta + \rho(B)Y_t] = \varepsilon_t$$

where B is the backshift operator, $\rho(B) = 1 - \rho_1 B - \rho_2 B^2 - \ldots - \rho_p B^p$, and $\theta(B) = 1 - \theta_1 B - \theta_2 B^2 - \ldots - \theta_q B^q$. Conditional to the historical information $(Y_N, \ldots, Y_1)$, and data initialization $(Y_0, \ldots, Y_{-p+1})$ and $(\varepsilon_0, \ldots, \varepsilon_{-q+1})$, the error sum-of-squares is defined by

$$S = \Sigma_{t=1,2,\ldots,N} \varepsilon_t^2$$

In order to utilize all N data observations, data initialization may be needed for the observations $Y_0, Y_{-1}, ..., Y_{-p+1}$ with $E(Y_t) = \delta / (1-\rho_1-...-\rho_p)$, and $\varepsilon_0, \varepsilon_{-1}, ..., \varepsilon_{-q+1}$ with $E(\varepsilon_t) = 0$.[14] In GPE, the data initialization used for the pre-sample observations is simply the sample mean of the series.

Techniques of nonlinear optimization may be applied directly to minimize the sum-of-squares objective function. The alternative is the maximum likelihood method, for which we need to make additional assumptions about the probability distribution of the error term. For each independent observation t, we assume the model error ε_t is normally distributed with zero mean and constant variance σ^2, that is $\varepsilon_t \sim nii(0,\sigma^2)$. Then the concentrated log-likelihood objective function is

$$ll = -N/2\ [1+ln(2\pi)-ln(N)+ln(\textstyle\sum_{t=1,2,...,N}\varepsilon_t^2)]$$

Using nonlinear optimization methods, maximizing the above function with respect to the parameters ρs, θs, and δ is straightforward (see Chapter VII for more details on maximum likelihood estimation of a nonlinear regression model). The GPE package implements the nonlinear maximum likelihood estimation for the ARMA error structure in a linear regression framework.

Note that the model specification posited above is only tentative, pending diagnostic checking on the estimated residuals. We do not know whether or not we have included sufficiently high orders of AR and MA terms in the model specification. In other words, we do not know whether our choice of orders, p for AR and q for MA, were adequate. The "correct" p and q are usually determined through an iterative process. We choose an initial number of AR and MA terms (usually at low values, zero or one) and estimate the model. We then use the diagnostic tests on the estimated residuals (e.g., Durbin-Watson, Breusch-Godfrey, Box-Pierce, and Ljung-Box) to determine if serial correlation is still present in the model. If we still have problems with serial correlation, we add AR or MA terms (i.e., increase the values of p and q), re-estimate the model and rerun the diagnostic tests on the "new" residuals. This process continues until the error term has been sufficiently "whitened." In so doing, we find the combination of AR and MA terms that removes the serial correlation from the model. Note that when performing the diagnostic checking on the estimated residuals, the degrees of freedom used to choose the critical value for each test statistic is N-(K+p+q), where K is the number of regression parameters.

Lesson 15.1: ARMA Analysis of Bond Yields

This example demonstrates univariate time series analysis. **bonds.txt** is a data file consisting of 5 years of monthly average yields on a Moody's Aaa rated corporate bond (see also Greene, 1999, Example 18.1). The original level series is nostationary, but it can be shown to be an integrated process of the first order (or I(1)) with no augmented lags (we leave this as an exercise, see Chapter XIV). Since the first difference of an I(1) process is stationary, deriving from the unit roots test equation, we will estimate the following second order autoregressive model:

$$Y_t = \rho_0 + \rho_1\ Y_{t-1} + \rho_2\ Y_{t-2} + u_t$$

---

[14] The alternative to data initialization is to estimate the unknown pre-sample observations of $\varepsilon_0, \varepsilon_{-1}, ..., \varepsilon_{-q+1}$ together with the model parameters. The problem becomes highly nonlinear and complicated.

where $u_t \sim ii(0,\sigma^2)$ or $nii(0,\sigma^2)$. We may examine the data series Y_t by plotting the correlogram of its autocorrelation and partial autocorrelation coefficients. For univariate analysis, the ACF and PACF of the time series will be identical to those of the residuals obtained from the mean-deviation regression. Up to the maximum number of lags specified for the ACF and PACF, Box-Pierce and Ljung-Box test statistics are useful for identifying the proper order of AR(p), MA(q), or ARMA(p,q) process. In addition, the Breusch-Godfrey LM test may be used to verify higher orders of autocorrelation, if any exist.

Although the entire diagnostic checking procedure is not shown here, by examining the autocorrelation and partial autocorrelation coefficients as well as the relevant diagnostic test statistics, we can show that an AR(2) specification is sufficient for the bond yield model. The result is consistent with that of the stationarity test. Using a time series of bond yields, a regression model with two (first and second) lagged dependent variables is estimated in the following program **lesson15.1**.

```
      /*
      ** Lesson 15.1: ARMA Analysis of Bond Yields
      */
1     use gpe2;
2     output file=gpe\output15.1 reset;

3     n=61;  @ 1990.01 - 1994.12 @
4     load bonds[n,2]=gpe\bonds.txt;

5     y=bonds[2:n,2];

6     call reset;
7     _names={"yields"};
8     _rstat=1;
9     _rplot=2;

10    _dlags=2;
      /*
      _ar=2;
      _iter=50;
      */
11    _bgtest=4;
12    _acf=12;
13    call estimate(y,0);

14    end;
```

The estimated model is summarized as follows (standard errors are in parentheses):

$$Y_t = \underset{(0.2107)}{0.4068} + \underset{(0.1107)}{1.1566} \, Y_{t-1} - \underset{(0.1102)}{0.2083} \, Y_{t-2}$$

Further study of the regression residuals using the ACF and PACF up to 12 lags does not reveal higher-order autocorrelated structure in this model. The other tests (Durbin-Watson test for the first lag and Breusch-Godfrey LM test up to the fourth lags) suggest that a structure beyond AR(2) may be presented. But if such structure does exist in this model, it is not reflected in the ACF and PACF. Conflicting results from the use of different diagnostic tests are not unusual in empirical analysis. Run this program, and see the output file output15.1 for details.

An alternative to including two lagged dependent variables in the model is to express residuals of the mean-deviation model as an AR(2) process:

$$Y_t = \mu + \varepsilon_t$$
$$\varepsilon_t = \phi_1 \varepsilon_{t-1} + \phi_2 \varepsilon_{t-2} + u_t$$

Or, equivalently

$$Y_t = \mu + \phi_1 \varepsilon_{t-1} + \phi_2 \varepsilon_{t-2} + u_t$$

We note that $\mu = \rho_0 /(1 - \rho_1 - \rho_2)$ from the earlier specification with lagged dependent variables. We now modify Lesson 15.1 by replacing line 10 of the program (_dlags=2) with the following two statements:

```
_ar=2;
_iter=50;
```

Estimation of autocorrelated error structures is inherently nonlinear, so we will need to ensure that the number of iterations is sufficient to converge on a solution. We note that the control variable _ar is used to specify the autocorrelation order of the model error. For a more general autoregressive and moving average model, the GPE control variable _arma should be used instead. _arma is a column vector with the first element being the autoregressive order, and the second being the moving average order of the model structure. In this example, _ar=2 is equivalent to _arma={2,0}. For a pure moving average model, you would set the first element of _arma to zero. For example, _arma={0,1} defines the first-order moving average process. See Appendix A for more information about the use of the GPE control variable _arma.

Running the revised **lesson15.1**, we obtain the following result (standard errors are in parentheses):

$$Y_t = \quad 7.877 \quad + \quad 1.1566 \, \varepsilon_{t-1} \quad - \quad 0.2083 \, \varepsilon_{t-2}$$
s.e. (0.3882) (0.08597) (0.08654)

Comparing the estimated autoregressive parameters with those of Lesson 15.1, we find the two sets of coefficients are very similar. In addition, diagnostic checking indicates that AR(2) is a sufficient specification for this model. We note that the divisor N (N=58 in this example) is used in calculating the standard errors for a nonlinear model.[15] Therefore, the resulting standard errors of the parameters are smaller in this model, as compared with the lagged dependent variables specification of Lesson 15.1.

The classical univariate ARMA analysis is easily extended to a more general regression model with multiple regressors. There are two approaches, as shown below.

ARMA Analysis for Regression Residuals

The full model consists of the following two equations:

---

[15] With the model of Lesson 15.1, the divisor used is N-K where K is 3.

$$Y_t = X_t\beta + \varepsilon_t$$
$$\phi(B)\varepsilon_t = \theta(B)u_t$$

Or, equivalently

$$Y_t = X_t\beta + \phi_1\varepsilon_{t-1} + \phi_2\varepsilon_{t-2} + \ldots + \phi_p\varepsilon_{t-p} - \theta_1 u_{t-1} - \theta_2 u_{t-2} - \ldots - \theta_q u_{t-q} + u_t$$

where $u_t \sim ii(0,\sigma^2)$ or $nii(0,\sigma^2)$, $t = 1,2,\ldots,N$. The model identification and estimation proceeds in the same way as univariate ARMA analysis. Regression parameters (βs) and ARMA parameters (ϕs and θs) must be simultaneously estimated through iterations of nonlinear functional (sum-of-squares or log-likelihood) optimization. For statistical inference, the degrees of freedom must account for all the unknown parameters in the model.

ARMAX Regression Model: Transfer Function Approach

The model to be estimated is

$$\rho(B)Y_t = X_t\beta + \varepsilon_t$$
$$\varepsilon_t = \theta(B)u_t$$

Or, equivalently

$$Y_t = X_t\beta + \rho_1 Y_{t-1} + \rho_2 Y_{t-2} + \ldots + \rho_p Y_{t-p} - \theta_1 u_{t-1} - \theta_2 u_{t-2} - \ldots - \theta_q u_{t-q} + u_t$$

where $u_t \sim ii(0,\sigma^2)$ or $nii(0,\sigma^2)$, $t = 1,2,\ldots,N$. We identify the proper autoregressive and moving average orders and estimate the model in a similar fashion to the classical univariate ARMA analysis. The difference between ARMA and ARMAX model specification lies in the treatment of autoregressive components of the error structure. For the former, the model error is specified solely by an ARMA representation. On the other hand, in an ARMAX model, lagged dependent variables are used in conjunction with only the moving averages of errors. In GPE, however, it is possible to include the autoregressive error terms in an ARMAX model for estimating non-stationary time series with ARMA error structure.

As mentioned earlier, in GPE, ARMA analysis is called with the input control variable _arma. _arma is a column vector containing at least two elements specifying the type of ARMA model to be estimated. The first element of _arma denotes autoregressive order of the ARMA process, while the second element denotes the moving average order. Specifying only the autoregressive portion and including a zero for the moving average portion yields a pure AR specification (vice versa for a pure MA specification). Optional initial values of the autoregressive and moving average coefficients may be appended to the vector _arma along with their respective orders. Supplying the initial values is useful for starting the iterative estimation process from non-zero values of ARMA coefficients. For example,

```
_arma = {1,1,0.5,0.1};
```

The model ARMA(1,1) is specified, with the initial values 0.5 for the AR(1) coefficient and 0.1 for the MA(1) coefficient. Nonlinear estimation of this model will begin from the specified set of starting values.

Lesson 15.2: ARMA Analysis of U.S. Inflation

In this example we will identify and estimate a time series regression model of U.S. inflation. The inflation rate in this example is measured as the quarterly rate of percent change in price:

$$\Delta P_t = 100 \, [ln(P_t) - ln(P_{t-1})]$$

Inflation is believed to be affected by excess monetary growth (i.e., monetary growth that is faster than the growth of real output) and by external economic shocks. Excess monetary growth is defined as $\Delta M_t - \Delta Y_t$, where

$$\Delta M_t = 100 \, [ln(M1_t) - ln(M1_{t-1})]$$
$$\Delta Y_t = 100 \, [ln(GNP_t) - ln(GNP_{t-1})]$$

The basic regression model of inflation is presented as follows:

$$\Delta P_t = \beta_0 + \beta_1(\Delta M_t - \Delta Y_t) + \varepsilon_t$$

The lagged values of the inflation rate (or the disturbance term) will serve to model the effects of external shocks to the economy. The data file **usinf.txt** consists of 136 quarterly observations (from 1950 Q1 to 1984 Q4) of data for price (implicit GNP deflator) P_t, money stock $M1_t$, and output (GNP) Y_t.

To keep the model simple, we include the first lag of the dependent variable in the regression and examine the patterns of ACF and PACF. Significant spikes (or non-zero values of autocorrelation and partial autocorrelation coefficients) appear up to the third or fourth lags for both functions, indicating a complicated structure in the model's error term. We will not go through the entire identification process here. Interested readers can "comment out" lines 15 to 18 in the program **lesson15.2** below, and decide the proper ARMA or ARMAX specification for themselves based on their observations of the behavior of the ACF and PACF.

```
   /*
   ** Lesson 15.2: ARMA Analysis of U.S. Inflation
   ** Greene (1999), Example 18.11
   */
1  use gpe2;
2  output file=gpe\output15.2 reset;

3  n=137;
4  load data[n,4]=gpe\usinf.txt;

5  y=ln(data[2:n,2]);
6  m=ln(data[2:n,3]);
7  p=ln(data[2:n,4]);
8  dp=packr(100*(p-lagn(p,1)));
9  dm=packr(100*(m-lagn(m,1)));
10 dy=packr(100*(y-lagn(y,1)));

11 call reset;
12 _rstat=1;
13 _rplot=2;
14 _acf=12;

15 _dlags=1;
16 _arma={0,3};
17 _method=5;
```

```
18  _iter=100;
19  call estimate(dp,lagn(dm-dy,1));

20  end;
```

The final model for estimation is a lagged dependent variable model (line 15) with a third-order moving average specification (line 16). Maximum likelihood estimation of the model is carried out using the QHC optimization method (line 17). The output of running **lesson15.2** is stored in the file output15.2.

In summary, the estimated model (with standard errors in parentheses) is

$$\Delta P_t = \quad 0.1008 \quad + \quad 0.0146\,(\Delta M_t\text{-}\Delta Y_t) \quad + \quad 0.9151\Delta P_{t\text{-}1}$$
$$\text{s.e.} \quad (0.0516) \qquad\quad (0.0199) \qquad\qquad\quad (0.0429)$$
$$\qquad\quad - 0.505\varepsilon_{t\text{-}1} \quad + \quad 0.0232\varepsilon_{t\text{-}2} \qquad + \quad 0.204\varepsilon_{t\text{-}3}$$
$$\qquad\quad (0.093) \qquad\qquad (0.0986) \qquad\qquad\quad (0.0884)$$

The lag of the dependent variable ($\Delta P_{t\text{-}1}$) plays an important role in the regression equation. Although the second lag of the moving average is insignificant, the first and third are significant. Further analysis of the ACF and PACF does not show autocorrelation in the regression residuals.

Autoregressive Conditional Heteroscedasticity

We have thus far concentrated on the classical time series modeling, which focuses on the expected value (mean) of the variable. In many financial and monetary economic applications, serial correlation over time is characterized not only in the mean but also in the conditional variance. The latter is the so-called autoregressive conditional heteroscedasticity or ARCH model. It is possible that the variance is *unconditionally* homogeneous in spite of the presence of *conditional* heteroscedasticity. Using GPE, analysis of ARCH effects is no more complicated than setting a few input control variables.

Consider the time series linear regression model:

$$Y_t = X_t\beta + \varepsilon_t$$

At time t, conditional to the available historical information H_t, we assume that the error structure follows a normal distribution: $\varepsilon_t|H_t \sim nii(0,\sigma^2_t)$ where the variance is written as:

$$\sigma^2_t = \alpha_0 + \delta_1\sigma^2_{t\text{-}1} + ... + \delta_p\sigma^2_{t\text{-}p} + \alpha_1\varepsilon^2_{t\text{-}1} + ... + \alpha_q\varepsilon^2_{t\text{-}q}$$
$$= \alpha_0 + \Sigma_{j=1,2,...p}\delta_j\sigma^2_{t\text{-}j} + \Sigma_{i=1,2,...q}\alpha_i\varepsilon^2_{t\text{-}i}$$

Let $\upsilon_t = \varepsilon^2_t\text{-}\sigma^2_t$, $\alpha_i = 0$ for $i > q$, $\delta_j = 0$ for $j > p$, and $m = \max(p,q)$. Then, the above serially correlated variance process may be conveniently rewritten as an ARMA(m,p) model for ε^2_t. That is,

$$\varepsilon^2_t = \alpha_0 + \Sigma_{i=1,2,...m}(\alpha_i+\delta_i)\varepsilon^2_{t\text{-}i} - \Sigma_{j=1,2,...p}\delta_j\upsilon_{t\text{-}j} + \upsilon_t$$

By assuming $E(\upsilon_t) = 0$, $E(\varepsilon^2_t)$ is the estimated variance of σ^2_t. This is the general specification of autoregressive conditional heteroscedasticity, or GARCH(p,q), according to Bollerslev (1986). If p = 0, this GARCH(0,q) process simply reduces to an ARCH(q) process:

$$\sigma^2_t = \alpha_0 + \Sigma_{i=1,2,...q} \alpha_i \varepsilon^2_{t-i}$$

ARCH(1) Process

The simplest case, pioneered by Engle (1982) sets q = 1 (while p = 0). This ARCH(1) process can be written as:

$$\sigma^2_t = \alpha_0 + \alpha_1 \varepsilon^2_{t-1}$$

The ARCH(1) model can be summarized as follows:

$$Y_t = X_t \beta + \varepsilon_t$$
$$\varepsilon_t = u_t(\alpha_0 + \alpha_1 \varepsilon^2_{t-1})^{1/2} \text{ where } u_t \sim nii(0,1)$$

This specification gives us the conditional mean and variance, $E(\varepsilon_t|\varepsilon_{t-1}) = 0$ and $\sigma^2_t = E(\varepsilon^2_t|\varepsilon_{t-1}) = \alpha_0 + \alpha_1 \varepsilon^2_{t-1}$, respectively. Note that the unconditional variance of ε_t is $E(\varepsilon^2_t) = E[E(\varepsilon^2_t|\varepsilon_{t-1})] = \alpha_0 + \alpha_1 E(\varepsilon^2_{t-1})$. If $\sigma^2 = E(\varepsilon^2_t) = E(\varepsilon^2_{t-1})$, then $\sigma^2 = \alpha_0/(1-\alpha_1)$, provided that $|\alpha_1| < 1$. In other words, the model may be free of general heteroscedasticity even when we assume that conditional heteroscedasticity is present.

ARCH-M(1) Model

An extension of the ARCH(1) model is ARCH(1) in mean, or ARCH-M(1) model, which adds the heterogeneous variance term directly into the regression equation (assuming a linear model):

$$Y_t = X_t \beta + \gamma \sigma^2_t + \varepsilon_t$$
$$\sigma^2_t = \alpha_0 + \alpha_1 \varepsilon^2_{t-1}$$

The last variance term of the regression may be expressed in log form $ln(\sigma^2_t)$ or in standard error σ_t. For example, $Y_t = X_t \beta + \gamma ln(\sigma^2_t) + \varepsilon_t$. Moreover, to ensure the model stability and positive values of variances, we will need to constrain σ^2_t by forcing $\alpha_0 > 0$ and $0 \leq \alpha_1 < 1$.

Hypothesis Testing for ARCH and GARCH Processes

As with ARMA modeling, specifying the correct order of the model is an important step in estimating the ARCH and GARCH processes. Luckily, the close connection between GARCH and ARMA allows us to compute the ARMA autocorrelation and partial autocorrelation coefficients based on the squares of standardized regression residuals $(\varepsilon_t/\sigma_t)^2$. The GPE control input variable _acf2 calculates the ACF, PACF, and the associated diagnostic test statistics on $(\varepsilon_t/\sigma_t)^2$ up to the number of lags we specified. For example, to examine 12 lags of ACF and PACF of $(\varepsilon_t/\sigma_t)^2$, use the statement:

```
_acf2 = 12;
```

The other testing procedure involves checking ARCH(q) against ARCH(0), or GARCH (p,q) against GARCH(p,0) for a given p. The Engle-Bollerslev LM Test of ARCH effects (Bollerslev, 1986) is carried out using the test statistic NR^2, where N is the sample size and R^2 (R-square statistic) is obtained from the ARCH(q) regression. The Engle-Bollerslev test statistic is distributed as a Chi-square with q degrees of freedom. The Engle-Bollerslev LM test of ARCH effects resembles the Breusch Godfrey LM test for AR effects. This is a cumulative test for no ARCH effects up to the order specified. Therefore, we need only to test for ARCH effects at a low order to confirm their existence. In GPE, the Engle-Bollerslev LM test procedure is called using the control variable _ebtest in a similar fashion to _acf2. For example, to test for ARCH effects up to the 6th order, use the statement:

```
_ebtest = 6;
```

For more information about the use of _acf2 and _ebtest, see Appendix A.

ARCH Model Estimation

Recall the normal log-likelihood function of a heteroscedastic regression model

$$ll = -\tfrac{1}{2} N\ ln(2\pi) - \tfrac{1}{2}\ \Sigma_{t=1,2,...,N}ln(\sigma^2_t) - \tfrac{1}{2}\ \Sigma_{t=1,2,...,N}(\varepsilon^2_t/\sigma^2_t)$$

with the general conditional heteroscedastic variance GARCH(p,q) process:

$$\sigma^2_t = \alpha_0 + \delta_1\sigma^2_{t-1} + \delta_2\sigma^2_{t-2} + ... + \delta_p\sigma^2_{t-p} + \alpha_1\varepsilon^2_{t-1} + \alpha_2\varepsilon^2_{t-2} + ... + \alpha_q\varepsilon^2_{t-q}$$

The parameter vector (α,δ) is estimated together with the regression parameters (e.g., $\varepsilon = Y - X\beta$) by maximizing the log-likelihood function, conditional to the data initialization $\varepsilon^2_0, \varepsilon^2_{-1}, ..., \varepsilon^2_{-q}, \sigma^2_0, \sigma^2_{-1}, ..., \sigma^2_{-p}$. In GPE, the data initialization used for the pre-sample observations is simply the sample variance of the error series $E(\varepsilon^2_t) = \Sigma_{t=1,2,...,N}\ \varepsilon^2_t/N$.

In estimating a GARCH model, the estimated variance for each observation must be positive. We could assume the following parameter restrictions:

$$\alpha_0 > 0;\ \alpha_i \geq 0,\ i=1,2,...q;\ \delta_j \geq 0,\ j=1,2,...,p$$

However, this set of restrictions is sufficient but not necessary (see Nelson and Cao, 1992) for the positive values of variances.

To estimate a model with ARCH or GARCH effects, we introduce the input control variable _garch. _garch is a column vector with at least two elements. The first element defines the autoregressive order of the GARCH model, while the second element is the moving average order of the model. The rest of components in the vector _garch, if given, specify the initial values of the GARCH parameters in accordance with the orders given, as well as the initial value of the constant term. The constant term in the variance equation is important because it may indicate a homoscedastic structure if all the other slope parameters are insignificant. For example,

```
_garch = {1,1};
```

specifies a GARCH(1,1) model. If we write instead,

```
_garch = {1,1,0.1,0.1,0.5};
```

then the initial values of the GARCH(1,1) are also given. The first two values of 0.1 are the initial values of autoregressive and moving average components of the GARCH (1,1) process, respectively. The last element, 0.5, is the constant. The nonlinear model estimation will begin from this set of starting values. Finally, we remark that GPE implementation of the GARCH model estimation includes another input variable _garchx to allow for external effects in the variance equation:

$$\sigma^2_t = \alpha_0 + \Sigma_{j=1,2,...p}\delta_j\sigma^2_{t-j} + \Sigma_{i=1,2,...q}\alpha_i\epsilon^2_{t-i} + X_t\gamma$$

where X_t is a data matrix of external variables which may influence the variances. γ is the corresponding parameter vector. Setting the data matrix to the variable _garchx will do the trick. For example,

```
_garchx = x;
```

where x is the data matrix of the external variables already in place, which must have the same number of observations as the residual variances. For more information about the use of _garch and _garchx, see Appendix A.

Lesson 15.3 ARCH Model of U.S. Inflation

In this example, we focus on univariate ARCH analysis of U.S. inflation. We have seen the ARMA regression analysis of U.S. inflation rate in Lesson 15.2. The data are read from the file **usinf.txt** as in Lesson 15.2, but we use only the price variable. Our study is based on the example given in Bollerslev (1986) and Greene (1999, Example 18.2).

We will test, identify, and estimate the appropriate GARCH variance structure for the variable ΔP_t, defined as the percentage change of implicit price GNP deflator. We specify 12 lags of ACF and PACF for the squared mean-deviation residuals and compute Engle-Bollerslev LM test statistics up to the sixth lag:

```
_acf2 = 12;
_ebtest = 6;
```

Just to be sure, the ARMA structure in the mean is also investigated by examining 12 lags of ACF and PACF for the mean-deviation residuals and 6 lags for Breusch-Godfrey LM test statistics:

```
_acf = 12;
_bgtest = 6;
```

We consider a three-lag autoregressive model of ΔP_t in conjunction with a GARCH(1,1) error process. If you would like to go through the model identification process, simply comment out lines 14 through 17 in the following **lesson15.3**.

```
    /*
    ** Lesson 15.3: ARCH Analysis of U.S. Inflation
    ** Greene (1999), Example 18.12
    */
1   use gpe2;
2   output file=gpe\output15.3 reset;
```

```
3  n=137;
4  load data[n,4]=gpe\usinf.txt;
5  p=ln(data[2:n,4]);
6  dp=packr(100*(p-lagn(p,1)));

7  call reset;
8  _rstat=1;
9  _rplot=2;

10 _acf=12;
11 _bgtest=6;
12 _acf2=12;
13 _ebtest=6;

14 _dlags=3;
15 _garch={1,1,0.5,0.5,0.1};
16 _method=5;
17 _iter=100;

18 call estimate(dp,0);

19 end;
```

We note that the initial values of the GARCH(1,1) parameters are used in order to successfully estimate the model (see line 15). Running **lesson15.3**, we obtain the following result (see the generated output file output15.3 for details):[16]

$$\Delta P_t = \quad 0.119 \quad + \quad 0.341\,\Delta P_{t-1} \quad + \quad 0.214\,\Delta P_{t-2} \quad + \quad 0.325\,\Delta P_{t-3}$$
$$\text{s.e.} \quad (0.056) \qquad (0.088) \qquad\qquad (0.088) \qquad\qquad (0.087)$$

$$\sigma^2_t = \quad 0.00573 \quad + \quad 0.882\,\sigma^2_{t-1} \quad + \quad 0.0799\,\varepsilon^2_{t-1}$$
$$\text{s.e.} \quad (0.0066) \qquad (0.056) \qquad\qquad (0.0496)$$

Based on the standard normal test, we see that σ^2_{t-1} is statistically different from zero, but the constant term and ε^2_{t-1} are not. The model may be re-estimated with GARCH(1,0) specification.

To be sure that the estimated GARCH(1,1) model does not have higher-order structures in either the ARMA or GARCH specifications, the following extract of output on diagnostic checking of the estimated model consists of: (1) ACF and PACF for the estimated residuals and Breusch-Godfrey LM test for ARMA specification; (2) ACF and PACF for the squared estimated standardized residuals and Engle-Bollerslev LM test for ARCH specification. With an exception at the twelfth lag of ACF and PACF for GARCH specification (possibly an outlier), the estimated GARCH(1,1) model is acceptable for describing the U.S. inflation rate.

```
Breusch-Godfrey LM Test for Autocorrelation
                    Chi-Sq        DF    Prob>Chi-Sq
AR(   1)            0.66868       1      0.41351
AR(   2)            0.79698       2      0.67133
AR(   3)            0.82301       3      0.84396
AR(   4)            1.5805        4      0.81229
AR(   5)            1.7334        5      0.88467
AR(   6)            2.3775        6      0.88192
Engle-Bollerslev LM Test for Autoregressive Conditional Heteroscedasticity
```

Based on Squared Standardized Residuals

		Chi-Sq	DF	Prob>Chi-Sq
ARCH(	1)	1.3974	1	0.23716
ARCH(	2)	2.0844	2	0.35269
ARCH(	3)	2.4708	3	0.48060
ARCH(	4)	3.5246	4	0.47415
ARCH(	5)	3.5422	5	0.61702
ARCH(	6)	3.8524	6	0.69665

Autocorrelation and Partial Autocorrelation Functions
ARMA Model Specification
Mean = 0.010305   Standard Error = 0.3924

Lag	AR	S.E.(AR)	PAR	S.E.(PAR)	Box-Pierce	Ljung-Box
1	0.065389	0.087410	0.065389	0.087039	0.56439	0.57732
2	0.034597	0.087514	0.030451	0.087039	0.72238	0.74017
3	0.031536	0.087600	0.027494	0.087039	0.85366	0.87653
4	0.041261	0.087747	0.036716	0.087039	1.0784	1.1118
5	0.012524	0.087761	0.0058822	0.087039	1.0991	1.1336
6	0.0021592	0.087761	-0.0021918	0.087039	1.0997	1.1343
7	-0.12321	0.089062	-0.12686	0.087039	3.1034	3.2823
8	-0.080462	0.089611	-0.068807	0.087039	3.9580	4.2058
9	-0.019052	0.089641	-0.0039795	0.087039	4.0059	4.2580
10	-0.011847	0.089653	0.0011377	0.087039	4.0245	4.2784
11	-0.095777	0.090425	-0.082072	0.087039	5.2353	5.6193
12	-0.067064	0.090801	-0.049412	0.087039	5.8290	6.2823

GARCH Model Specification based on Squared Standardized Residuals
Mean = 1.0197   Standard Error = 1.4008

Lag	AR	S.E.(AR)	PAR	S.E.(PAR)	Box-Pierce	Ljung-Box
1	-0.10274	0.087953	-0.10274	0.087039	1.3933	1.4252
2	0.082417	0.088536	0.072628	0.087039	2.2899	2.3494
3	-0.069017	0.088943	-0.054563	0.087039	2.9186	3.0025
4	0.10580	0.089891	0.090016	0.087039	4.3961	4.5492
5	-0.015788	0.089912	0.010947	0.087039	4.4290	4.5839
6	-0.030121	0.089988	-0.048974	0.087039	4.5488	4.7113
7	-0.050698	0.090204	-0.047526	0.087039	4.8880	5.0750
8	0.095577	0.090968	0.085506	0.087039	6.0939	6.3781
9	0.00024805	0.090968	0.019248	0.087039	6.0939	6.3781
10	-0.056418	0.091233	-0.067360	0.087039	6.5140	6.8396
11	-0.12419	0.092505	-0.12321	0.087039	8.5499	9.0942
12	0.21915	0.096358	0.20097	0.087039	14.889	16.173

At this point, you may be wondering whether there exist ARCH effects for the inflation rate model we considered earlier in Lesson 15.2. The mixture of ARMA and ARCH effects may be identified and estimated for the model. We leave the validation of ARCH effects in Lesson 15.2 to interested readers.

Lesson 15.4 ARCH Model of Deutschemark-British Pound Exchange Rate

This example investigates the "long-run volatility" persistence of the Deutschemark-British pound exchange rate (see Bollerslev and Ghysels, 1986). Daily exchange rate data from January 3, 1984 to December 31, 1991 (1974 observations) are used (see data text file **dmbp.txt**). The model of interest is

$$Y_t = 100 \ [ln(P_t) - ln(P_{t-1})] = \mu + \varepsilon_t$$

where P_t is the bilateral spot Deutschemark-British pound exchange rate. Thus Y_t is the daily nominal percentage returns from exchanging the two currencies. Similar to

---

[16] Because we use a different set of U.S. inflation rate data, the estimated model does not match with the Example 18.2 of Greene (1999).

the testing procedure carried out in Lesson 15.3, we will identify and estimate the appropriate GARCH variance structure for the variable Y_t. Because of the large data sample, longer lags may be used for the tests with ACF and PACF.[17] We leave out the details of identification and report only the chosen model for estimation.

We find that the mean returns of Deutschemark-British pound exchange are essentially zero, and there is no evidence of ARMA structure. However, a high order ARCH or a mixed GARCH process is suggested. Therefore, in **lesson15.4**, the model is estimated with GARCH(1,1) effects (see line 14). We keep the code section of model identification (lines 10 through 13) for the purpose of performing diagnostic tests on the estimated model.

```
    /*
    ** Lesson 15.4: GARCH(1,1) Model of DM/BP Exchange Rate
    ** Bollerslev and Ghysels (1996), JBES, 307-327.
    */
1   use gpe2;
2   output file=gpe\output15.4 reset;

    @ Deutschemark/British Pound Exchange Rate @
3   n=1974; @ 1-3-1984 to 12-31-1991 @
4   load data[n,2]=gpe\dmbp.txt;

5   x=data[.,1];

6   call reset;
7   _names={"xrate"};
8   _rstat=1;
9   _rplot=2;

    @ model identification @
10  _acf2=12;
11  _ebtest=6;
12  _acf=12;
13  _bgtest=6;

    @ model estimation @
14  _garch={1,1};
15  _method=6;
16  _iter=100;

17  call estimate(x,0);

18  end;
```

Using the modified QHC method (line 15), the result of maximum likelihood estimation of the GARCH(1,1) model is given below:

```
Least Squares Estimation
------------------------
Dependent Variable = XRATE
Estimation Range =  1         1974
Number of Observations = 1974
Mean of Dependent Variable = -0.016427
Standard Error of Dependent Variable = 0.47024

Maximum Likelihood Estimation for Nonlinear Error Structure
GARCH( 1, 1) Autoregressive Conditional Heteroscedasticity Process
```

---

[17] As the size of the data is beyond the limit of GAUSS Light, the professional version of GAUSS should be used.

```
Maximum Number of Iterations = 100
Step Size Search Method = 0
Convergence Criterion = 0
Tolerance = 0.001

Initial Result:
Log Likelihood =      -1722.8
Parameters =    -0.016427      0.00000       0.00000       0.10000

Using Modified Quadratic Hill-Climbing Algorithm
Iteration =  1   Step Size =  2.3579  Log Likelihood =      -1305.1
Parameters =    -0.013777      0.072340      0.015314      0.16692
...
Iteration = 11   Step Size =  1.0000  Log Likelihood =      -1106.6
Parameters =    -0.0061905     0.80598       0.15313       0.010761

Final Result:
Iterations = 11           Evaluations = 596148
Log Likelihood =       -1106.6
Parameters =    -0.0061905     0.80598       0.15313       0.010761
Gradient Vector =       0.067109      -3.2813       -2.7642       -17.896


                 Parameter     Std.Error      t-Ratio
HAR( 1)          0.80598       0.073406       10.980
HMA( 1)          0.15313       0.054232       2.8236
CONSTANT         0.010761      0.0065879      1.6334

NOTE: R-Square, AOV are computed from original series.

R-Square = -0.00047409  R-Square Adjusted = -0.00047409
Standard Error of the Estimate = 0.47036
Log-Likelihood = -1106.6
Log Ammemiya Prediction Criterion (APC) =  -1.5080
Log Akaike Information Criterion (AIC) =  -1.5080
Log Schwarz Bayesian Information Criterion (BIC) =  -1.5052
```

Sum of Squares	SS	DF	MSS	F	Prob>F
Explained	3.7079E-029	0			
Residual	436.50	1973	0.22123		
Total	436.29	1973	0.22113		

Variable Name	Estimated Coefficient	Standard Error	t-Ratio 1973 DF	Prob >|t|	Partial Regression
CONSTANT	-0.0061905	0.0091932	-0.67338	0.50079	0.00022977

```
Variance-Covariance Matrix of Coefficients
CONSTANT       8.4515E-005
               CONSTANT

Correlation Matrix of Coefficients
CONSTANT           1.0000
               CONSTANT

Squared Correlation of Observed and Predicted = 5.3640E-006
Sum of Squared Residuals = 436.50
Sum of Absolute Residuals = 647.59
Sum of Residuals = -2.02064E+001
First-Order Rho = 0.0098581
Durbin-Watson Test Statistic = 1.9796
```

The GARCH(1,1) model is summarized as follows:

$$\sigma_t^2 = \quad 0.01076 \quad + \quad 0.80598\ \sigma_{t-1}^2 \quad + \quad 0.15313\ \varepsilon_{t-1}^2$$
s.e. $\quad (0.0066) \qquad (0.0734) \qquad\qquad (0.0542)$

With the exception of the constant term, all other parameters are significantly different from zero based on the standard normal test.

 If the underlying assumption of normal distribution for the model is questionable, the estimated variance-covariance matrix may be adjusted. This is easily done by setting the control variable _vcov=3 before calling the estimate statement (line 17). As the result of quasi-maximum likelihood estimation, the *robust* standard errors for the parameters are computed. See Appendix A for more details.

Diagnostic checking on the estimated GARCH(1,1) model does not suggest a higher-order ARMA or GARCH specification. All the statistical tests presented below confirm that the estimated GARCH(1,1) model describes the volatility of the returns of the Deutschemark-British pound exchange rate reasonably well.

Breusch-Godfrey LM Test for Autocorrelation

		Chi-Sq	DF	Prob>Chi-Sq
AR(	1)	0.17342	1	0.67709
AR(	2)	1.4489	2	0.48458
AR(	3)	3.8242	3	0.28109
AR(	4)	4.5111	4	0.34124
AR(	5)	5.2147	5	0.39025
AR(	6)	5.2316	6	0.51447

Engle-Bollerslev LM Test for Autoregressive Conditional Heteroscedasticity
Based on Squared Standardized Residuals

		Chi-Sq	DF	Prob>Chi-Sq
ARCH(	1)	2.5119	1	0.11299
ARCH(	2)	2.6312	2	0.26832
ARCH(	3)	4.2403	3	0.23666
ARCH(	4)	4.2406	4	0.37442
ARCH(	5)	4.2422	5	0.51510
ARCH(	6)	6.7980	6	0.33993

Autocorrelation and Partial Autocorrelation Functions
ARMA Model Specification
Mean = -0.010236   Standard Error = 0.47024

Lag	AR	S.E.(AR)	PAR	S.E.(PAR)	Box-Pierce	Ljung-Box
1	0.0093663	0.022509	0.0093663	0.022507	0.17318	0.17344
2	-0.025323	0.022524	-0.025413	0.022507	1.4390	1.4418
3	0.034169	0.022550	0.034675	0.022507	3.7436	3.7523
4	0.019958	0.022559	0.018659	0.022507	4.5299	4.5409
5	0.017487	0.022566	0.018896	0.022507	5.1335	5.1468
6	-0.0023945	0.022566	-0.0029546	0.022507	5.1449	5.1581
7	-0.016242	0.022572	-0.016632	0.022507	5.6656	5.6812
8	0.016314	0.022578	0.014906	0.022507	6.1910	6.2093
9	0.016177	0.022584	0.014567	0.022507	6.7076	6.7288
10	0.011128	0.022587	0.012590	0.022507	6.9520	6.9747
11	-0.037358	0.022618	-0.037292	0.022507	9.7069	9.7478
12	-0.0013434	0.022618	-0.0011303	0.022507	9.7105	9.7514

GARCH Model Specification based on Squared Standardized Residuals
Mean = 0.99779   Standard Error = 2.35

Lag	AR	S.E.(AR)	PAR	S.E.(PAR)	Box-Pierce	Ljung-Box
1	0.035668	0.022536	0.035668	0.022507	2.5113	2.5152
2	-0.0064933	0.022537	-0.0077754	0.022507	2.5946	2.5986
3	-0.029035	0.022556	-0.028562	0.022507	4.2587	4.2669
4	-0.0016120	0.022556	0.00040097	0.022507	4.2638	4.2720
5	-0.00056223	0.022556	-0.00090229	0.022507	4.2644	4.2726
6	-0.035159	0.022584	-0.036022	0.022507	6.7046	6.7228

7	−0.025093	0.022598	−0.022674	0.022507	7.9475	7.9714
8	−0.013861	0.022602	−0.012704	0.022507	8.3268	8.3526
9	−0.0019132	0.022602	−0.0033856	0.022507	8.3340	8.3598
10	0.018812	0.022610	0.017422	0.022507	9.0326	9.0627
11	−0.013855	0.022615	−0.016063	0.022507	9.4116	9.4441
12	−0.016590	0.022621	−0.016835	0.022507	9.9548	9.9913

XVI
Panel Data Analysis

We have seen two popular types of data used in econometric analysis: time-series and cross-sectional data. However, in some circumstances, the economic data may be a composition of time series and cross sections (i.e., the observations of several individuals over time). International statistics, company surveys, and longitudinal data sets are common examples. Modeling these panel data sets calls for some quite complex stochastic specifications. In this chapter, we introduce the basic programming techniques for panel data analysis.

For each cross section (individual) $i=1,2,...N$ and each time period (time) $t=1,2,...T$, we write the regression equation as follows:

$$Y_{it} = X_{it}\beta_{it} + \varepsilon_{it}$$

Suppose that the regressors X_{it} include a constant term. Let $\beta_{it} = \beta$ and assume $\varepsilon_{it} = u_i + v_t + e_{it}$. Note that we assume the identical β for all i and t, and consider their differences in the components of the error term ε_{it}. Here u_i represents the individual difference in intercept (so that the *individual effect* is β_0+u_i, where β_0 is the intercept parameter in β) and v_t is the time difference in intercept (so that the *time effect* is β_0+v_t). Two-way analysis includes both time and individual effects. Throughout much of this chapter, however, we will assume $v_t = 0$. That is, there is no time effect and only the one-way individual effects will be analyzed.

We further assume that e_{it} is a classical error term, with zero mean, homogeneous variance, and there is neither serial correlation nor contemporaneous correlation. That is, the error term is not correlated across individuals or time periods. Also, e_{it} is assumed to be uncorrelated with the regressors X_{it}. That is,

$$E(e_{it}) = 0$$
$$E(e_{it}^2) = \sigma^2_e$$
$$E(e_{it}e_{jt}) = 0, \text{ for } i{\neq}j$$
$$E(e_{it}e_{i\tau}) = 0, \text{ for } t{\neq}\tau$$
$$E(X_{it}e_{it}) = 0$$

Fixed Effects Model

Assume that the error component u_i, the individual difference, is fixed (or *nonstochastic*), but varies across individuals. In this case, the model error simply reduces to $\varepsilon_{it} = e_{it}$. The model is expressed as:

$$Y_{it} = (X_{it}\beta_{it} + u_i) + e_{it}$$

where u_i is interpreted to be the *change* in the intercept from individual to individual. As defined earlier, the individual effect is u_i plus the intercept, and this model is known as the *fixed effects* model. To estimate a model with individual fixed effects, consider the following equation:

$$Y_{it} = (X_{it}\beta + u_i) + \varepsilon_{it} \ (i=1,2,...,N; \ t=1,2,...,T)$$

Let $Y_i = [Y_{i1}, Y_{i2}, ..., Y_{iT}]'$, $X_i = [X_{i1}, X_{i2}, ..., X_{iT}]'$, $\varepsilon_i = [\varepsilon_{i1}, \varepsilon_{i2}, ..., \varepsilon_{iT}]'$, and $\upsilon_i = [u_i, u_i, ..., u_i]'$ (a column vector of T elements of u_i). The pooled (stacked) model is

$$\begin{bmatrix} Y_1 \\ Y_2 \\ ... \\ Y_N \end{bmatrix} = \begin{bmatrix} X_1 \\ X_2 \\ ... \\ X_N \end{bmatrix} \beta + \begin{bmatrix} \upsilon_1 \\ \upsilon_2 \\ ... \\ \upsilon_N \end{bmatrix} + \begin{bmatrix} \varepsilon_1 \\ \varepsilon_2 \\ ... \\ \varepsilon_N \end{bmatrix}, \text{ or}$$

$$Y = X\beta + \upsilon + \varepsilon$$

Dummy Variables Approach

Define $D = [D_1, D_2, ..., D_{N-1}]$ with the element $D_i = [D_{i1}, D_{i2}, ..., D_{iT}]'$ and

$$D_{it} = \begin{array}{l} 1 \text{ if } (i-1) \times T + 1 \le i \times t \le i \times T \\ 0 \text{ otherwise} \end{array}$$

Ordinary least squares can be used to estimate the model with dummy variables as follows:

$$Y = X\beta + D\delta + \varepsilon$$

Since X includes a constant term, we will only need N-1 dummy variables for estimation and the estimated δ measures the individual *change* from the intercept. The individual effects are then computed as the sum of the intercept coefficient and the estimated dummy variable parameter for each individual.

Deviation Approach

Although the dummy variable approach is simple, the size of the problem may become difficult to handle if the number of cross sections (individuals) is large. An alternative is the deviation approach.

Let $Y^m_i = (\Sigma_{t=1,2,...,T} Y_{it})/T$, $X^m_i = (\Sigma_{t=1,2,...,T} X_{it})/T$, and $e^m_i = (\Sigma_{t=1,2,...,T} e_{it})/T$. By estimating the following mean deviation model, we can obtain *within-estimates* of the parameters:

$$(Y_{it} - Y^m_i) = (X_{it} - X^m_i)\beta + (e_{it} - e^m_i)$$

Or, equivalently

$$Y_{it} = X_{it}\beta + (Y^m_i - X^m_i\beta) + (e_{it} - e^m_i)$$

Note that the constant term drops out due to the deviation transformation. As a result, we can conclude the individual effects as $u_i = Y^m_i - X^m_i\beta$. The variance-covariance matrix of individual effects can be estimated as follows:

$$Var(u_i) = v/T + X^m_i [Var(\beta)] X^{m'}_i$$

where v is the estimated variance of the mean deviation regression with NT-N-K degrees of freedom. Note that K is the number of explanatory variables not counting the constant term.

We can also estimate the model by using only the calculated individual means (as opposed to the deviations from the mean):

$$Y^m_i = X^m_i\beta + u_i + e^m_i$$

The parameter estimates produced from this specification are referred to as the *between-estimates*, and are related to the *within-estimates* of the parameters.

Hypothesis Testing for Fixed Effects

With the dummy variable model, we can test the null hypothesis that $\delta = 0$ (i.e., that there are no fixed effects) using the standard Wald F-test. The equivalent test statistic for the deviation model is computed from the restricted (pooled model) and unrestricted (mean deviation model) sum-of-squared residuals. That is, the statistic

$$\frac{\dfrac{RSS_R - RSS_U}{N-1}}{\dfrac{RSS_U}{NT-N-K}}$$

follows an F distribution with N-1 and NT-N-K degrees of freedom.

Lesson 16.1: One-Way Panel Data Analysis: Dummy Variable Approach

As an example of one-way panel data analysis, we will duplicate a study of efficiency in production of airline services presented in Greene (1999), Chapter 14. The data file **airline.txt** consists of 6 firms for 15 years (1970 to 1984) with the following variables:

I Cross section index: 6 airline firms
T Time index: 15 years from 1970 to 1984
C Cost (total cost of services)
Q Output (revenue passenger miles)
PF Fuel price
LF Load factor (rate of capacity utilization, measured as the average rate at which seats on the airline's planes are filled)

For panel data analysis, allowing for individual effects, the model for the total cost of production is:

$$ln(C_{it}) = \quad \alpha_i + \beta_1\, ln(Q_{it}) + \beta_2\, ln(PF_{it}) + \beta_3\, ln(LF_{it}) + \varepsilon_{it}$$

We notice that the intercept α_i is taken to be constant over time t and specific to the individual firm i. The interpretation of slope parameters is straightforward in that

$\beta_1 > 0$, $\beta_2 > 0$, and $\beta_3 < 0$. Moreover, the economies of scale defined as $\left(\dfrac{1}{\beta_1} - 1\right)$, measures the efficiency of production.

The following program implements the fixed effects analysis using dummy variables. For a typical regression, we need only to include five dummy variables for the case of six firms. The estimated parameters associated with dummy variables represent the *change* from the intercept (or the base case). If you are interested in the fixed effects for each individual firm, you may use the full set of 6 dummy variables in the regression equation without including the intercept. Since the use of dummy variables in the regression was explained earlier in Chapter IV, this program is easy to follow. In passing, note the use of a GAUSS built-in command dummybr to generate the necessary dummy variables (see line 18).

```
     /*
     Lesson 16.1: One-Way Panel Data Analysis, Dummy Variable Approach
     Cost of Production for Airline Services I
     */
 1   use gpe2;
 2   output file = gpe\output16.1 reset;
 3   load data[91,6] = gpe\airline.txt;
 4   panel=data[2:91,1:2];    @ panel definition @
 5   n=6;
 6   t=15;

     @ stacked data series, by sections @
 7   cs=ln(data[2:91,3]);     @ log cost (stacked) @
 8   qs=ln(data[2:91,4]);     @ log output (stacked) @
 9   pfs=ln(data[2:91,5]);    @ log fuel price (stacked) @
10   lfs=data[2:91,6];        @ load factor (stacked) @

11   call reset;
12   _names = {"c","q","pf","lf","d1","d2","d3","d4","d5","d6"};

     /* pooled estimates */
13   ys=cs;
14   xs=qs~pfs~lfs;
15   call estimate(ys,xs);
16   rssr=__rss;
17   dfr=__df;

     @ use one less dummy variables with intercept @
18   d=dummybr(panel[.,1],seqa(1,1,n-1));
19   call estimate(ys,xs~d);
20   rssur=__rss;
21   dfur=__df;

22   f=((rssr-rssur)/(dfr-dfur))/(rssur/dfur);
23   print "Wald F Test Statistic";
24   print "for No Fixed Individual Effects = " f;

25   end;
```

The estimation results include the pooled regression and the dummy variable regression. The Wald F-test statistic for fixed effects is computed from the estimated sum-of-squares of the restricted (pooled) and unrestricted (dummy variables) regressions (see line 22 in the program). Here is the output of running **lesson16.1**:

```
Least Squares Estimation
------------------------
Dependent Variable = C
```

```
Estimation Range =   1              90
Number of Observations = 90
Mean of Dependent Variable = 13.366
Standard Error of Dependent Variable = 1.1320


R-Square = 0.98829      R-Square Adjusted = 0.98788
Standard Error of the Estimate = 0.12461
Log-Likelihood = 61.770
Log Ammemiya Prediction Criterion (APC) =   -4.1216
Log Akaike Information Criterion (AIC) =    -4.1217
Log Schwarz Bayesian Information Criterion (BIC) =  -4.0106
```

Sum of Squares	SS	DF	MSS	F	Prob>F
Explained	112.71	3	37.568	2419.3	6.5875E-083
Residual	1.3354	86	0.015528		
Total	114.04	89	1.2814		

Variable Name	Estimated Coefficient	Standard Error	t-Ratio 86 DF	Prob >|t|	Partial Regression
Q	0.88274	0.013255	66.599	8.7911E-076	0.98098
PF	0.45398	0.020304	22.359	1.3601E-037	0.85322
LF	-1.6275	0.34530	-4.7133	9.3090E-006	0.20529
CONSTANT	9.5169	0.22924	41.514	1.1294E-058	0.95247

```
Least Squares Estimation
------------------------
Dependent Variable = C
Estimation Range =   1              90
Number of Observations = 90
Mean of Dependent Variable = 13.366
Standard Error of Dependent Variable = 1.1320


R-Square = 0.99743      R-Square Adjusted = 0.99718
Standard Error of the Estimate = 0.060105
Log-Likelihood = 130.09
Log Ammemiya Prediction Criterion (APC) =   -5.5280
Log Akaike Information Criterion (AIC) =    -5.5287
Log Schwarz Bayesian Information Criterion (BIC) =  -5.2787
```

Sum of Squares	SS	DF	MSS	F	Prob>F
Explained	113.75	8	14.219	3935.8	1.5066E-101
Residual	0.29262	81	0.0036126		
Total	114.04	89	1.2814		

Variable Name	Estimated Coefficient	Standard Error	t-Ratio 81 DF	Prob >|t|	Partial Regression
Q	0.91928	0.029890	30.756	1.9519E-046	0.92112
PF	0.41749	0.015199	27.468	8.3708E-043	0.90305
LF	-1.0704	0.20169	-5.3071	9.5003E-007	0.25801
D1	-0.087062	0.084199	-1.0340	0.30421	0.013027
D2	-0.12830	0.075728	-1.6942	0.094071	0.034223
D3	-0.29598	0.050023	-5.9169	7.5281E-008	0.30179
D4	0.097494	0.033009	2.9535	0.0041106	0.097225
D5	-0.063007	0.023892	-2.6372	0.010020	0.079071
CONSTANT	9.7930	0.26366	37.142	1.2279E-052	0.94454

```
Wald F Test Statistic
for No Fixed Individual Effects =       57.732
```

Given the critical value of the distribution $F(5, 81)$ at 5% level of significance, it is clear that the cost structures among the six airline firms are somewhat different. In other words, we fail to reject the null hypothesis that there are *no* fixed effects. The fixed effects are calculated by adding the parameters of the dummy variables to the intercept.

Remember that an alternative is to include all six dummy variables and estimate the model without an intercept. That is, replace line 18 with the following two statements:

```
_const=0;
d=dummybr(panel[.,1],seqa(1,1,n));
```

The individual fixed effects are summarized in the following table (numbers in parentheses are the estimated standard errors):

Firm	Individual Effect
1	9.7059 (0.19312)
2	9.6647 (0.19898)
3	9.4970 (0.22496)
4	9.8905 (0.24176)
5	9.7300 (0.26094)
6	9.7930 (0.26366)

Random Effects Model

Consider the model with individual effects: $Y_{it} = X_{it}\beta_{it} + u_i + e_{it}$. We now assume that the error component u_i, the individual difference, is random (or *stochastic*) and satisfies the following assumptions:

$E(u_i) = 0$ (zero mean)
$E(u_i^2) = \sigma_u^2$ (homoscedasticity)
$E(u_iu_j) = 0$ for $i{\neq}j$ (no cross-section correlation)
$E(u_ie_{it}) = E(u_ie_{jt}) = 0$ (independent from each e_{it} or e_{jt})

Then, the model error is $\varepsilon_{it} = u_i + e_{it}$, which has the following structure:

$E(\varepsilon_{it}) = E(u_i + e_{it}) = 0$
$E(\varepsilon_{it}^2) = E((u_i + e_{it})^2) = \sigma_u^2 + \sigma_e^2$
$E(\varepsilon_{it}\varepsilon_{i\tau}) = E((u_i + e_{it})(u_i + e_{i\tau})) = \sigma_u^2$, for $t{\neq}\tau$
$E(\varepsilon_{it}\varepsilon_{jt}) = E((u_i + e_{it})(u_j + e_{jt})) = 0$, for $i{\neq}j$

In other words, for each cross section i, the variance-covariance matrix of the model error $\varepsilon_i = [\varepsilon_{i1}, \varepsilon_{i2}, ...,\varepsilon_{iT}]'$ is the following T×T matrix:

$$\Sigma = \begin{bmatrix} \sigma_e^2 + \sigma_u^2 & \sigma_u^2 \cdots & \sigma_u^2 \\ \sigma_u^2 & \sigma_e^2 + \sigma_u^2 \cdots & \sigma_u^2 \\ \cdots & \cdots \cdots & \cdots \\ \sigma_u^2 & \sigma_u^2 \cdots \sigma_e^2 + \sigma_u^2 \end{bmatrix} = \sigma_e^2 I + \sigma_u^2$$

If we let ε be an NT-element vector of the stacked errors $\varepsilon_1, \varepsilon_2, ..., \varepsilon_N$, then $E(\varepsilon) = 0$ and $E(\varepsilon\varepsilon') = \Sigma \otimes I$, where I is an N×N identity matrix and Σ is the T×T variance-covariance matrix defined above.

Recall the pooled model for estimation, $Y = X\beta + \varepsilon$, where $\varepsilon = [\varepsilon_1,\varepsilon_2,...,\varepsilon_N]$, $\varepsilon_i = [\varepsilon_{i1},\varepsilon_{i2},...,\varepsilon_{iT}]'$, and the random error has two components: $\varepsilon_{it} = u_i + e_{it}$. By assumption, $E(\varepsilon) = 0$, and $E(\varepsilon\varepsilon') = \Sigma \otimes I$. The generalized least squares estimate of β is

$$\beta = [X'(\Sigma^{-1} \otimes I)X]^{-1}X'(\Sigma^{-1} \otimes I)y$$

Since Σ^{-1} can be derived from the estimated variance components σ^2_e and σ^2_u, in practice the model is estimated using the following *partial deviation approach*.

1. Estimate the model $Y = X\beta + \varepsilon$ as a fixed effects model, using the dummy variable approach, to obtain the estimated variance σ^2_e.

2. Assuming the randomness of u_i, estimate the *between* parameters of the model:

$$Y^m_i = X^m_i\beta + (u_i + e^m_i)$$

where the error structure of $u_i + e^m_i$ satisfies:

$$E(u_i + e^m_i) = 0$$
$$E((u_i + e^m_i)^2) = \sigma^2_u + (\sigma^2_e/T)$$
$$E((u_i + e^m_i)(u_j + e^m_j)) = 0, \text{ for } i \neq j$$

Let $v = \sigma^2_e$ and $v_1 = T\sigma^2_u + \sigma^2_e$. Define $w = 1 - (v/v_1)^{1/2}$.

3. Use w to transform (partial deviations) the data as follows:

$$Y^*_{it} = Y_{it} - w\, Y^m_i$$
$$X^*_{it} = X_{it} - w\, X^m_i$$

Then the model for estimation becomes:

$$Y^*_{it} = X^*_{it}\beta + \varepsilon^*_{it}$$

where $\varepsilon^*_{it} = (1-w)\, u_i + e_{it} - w\, e^m_i$. Or, equivalently

$$Y_{it} = X_{it}\beta + w\, (y^m_i - X^m_i\beta) + \varepsilon^*_{it}$$

It is easy to validate that

$$E(\varepsilon^*_{it}) = 0$$
$$E(\varepsilon^{*2}_{it}) = \sigma^2_e$$
$$E(\varepsilon^*_{it}\varepsilon^*_{i\tau}) = 0 \text{ for } t \neq \tau$$
$$E(\varepsilon^*_{it}\varepsilon^*_{jt}) = 0 \text{ for } i \neq j$$

The least squares estimate of $[w\,(Y^m_i - X^m_i\beta)]$ is interpreted as the *change* in the individual effects.

Hypothesis Testing for Random Effects

To test the null hypothesis of no correlation between the error terms $u_i + e_{it}$ and $u_i + e_{i\tau}$, we will use the following Breusch-Pagan LM test statistic based on the estimated residuals of the restricted (pooled) model, ε_{it} ($i=1,2,...N$, $t=1,2,...,T$). The LM test statistic is distributed as a Chi-square with one degree of freedom (note that $\varepsilon^m_i = \Sigma_{t=1,2,\dots,T}\varepsilon_{it}/T$):

$$\frac{NT}{2(T-1)}\left[\left(\Sigma_{i=1,2,\dots,N}\left(\Sigma_{t=1,2,\dots,T}\varepsilon_{it}\right)^2\right)\Big/\left(\Sigma_{i=1,2,\dots,N}\Sigma_{t=1,2,\dots,T}\varepsilon_{it}^2\right)-1\right]^2$$

or,

$$\frac{NT}{2(T-1)}\left[\left(\Sigma_{i=1,2,\dots,N}\left(T\varepsilon^m_i\right)^2\right)\Big/\left(\Sigma_{i=1,2,\dots,N}\Sigma_{t=1,2,\dots,T}\varepsilon_{it}^2\right)-1\right]^2$$

Hausman Specification Test for Fixed or Random Effects

We have discussed the fixed and random effects models, and now you may be wondering exactly what the difference is between the two models. How does one decide to estimate a fixed vs. random effects model? The Hausman specification test answers this question. It tests the null hypothesis that there is no difference between the fixed and random effects models. Failure to reject the null hypothesis usually implies that the fixed effects model is safe to use.

The Hausman test begins by noting that the difference between the fixed and random effects models is in their respective covariance matrices. Let b_{fixed} be the estimated slope parameters of the fixed effects model (using the dummy variable approach), and let b_{random} be the estimated slope parameters of the random effects model. Similarly, let $Var(b_{fixed})$ and $Var(b_{random})$ be the estimated covariance matrices for the fixed and random effects models, respectively. The Hausman specification test statistic is:

$$(b_{random}-b_{fixed})'[Var(b_{random})-Var(b_{fixed})]^{-1}(b_{random}-b_{fixed})$$

The Hausman test statistic is distributed as a Chi-square with degrees of freedom equal to the number of slope parameters.

Lesson 16.2: One-Way Panel Data Analysis: Deviation Approach

We continue the previous example on the cost of airline services production. Instead of using the dummy variable approach, we apply the deviation approach to investigate the fixed effects and random effects. Recall that the main difference between fixed and random effects lies in the assumption of the covariance structure of the model. For the fixed effects model, *total* deviations of the data series from the group means are used. For the random effects model, on the other hand, partial deviations are employed. The deviation approach for one-way panel data analysis is implemented in a GPE module program: **PANEL1.GPE**. In order to compute the fixed effects and random effects, we run four regressions: pooled regression, between-groups or means regression, within-groups full deviations regression, and within-groups partial deviations regression. Three sets of hypothesis testing are performed: Wald F-test for fixed effects, LM test for random effects, and Hausman specification test comparing fixed and random effects. At the end, a summary of the panel data analysis is presented, including the estimated individual intercept parameters for both the fixed and random effects models. **PANEL1.GPE** is installed in the GPE subdirectory. The interested reader can examine the code to make sense of the implementation (see also Appendix B-3). **PANEL1.GPE** can be included in any part of your program with a compiler directive #include such as:

```
#include gpe\panel1.gpe;
```

We put the include directive at the end of program (see line 15 of **lesson16.2**). Then one-way panel data analysis is called with the statement:

```
call panel1(y,x,n,t);
```

where y is the dependent variable and x is the data matrix of explanatory variables. Both y and x are stacked according to the panel definition of n blocks (cross sections) of t observations (time periods). To analyze fixed and random effects for the airline services example, the program of Lesson 16.2 is given below:

```
     /*
     Lesson 16.2: One-Way Panel Data Analysis, Deviation Approach
     Cost of Production for Airline Services II
     */
1    use gpe2;
2    output file = gpe\output16.2 reset;
3    load data[91,6] = gpe\airline.txt;
4    panel=data[2:91,1:2];    @ panel definition @
5    n=6;
6    t=15;

     /* stacked data series, by sections */
7    cs=ln(data[2:91,3]);     @ log cost (stacked) @
8    qs=ln(data[2:91,4]);     @ log output (stacked) @
9    pfs=ln(data[2:91,5]);    @ log fuel price (stacked) @
10   lfs=data[2:91,6];        @ load factor (stacked) @
11   call reset;
12   _names = {"c","q","pf","lf"};
13   call panel1(cs,qs~pfs~lfs,n,t);

14   end;

15   #include gpe\panel1.gpe;
```

There are four sets of regression output, but we will present only the important results of fixed effects and random effects models here:

```
Least Squares Estimation
------------------------
Dependent Variable = C
Estimation Range =  1          90
Number of Observations = 90
Mean of Dependent Variable = -6.3159E-016
Standard Error of Dependent Variable = 0.66503

R-Square = 0.99257      R-Square Adjusted = 0.99231
Standard Error of the Estimate = 0.058332
Log-Likelihood = 130.09
Log Ammemiya Prediction Criterion (APC) =  -5.6397
Log Akaike Information Criterion (AIC) =  -5.6398
Log Schwarz Bayesian Information Criterion (BIC) =  -5.5287
```

Sum of Squares	SS	DF	MSS	F	Prob>F
Explained	39.068	3	13.023	3827.3	2.1614E-091
Residual	0.29262	86	0.0034026		
Total	39.361	89	0.44226		

Variable	Estimated	Standard	t-Ratio	Prob	Partial

Name	Coefficient	Error	86 DF	>|t|	Regression
Q	0.91928	0.029008	31.691	3.3110E-049	0.92112
PF	0.41749	0.014751	28.303	2.3780E-045	0.90305
LF	-1.0704	0.19574	-5.4685	4.3807E-007	0.25801
CONSTANT	-6.1586E-016	0.0061487	-1.0016E-013	1.0000	1.1666E-028

```
Least Squares Estimation
------------------------
Dependent Variable = C
Estimation Range =   1          90
Number of Observations = 90
Mean of Dependent Variable = 1.6482
Standard Error of Dependent Variable = 0.67455

R-Square = 0.99231     R-Square Adjusted = 0.99204
Standard Error of the Estimate = 0.060192
Log-Likelihood = 127.26
Log Ammemiya Prediction Criterion (APC) =  -5.5769
Log Akaike Information Criterion (AIC) =  -5.5770
Log Schwarz Bayesian Information Criterion (BIC) =  -5.4659
```

Sum of Squares	SS	DF	MSS	F	Prob>F
Explained	40.185	3	13.395	3697.1	9.4659E-091
Residual	0.31159	86	0.0036231		
Total	40.497	89	0.45502		

Variable Name	Estimated Coefficient	Standard Error	t-Ratio 86 DF	Prob >|t|	Partial Regression
Q	0.90668	0.025625	35.383	4.9455E-053	0.93572
PF	0.42278	0.014025	30.145	1.7169E-047	0.91354
LF	-1.0645	0.20007	-5.3206	8.1016E-007	0.24765
CONSTANT	1.1873	0.025916	45.811	3.4012E-062	0.96064

The end of the estimation output produces a summary of the panel data analysis. Three sets of hypothesis testing for fixed and random effects are given. Based on the Wald F-test and the Breusch-Pagan LM test, it is clear that there exist both fixed effects and random effects for this model. Based on the Hausman specification test, however, there is no significant difference between the fixed and random effects.

```
Panel Data Model Estimation Procedure:
(1) Pooled Regression
(2) Between-Groups Regression
(3) Fixed Effects (Within-Groups) Regression
(4) Random Effects (Weighted Within-Groups) Regression

Wald F Test Statistic for No Fixed One-Way Effects
F(   5,   81) =       57.732

Breusch-Pagan LM Test Statistic for No One-Way Effects
Chi-Sq(   1) =       334.85

Hausman's Test for Fixed and Random Effects
Chi-Sq(   3) =       0.75471

Within-Groups Estimates:
      Fixed         S.E.        Random        S.E.
    0.91928      0.029890     0.90668      0.026404
    0.41749      0.015199     0.42278      0.014451
   -1.0704       0.20169     -1.0645       0.20615
-6.1586e-016     0.0063356    1.1873       0.026704

One-Way Effects:
```

Section/Period	Fixed	S.E.	Random	S.E.
1.0000	9.7059	0.19323	9.6378	0.18313
2.0000	9.6647	0.19908	9.5979	0.18716
3.0000	9.4970	0.22505	9.4408	0.20686
4.0000	9.8905	0.24185	9.7780	0.21918
5.0000	9.7300	0.26102	9.6299	0.23371
6.0000	9.7930	0.26374	9.6831	0.23544

Finally, within-groups estimates of the slope parameters and the individual intercept parameters are presented for the fixed effects and random effects models, respectively. Note that the estimated fixed effects, derived from the deviation approach, are the same as those of dummy variables approach. Furthermore, the random effects are similar to the fixed effects, reinforcing the result of the Hausman specification test that there is no significant difference between the two models.

Notice that the procedure panel1 is designed for study of individual (cross-section) effects. To study the time effects, swap the panel definition n and t and rearrange the stacked data series accordingly. For example, in **lesson16.2**, you can insert the following statements (with comments for clarity) between lines 10 and 11:

```
@ re-arrange data, then swap n and t @
cs=vec(reshape(cs,n,t));
qs=vec(reshape(qs,n,t));
pfs=vec(reshape(pfs,n,t));
lfs=vec(reshape(lfs,n,t));
n=15;
t=6;
```

We leave the estimation and interpretation of the time period effects as an exercise.

Once you understand and master the idea of one-way panel data analysis, it is straightforward to extend it to two-way analysis. Both cross-section and time period effects are analyzed simultaneously under the respective assumptions of fixed effects and random effects. Greene (1999) presented such an extension as two exercises in Chapter 14. We implement the two-way analysis in the module program **PANEL2.GPE**, which extends the module **PANEL1.GPE** for one-way analysis used in Lesson 16.2. You may want to examine the code of **PANEL2.GPE** in comparison with the outlined formula of Greene (1999), pp. 587-589. In essence, the two-way analysis runs five regressions: a pooled regression, two between-groups (time periods and cross sections) regressions, and two within-groups (full deviations and partial deviations) regressions. From these regression estimations, we calculate overall, cross section, and time period effects. As with one-way analysis, statistics for testing fixed effects, random effects, and for comparing fixed and random effects are computed. The module program **PANEL2.GPE** hides the details of implementation from all but the most curious eyes. **PANEL2.GPE** can be found in Appendix B-4 and it is installed in the GPE subdirectory.

Lesson 16.3: Two-Way Panel Data Analysis

Extending the analysis of one-way effects, in this example we re-estimate the airline services production model to consider the two-way effects. We include **PANEL2.GPE** at the end of the program. Similar to the one-way analysis, two-way analysis is done with the statement (see line 14 of **lesson16.3** below):

```
call panel2(y,x,n,t);
```

where y, the dependent variable, and x, the independent variables, are stacked according to the panel definition of n blocks (cross sections) of t observations (time periods). The rest of the program for two-way analysis is identical to the previous lesson for one-way analysis.

```
/*
Lesson 16.3: Two-Way Panel Data Analysis
Cost of Production for Airline Services III
*/
1   use gpe2;
2   output file = gpe\output16.3 reset;
3   load data[91,6] = gpe\airline.txt;
4   panel = data[2:91,1:2];   @ panel definition @
5   n=6;
6   t=15;

    /* stacked data series, by sections */
7   cs = ln(data[2:91,3]);    @ log cost (stacked) @
8   qs = ln(data[2:91,4]);    @ log output (stacked) @
9   pfs = ln(data[2:91,5]);   @ log fuel price (stacked) @
10  lfs = data[2:91,6];       @ load factor (stacked) @
11  xs = qs~pfs~lfs;

12  call reset;
13  _names = {"c","q","pf","lf"};

14  call panel2(cs,xs,n,t);

15  end;

16  #include gpe\panel2.gpe;
```

It takes five regression estimations to carry out two-way panel data analysis. To save space, we will report only the summary information as follows:

```
Panel Data Model Estimation Procedure:
(1) Pooled Regression
(2) Between-Groups (Cross Sections) Regression
(3) Between-Groups (Time Periods) Regression
(4) Fixed Effects (Within-Groups) Regression
(5) Random Effects (Weighted Within-Groups) Regression

Wald F Test Statistic for No Fixed Two-Way Effects
F( 19, 67) =        23.102

Breusch-Pagan LM Test Statistic for No Two-Way Effects
Chi-Sq( 2) =         336.40

Hausman's Test for Fixed and Random Effects
Chi-Sq( 3) =         183.54

Within-Groups Estimates:
       Fixed        S.E.        Random        S.E.
     0.81725     0.031851       0.90237     0.029742
     0.16861      0.16348       0.42418     0.016306
    -0.88281      0.26174       -1.0531      0.22948
 6.1829e-016    0.0054155        1.0109     0.025968

Two-Way Effects:
                   Fixed        Random
     Overall      12.667        1.0031

Cross Sections Effects:
```

Sections	Fixed	Random
1.0000	0.12833	7.9348
2.0000	0.065495	7.8933
3.0000	-0.18947	7.7292
4.0000	0.13425	8.0709
5.0000	-0.092650	7.9171
6.0000	-0.045956	7.9710

Time Periods Effects:

Periods	Fixed	Random
1.0000	-0.37402	-0.0023032
2.0000	-0.31932	0.00074765
3.0000	-0.27669	0.0030529
4.0000	-0.22304	0.0049901
5.0000	-0.15393	0.00044843
6.0000	-0.10809	-0.0013027
7.0000	-0.076864	-0.0011691
8.0000	-0.020733	-0.00015766
9.0000	0.047220	0.0025912
10.000	0.091728	-0.0018190
11.000	0.20731	-0.0018378
12.000	0.28547	0.00047461
13.000	0.30138	0.0022213
14.000	0.30047	0.0027990
15.000	0.31911	0.0043389

From the two-way analysis, we can see that the model exhibits significant fixed effects and random effects. The magnitude and the pattern of the two effects are different. From examining the "Time Periods Effects" in the output, we see that the fixed effects are larger than the random effects. On the other hand, we see that for the "Cross Sections Effects," the magnitude of the random effects is greater than that of the fixed effects.

Remember that to analyze one-way (time or individual) effects, **PANEL1.GPE** should be included. **PANEL2.GPE** is used for analyzing two-way (time and individual) effects.

Seemingly Unrelated Regression System

The classical panel data analysis investigates only the intercept difference across individuals or time periods. Consider a more general specification of the model:

$$Y_{it} = X_{it}\beta_i + \varepsilon_{it} \ (i=1,2,...,N; \ t=1,2,...,T)$$

Let $Y_i = [Y_{i1}, Y_{i2},...,Y_{iT}]'$, $X_i = [X_{i1}, X_{i2},...,X_{iT}]'$, and $\varepsilon_i = [\varepsilon_{i1}, \varepsilon_{i2},...,\varepsilon_{iT}]'$. The stacked N equations (T observations each) system is $Y = X\beta + \varepsilon$, or

$$\begin{bmatrix} Y_1 \\ Y_2 \\ ... \\ Y_N \end{bmatrix} = \begin{bmatrix} X_1 & 0 & ... & 0 \\ 0 & X_2 & ... & 0 \\ ... & ... & ... & ... \\ 0 & 0 & ... & X_N \end{bmatrix} \beta + \begin{bmatrix} \varepsilon_1 \\ \varepsilon_2 \\ ... \\ \varepsilon_N \end{bmatrix}$$

Notice that not only the intercept but also the slope terms of the estimated parameters are different across individuals. Of course, the restrictions of identical slope terms across individuals may be imposed for direct comparison with the classical methods. The error structure of the model is summarized as follows:

$E(\varepsilon) = 0$
$E(X\varepsilon) = 0$
$E(\varepsilon\varepsilon') = \Sigma \otimes I$

where $\Sigma = [\sigma_{ij}, i,j=1,2,...N]$ is the NxN variance-covariance matrix and I is a TxT identity matrix. Notice that contemporaneous correlation across individuals is assumed, although the assumption of no serial correlation is implied. The error structure of this model is different than that of the random effects model described above.

System estimation techniques such as 3SLS and FIML should be used for parameter estimation in this kind of model, which is seemingly unrelated regression estimation in the current context. The SUR estimation method was discussed in Chapter XIII. Denote b and S as the estimated β and Σ, respectively. Then,

$b = [X'(S^{-1}\otimes I)X]^{-1}X'(S^{-1}\otimes I)y$
$Var(b) = [X'(S^{-1}\otimes I)X]^{-1}$

and $S = ee'/T$, where $e = y-Xb$ is the estimated error ε.

The advantage of the SUR estimation method for panel data analysis is that it not only allows the intercept difference between individuals (as in the fixed and random effects models), but also allows the slope to vary among individuals. If the slope parameters are assumed to be constant across individuals, the method differs from the random effects model in the fundamental assumption of the covariance structure. By allowing cross-section correlation, the restricted SUR method is more general than the classical random effects model.

Lesson 16.4: Panel Data Analysis for Investment Demand: Deviation Approach

To demonstrate the different approaches for panel data analysis, we consider the following classical example of investment demand (Greene, 1999, Chap. 15; Grunfeld and Griliches, 1960; Boot and deWitt, 1960):

$I_{it} = \alpha_i + \beta_{1i} F_{it} + \beta_{2i} C_{it} + \varepsilon_{it}$

Where | i | 5 firms: General Motors, Chrysler, General Electric, Westinghouse, and United Steel.
| t | 20 years: 1935-1954.
| I_{it} | Gross investment.
| F_{it} | Market value.
| C_{it} | Value of the stock of plant and equipment.

The panel data of 20 years for 5 companies are available in 5 separate files, one for each company. The data files used are: **ifcgm.txt** (General Motor), **ifcch.txt** (Chrysler), **ifcge.txt** (General Electric), **ifcwe.txt** (Westinghouse), **ifcus.txt** (United Steel).

First we assume that $\beta_{1i} = \beta_1$ and $\beta_{2i} = \beta_2$ for all firms. In other words, we are estimating the restricted SUR model by assuming that the slope parameters do not vary across firms. To estimate and compare the fixed effects and random effects for the model, we use the following program which is essentially the same as that of

lesson16.2. Since the five company data sets are read in separately as time series, some manipulation is necessary to convert them into a stacked vector of dependent variables and a stacked matrix of independent variables (see lines 8 through 14 in **lesson16.4** below). The stacked data format is required in order to use the **PANEL1.GPE** module program.

```
    /*
    Lesson 16.4: Panel Data Analysis for Investment Demand
    Deviation Approach
    */
1   use gpe2;
2   output file = gpe\output16.4 reset;

3   load gmc[21,4] = gpe\ifcgm.txt;
4   load chc[21,4] = gpe\ifcch.txt;
5   load gec[21,4] = gpe\ifcge.txt;
6   load wec[21,4] = gpe\ifcwe.txt;
7   load usc[21,4] = gpe\ifcus.txt;
8   i=gmc[2:21,2]~chc[2:21,2]~gec[2:21,2]~wec[2:21,2]~usc[2:21,2];
9   f=gmc[2:21,3]~chc[2:21,3]~gec[2:21,3]~wec[2:21,3]~usc[2:21,3];
10  c=gmc[2:21,4]~chc[2:21,4]~gec[2:21,4]~wec[2:21,4]~usc[2:21,4];

11  n=5;    @ 5 cross sections (firms) @
12  t=20;   @ 20 time periods (years) @

    @ stacked data series, by firms @
13  ys = vec(i);
14  xs = vec(f)~vec(c);

15  call reset;
16  _names={"i","f","c"};

17  call panel1(ys,xs,n,t);

18  end;

19  #include gpe\panel1.gpe;
```

As described earlier, using the module **PANEL1.GPE** to estimate the one-way fixed and random effects gives us four sets of regression output: the pooled regression, between-groups means regression, within-groups full deviations regression, and within-groups partial deviations regression. You should check the details of each regression output. We present only the summary results of the analysis.

```
Panel Data Model Estimation Procedure:
(1) Pooled Regression
(2) Between-Groups Regression
(3) Fixed Effects (Within-Groups) Regression
(4) Random Effects (Weighted Within-Groups) Regression

Wald F Test Statistic for No Fixed One-Way Effects
F(   4,  93) =       58.956

Breusch-Pagan LM Test Statistic for No One-Way Effects
Chi-Sq(   1) =       453.82

Hausman's Test for Fixed and Random Effects
Chi-Sq(   2) =       0.033043
Within-Groups Estimates:
      Fixed          S.E.        Random         S.E.
    0.10598       0.015891      0.10489       0.015112
    0.34666       0.024161      0.34602       0.024770
```

-1.6507e-014	6.9118	-8.8082	8.1293	

One-Way Effects:

Section/Period	Fixed	S.E.	Random	S.E.
1.0000	-76.067	66.886	-69.356	58.234
2.0000	-29.374	19.814	-33.176	19.376
3.0000	-242.17	33.321	-213.56	31.028
4.0000	-57.899	19.703	-57.575	19.263
5.0000	92.539	33.947	72.218	31.535

It is interesting to find the classical estimates of fixed effects and random effects are similar. This is consistent with the very small Hausman specification test statistic shown in the output.

Lesson 16.5: Panel Data Analysis for Investment Demand: SUR Method

By restricting $\beta_{1i} = \beta_1$ and $\beta_{2i} = \beta_2$ for all firms, the restricted SUR estimation method is used in direct comparison with the classical methods of panel data analysis. In Chapter XIII we implemented and estimated a system of linear demand equations using the SUR estimation method. The use of the input control variable _eq in estimating the simultaneous linear equations system was discussed in detail in Chapter XIII. In Chapter III we introduced the implementation of restricted least squares with the use of input control variable _restr. Parameter restrictions across equations in a linear equations system were again discussed in Chapter XIII. You may want to review these chapters and the relevant examples before working on this lesson.

In Lesson 16.5, the restricted SUR method is estimated using iterative three-stage least squares (_method=3). The result is the same as full information maximum likelihood.

```
      /*
      Lesson 16.5: Panel Data Analysis for Investment Demand Function
      Seemingly Unrelated Regression Estimation
      */
 1    use gpe2;
 2    output file = gpe\output16.5 reset;

 3    load gmc[21,4] = gpe\ifcgm.txt;
 4    load chc[21,4] = gpe\ifcch.txt;
 5    load gec[21,4] = gpe\ifcge.txt;
 6    load wec[21,4] = gpe\ifcwe.txt;
 7    load usc[21,4] = gpe\ifcus.txt;
 8    i=gmc[2:21,2]~chc[2:21,2]~gec[2:21,2]~wec[2:21,2]~usc[2:21,2];
 9    f=gmc[2:21,3]~chc[2:21,3]~gec[2:21,3]~wec[2:21,3]~usc[2:21,3];
10    c=gmc[2:21,4]~chc[2:21,4]~gec[2:21,4]~wec[2:21,4]~usc[2:21,4];

11    yvar=i;
12    xvar=f~c;

13    call reset;

14    _names={"i-gm","i-ch","i-ge","i-we","i-us",
              "f-gm","f-ch","f-ge","f-we","f-us",
              "c-gm","c-ch","c-ge","c-we","c-us"};
            @ I  I  I  I  I  F F F F F C C C C C 1@
15    _eq = {-1  0  0  0  0  1 0 0 0 0 1 0 0 0 0,
             0 -1  0  0  0  0 1 0 0 0 0 1 0 0 0,
             0  0 -1  0  0  0 0 1 0 0 0 0 1 0 0,
             0  0  0 -1  0  0 0 0 1 0 0 0 0 1 0,
```

```
               0   0   0   0 -1   0 0 0 0 1 0 0 0 0 1};

               @ F  C|F  C|F  C|F  C|F  C|q @
16 | _restr = {-1 0 1 0 0 0 0 0 0 0 0,
               -1 0 0 0 1 0 0 0 0 0 0,
               -1 0 0 0 0 0 1 0 0 0 0,
               -1 0 0 0 0 0 0 0 1 0 0,
                0 -1 0 1 0 0 0 0 0 0 0,
                0 -1 0 0 0 1 0 0 0 0 0,
                0 -1 0 0 0 0 0 1 0 0 0,
                0 -1 0 0 0 0 0 0 0 1 0};

17 | _iter=200;
18 | _method=3;
19 | call estimate(yvar,xvar);

20 | end;
```

You should run the program to get the full report of the estimation results. The output of the restricted SUR estimation is lengthy, but can be summarized as follows:

```
Simultaneous Linear Equations Estimation
----------------------------------------
Number of Endogenous Variables = 5
Number of Predetermined Variables = 11
Number of Stochastic Equations = 5
Number of Observations = 20
Estimation Range =  1          20

Three Stages Least Squares Estimation
Maximum Number of Iterations = 200
Tolerance = 0.001
...
System R-Square = 0.59471
Log-Likelihood = -490.75300
```

Equation Name	Variable Name	Estimated Coefficient	Asymptotic Std Error	t-Ratio
I-GM	F-GM	0.033825	0.0063427	5.3330
	C-GM	0.15536	0.016608	9.3541
	CONSTANT	360.69	51.871	6.9536
I-CH	F-CH	0.033825	0.0063427	5.3330
	C-CH	0.15536	0.016608	9.3541
	CONSTANT	43.839	6.9344	6.3220
I-GE	F-GE	0.033825	0.0063427	5.3330
	C-GE	0.15536	0.016608	9.3541
	CONSTANT	-25.543	13.842	-1.8454
I-WE	F-WE	0.033825	0.0063427	5.3330
	C-WE	0.15536	0.016608	9.3541
	CONSTANT	6.8931	4.7102	1.4634
I-US	F-US	0.033825	0.0063427	5.3330
	C-US	0.15536	0.016608	9.3541
	CONSTANT	292.18	27.650	10.567

```
Asymptotic Variance-Covariance Matrix of Equations
I-GM    39110.
I-CH    3359.9      575.64
I-GE    312.36     -49.662     670.86
I-WE    317.11      30.538     178.24     96.919
I-US    9742.5     1695.0      919.47    622.51    12240.
         I-GM        I-CH       I-GE      I-WE      I-US
```

To compare the fixed effects, random effects, and SUR method, the estimated parameters of the investment function are tabled together. The individual effects for three methods (under different covariance assumptions) are shown in the rows of intercept terms for each firm. Numbers in parentheses are the estimated standard errors.

		Fixed Effects	Random Effects	SUR Method
Slope	F	0.10598 (0.01589)	0.10489 (0.01511)	0.033825 (0.006343)
	C	0.34666 (0.02416)	0.34602 (0.02477)	0.15536 (0.01661)
Intercept	GM	-76.067 (66.886)	-69.356 (58.234)	360.69 (51.871)
	CH	-29.374 (19.814)	-33.176 (19.376)	43.839 (6.9344)
	GE	-242.17 (33.321)	-213.56 (31.028)	-25.543 (13.842)
	WE	-57.899 (19.703)	-57.575 (19.263)	6.8931 (4.7102)
	US	92.539 (33.947)	72.218 (31.535)	292.18 (27.650)

Although the estimates from the models of fixed effects and random effects are similar, the parameter estimates obtained from the SUR estimation method are quite different. The impact of different covariance assumptions when estimating the model is obvious. Since the SUR method is typically applied to estimating a model with varying slope as well as intercept terms, we can easily estimate the unrestricted model by removing (or commenting out) the restriction statement in line 16 of **lesson16.5** above. By comparing the results to those of the restricted model, the validity of the assumption of constant slopes may be tested. The following table presents the comparison results of restricted and unrestricted estimates (standard errors are in parentheses). The large Likelihood Ratio statistic of the two models, calculated as $2 \times [-459.092 - (-490.753)] = 63.322$, leads us to the conclusion that the slope parameters are not the same across the five firms under consideration.

Eq.	Variable	Unrestricted Model	Restricted Model
I-GM	F	0.12195 (0.020243)	0.033825 (0.006343)
	C	0.38945 (0.031852)	0.15536 (0.01661)
	Constant	-173.04 (84.280)	360.69 (51.871)
I-CH	F	0.067451 (0.017102)	0.033825 (0.006343)
	C	0.30507 (0.026067)	0.15536 (0.01661)
	Constant	2.3783 (11.631)	43.839 (6.9344)
I-GE	F	0.037019 (0.01177)	0.033825 (0.006343)
	C	0.11695 (0.021731)	0.15536 (0.01661)
	Constant	-16.376 (24.961)	-25.543 (13.842)
I-WE	F	0.053861 (0.010294)	0.033825 (0.006343)
	C	0.026469 (0.037038)	0.15536 (0.01661)
	Constant	4.4891 (6.0221)	6.8931 (4.7102)
I-US	F	0.0886 (0.045278)	0.033825 (0.006343)
	C	0.3093 (0.11783)	0.15536 (0.01661)
	Constant	138.01 (94.608)	292.18 (27.650)
Log-Likelihood		-459.092	-490.753

In summary, we have presented the classical methods of panel data analysis: fixed effects and random effects. A more general SUR approach was introduced, which allowed us to consider contemporaneous correlation across individuals, which the classical methods ignore. Misspecification issues such as autocorrelation and heteroscedasticity in panel data are important. In Chapter X we discussed the problem of autocorrelation associated with time series, while heteroscedasticity in cross-sectional models was covered in Chapter IX. The combination of autocorrelation and heteroscedasticity is common in models for panel data. The treatment of autocorrelation for time-period effects and heteroscedasticity for cross-section effects would be an integrated and complicated application of this and the two aforementioned chapters, which we will not discuss here.

XVII

Least Squares Prediction

The art of forecasting lies in building a practical model for real world application, and in the preceding chapters, we have presented all the tools necessary to do so in GPE. This chapter introduces the few remaining GPE control variables dedicated solely to least squares prediction and time series forecasting.

Least squares prediction is nothing more than the extrapolation of the estimated regression model from a set of historical observations into the unknown future. It is assumed that given the stable model structure, the future state is predictable from the replication of history.

Predicting Economic Growth

In this chapter, we will consider a "conventional wisdom" that the future state of the economy (measured in terms of real GDP growth) is predictable by an index called the Composite Economic Leading Indicator, which is assembled and updated monthly by the U.S. Department of Commerce. The Indicator is a weighted average of 11 short-run economic factors, such as stock prices and average hours worked. It is often reported in the media that this Leading Indicator can predict the direction of the economy 3 to 9 months into the future.

The lessons in this chapter use the data file **gdp96.txt**. It consists of four variables: QUARTER (quarterly index), GDP (Gross Domestic Product in billions of dollars), PGDP (Implicit Price Deflator of GDP, 1996 = 100), and LEADING (Composite Economic Leading Indicator, 1987 = 100). We note that LEADING is the quarterly average of the monthly series.

The target variable is the annual growth rate of real GDP. The following GAUSS statements generate the required data series of GDP growth:

```
rgdp = 100*gdp./pgdp;
growth = 100*(rgdp-lagn(rgdp,4))./lagn(rgdp,4);
```

First, Real Gross Domestic Product is expressed in billions of 1996 dollars. Then, GDP growth is measured as the annual percentage rate of change in real GDP from the same quarter last year. Although the causal relationship of the variables LEADING and GROWTH is well grounded, we have to make sure that these two variables are cointegrated. It turns out that both variables are stationary or I(0) processes and thus do not have unit roots. Moreover, the two variables are cointegrated. We leave the details of the unit roots and cointegration tests of LEADING and GROWTH as exercises. See also Chapter XVI for a thorough review.

We are now ready to construct a working model suitable for short-run structural estimation and prediction. Since forecasting is a time-sensitive business, we reserve the last four quarters of data for ex-post forecast evaluation. In other words, we are going to estimate the model using data through 1999, and see how well the model predicts real GDP growth in the last four quarters of 2000. We will need to construct a working model not only for historical estimation but also for forecasting.

If the variable LEADING can actually predict GROWTH several quarters ahead, then a distributed lag structure must be specified. As a result of trial and error, we have found that both the current and one-year (four quarters) lag of LEADING are useful in explaining historical GROWTH. In addition, the momentum effect of GDP growth is captured with a lagged dependent variable. The model error is identified to be a MA(4) process. By construction, the explanatory variable LEADING is the quarterly average of the monthly series. The specification of fourth-order moving average for the model error term should not, therefore, be surprising. Of course, this may not be the only working specification of the model you can construct. Throughout this book we have given examples of model building. We leave the process of finding the best model for forecasting to you. However, we emphasize the importance of using GPE variables such as _pdl and _dlags to determine the short run dynamics of the model structure.

We now turn to new forecasting features of the GPE package. In GPE, the work of least squares prediction is done by a procedure called forecast. Forecasts are usually computed after the estimation of the model. Calling forecast is similar to calling estimate. In calling forecast, you need to specify only the dependent and independent variables (in that order). The estimated parameters and the associated covariance matrix of the previously estimated model are used to compute the forecasts for the same model. The alternative is that you may specify a vector of estimated regression coefficients and the associated covariance matrix including those of autocorrelated error structure if the model is so specified. The forecasting period defaults to begin one observation after the estimation period ends and continues to the end of the data series. If future observations of the dependent variable become available, ex-post forecast error statistics based on the results of least squares prediction can be used for model evaluation.

If there are longer series of right-hand side explanatory variables, ex-ante forecasts can be computed upon request. The GPE control variables _fbegin and _fend are used to specify the beginning and ending of the multiple steps ahead of forecasts. In most cases, ex-ante forecasting depends on scenario assumptions made regarding the explanatory independent variables. If the Composite Economic Leading Indicator can predict the economy three to nine months ahead as claimed, our model certainly can point out the direction of GROWTH about one year in advance of LEADING. Furthermore, by making scenario assumptions about the variable LEADING (for example assuming no change in LEADING for the next year or so) we can predict the future value of GROWTH even further out on the horizon.

Lesson 17.1: Ex-Post Forecasts and Forecast Error Statistics

Here is the program predicting economic growth with the Composite Economic Leading Indicator:

```
/*
** Lesson 17.1: Ex-Post Forecasts and
** Forecast Error Statistics
*/
1  use gpe2;
2  output file = gpe\output17.1 reset;
```

```
 3  n=169;   @ 1959.1 to 2000.4 @
 4  load z[n,4] = gpe\gdp96.txt;
 5  gdp = z[2:n,2];
 6  pgdp = z[2:n,3];
 7  leading = z[2:n,4];
 8  rgdp = 100*gdp./pgdp;
 9  growth = 100*(rgdp-lagn(rgdp,4))./lagn(rgdp,4);
10  xvar = leading~lagn(leading,4);

    /* Model Estimation */
11  call reset;
12  _rstat=1;
13  _dlags=1;
    /*
    _bgtest=4;
    _ebtest=4;
    _acf=12;
    _acf2=12;
    */
14  _arma={0,4};
15  _iter=100;
16  _method=5;

17  _begin=9;   @ 1961Q1 @
18  _end=164;   @ 1999Q4 @
19  call estimate(growth,xvar);

    /* Forecasting */
20  _fstat=1;
21  _fplot=1;
    @ _dynamic=1; @
22  call forecast(growth,xvar);

23  end;
```

The program is divided into two main sections: estimation and forecasting. Notice that line 10 assigns the matrix of independent variables to the variable XVAR. XVAR is then passed to both estimate (line 19) and forecast (line 22). Modifying the independent variable matrix can quickly be done by editing only line 10.

The distributed lag structure of the model includes a one year (four quarters) lag of the independent variable LEADING (line 10) and a one quarter lag of the dependent variable GROWTH (line 13). The first year (four quarters) of the data series is lost via variable transformation. Through model identification, we determine that the error structure follows an MA(4) process. Using the QHC method for maximum likelihood estimation (lines 15-16), the model is estimated from the first quarter of 1961 (or the 9th observation) to the fourth quarter of 1999 (or the 164th observation):

```
_begin = 9;
_end = 164;
```

The _begin statement (line 17) safely blocks out the unusable data series for estimation, while _end statement (line 18) reserves the rest of the data series (all of the four quarters of 2000) for ex-post forecast evaluation. The output of the estimated model follows:

```
Least Squares Estimation
- - - - - - - - - - - - - - - - - - - - - - -
```

```
Dependent Variable = Y
Estimation Range =  9        164
Number of Observations = 156
Mean of Dependent Variable = 3.4640
Standard Error of Dependent Variable = 2.4074

Maximum Likelihood Estimation for Nonlinear Error Structure
ARMA( 0, 4) Autoregressive Moving Average Process

Maximum Number of Iterations = 100
Step Size Search Method = 0
Convergence Criterion = 0
Tolerance = 0.001

Initial Result:
Log Likelihood =      -200.06
Parameters =        0.72598       0.32261       -0.32815        1.0222        0.00000
0.00000      0.00000      0.00000

Using Quadratic Hill-Climbing Algorithm
Iteration = 1    Step Size = 1.7716  Log Likelihood =      -174.57
Parameters =        0.75262       0.29208       -0.29795        1.0070       -0.13915
-0.23366     -0.051020      0.62600
...
Iteration = 28   Step Size = 1.0000  Log Likelihood =      -173.74
Parameters =        0.77187       0.29116       -0.29460        0.72984      -0.12845
-0.17370     -0.028399      0.70138

Final Result:
Iterations = 28           Evaluations = 281112
Log Likelihood =      -173.74
Parameters =        0.77187       0.29116       -0.29460        0.72984      -0.12845
-0.17370     -0.028399      0.70138
Gradient Vector =      -0.029735       -0.75954      -0.74884      -0.0092271    -
0.00032321   -0.00026542   -0.00020601   -0.00025569
```

	Parameter	Std.Error	t-Ratio
MA(1)	-0.12845	0.075524	-1.7007
MA(2)	-0.17370	0.074877	-2.3198
MA(3)	-0.028399	0.080335	-0.35350
MA(4)	0.70138	0.076126	9.2134

```
NOTE: R-Square, AOV are computed from original series.

R-Square = 0.90568      R-Square Adjusted = 0.90382
Standard Error of the Estimate = 0.74659
Log-Likelihood = -173.74
Log Ammemiya Prediction Criterion (APC) =   -0.55915
Log Akaike Information Criterion (AIC) =   -0.55916
Log Schwarz Bayesian Information Criterion (BIC) =   -0.48096
```

Sum of Squares	SS	DF	MSS	F	Prob>F
Explained	851.19	3	283.73	509.02	4.8917E-079
Residual	84.725	152	0.55740		
Total	898.31	155	5.7955		

Variable Name	Estimated Coefficient	Standard Error	t-Ratio 152 DF	Prob >|t|	Partial Regression
Y-1	0.77187	0.038674	19.958	2.5838E-044	0.72380
X1	0.29116	0.034954	8.3299	1.0880E-014	0.31342
X2	-0.29460	0.034512	-8.5361	0.00000	0.32404
CONSTANT	0.72984	0.32619	2.2375	0.026708	0.031887

```
Squared Correlation of Observed and Predicted = 0.90615
Sum of Squared Residuals = 84.725
Sum of Absolute Residuals = 87.607
```

274

```
Sum of Residuals = 8.18894E-001
First-Order Rho = -0.018649
Durbin-Watson Test Statistic = 1.9838
Durbin-H Statistic = 0.11530
```

 Although the estimated model with MA(4) error structure looks satisfactory, add the following few lines before the estimation call (line 19):

```
_bgtest = 4;
_ebtest = 4;
_acf = 12;
_acf2 = 12;
```

and rerun the model to verify the serial correlation problem in the conditional mean and variance,[18] if any.

The next section of the program (lines 20 to 22), calls for least squares prediction based on the estimated model. Simply calling forecast specifies the default prediction period, which begins after the last observation used in the regression estimation, and ends with the end of the sample. We note that the beginning and end of the prediction period can be controlled by two GPE input variables, _fbegin and _fend, respectively.

 In almost all cases, regression coefficients and the associated covariance matrix from the previously estimated model are used for prediction. The alternative is to set the forecast input variable named _b to the estimation output variable __b for specifying the estimated regression parameters (and possibly including the estimated parameters of the autocorrelated error structure). Similarly, for the purpose of computing the variance of the forecasts, the estimated variance-covariance matrix __vb of the regression parameters must be used. Thus we set the forecast input variable _vb to the estimation output variable __vb. This is the required parameter information for the GPE procedure forecast (line 22) to carry out the forecasting task for an estimated model.

Ex-post forecast error statistics are computed by setting the input control variable _fstat=1 (line 20). This control variable is similar to its counterpart, _rstat, used for estimate. In addition, plotting of the forecasts and actuals can provide a visual clues as to the model's performance. This is done in line 21 by setting the input control variable _fplot = 1.

Here is the forecast output:

```
Least Squares Prediction
------------------------
Dependent Variable = Y
Prediction Range =   165        168
Using Regression Coefficients:
      0.77187        0.29116      -0.29460       0.72984      -0.12845      -0.17370
  -0.028399        0.70138

  Observation      Observed      Predicted      Residual     Std.Error
          165       5.29216       5.40534       -0.11318       0.75492
```

---

[18] The dynamic model may be correlated in terms of conditional variance, identifiable with ARCH or GARCH specification.

166	6.09665	5.73282	0.36383	1.01130
167	5.21095	5.19941	0.01154	1.20549
168	3.41463	3.75958	-0.34495	1.31388

R-Square Between Observed and Predicted = 0.98040
Mean Error (ME) = -0.020691
Mean Absolute Error (MAE) = 0.20837
Mean Squared Error (MSE) = 0.066077
Root Mean Squared Error (RMSE) = 0.25705
Mean Absolute Percent Error (MAPE) = 4.6075
Mean Squared Percent Error (MSPE) = 35.573
Root Mean Squared Percent Error (RMSPE) = 5.9643
Theil Inequality Coefficient = 0.025252
Decomposition:
  Proportion Due to Bias = 0.0064791
  Proportion Due to Variance = 0.77294
  Proportion Due to Covariance = 0.22058
  Proportion Due to Regression = 0.70829
  Proportion Due to Disturbance = 0.28523

Each observation in the forecast period is listed, complete with observed and predicted values. Residuals (or forecast errors) and their standard errors are also given. Since we have put aside the last six quarters of the GROWTH data series to be compared with the forecasts, ex-post forecast error statistics, including mean squared error and its components, are computed from the last six quarters of GDP growth. Moreover, forecasts in pairs with actuals are plotted together with the band of two standard errors. We note that the upper and lower bounds of forecast are the minimal spread of the prediction. In reality, the forecast interval tends to be much wider due to additional non sampling errors. Econometrics texts describe the model evaluation based on this set of forecast error statistics in detail. We leave judgment of the model's performance to you.

It can be shown that the method of least squares yields the best, linear, and unbiased predictor. Since the model is dynamic in nature (with a lagged dependent variable), we have an option to perform a dynamic forecast. A dynamic forecast is obtained by using the *predicted* lagged dependent variable on the right-hand side of the forecasting equation, instead of the *actual* lagged dependent variable. Let's turn on the dynamic option of least squares prediction:

```
_dynamic = 1;
```

Make sure that the dynamic option is added before calling forecast, and run the program to see the result:

```
Least Squares Prediction
------------------------
Dependent Variable = Y
Prediction Range =   165       168
Using Regression Coefficients:
    0.77187       0.29116      -0.29460       0.72984      -0.12845      -0.17370
   -0.028399      0.70138

NOTE: Dynamic Prediction Computed.
```

Observation	Observed	Predicted	Residual	Std.Error
165	5.29216	5.40534	-0.11318	0.75492
166	6.09665	5.47912	0.61753	1.01065
167	5.21095	4.15381	1.05715	1.20145
168	3.41463	2.96447	0.45016	1.31095

```
R-Square Between Observed and Predicted = 0.83621
Mean Error (ME) = 0.50292
Mean Absolute Error (MAE) = 0.55950
Mean Squared Error (MSE) = 0.42859
Root Mean Squared Error (RMSE) = 0.65467
Mean Absolute Percent Error (MAPE) = 11.434
Mean Squared Percent Error (MSPE) = 173.13
Root Mean Squared Percent Error (RMSPE) = 13.158
Theil Inequality Coefficient = 0.067379
Decomposition:
  Proportion Due to Bias = 0.59013
  Proportion Due to Variance = 0.0060607
  Proportion Due to Covariance = 0.40381
  Proportion Due to Regression = 0.042433
  Proportion Due to Disturbance = 0.36744
```

As expected, the model performance deteriorates when we forecast farther ahead into the future. This is because the predicted value of the lagged dependent variable is used in place of the actual value of the lagged dependent variable. Including the predicted value of the lagged dependent variable simply means that each forecast error is compounded over the forecast period. One important characteristic of the dynamic forecast is that the further in the future we try to predict, the less reliable the forecasts we get.

Lesson 17.2: Ex-Ante Forecasts

Forecasting is a time sensitive business. At the time of this writing, new information on the Composite Economic Leading Indicator may become available. We could modify the data file **gdp96.txt**, or just add the new data into the program. The latter is especially helpful to carry out scenario ex-ante forecasts. That is, we extend the data further by making a scenario assumption about the Leading Indicator to predict GDP growth in accordance with the assumption. For example, a "constant scenario" would assume no change (from the last year average) in the variable LEADING for the next year or so. Then, in line 7 of **lesson17.2**, the hypothesized observations of LEADING are appended at the end of historical data series as follows:

```
leading = z[2:n,4]|108.8|108.8|108.8|108.8;
```

Recall that the variable z is the original data matrix read from the data file **gdp96.txt**. Similarly, we could create a "pessimistic scenario" similar to the following, in which the variable LEADING declines at 2 percent over the next year:

```
leading = z[2:n,4]|108.2|107.7|107.1|106.6;
```

Or, we could assume an "optimistic scenario" (2 percent annual growth rate) as well:

```
leading = z[2:n,4]|109.3|109.9|110.4|110.9;
```

In other words, ex-ante forecasts are nothing but a crystal-ball prediction about uncertain future conditions. To keep the model performance in line with the available information, we do not use the dynamic features of the least squares prediction during the ex-post forecast periods. Dynamic forecast is automatic anyway, during the ex-ante forecast periods, since the value of the lagged dependent variable is not available and must first be predicted for the period that follows.

The following program is almost identical to that of Lesson 17.1. Pay attention to the change we made in line 7 assuming a scenario for ex-ante forecast:

```
      /*
      ** Lesson 17.2: Ex-Ante Forecasts
      */
1     use gpe2;
2     output file = gpe\output17.2 reset;

3     n=169;  @ 1951.1 to 2000.4 @
4     load z[n,4] = gpe\gdp96.txt;
5     gdp = z[2:n,2];
6     pgdp = z[2:n,3];

      /* pessimistic scenario (-2% AGR) */
      @ leading = z[2:n,4]|108.2|107.7|107.1|106.6; @
      /* constant scenario (0% AGR) */
7     leading = z[2:n,4]|108.8|108.8|108.8|108.8;
      /* optimistic scenario (+2% AGR) */
      @ leading = z[2:n,4]|109.3|109.9|110.4|110.9; @

8     rgdp = 100*gdp./pgdp;
9     growth = 100*(rgdp-lagn(rgdp,4))./lagn(rgdp,4);
10    xvar = leading~lagn(leading,4);

      /* Model Estimation */
11    call reset;
12    _rstat=1;
13    _dlags=1;
14    _arma={0,4};
15    _iter=100;
16    _method=5;
17    _begin=9;  @ 1961Q1 @
18    _end=164;  @ 1999Q4 @
19    call estimate(growth,xvar);

      /* Forecasting */
20    _fstat=1;
21    _fplot=1;
      @ _dynamic=1; @
22    call forecast(growth,xvar);

23    end;
```

Here is the forecasting output of the "constant scenario":

```
Least Squares Prediction
------------------------
Dependent Variable = Y
Prediction Range =   165        172
Using Regression Coefficients:
     0.77187        0.29116     -0.29460       0.72984      -0.12845      -0.17370
    -0.028399       0.70138

NOTE: Dynamic Prediction Computed.

Observation      Observed      Predicted      Residual     Std.Error
        165       5.29216       5.40534       -0.11318       0.75492
        166       6.09665       5.73282        0.36383       1.01130
        167       5.21095       5.19941        0.01154       1.20549
        168       3.41463       3.75958       -0.34495       1.31388
        169                     2.52032                      1.31668
        170                     1.88011                      1.31846
        171                     1.52147                      1.31970
        172                     1.50094                      1.32089
```

```
R-Square Between Observed and Predicted = 0.98040
Mean Error (ME) = -0.020691
Mean Absolute Error (MAE) = 0.20837
Mean Squared Error (MSE) = 0.066077
Root Mean Squared Error (RMSE) = 0.25705
Mean Absolute Percent Error (MAPE) = 4.6075
Mean Squared Percent Error (MSPE) = 35.573
Root Mean Squared Percent Error (RMSPE) = 5.9643
Theil Inequality Coefficient = 0.025252
Decomposition:
  Proportion Due to Bias = 0.0064791
  Proportion Due to Variance = 0.77294
  Proportion Due to Covariance = 0.22058
  Proportion Due to Regression = 0.70829
  Proportion Due to Disturbance = 0.28523
```

Similarly, we run the other two scenarios, pessimistic (LEADING decreases) and optimistic (LEADING increases), respectively. Instead of listing each of the forecasting results, we compare the respective ex-ante forecasts in the following table:

Predicted GDP Growth (%, annual rate)	Pessimistic (low) Scenario	Constant Scenario	Optimistic (high) Scenario
2001.1	2.35	2.52	2.67
2001.2	1.43	1.88	2.31
2001.3	0.68	1.52	2.32
2001.4	0.21	1.50	2.73

Furthermore, the following graph summarizes the ex-post and ex-ante forecasts for three different scenarios. The picture can tell a complicate story more clearly.

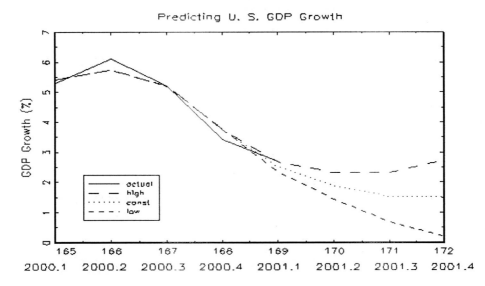

What you can say about the predictability of the Composite Economic Leading Indicator? No matter which scenario is used the economy appears to be heading towards a period of adjustment. Will the downward trend continue? Only under the optimistic view, the economy could recover in the third quarter of 2001. It will certainly depend on an effective government policy to revive the growth. Only time will tell!

Epilogue

 This is not the end of *Gauss Programming for Econometricians and Financial Analysts!*

It is just the beginning. Many extensions of econometric estimation, testing, and forecasting techniques discussed in this book can be done with GPE. Taking advantage of GPE output variables for each call to the main routine `estimate` or `forecast`, you can write add-on programs to do advanced applications as we did with the GPE application modules in Appendix B. Within the scope of econometric models we have discussed so far, you can experiment with the following extensions:

- Nonlinear ARCH-M Model Estimation and Prediction
- Qualitative Choice Model with Heteroscedasticity
- Panel Data Analysis with Heteroscedasticity and Autocorrelation

Many important topics in econometrics we did not cover here would certainly be good candidates for GAUSS implementation. To name a few examples:

- Monte Carlo Simulations and Bootstrapping Methods
- Nonparametric Regression Analysis
- Baysian Estimation and Inference
- Benchmarking Econometric Computation

Beyond GPE, you may feel ready to write your own codes for econometric and statistical applications. More than 400 GAUSS commands, procedures, and functions are available at your disposal as part of the GAUSS programming environment. As a consequence, we have seen powerful procedures being developed over the past years.

Whatever your eventual goals, you will probably agree that learning econometrics with GPE is certainly the right first step. We have demonstrated that GAUSS is a programming environment built on the convenient syntax and operations of matrix algebra. As you step through each lesson, learning to master GPE, you also learn GAUSS and econometrics. From here, the next step is up to you!

Appendix   A
GPE Control Variables

There are two types of global control variables in GPE: input control variables and output control variables. For reference purposes, consider the following general regression equation:

$$F(Z, \beta) = \varepsilon$$

where Z is the data matrix of variables and β is the vector of parameters, which define the functional form F. ε is the error structure of the model. Z can be further decomposed as $Z = [Y, X]$ with Y denoting the endogenous (dependent) variables and X the predetermined (independent) variables. If Y consists of more than one column, it is a system of linear equations. For a classical regression model, $Y = f(X, \beta) + \varepsilon$ or $F(Z, \beta) = Y - f(X, \beta) = \varepsilon$. The simple case of single linear regression equation is written as:

$$Y = X\beta + \varepsilon$$

where Y is the left-hand side (LHS) or dependent variable, and X denotes the right-hand side (RHS) explanatory or independent variables. β is the vector of estimated parameters, and ε is the vector of estimated residuals.

Input Control Variables

Input control variables must be initialized before calling one of the main econometric routines: `estimate` or `forecast`. To initialize all the global control variables, call `reset`.

Three categories of input control variables are listed below: general-purpose input control variables, `estimate` input control variables, and `forecast` input control variables. Unless otherwise specified, setting each variable to 1 (that is, true or yes) activates or turns on the optional behavior specified. If the variable is not defined or specified, then its default value is assumed.

General Purpose Input Control Variables

Variable	Description
`_cmplx`	Complex number computation. `_cmplx = 0` (default): Do not allow for complex number computation, therefore a negative argument for LN, LOG, and SQRT is not permitted; `_cmplx = 1`: Allow for complex number computation.

_legend	When a graph is requested (_rplot>0, see below), _legend = 1 (default): Show legends for graph plots; _legend = 0: No legends will be shown.
_pause	Pause the output before displaying graphs. _pause = 0 (default): No waiting prompt; _pause = 1: Wait for a keystroke to display graphs.
_print	Control screen output. _print = 1 (default): Direct full output to screen; _print = 0: Direct partial output to screen. Verbose iteration outputs from a nonlinear or iterative model are suppressed; _print = -1: Suppress all screen output. Suppressing the screen output will force _rplot = 0 and _fplot = 0 (see below), but it will have no effect on sending output to a file or printer if requested.

ESTIMATE Input Control Variables

Variable	Description
_acf	Specify the number of lags for computing autocorrelation and partial autocorrelation coefficients from the estimated regression residuals. Useful for testing the ARMA error structure. Display and plot the functions if _rplot > 0 (see below). In addition, standard errors of coefficients and Box-Pierce and Ljung-Box portmanteau test statistics are presented up to the number of lags specified in _acf. For example, 12 lags of autocorrelation and partial autocorrelation functions are requested by setting: _acf = 12; The default is _acf = 0. As an option for computing autocorrelation coefficients and the associated standard errors using regression method, the second element of the vector _acf may be set to a positive value, with the first element indicating the number of lags requested. For example: _acf = {12,1};
_acf2	Same as _acf except that the autocorrelation and partial autocorrelation coefficients are computed from the squared standardized residuals. Useful for testing the GARCH error structure. _acf2 = 0 is the default.
_ar	Specify the order of an autoregressive (AR) error structure. If an additional moving average process is desired for an autoregressive moving average ARMA structure, use the variable _arma instead (see below). Optional initial values of the autocorrelation coefficients may be appended at the end of _ar for estimation. Providing the initial values is useful for starting a search from non-zero values of autocorrelation coefficients. For example: _ar = 1; _ar = {1, 0.5}; @ with initial value of AR(1) parameter @ _ar = 0; @ (the default) @

_arma   Specify the orders of an autoregressive moving average (ARMA) error structure. It is a column vector consisting of at least two elements. The first element denotes the order of autoregressive portion of the ARMA process, while the second element is the order of moving average portion. If only the autoregressive portion is given, it is exactly the AR model (see _ar above). The model is estimated using the maximum likelihood method conditional to the initialization of pre-sample series, which is the sample mean of the error series. Optional initial values of the autoregressive and moving average coefficients may be appended at the end of _arma for estimation. Giving the initial values is useful for starting a search from non-zero values of ARMA coefficients. For example:

```
_arma = {1, 0}; @ this is identical to: _ar = 1; @
_arma = {0, 1};
_arma = {1, 1, 0.5, -0.5}; @ initial values of
ARMA(1,1) parameters @
_arma = {0, 0}; @ (the default) @
```

_b   A column vector of initial parameter values for nonlinear model estimation.

_begin   Specify the starting observation number for estimation.
_begin = 1 is the default.

_bjtest   Bera-Jarque test for residual normality.
_bjtest = 0 (default): Skip the test;
_bjtest = 1: Perform the test.

_bgtest   Breusch Godfrey test for higher-order autocorrelation.
_bgtest = 0 (default): Skip the test;
_bgtest = p (>0): Perform the test for autocorrelation up to the p-th order. The number p (>0) is the highest order tested.

_bptest   Breusch Pagan and White tests for heteroscedasticity.
_bptest = 0 (default): Skip the test;
_bptest = 1: Perform Breusch-Pagan and White tests for general heteroscedasticity. For the Breusch-Pagan test, all explanatory variables including constant term (i.e., X) are the RHS variables of the auxiliary test regression. For the White test, all explanatory variables and their squares and cross product including constant term are the RHS variables of the auxiliary test regression.

_const   Specify a constant term for a regression model.
_const = 1 (default): Constant term is added in the regression;
_const = 0: No constant is added.

For a system model, this is a column vector of 0 (no constant) or 1 (with constant) associated with each equation.

_conv   Convergence criteria for nonlinear model estimation.
_conv = 0 (default): Convergence in function value and solution;
_conv = 1: Convergence in function value, solution, and zero

gradient. All convergence criteria are checked relative to the tolerance level _tol (see below).

_corr   Compute condition number of explanatory variables and correlation matrix of dependent and explanatory variables, useful for multicollinearity analysis.
_corr = 0 (default): Do not compute the statistics;
_corr = 1: Compute and show the statistics.

_dlags   A scalar or a 2x1 column vector to specify the use of lagged dependent variables. As a scalar, it is the order of the regular lagged dependent variables in use. As a 2x1 column vector, a seasonal lagged dependent variables model is identified with order _dlags[1] and seasonal span _dlags[2] (require _dlags[2]>0). Normally, _dlags[2] = 4 for a model with quarterly data series, while _dlags[2] = 12 for the monthly case. _dlags[1] or the scalar _dlags is always the order number. For a pure (regular or seasonal) lagged dependent variables model, set RHS variable X = 0 in calling the estimate procedure and specify the column vector _dlags accordingly. For example:
_dlags = q; @ or equivalently, _dlags = {q,1} @
_dlags = {q,s};
Where q is the order of autocorrelation and s is the seasonal span.
_dlags = 0 is the default.

For a system model, _dlags is a gxg matrix with the value of its entry indicating the number of lags for each endogenous variable (column) in each equation (row). A zero ij-element of _dlags signifies that no lag is used for the j-th variable in the i-th equation. Here, g is the number of endogenous variables or equations.

_drop   Drop the first few observations for model estimation. Depending on the method of estimation, initial unusable observations may be dropped automatically.
_drop = 1: Drop the first observation or the first seasonal span of observations for AR model estimation;
_drop = 0 (default): Keep the first observation or the first seasonal span of observations for AR model estimation with appropriate data transformation.

_ebtest   Engle-Bollerslev test for higher-order autoregressive conditional heteroscedasticity (ARCH).
_ebtest = 0 (default): Skip the test;
_ebtest = q (>0): Perform the test for ARCH structure up to the q-th order. The number q (>0) is the highest order tested.

_end   Specify the ending observation number for estimation.
_end = rows(y) is the default.

_eq   Specify the stochastic equation specification matrix for system model estimation. This is a gx(gs+ks) matrix with elements -1, 0, and 1 arranged in accordance with the order of endogenous variables followed by the predetermined variables. Note that g is the number of stochastic equations, gs is the number of endogenous variables (gs>=g), while ks is the number of predetermined variables. In the stochastic equation specification matrix _eq, an element -1 indicates the LHS endogenous variable. Only one -1 entry is allowed in each equation. An element 1 indicates the use of an endogenous and/or a predetermined variable on the RHS of an equation. An element 0 indicates the corresponding unused variable. If _eq is not specified, or _eq = 0 by default, a seemingly unrelated system is assumed. That is, g=gs and -1 in the gs diagonals and 1 in the next gsxks predetermined variables portion of the matrix. Normally constant terms are not included in the equation specification.

_garch   Specify the orders of a generalized autoregressive conditional heteroscedasticity (GARCH) error structure. It is a column vector consisting of at least two elements. The first element denotes the order of autoregressive (variances) portion of GARCH process, while the second element is the order of moving average (squared errors) portion. The model is estimated using maximum likelihood method conditional to the initialization of pre-sample series, which is the sample variance of the error series. The optional initial value of GARCH coefficients may be appended at the end of _garch for estimation. Be reminded that there is always a constant for the GARCH process. The constant is the last term of GARCH parameters. Giving the initial values is useful for starting a search from non-zero values of GARCH coefficients. For example:
```
_garch = {1, 0};
_garch = {0, 1};
_garch = {1, 1, 0.5, 0.5, 0.5}; @ with initial values
of GARCH(1,1) @
_garch = {0, 0}; @ (the default) @
```

_garchx   Specify additional variables included in the GARCH variance equation (see _garch above). This may be a data matrix of multiple variables. The variables must be defined with the same number of rows or observations as that of the regression residuals.

_hacv   Compute heteroscedasticity and autocorrelation-consistent variance-covariance matrix and perform adjustment to standard error and t-ratio of estimated coefficients accordingly. This may be a column vector up to 3 elements.
_hacv = 0 (default): No adjustment;
_hacv = 1: Compute heteroscedasticity-consistent variance-covariance matrix;
_hacv = {0,p}: Compute p-th order autocorrelation-consistent variance-covariance matrix with declining weights of autocovariances (Newey-West estimators), p=1,2,...;
_hacv = {1,p}: Compute heteroscedasticity and p-th order autocorrelation-consistent variance-covariance matrix with declining weights of autocovariances (Newey-West estimators), p=1,2,....;
_hacv = {1,p,1}: Compute heteroscedasticity and p-th order autocorrelation-consistent variance-covariance matrix with the equal weighted autocovariances, p=1,2,....; Therefore, _hacv = {0,p} is the same as _hacv = {0,p,0} and _hacv = {1,p} is the same as

_hacv = {1,p,0}.

Note: If _hacv is used in conjunction with the instrumental variable estimation (see, _ivar below) in setting the number of iterations (see, _iter below) to achieve the convergence of estimated parameters, this is essentially the generalized method of moments (GMM). _hacv is meaningful only when there is a potential misspecification problem of autoregresive and/or heteroscedastic error structure.

_hacv may be used in conjunction with the system model estimation. If the method of 2SLS (see _method below) is requested with non-zero _hacv, then two stage GMM estimation is performed. Similarly, if the method of 3SLS is requested with non-zero _hacv, then three stage GMM estimation is performed. However, the computed variance-covariance matrix for the system may become non-positive definite due to excess numerical rounding errors or the improper autocovariance structures specified.

_id   Specify the identity equation specification matrix for a system model. Similar size and setup as _eq (see above) except that its entries can be any value as required. If _id is not specified, or _id = 0 by default, there is no identity. Note: gs=rows(_eq|_id) to ensure the system compatibility.

_iter   Maximum number of iterations requested for iterative or nonlinear model estimation.
_iter = 1 is the default.

_ivar   Instrumental variable estimation requested with instrumental variables specified in matrix _ivar. If _dlags[1] > 0, _ivar may be given with a positive scalar (i.e. _ivar = 1) and perform instrumental variable estimation with the internal instrumental variables obtained from the explanatory variables and their lags. If the matrix form of _ivar is specified, the external instrumental variables are used for that cols(_ivar) >= cols(X) + _const and rows(_ivar) >= rows(X). Constant term is automatically included in _ivar.
_ivar = 0 is the default.

For a system model, external instrumental variable estimation may be requested with the instrumental variables specified in matrix _ivar. The data matrix _ivar will be combined with all predetermined variables to form the basis for instrumental variable estimation.

_ivar may be used together with _iter and _hacv (see above) to produce the GMM estimation.

_ma   Specify the order of a moving average (MA) error structure. If an additional autoregressive process is desired for an ARMA structure, use the variable _arma instead (see above). Optional initial values of the moving average coefficients may be appended at the end of _ma for estimation. Providing the initial values is useful for starting search from non-zero values of moving average coefficients. For example:

```
_ma = 1;
_ma = {1,  0.5}; @ with  initial  value  of  MA(1)
parameter @
_ma = 0; @ (the default) @
```

_method   Specify the estimation method for an AR model.
`_method` = 0 (default): Cochrane-Orcutt iterative LS method;
`_method` = {0,1}: Cochrane-Orcutt iterative ML method;
`_method` = 1: Beach-MacKinnon iterative ML method (for `_ar` = 1 only, and `_drop` = 0 is in effect);
`_method` = 2 or {2,0}: Hildreth-Lu grid search LS method (for `_ar` = 1 only);
`_method` = {2,1}: Hildreth-Lu grid search ML method (for `_ar` = 1 only).
Note: higher AR order (`_ar` > 1) can only use `_method` = 0 or `_method` = {0,1}.

Specify the estimation method for a system model.
`_method` = 0 (default): Ordinary least squares (biased);
`_method` = 1: Limited information maximum likelihood;
`_method` = 2: Two stage least squaes;
`_method` = 3: Three-stage least squares;
`_method` = 4: Full information maximum likelihood.
Note: LIML and FIML are not true nonlinear maximum likelihood estimation. Instead they are types of instrumental variables estimation.

Specify the estimation method for a nonlinear model (including a linear model with nonlinear error structure such as ARMA and GARCH).
`_method` = 0 (default): Steep-ascent or decent method for mathematical optimization; Gauss-Newton method for nonlinear least squares estimation; Berndt-Hall-Hall-Hausman (BHHH) method for maximum likelihood estimation;
`_method` = 1: Quasi-Newton BFGS update method;
`_method` = 2: Quasi-Newton DFP update method;
`_method` = 3: Greenstadt method;
`_method` = 4: Newton-Raphson method;
`_method` = 5: Quadratic hill-climbing method;
`_method` = 6: Modified quadratic hill-climbing method.

_names   Specify a vector of character names for variables (linear model) or parameters (nonlinear model) as appeared in a regression equation.

_nlopt   Specify a nonlinear optimization problem.
`_nlopt` = 0 (default): Mathematical minimization of a scalar-valued function or nonlinear least squares estimation based on a vector-valued component error function;
`_nlopt` = 1: Mathematical maximization of a scalar-valued function or maximum likelihood estimation based on a vector-valued component error function;
`_nlopt` = 2: Maximum likelihood estimation based on a vector-valued component log-likelihood function.

_pdl   Specify a polynomial distributed lag model if _pdl is defined as a rows(_pdl)x3 matrix. Each row of _pdl consists three elements: {q p r} where q = lags, p = orders, and r = endpoint restrictions: -1 (beginning), 1 (ending), 2 (both), and 0 (no restriction), for each RHS variable. Requires rows(_pdl) = cols(X), and cols(_pdl) = 3: _pdl = 0 is the default.

_restart   Number of times to restart estimation for iterative or nonlinear models when function value does not improve. Maximum value of _restart is 10. _restart = 0 is the default.

_restr   Perform restricted least squares estimation with the linear restrictions defined in accordance with the form: Rb = q, or [R1 R0][b1 b0]' = q, where b1 is the vector of slope coefficients and R1 is the restriction matrix corresponds to b1. Similarly, b0 is the intercept and R0 corresponds to b0. q is the vector of restricted values. Linear restrictions involving intercept should be specified in conjunction with _const = 0. If _restr is specified, then _restr = [R1 q]. Requires rows(_restr) = number of restrictions, and cols(_restr) = cols(X). _restr = 0 is the default.

For a system model, restrictions in the matrix R are stacked horizontally in accordance with the equations, while the vertical rows indicate the number of restrictions imposed. Own or cross equation restrictions can be coded easily. In general restrictions on the constant terms are not required.

_rlist   List regression residual series.
_rlist = 0 (default): Skip listing the series;
_rlist = 1: List observed, predicted, and least squares residual series;
_rlist = 2: In addition to listing least squares residual series, studentized residuals and leverage information are provided. Useful for checking influential observations and outliers.

_rplot   Plot regression residual series.
_rplot = 0 (default): No plots;
_rplot = 1: Plot residuals only;
_rplot = 2: Plot both observed and predicted, and residuals.
Also for plotting autocorrelation and partial autocorrelation functions if requested (see _acf above), a positive value of _rplot is needed.

_rstat   Report regression residual statistics.
_rstat = 0 (default): Do not report the statistics;
_rstat = 1: Report residual statistics, including DW, DH whenever appropriate.

_step   Specify step size of line search method for iterative or nonlinear model estimation.
_step = 0 (default): Cut back (half) step size is used;
_step = 1: Quadratic step size is used.

_tol   Set the convergence tolerance level for iterative or nonlinear model estimation.
_tol = 0.001 is the default.

_vcov   Report the estimated variance-covariance matrix.
_vcov = 0 (default): Do not report the variance-covariance matrix;
_vcov = 1: Report variance-covariance matrix and correlation matrix of the estimated coefficients.

For a nonlinear model,
_vcov = 1: Variance-covariance matrix is derived from the method dependent approximated hessian (information matrix);
_vcov = 2: Variance-covariance matrix is derived from the estimated hessian.
_vcov = 3: Robust variance-covariance matrix, if available, is derived from the maximum likelihood estimation of component error or log-likelihood function.

_weight   Perform weighted least squares estimation with the weighting variable defined in _weight. _weight must be a column vector and rows(_weight) >= rows(X).
_weight = 0 is the default.

FORECAST Input Control Variables

In addition to the estimate input variables which control the model specification (e.g., _ar, _arma, _dlags, _pdl, etc.), the following are the FORECAST input variables:

Variable	Description
_b	Parameter estimates for computing the forecasts. Depending on the model specification, it may include the estimated coefficients of AR or ARMA error structures. Forecasting with GARCH innovations is not implemented.
_dynamic	Dynamic forecasts for lagged dependent variables model. _dynamic = 0 (default): Do not perform dynamic forecasts; _dynamic = 1: Perform dynamic forecasts. Dynamic forecast uses previous predicted lagged dependent variables.
_fbegin	Start of forecast observation number. _fbegin = _end +1 is the default.
_fend	End of forecast observation number. _fend = rows(X) is the default.
_fplot	Plots predicted or forecast series. _fplot = 0 (default): Do not plot the series; _fplot = 1: Plot predicted or forecast series.
_fstat	Computes ex-post forecast error statistics.

          _fstat = 0 (default): Do not compute the statistics.
          _fstat = 1: Compute and report the statistics.

_unlog   Computes unlogged series of forecasts.
          _unlog = 0 (default): Do not compute unlogged series of forecasts;
          _unlog = 1: Compute unlogged series of forecasts, assuming the original series has been log transformed.

_vb   Compute and report the estimated variance-covariance matrix of the basic model (not including the variance-covariance matrix of AR or ARMA error structure if specified).

Note: forecast is not available for nonlinear models.

Output Control Variables

Output control variables are available after calling the procedure estimate or forecast. They may be used later in the program for further analysis. Depending on the input variables specified, not all the output variables will be available. Calling reset assigns all output variables to zero. Each call to estimate or forecast assigns new values to output variables.

ESTIMATE Output Control Variables

Variable	Description
__ar	Estimated coefficients of the autocorrelated error structure. Depending on the model specification, it may include AR or ARMA, and GARCH coefficients in that order.
__b	Estimated regression coefficients (and possibly including the coefficients for the autocorrelated error structure, that is __ar, if the model is so specified).
__dh	Estimated Durbin-H statistic.
__dw	Estimated Durbin-Watson statistic.
__e	Estimated regression residuals; for nonlinear scalar-valued function optimization, this is the function value at the solution.
__g	Gradient vector of nonlinear objective function evaluated at the solution.
__h	Hessian matrix of nonlinear objective function evaluated at the solution.
__hat	Diagonal vector of Hat-matrix, $X(X'X)^{-1}X'$, or leverage.
__ll	Maximum log likelihood function value.
__r2	R-square (goodness of fit of the regression).

__r2a   Adjusted R-square.

__rss   Residual or error sums-of-squares.

__v   Estimated regression variance.

FORECAST Output Control Variables

Variable	Description
__f	Predicted or forecast series.
__mape	Mean absolute percent of forecast errors.
__mse	Mean sum squares of forecast errors.
__rmspe	Root mean absolute percent of forecast errors.
__u1	Theil inequality coefficient ($0 <= $__u1$ <= 1$).
__uc	Covariance proportion of mean sum squares of errors.
__ue	Disturbance proportion of mean sum squares of errors.
__um	Bias proportion of mean sum squares of errors.
__ur	Regression proportion of mean sum squares of errors.
__us	Variance proportion of mean sum squares of errors.
__vf	Variance of predicted or forecast series.

Note: forecast is not available for nonlinear models.

Appendix   B
GPE Application Modules

Each of the GPE application modules is given AS IS. The user is free to use and to make changes as needed for different purposes. However, the usual disclaimer applies. In particular, the following copyright statement must be presented as long as all or part of the program code is used in your work:

© **Copyright 2001 by Kuan-Pin Lin and Applied Data Associates**
All Rights Reserved.

THIS SOFTWARE PRODUCT IS PROPRIETARY SOURCE CODE OF APPLIED DATA ASSOCIATES. THIS FILE HEADER MUST ACCOMPANY ALL FILES USING ANY PORTION, IN WHOLE OR IN PART, OF THIS SOURCE CODE. THIS SOFTWARE PRODUCT IS DESIGNED TO BE USED WITH GPE2 AND GAUSS. IF YOU USE THIS SOURCE CODE FOR RESEARCH AND DEVELOPMENT, A PROPER REFERENCE IS REQUIRED. IF YOU WISH TO DISTRIBUTE ANY PORTION OF THE PROPRIETARY SOURCE CODE, IN WHOLE OR IN PART, YOU MUST FIRST OBTAIN WRITTEN PERMISSION FROM THE AUTHOR.

Application Module B-1: GMM.GPE

```
/*
** GMM.GPE: Nonlinear GMM Estimation
**
** ==> call estimate(&gmmqw,x);
** or
** ==> call estimate(&gmmq,x);
**
** A set of moment functions must be defined as a procedure with the
** name mf(x,b). The result is an nxl matrix of moments. n is the
** number of sample observations; l is the number of moment equations;
** x is the data matrix and b is the parameter vector.
**
** A global variable gmmw is used to define the weighting matrix for
** the GMM criterion function (to be minimized). gmmw is initially
** an identity matrix or 1 for the 1st GMM estimation; gmmw should be
** set to gmmv(x,b), the inverse of the variance-covariance matrix of
** moments functions, for the 2nd GMM estimation.
**
** gmmqw is the objective function with externally defined weighting
** matrix gmmw, the result is a consistent GMM estimation.
**
** gmmq is the objective function with internally estimated weighting
** matrix, the result is an efficient GMM estimation.
**
** GMM estimation is usually called in the following steps:
**
** ==> call estimate(&gmmqw,x);
** ==>
** ==> _b=__b;
** ==> gmmw=gmmv(x,_b);
** ==> call estimate(&gmmqw,x);
** ==>
** ==> _b=__b;
** ==> call estimate(&gmmq,x);
```

```
**  ==>
**  ==> call gmmout(x,__b);
*/

declare gmmw ?= 1;

/*
Sample average of moments
*/
proc gmmm(x,b);
    local m,d;
    m=meanc(mf(x,b));
    retp(m);
endp;

/*
Covariance matrix of sample averages of moments
considering White-Newey-West autocovariances
depending on global _hacv
*/
proc gmmv(x,b);
    local n,m,v,s,j;
    n=rows(x);
    m=mf(x,b)/n;
    v=m'm;          @ hetero. variances @
    j=1;
    do until j>_hacv[2]; @ autocovariances @
        s=m'*missrv(lagn(m,j),0);
        v=v+(1-j/(_hacv[2]+1))*(s+s');
        j=j+1;
    endo;
    retp(v);
endp;

/*
GMM criterion function: depending on global gmmw
Weighted sum of squared sample averages of moments
*/
proc gmmqw(x,b);
    local m;
    m=gmmm(x,b);
    retp(m'*gmmw*m);
endp;

/*
GMM criterion function: general
Weighted sum of squared sample averages of moments
*/
proc gmmq(x,b);
    local m;
    m=gmmm(x,b);
    gmmw=invpd(gmmv(x,b));
    retp(m'*gmmw*m);
endp;

proc (0) = gmmout(x,b);
    local m,v,q,g,vb;
    m=gmmm(x,b);
    v=gmmv(x,b);
    q=m'*invpd(v)*m;
    g=gradp2(&gmmm,x,b);
    vb=invpd(g'*gmmw*g)*g'*gmmw*v*gmmw'*g*invpd(g'*gmmw*g);
    print;
    print "GMM Estimation Result";
    print "=====================";
    print "   Parameter   Std. Error      t-Ratio";;
    print b~sqrt(diag(vb))~b./sqrt(diag(vb));
```

```
    print;
    print "Hansen Test Statistic of the Moment Restrictions";
    print ftos(rows(m)-rows(b),"Chi-Sq(%*.*lf) = ",4,0);;
    print q;
    __vb=vb; @ using the GMM var-cov matrix @
endp;
```

Application Module B-2: JOHANSEN.GPE

```
/*
** JOHANSEN.GPE - Cointegration test procedure
** based on Johansen's VAR approach
**
** ==> call johansen(z,p,c);
** or
** ==> {lr,lrsum} = johansen(z,p,c);
**
** z is the data matrix for cointegration analysis, p is number of lags
** of VAR structure, c is the model indicator (0=no constant, 1=drift,
** 2=trend drift). outputs are two vectors of maximum eigenvalue and
** trace test statistics, lr and lrsum, respectively.
*/

proc (2) = johansen(z,p,c);
    local m,n,j,z1,dz,y1,dy,y,x,u,v,suu,svv,suv,svu;
    local r,lr,lrsum,msk,fmt,one,e;

    m=cols(z);              @ number of variables @
                            @ maximal lags in the test regression @
    z1=lagn(z,1);           @ lag of data matrix, at least p=1 @
    dz=z-z1;                @ construct difference data matrix @
    j=1;
    do until j>=p;          @ use up to p-1 lags of differences @
        dz=dz~lagn(z-z1,j);
        j=j+1;
    endo;

    y=packr(z1~dz);         @ combined data matrix @
    n=rows(y);              @ number of usable observations @
    y1=y[.,1:m];            @ lag of y data matrix @
    dy=y[.,m+1:2*m];        @ difference of y data matrix @

    one=ones(n,1);
    if p>1;                 @ VAR(p), p>1 @
        x=y[.,2*m+1:cols(y)]; @ RHS x data matrix @
        if c>0;
            if c==1;        @ with drift only @
                e=one-x*(one/x);
            endif;          @ constant regression residuals @
            if c==2;        @ with trend drift @
                x=x~one;
            endif;
        endif;
                            @ auxiliary regression residuals @
        u=dy-x*(dy/x);      @ (1) difference regression @
        v=y1-x*(y1/x);      @ (2) lag regression @
    else;                   @ p==1, or VAR(1) @
        if c>0;
            u=dy-meanc(dy)';
            v=y1-meanc(y1)';
            if c==1; e=one; endif;
        else;
            u=dy; v=y1;
        endif;
    endif;
```

```
    if c==1; v=e~v; endif;
    suu=u'u/n;              @ var-cov matrices @
    svv=v'v/n;
    suv=u'v/n;
    svu=suv';
    r=eig(invpd(suu)*suv*invpd(svv)*svu); @ compute eigenvalue @
    r=rev(sortc(r,1));      @ sort eigvalues in increasing order @
    lr=-n*ln(1-r);          @ likelihood ratio test @
    lrsum=rev(cumsumc(rev(lr))); @ trace test statistic @

    msk={1 1 1 1};          @ print cointegration test results @
    fmt={"*.*lf" 8 0,"*.*lf" 5 0,"#*.*lg" 12 5,"#*.*lg" 12 5};
    print ftos(c+1,"\lCointegration Test (Model %-*.*lf):",1,0);
    print "Cointegrating  Eigv. Test  Trace Test";
    print "    Rank    DF    Statistic    Statistic";
    call printfm
        (real(seqa(0,1,m)~(m-seqa(0,1,m))~lr~lrsum),msk,fmt);
    retp(lr,lrsum);
endp;
```

Application Module B-3: PANEL1.GPE

```
/*
** PANEL1.GPE - one-way panel data analysis
**
** ==> call panel1(ys,xs,n,t);
** ys and xs are stacked of dependent and independent variables;
** one-way effects is computed for fixed and random models.
** ys and xs must be arranged in n blocks (cross sections) of t
** observations (time periods). it is used to study the individual
** (cross section) effects; to study the period (time periods)
** effects, re-arrange ys and xs then swap n and t.
**
** make sure to call reset, and define the variable names in _names.
*/

proc (0) = panel1(ys,xs,n,t);
    local y,x,ym,xm,yms,xms,k;
    local rssr,rssur,dfr,dfur,bp,wf,v1,v,w,h;
    local b1,b2,vb1,vb2,a1,a2,va1,va2,xm1,xm2;

    /* panel data processing */
    k=cols(xs);
    @ ys,xs: stacked data series @
    @ y,x: panel data series @
    y=reshape(ys,n,t)';
    x=reshape(vec(xs),n*k,t)';
    @ ym,xm: group means @
    ym=meanc(y);
    xm=reshape(meanc(x),k,n)';
    @ yms,xms: stacked group means @
    yms=vec(reshape(ym,t,n));
    xms=reshape(reshape(xm',k*t,n)',n*t,k);

    /* pooled (restricted) regression */
    call estimate(ys,xs);
    rssr=__rss;
    dfr=__df;
    @ testing for random one-way effects @
    bp=(n*t/2)*(1/(t-1))*(
        (sumc(sumc(reshape(__e,n,t)')^2)/sumc(sumc(__e^2))-1)^2);

    /* between-group (mean) regression */
    call estimate(ym,xm);
    v1=t*__v;
```

```
    /* within-group (mean deviation) regression */
    @ unrestricted regression @
    call estimate(ys-yms,xs-xms);
    rssur=__rss;
    dfur=__df-(n-1);
    v=__v*(__df/dfur); @ df adjusted variance @
    @ testing for fixed one-way effects @
    wf=((rssr-rssur)/(dfr-dfur))/(rssur/dfur);

    /* fixed effects model */
    b1=__b;
    vb1=__vb*(__df/dfur);
    xm1=xm~(-ones(n,1));
    a1=ym-xm1*b1; @ section/period difference @
    va1=v/t+xm1*vb1*xm1';

    /* random effects model */
    w=1-minc(sqrt(v/v1)|1);
    @ if w==1, it is fixed effects model @
    @ if w==0, it is a pooled model (no effects) @
    call estimate(ys-w*yms,xs-w*xms);
    b2=__b;
    vb2=__vb*(__df/dfur);
    if w>0;
        xm2=xm~((-1/w)*ones(n,1));
        a2=w*(ym-xm2*b2);
        va2=(w^2)*(v/t+xm2*vb2*xm2');
    else;
        a2=zeros(n,1);
        va2=zeros(n,n);
    endif;
    h=(b1[1:k]-b2[1:k])'*inv(vb1[1:k,1:k]-vb2[1:k,1:k])*(b1[1:k]-b2[1:k]);

    /* print output */
    print;
    print "Panel Data Model Estimation Procedure:";
    print "(1) Pooled Regression";
    print "(2) Between-Groups Regression";
    print "(3) Fixed Effects (Within-Groups) Regression";
    print "(4) Random Effects (Weighted Within-Groups) Regression";
    print;
    print "Wald F Test Statistic for No Fixed One-Way Effects";
    print ftos(dfr-dfur,"F(%*.*f,",4,0);;
    print ftos(dfur,"%*.*f) = ",4,0);;
    print wf;
    print;
    print "Breusch-Pagan LM Test Statistic for No One-Way Effects";
    print ftos(1,"Chi-Sq(%*.*f) = ",4,0);;
    print bp;
    print;
    print "Hausman's Test for Fixed and Random Effects";
    print ftos(k,"Chi-Sq(%*.*f) = ",4,0);;
    print abs(h);
    print;
    print "Within-Groups Estimates:";
    print "        Fixed       S.E.        Random      S.E.";;
    print b1~sqrt(diag(vb1))~b2~sqrt(diag(vb2));
    print;
    print "One-Way Effects:";
    print "Section/Period    Fixed       S.E.        Random      S.E.";;
    print seqa(1,1,n)~a1~sqrt(diag(va1))~a2~sqrt(diag(va2));
endp;
```

Application Module B-4: PANEL2.GPE

```
/*
** PANEL2.GPE - two-way panel data analysis
**
** ==> call panel2(ys,xs,n,t);
** ys and xs are stacked of dependent and independent variables;
** two-way effects is computed for fixed and random models.
** ys and xs must be arranged in n blocks (cross sections) of t
** observations (time periods).
**
** make sure to call reset, and define the variable names in _names.
*/

proc (0) = panel2(ys,xs,n,t);
    local ymi,xmi,ymis,xmis,ystar,xstar,k;
    local ymt,xmt,ymts,xmts,ymm,xmm,y,x;
    local rssr,rssur,dfr,dfur,bp,wf,v1,v2,v3,v,w1,w2,w3,h;
    local b1,b2,vb1,vb2,a1i,a1t,a2i,a2t,c1,c2;

    /* panel data processing (complicated, do not change) */
    k=cols(xs);
    @ ys,xs: stacked data series @
    @ y,x: panel data series @
    y=reshape(ys,n,t)';
    x=reshape(xs',n*k,t)';
    @ xt=reshape(xs,n,k*t); @

    @ ymi,xmi: cross section means @
    ymi=meanc(y);
    xmi=reshape(meanc(x),k,n)';
    @ ymt,xmt: time period means @
    ymt=meanc(y');
    @ xmt=reshape(meanc(xt),t,k); @
    xmt=reshape(meanc(reshape(xs,n,k*t)),t,k);

    @ ymm,xmm: overall means @
    ymm=meanc(ymi)';
    xmm=meanc(xmi)';

    @ ymis,xmis: stacked section means @
    ymis=vec(reshape(ymi,t,n));
    xmis=reshape(reshape(xmi',k*t,n)',n*t,k);
    @ ymts,xmts: stacked time period means @
    ymts=reshape(ymt,n*t,1);
    xmts=reshape(xmt,n*t,k);

    /* pooled (restricted) regression */
    call estimate(ys,xs);
    rssr=__rss;
    dfr=__df;

    @ testing for two-way effects @
    bp=(n*t/2)*(
    (1/(t-1))*((sumc(sumc(reshape(__e,n,t)')^2)/sumc(sumc(__e^2))-1)^2)+
    (1/(n-1))*((sumc(sumc(reshape(__e,n,t))^2)/sumc(sumc(__e^2))-1)^2));

    @ between-groups (cross sections) means regression @
    call estimate(ymi,xmi);
    v1=t*__v;

    @ between-groups (time periods) means regression @
    call estimate(ymt,xmt);
    v2=n*__v;

    /* fixed effects model */
```

```
@ within-groups (cross sections and time periods) regression @
ystar=ys-ymis-ymts+ymm;
xstar=xs-xmis-xmts+xmm;
call estimate(ystar,xstar);
rssur=__rss;
dfur=__df-(n-1)-(t-1); @ adjust df @
v=__v*(__df/dfur);

@ testing for fixed two-way effects @
wf=((rssr-rssur)/(dfr-dfur))/(rssur/dfur);

b1=__b;
vb1=__vb*(__df/dfur);
c1=ymm-xmm*b1[1:k];    @ overall effects, note: b1[k+1]=0 @
a1i=(ymi-ymm)-(xmi-xmm)*b1[1:k]; @ cross sections effects @
a1t=(ymt-ymm)-(xmt-xmm)*b1[1:k]; @ time periods effects @

/* random effects model */
v3=v1+v2-v;
w1=1-minc(sqrt(v/v1)|1);
w2=1-minc(sqrt(v/v2)|1);
w3=w1+w2-(1-minc(sqrt(v/v3)|1));
ystar=ys-w1*ymis-w2*ymts+w3*ymm;
xstar=xs-w1*xmis-w2*xmts+w3*xmm;
call estimate(ystar,xstar);

b2=__b;
vb2=__vb*(__df/dfur);
c2=w3*((ymm-xmm)*b2[1:k])+b2[k+1]; @ overall effect @
a2i=(w1*ymi-w3*ymm)-(w1*xmi-w3*xmm)*b2[1:k]; @ individual effects @
a2t=(w2*ymt-w3*ymm)-(w2*xmt-w3*xmm)*b2[1:k]; @ period effects @
h=(b1[1:k]-b2[1:k])'*inv(vb1[1:k,1:k]-vb2[1:k,1:k])*(b1[1:k]-b2[1:k]);

/* print output */
print;
print "Panel Data Model Estimation Procedure:";
print "(1) Pooled Regression";
print "(2) Between-Groups (Cross Sections) Regression";
print "(3) Between-Groups (Time Periods) Regression";
print "(4) Fixed Effects (Within-Groups) Regression";
print "(5) Random Effects (Weighted Within-Groups) Regression";
print;
print "Wald F Test Statistic for No Fixed Two-Way Effects";
print ftos(dfr-dfur,"F(%*.*f,",4,0);;
print ftos(dfur,"%*.*f) = ",4,0);;
print wf;
print;
print "Breusch-Pagan LM Test Statistic for No Two-Way Effects";
print ftos(2,"Chi-Sq(%*.*f) = ",4,0);;
print bp;
print;
print "Hausman's Test for Fixed and Random Effects";
print ftos(k,"Chi-Sq(%*.*f) = ",4,0);;
print abs(h);
print;
print "Within-Groups Estimates:";
print "        Fixed         S.E.         Random          S.E.";;
print b1~sqrt(diag(vb1))~b2~sqrt(diag(vb2));
print;
print "Two-Way Effects:";
print "                      Fixed        Random";
print "      Overall " c1~c2;
print;
print "Cross Sections Effects:";
print "    Sections        Fixed         Random";;
print seqa(1,1,n)~a1i~a2i;
print;
```

```
    print "Time Periods Effects:";
    print "     Periods      Fixed      Random";;
    print seqa(1,1,t)~a1t~a2t;
endp;
```

Appendix   C
Statistical Tables

Statistical tables for normal distribution, t distribution, Chi-squared distribution, and F distribution are available from most statistics references. Durbin-Watson bounds test statistics are readily available in econometric textbooks. In this appendix, we list only the not-so-popular statistical tables for testing unit roots and cointegration as discussed in Chapter XVI.

Table C-1. Critical Values for the Dickey-Fuller Unit Root Test Based on t-Statistic

Model

Model I: $\Delta X_t = (\rho-1) X_{t-1} + \Sigma_{i=1,2,...} \rho_i \Delta X_{t-i} + \varepsilon_t$

Model II: $\Delta X_t = \alpha + (\rho-1) X_{t-1} + \Sigma_{i=1,2,...} \rho_i \Delta X_{t-i} + \varepsilon_t$

Model III: $\Delta X_t = \alpha + \beta t + (\rho-1) X_{t-1} + \Sigma_{i=1,2,...} \rho_i \Delta X_{t-i} + \varepsilon_t$

Test Statistic

τ_ρ t-statistic (non-symmetric distribution, testing $\rho = 1$)

τ_α t-statistic (symmetric distribution, testing $\alpha = 0$ given $\rho = 1$)

τ_β t-statistic (symmetric distribution, testing $\beta = 0$ given $\rho = 1$)

Source

Fuller (1976, p. 373); Dickey and Fuller (1981).

Model	Statistic	N	1%	2.5%	5%	10%
I	τ_ρ	25	-2.66	-2.26	-1.95	-1.60
		50	-2.62	-2.25	-1.95	-1.61
		100	-2.60	-2.24	-1.95	-1.61
		250	-2.58	-2.23	-1.95	-1.61
		500	-2.58	-2.23	-1.95	-1.61
		>500	-2.58	-2.23	-1.95	-1.61
II	τ_ρ	25	-3.75	-3.33	-3.00	-2.62
		50	-3.58	-3.22	-2.93	-2.60
		100	-3.51	-3.17	-2.89	-2.58
		250	-3.46	-3.14	-2.88	-2.57
		500	-3.44	-3.13	-2.87	-2.57
		>500	-3.43	-3.12	-2.86	-2.57
III	τ_ρ	25	-4.38	-3.95	-3.60	-3.24
		50	-4.15	-3.80	-3.50	-3.18
		100	-4.04	-3.73	-3.45	-3.15
		250	-3.99	-3.69	-3.43	-3.13
		500	-3.98	-3.68	-3.42	-3.13
		>500	-3.96	-3.66	-3.41	-3.12
II	τ_α	25	3.41	2.97	2.61	2.20
		50	3.28	2,89	2.56	2.18
		100	3.22	2.86	2.54	2.17
		250	3.19	2.84	2.53	2.16
		500	3.18	2.83	2.52	2.16
		>500	3.18	2.83	2.52	2.16
III	τ_α	25	4.05	3.59	3.20	2.77
		50	3.87	3.47	3.14	2.75
		100	3.78	3.42	3.11	2.73
		250	3.74	3.39	3.09	2.73
		500	3.72	3.38	3.08	2.72
		>500	3.71	3.38	3.08	2.72
III	τ_β	25	3.74	3.25	2.85	2.39
		50	3.60	3.18	2.81	2.38
		100	3.53	3.14	2.79	2.38
		250	3.49	3.12	2.79	2.38
		500	3.48	3.11	2.78	2.38
		>500	3.46	3.11	2.78	2.38

Table C-2. Critical Values for the Dickey-Fuller Unit Root Test Based on F-Statistic

Model

Model II: $\Delta X_t = \alpha + (\rho - 1) X_{t-1} + \Sigma_{i=1,2,...} \rho_i \Delta X_{t-i} + \varepsilon_t$

Model III: $\Delta X_t = \alpha + \beta t + (\rho - 1) X_{t-1} + \Sigma_{i=1,2,...} \rho_i \Delta X_{t-i} + \varepsilon_t$

Test Statistic

ϕ_1 F-statistic (testing $\alpha = 0$ and $\rho = 1$ on Model II)
ϕ_2 F-statistic (testing $\alpha = 0$, $\beta = 0$, and $\rho = 1$ on Model III)
ϕ_3 F-statistic (testing $\beta = 0$ and $\rho = 1$ on Model III)

Source

Dickey and Fuller (1981).

Model	Statistic	N	1%	2.5%	5%	10%
II	ϕ_1	25	7.88	6.30	5.18	4.12
		50	7.06	5.80	4.86	3.94
		100	6.70	5.57	4.71	3.86
		250	6.52	5.45	4.63	3.81
		500	6.47	5.41	4.61	3.79
		>500	6.43	5.38	4.59	3.78
III	ϕ_2	25	8.21	6.75	5.68	4.67
		50	7.02	5.94	5.13	4.31
		100	6.50	5.59	4.88	4.16
		250	6.22	5.40	4.75	4.07
		500	6.15	5.35	4.71	4.05
		>500	6.09	5.31	4.68	4.03
III	ϕ_3	25	10.61	8.65	7.24	5.91
		50	9.31	7.81	6.73	5.61
		100	8.73	7.44	6.49	5.47
		250	8.43	7.25	6.34	5.39
		500	8.34	7.20	6.30	5.36
		>500	8.27	7.16	6.25	5.34

Table C-3. Critical Values for the Dickey-Fuller Cointegration t-Statistic τ_ρ Applied on Regression Residuals

Model

$Y_t = \alpha + X_t \beta + \varepsilon_t$

$\Delta\varepsilon_t = (\rho-1) \varepsilon_{t-1} + \Sigma_{i=1,2,...} \rho_i \Delta\varepsilon_{t-i} + u_t$

K = Numbers of variables in the cointegration tests, i.e., $[Y_t, X_t]$.

t = 1,2,…, N (500).

Model 2: $E(Y_t) = E(X_t) = 0$ (both X and Y have no drift).

Model 2a: $E(X_t) \neq 0$ (at least one variable in X has drift).

Model 3: $E(Y_t) \neq 0$ but $E(X_t) = 0$ (only Y has drift).

Test Statistic

τ_ρ t-statistic (testing $\rho = 1$)

Source

Phillips and Ouliaris (1990).

Model	K	1%	2.5%	5%	10%
2	2	-3.96	-3.64	-3.37	-3.07
	3	-4.31	-4.02	-3.77	-3.45
	4	-4.73	-4.37	-4.11	-3.83
	5	-5.07	-4.71	-4.45	-4.16
	6	-5.28	-4.98	-4.71	-4.43
2a	2	-3.98	-3.68	-3.42	-3.13
	3	-4.36	-4.07	-3.80	-3.52
	4	-4.65	-4.39	-4.16	-3.84
	5	-5.04	-4.77	-4.49	-4.20
	6	-5.36	-5.02	-4.74	-4.46
	7	-5.58	-5.31	-5.03	-4.73
3	2	-4.36	-4.07	-3.80	-3.52
	3	-4.65	-4.39	-4.16	-3.84
	4	-5.04	-4.77	-4.49	-4.20
	5	-5.36	-5.02	-4.74	-4.46
	6	-5.58	-5.31	-5.03	-4.73

Note: For the case of two variables in Model 2a, X is trended but Y is not. It is asymptotically equivalent to ADF unit root test for Model III (see Table C-1, τ_ρ for N=500). If only Y has drift (Model 3), the cointegration equation can be expressed as $Y_t = \alpha + \gamma t + X_t \beta + \varepsilon_t$. Therefore, the same critical values of Model 2a apply to Model 3 for one extra variable t (but do not count for K).

Table C-4. Critical Values for Unit Root and Cointegration Tests Based on Response Surface Estimates

Critical values for unit root and cointegration tests can be computed from the equation:

$$CV(K, Model, N, e) = b + b_1 (1/N) + b_2 (1/N)^2$$

Notation

Model: 1=no constant; 2=no trend; 3=with trend;
K: Number of variables in cointegration tests (K=1 for unit root test);
N: Number of observations or sample size;
e: Level of significance, 0.01, 0.05, 0.1.

Source

MacKinnon (1991).

K	Model	e	b	b_1	b_2
1	1	0.01	-2.5658	-1.960	-10.04
1	1	0.05	-1.9393	-0.398	0.00
1	1	0.10	-1.6156	-0.181	0.00
1	2	0.01	-3.4335	-5.999	-29.25
1	2	0.05	-2.8621	-2.738	-8.36
1	2	0.10	-2.5671	-1.438	-4.48
1	3	0.01	-3.9638	-8.353	-47.44
1	3	0.05	-3.4126	-4.039	-17.83
1	3	0.10	-3.1279	-2.418	-7.58
2	2	0.01	-3.9001	-10.534	-30.03
2	2	0.05	-3.3377	-5.967	-8.98
2	2	0.10	-3.0462	-4.069	-5.73
2	3	0.01	-4.3266	-15.531	-34.03
2	3	0.05	-3.7809	-9.421	-15.06
2	3	0.10	-3.4959	-7.203	-4.01
3	2	0.01	-4.2981	-13.790	-46.37
3	2	0.05	-3.7429	-8.352	-13.41
3	2	0.10	-3.4518	-6.241	-2.79
3	3	0.01	-4.6676	-18.492	-49.35
3	3	0.05	-4.1193	-12.024	-13.13
3	3	0.10	-3.8344	-9.188	-4.85
4	2	0.01	-4.6493	-17.188	-59.20
4	2	0.05	-4.1000	-10.745	-21.57
4	2	0.10	-3.8110	-8.317	-5.19
4	3	0.01	-4.9695	-22.504	-50.22
4	3	0.05	-4.4294	-14.501	-19.54
4	3	0.10	-4.1474	-11.165	-9.88
5	2	0.01	-4.9587	-22.140	-37.29
5	2	0.05	-4.4185	-13.461	-21.16
5	2	0.10	-4.1327	-10.638	-5.48
5	3	0.01	-5.2497	-26.606	-49.56
5	3	0.05	-4.7154	-17.432	-16.50
5	3	0.10	-4.4345	-13.654	-5.77
6	2	0.01	-5.2400	-26.278	-41.65
6	2	0.05	-4.7048	-17.120	-11.17
6	2	0.10	-4.4242	-13.347	0.00
6	3	0.01	-5.5127	-30.735	-52.50
6	3	0.05	-4.9767	-20.883	-9.05
6	3	0.10	-4.6999	-16.445	0.00

Table C-5: Critical Values for the Johansen's Cointegration Likelihood Ratio Test Statistics

Notations

VAR Model: 1=no constant; 2=drift; 3=trend drift
N: Sample Size, 400
M: Number of Variables
r: Number of Cointegrating Vectors or Rank
Degree of Freedom = M-r

Source

Johansen (1988), Johansen and Juselius (1990), and Osterwald-Lenum (1992).

	Model	M-r	1%	2.5%	5%	10%	20%	50%
λ_{max}	1	1	6.51	4.93	3.84	2.86	1.82	0.58
	1	2	15.69	13.27	11.44	9.52	7.58	4.83
	1	3	22.99	20.02	17.89	15.59	13.31	9.71
	1	4	28.82	26.14	23.80	21.58	18.97	14.94
	1	5	35.17	32.51	30.04	27.62	24.83	20.16
	2	1	11.576	9.658	8.083	6.691	4.905	2.415
	2	2	18.782	16.403	14.595	12.783	10.666	7.474
	2	3	26.154	23.362	21.279	18.959	16.521	12.707
	2	4	32.616	29.599	27.341	24.917	22.341	17.875
	2	5	38.858	35.700	33.262	30.818	27.953	23.132
	3	1	6.936	5.332	3.962	2.816	1.699	0.447
	3	2	17.936	15.810	14.036	12.099	10.125	6.852
	3	3	25.521	23.002	20.778	18.697	16.324	12.381
	3	4	31.943	29.335	27.169	24.712	22.113	17.719
	3	5	38.341	35.546	33.178	30.774	27.899	23.211
λ_{trace}	1	1	6.51	4.93	3.84	2.86	1.82	0.58
	1	2	16.31	14.43	12.53	10.47	8.45	5.42
	1	3	29.75	26.64	24.31	21.63	18.83	14.30
	1	4	45.58	42.30	39.89	36.58	33.16	27.10
	1	5	66.52	62.91	59.46	55.44	51.13	43.79
	2	1	11.576	9.658	8.083	6.691	4.905	2.415
	2	2	21.962	19.611	17.844	15.583	13.038	9.355
	2	3	37.291	34.062	31.256	28.436	25.445	20.188
	2	4	55.551	51.801	48.419	45.248	41.623	34.873
	2	5	77.911	73.031	69.977	65.956	61.566	53.373
	3	1	6.936	5.332	3.962	2.816	1.699	0.447
	3	2	19.310	17.299	15.197	13.338	11.164	7.638
	3	3	35.397	32.313	29.509	26.791	23.868	18.759
	3	4	53.792	50.424	47.181	43.964	40.250	33.672
	3	5	76.955	72.140	68.905	65.063	60.215	52.588

References

GAUSS for Windows User Guide (Version 3.5), 2000, Aptech Systems, Inc.
GAUSS Language Reference (Version 3.5), 2000, Aptech Systems, Inc.

E. Berndt and D. Wood, 1975, "Technology, Prices, and the Derived Demand for Energy," *Review of Economics and Statistics*, 259-268.

T. Bollerslev, 1986, "Generalized Autoregressive Conditional Heteroskedasticity," *Journal of Econometrics*, 31, 307-327.

T. Bollerslev and E. Ghysels, 1996, "Periodic Autoregressive Conditional Heteroscedasticity," *American Statistical Association Journal of Business and Economic Statistics*, 14, 139-151.

J. Boot and G. deWitt, 1960, "Investment Demand: An Empirical Contribution to the Aggregation Problem," *International Economic Review*, 1, 3-30.

J. Y. Campbell, A. W. Lo, and A. C. Mackinlay, 1977, *The Econometrics of Financial Markets*, Princeton University Press.

R. Davidson and J. G. MacKinnon, 1973, *Estimation and Inference in Econometrics*, Oxford University Press.

D. A. Dickey and W. A. Fuller, 1981, "Likelihood Ratio Statistics for Autoregressive Time Series with a Unit Root," *Econometrica*, 49, 1057-1072.

P. J. Dhrymes, 1970, *Econometrics*, Harper & Row.

R. Engle and C. Granger, 1987, "Co-integration and Error Correction: Representation, Estimation and Testing," *Econometrica*, 35, 251-276.

R. F. Engle, 1982, ""Autoregressive Conditional Heteroscedasticity with Estimates of the Variance of United Kingdom Inflation," *Econometrica*, 50, 987-1006.

R. F. Engle, D. M. Lilien, and R. P. Robins, 1987, "Estimating Time-Varying Risk Premia in the Term Structure: the ARCH-M Model," *Econometrica* 55, 391-407.

R. Fair, 1978, "A Theory of Extramarital Affairs," *Journal of Political Economy*, 86, 45-61.

W. A. Fuller, 1976, *Introduction to Statistical Time Series*, John Wiley.

S. Goldfeld and R. Quandt, 1972, *Nonlinear Methods in Econometrics*, Chapter 1: Numerical Optimization, North-Holland, 1-38.

W. H. Greene, 1999, *Econometric Analysis*, 4th ed., Prentice Hall.

W. H. Greene, 1997, *Econometric Analysis*, 3rd ed., Prentice Hall.

Y. Grunfeld and Z. Griliches, 1960, "Is Aggregation Necessarily Bad?" *Review of Economics and Statistics*, 42, 1-13.

A. Hall, 1993, "Some Aspects of Generalized Method of Moments Estimation," *Handbook of Statistics*, Vol. 11, ed. by G. S. Maddala, C. R. Rao, and H. D. Vinod, Elsevier Science Publishers, North-Holland, 393-417.

R. Hall, 1978, "Stochastic Implications of the Life Cycle-Permanent Income Hypothesis: Theory and Evidence," *Journal of Political Economy* 86, 971-987.

J. D. Hamilton, 1994, *Time Series Analysis*, Princeton University Press.

L. P. Hansen and K. J. Singleton, 1982, "Generalized Instrumental Variables Estimation of Nonlinear Rational Expectations Models," *Econometrica* 50, 1269-1286.

J. Hausman, 1975, "An Instrumental Variable Approach to Full-Information Estimators for Linear and Certain Nonlinear Models," *Econometrica*, 727-738.

F. Hayashi, 2000, *Econometrics*, Princeton University Press.

S. Johansen, 1988, "Statistical Analysis of Cointegration Vectors," *Journal of Economic Dynamics and Control*, 12, 231-254.

S. Johansen and K. Juselius, 1990, "Maximum Likelihood Estimation and Inference on Cointegration with Applications to the Demand for Money," *Oxford Bulletin of Economics and Statistics*, 52, 169-210.

G. G. Judge, R. C. Hill, W. E. Griffiths, H. Lutkempohl, and T.-C. Lee, 1988, *Introduction to the Theory and Practice of Econometrics,* 2nd ed., John Wiley and Sons.

G. G. Judge, R. C. Hill, W. E. Griffiths, and T.-C. Lee, 1985, *Theory and Practice of Econometrics*, 2nd ed., John Wiley and Sons.

L. Klein, 1950, *Economic Fluctuations in the United States: 1921-1941*, John Wiley and Sons.

J. G. MacKinnon, 1991, "Critical Values for Cointegration Tests," in *Long-Run Economic Relationships: Readings in Cointegration*, ed. by R. F. Engle and G. W. Granger, Oxford University Press, 267-276.

T. C. Mills, 1999, *The Econometric Modeling of Financial Time Series*, 2nd ed., Cambridge University Press.

R. C. Mittelhammer, G. G. Judge, and D. J. Miller, 2000, *Econometric Foundations*, Cambridge University Press.

D. B. Nelson, 1991, "Conditional Heteroscedasticity in Asset Returns, A New Approach," *Econometrica*, 59, 347-370.

D. B. Nelson and C. Q. Cao, 1992, "Inequality Constraints in the Univariate GARCH Model," *Journal of Business and Economic Statistics*, 10, 229-235.

M. Ogaki, 1993, "Generalized Method of Moments: Econometric Applications," *Handbook of Statistics*, Vol. 11, ed. by G. S. Maddala, C. R. Rao, and H. D. Vinod, Elsevier Science Publishers, North-Holland, 455-488.

M. Osterwald-Lenum, 1992, "A Note with Quantiles of the Asymptotic Distribution of the Maximum Likelihood Cointegration Rank Test Statistics," *Oxford Bulletin of Economics and Statistics*, 54, 461-471.

P. C. B. Phillips and S. Ouliaris, 1990, "Asymptotic Properties of Residual Based Tests for Cointegration," *Econometrica*, 58, 165-193.

R. E. Quandt, 1983, "Computational Problem and Methods," *Handbook of Econometrics*, Vol. I, ed. by Z. Griliches and M. D. Intriligator, Chapter 12, 699-764, North-Holland.

L. Spector and M. Mazzeo, 1980, "Probit Analysis and Economic Education," *Journal of Economic Education*, 11, 37-44.

Index

ELECTRONIC MEDIA TRANSMITTAL AND GAUSS Light™ SOFTWARE
Terms and Conditions of Use for the CD-ROM Accompanying
COMPUTATIONAL ECONOMETRICS
GAUSS Programming for Econometricians and Financial Analysts

NOTICE: DO NOT UNSEAL THE ENVELOPE ENCLOSING THE CD-ROM (MEDIA) OR USE THE MEDIA OR ITS CONTENTS BEFORE READING THESE TERMS AND CONDITIONS OF USE. PUBLISHER AUTHORIZES USE OF THE MEDIA AND CONTENTS ONLY UNDER THESE TERMS AND CONDITIONS OF USE. IF RECIPIENT DOES NOT WISH TO BE BOUND BY THESE TERMS AND CONDITIONS OF USE, RECIPIENT IS PROHIBITED FROM USING THE MEDIA AND CONTENTS, AND RECIPIENT SHALL RETURN THE MEDIA AND CONTENTS TO PUBLISHER. RECIPIENT'S UNSEALING OF THE ENVELOPE AND/OR USE OF THE MEDIA OR CONTENTS SIGNIFIES RECIPIENT'S AGREEMENT TO THESE TERMS AND CONDITIONS OF USE.

1. ACCEPTANCE OF TERMS. Recipient's unsealing of the envelope enclosing the Media and Contents or use of the Media or Contents subjects Recipient to all terms and conditions of use described in this document and also all terms and conditions of the GAUSS Light™ License displayed in the Media. Publisher and Aptech authorize use of the Media and Contents only as set forth herein and within the GAUSS Light™ License.

2. NO WARRANTIES: Publisher and Aptech do not warrant the accuracy of the Contents as contained in the Media against data corruption, computer viruses, errors in file transfer data, unauthorized revisions to the files, or any other alterations or data destruction to the file(s). The Media and its Contents are transmitted as is. Publisher and Aptech shall not have any liability for Recipient's use of the Media or its Contents, including without limitation, any transmittal of bugs, viruses, or other destructive or harmful programs, scripts, applets or files to the computers or networks of the Recipient. Recipient acknowledges and agrees that Recipient is fully informed of the possibility of the Media or its Contents being harmful to Recipient's computers or networks and the possibility that the Contents may not be an exact and virus-free copy of masters by Publisher or Aptech. Recipient also acknowledges, agrees, and warrants that Recipient shall be solely responsible for inspection and testing of the Media and the Contents for bugs, viruses, or other destructive or harmful programs, scripts, applets or files, before accessing or using the Media or Contents.

3. NO IMPLIED WARRANTIES. THERE ARE NO IMPLIED WARRANTIES, INCLUDING WARRANTIES OF MERCHANTABILITY OR FITNESS FOR A PARTICULAR PURPOSE, WITH RESPECT EITHER TO THE MEDIA OR THE CONTENTS.

4. LIMITATIONS ON LIABILITY AND REMEDIES. Publisher and Aptech shall have no liability for any general damages, direct or indirect damages, special damages, exemplary damages, statutory damages, punitive damages, or consequential damages, including without limitation, lost profits, interruption of business, for any use of the Media or Contents. Recipient's sole and exclusive remedy for any claim based on Recipient's use of the Media or Contents shall be either (a) the delivery of another copy of the Contents on replacement Media, or (b) the costs of a physical replacement Media (for example, the costs of a diskette, tape or other back-up media) but Publisher shall have sole discretion to elect which remedy to provide. There shall be no other remedies, whether in law or equity.

5. GAUSS LIGHT SOFTWARE LICENSE: Installation and use of this software is subject to and governed by the License Agreement displayed in the Media. By installing and using the

GAUSS Light™ Software, Recipient indicates his or her acceptance of, and Recipient is subject to, all such terms and conditions of the License Agreement. Violation of the License Agreement is also a violation of the copyright laws.

GAUSS Light™ Software is furnished by:

Aptech Systems, Inc. ("Aptech")
28304 SE Kent-Kangley Rd
Maple Valley, WA 98038
Phone: 425-432-7855
FAX: 425-432-7832
Email: info@aptech.com
www.aptech.com

GAUSS Light™ Software is published by:

Etext.net ("Publisher")
P. O. Box 269
Venice, CA 90294
Phone: 310-452-3007
FAX: 310-664-0128
Email: etext@etext.net
www.etext.net